D0486196

Hiking in the
SIERRA NEVADA

John Mock
Kimberley O'Neil

LONELY PLANET PUBLICATIONS
Melbourne • Oakland • London • Paris

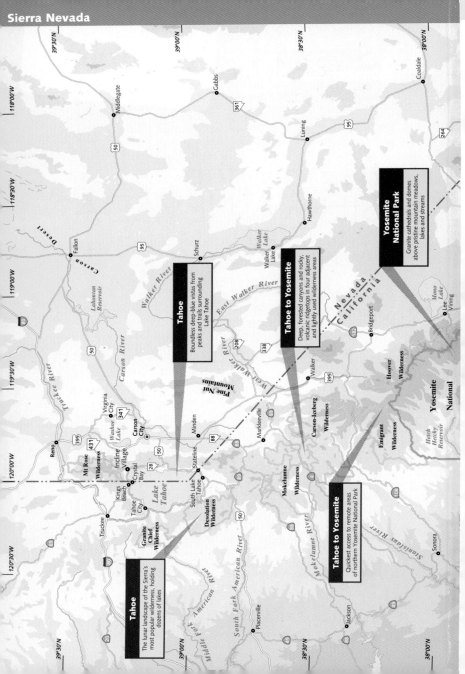

Tahoe

The lunar landscape of the Sierra's most popular wilderness, holding dozens of lakes

Tahoe to Yosemite

Quickest access to remote areas of northern Yosemite National Park

Tahoe

Boundless deep-blue vistas from peaks and trails surrounding Lake Tahoe

Tahoe to Yosemite

Deep, forested canyons and rocky, volcanic ridgetops in four adjacent and lightly used wilderness areas

Yosemite National Park

Granite cathedrals and domes above pristine mountain meadows, lakes and streams

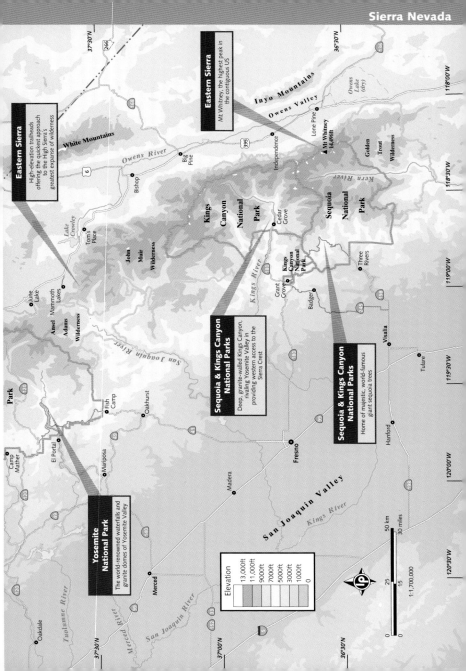

Eastern Sierra
High-elevation trailheads offering the quickest approach to the High Sierra's greatest expanse of wilderness

Eastern Sierra
Mt Whitney, the highest peak in the contiguous US

Sequoia & Kings Canyon National Parks
Deep, granite-walled Kings Canyon, rivaling Yosemite Valley in providing western access to the Sierra Crest

Sequoia & Kings Canyon National Parks
Home of majestic, world-famous giant sequoia trees

Yosemite National Park
The world-renowned waterfalls and granite domes of Yosemite Valley

White Mountains

Owens River

Inyo Mountains

Owens Valley

Owens Lake (dry)

Lone Pine

▲ Mt Whitney 14,496ft

Independence

Golden Trout Wilderness

Kern River

Big Pine

Bishop

Lake Crowley

Tom's Place

John Muir Wilderness

Kings Canyon National Park

Cedar Grove

Sequoia National Park

Three Rivers

Kings River

Grant Grove

Kings Canyon National Park

Badger

June Lake

Mammoth Lakes

Ansel Adams Wilderness

San Joaquin River

Visalia

Tulare

Hanford

Fish Camp

Oakhurst

Park

Camp Mather

El Portal

Mariposa

Madera

Fresno

Kings River

San Joaquin Valley

Merced

Tuolumne River

Merced River

San Joaquin River

Oakdale

Elevation
13,000ft
11,000ft
9000ft
7000ft
5000ft
3000ft
1000ft
0

50 km
30 miles
0 25
15
1:1,700,000

37°30′N
36°30′N
118°00′W
118°30′W
119°00′W
119°30′W
120°00′W
120°30′W
37°00′N
36°30′N

Hiking in the Sierra Nevada
1st edition – June 2002

Published by
Lonely Planet Publications Pty Ltd ABN 36 005 607 983
90 Maribyrnong St, Footscray, Victoria 3011, Australia

Lonely Planet Offices
Australia Locked Bag 1, Footscray, Victoria 3011
USA 150 Linden St, Oakland, CA 94607
UK 10a Spring Place, London NW5 3BH
France 1 rue du Dahomey, 75011 Paris

Photographs
Many of the images in this guide are available for licensing from
Lonely Planet Images.
email: lpi@lonelyplanet.com.au
Web site: www.lonelyplanetimages.com

Main front cover photograph
Half Dome, Yosemite National Park (Richard I'Anson)

Small front cover photograph
Hiker above Wolf Creek (John Mock)

ISBN 1 74059 272 7

text & maps © Lonely Planet Publications Pty Ltd 2002
photos © photographers as indicated 2002

Printed through Colorcraft Ltd, Hong Kong
Printed in China

CONTENTS

2   Contents

TAHOE TO YOSEMITE   125

YOSEMITE NATIONAL PARK   163

SEQUOIA & KINGS CANYON NATIONAL PARKS   213

EASTERN SIERRA   240

LONG-DISTANCE TRAILS   283

GLOSSARY   296
INDEX   298
MAP LEGEND   304

The Maps

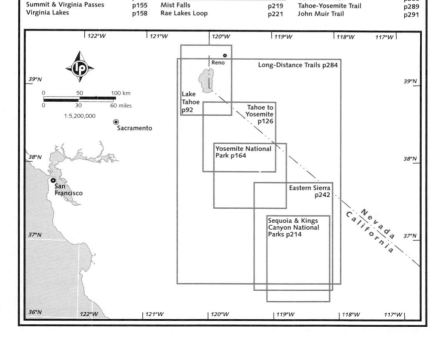

The Hikes	Duration	Standard	Season
Lake Tahoe			
Mt Judah Loop	3–3½ hours	easy	mid-June–mid-October
Donner Pass to Squaw Valley	7½–8½ hours	moderate-hard	mid-June–mid-October
Ellis Peak	3–3½ hours	easy-moderate	July–mid-October
Rubicon Trail	2–2½ hours	easy	mid-May–mid-September
Grass Lake	2½ hours	easy	July–mid-October
Half Moon Lake	2 days	easy-moderate	July–September
Mt Tallac	6–7 hours	hard	July–September
Dicks & Phipps Passes	4 days	moderate	July–September
Mt Rose	6–8 hours	moderate	July–mid-October
Tahoe Meadows to Spooner Summit	2 days	easy-moderate	mid-June–October
Freel Peak	2 days	easy-moderate	July–mid-October
Echo Summit to Carson Pass	2 days	easy-moderate	mid-June–October
Tahoe to Yosemite			
Winnemucca & Round Top Lakes	2–2½ hours	easy-moderate	mid-June–October
Fourth of July Lake	2 days	moderate	mid-June–September
Carson Pass to Ebbetts Pass	4 days	moderate	mid-June–September
Noble Lake	3½–4½ hours	easy-moderate	June–October
Falls Meadow	2 days	moderate	mid-May–October
St Marys Pass	1–1½ hours	easy	July–September
Brown Bear & Bond Passes	6 days	moderate	mid-June–September
Sawtooth Ridge	6 days	moderate-hard	July–mid-September
East Lake	4 hours	easy-moderate	mid-June–October
Summit & Virginia Passes	2 days	moderate-hard	July–October

Fees & Permits	Transport	Features	Page
no permit	no	Half-day hike to gentle, rolling summit, with superb Donner Lake views	95
no permit	finish only	Miles of ridgetop views while traversing Tinker Knob and Granite Chief Wilderness	96
no permit	no	Spectacular ridge walk and viewpoint above Tahoe's quiet west shore	100
day use $2, no permit	finish only	Lets you peer into crystalline water from Tahoe's only shoreline trail	102
free permit	no	Waterfall tumbling into rockbound island-dotted lake, ideal for swimming	105
res fee $5, camping fee $10 max	no	Secluded cirque lake in heart of Desolation Wilderness	106
free permit	no	Trail to summit of rocky peak, with stunning vistas of Desolation Wilderness and Lake Tahoe	109
res fee $5, camping fee $10 max	finish only	Traverses lunar landscape of Desolation Wilderness, crossing two passes	111
no permit	no	Trail to summit of Tahoe's third-highest peak, with stunning vistas	114
no permit	no	Ridgetop traverse of Carson Range; most scenic segment of Tahoe Rim Trail	116
no permit	no	A hike beneath Tahoe's highest peak, with optional cross-country excursion to summit	118
no permit	no	A stroll through meadows and wildflowers to beautiful lake; great overnight hike	121
no permit	no	Wildflowers, sparkling streams, picturesque lakes, rock-crowned ridges, sweeping vistas	127
free permit	no	Loop hike to sparkling subalpine lake beneath volcanic peak in remote wilderness	129
free permit	no	Traverses Mokelumne Wilderness past lakes and dramatic rock formations	131
no permit	no	Has wildflowers lining forested upper slopes of Noble Canyon under dramatic Highland Peak	134
free permit	no	Eastern Sierra's deepest and wildest canyon, in spectacularly remote Carson-Iceberg Wilderness	136
no permit	no	Fabulous viewpoint above Sonora Pass, with side trip to Sonora Peak summit	142
free permit	no	Two passes along pioneer route from western Sierra to Yosemite National Park	145
res fee $3	no	Granite towers and canyons of northern Yosemite National Park; crosses three passes	148
no permit	no	Sparkling blue lakes beneath vibrant red and ochre peaks of Hoover Wilderness	152
free permit, $3 permit reservation fee	no	Loop through Hoover Wilderness to pristine Yosemite's Virginia Canyon; crosses two passes	154

The Hikes	Duration	Standard	Season
Virginia Lakes	3 hours	easy-moderate	mid-June–October
Gardisky Lake	1–1½ hours	easy-moderate	mid-June–October
Yosemite National Park			
Vernal Fall	2–3 hours	easy-moderate	May–November
Nevada Fall	4–5 hours	moderate	May–November
Yosemite Falls	5–6 hours	moderate-hard	mid-May–mid-November
Four Mile & Panorama Trails	6½–8 hours	moderate-hard	July–October
Half Dome	2 days	hard	late May–mid-October
Sentinel Dome & Taft Point	2½–3 hours	easy	mid-May–November
North Dome	4½–5 hours	easy-moderate	mid-June–mid-October
Mt Hoffmann	4–5 hours	moderate	July–October
Clouds Rest	6–7 hours	moderate-hard	mid-June–October
Tenaya Lake to Yosemite Valley	2 days	moderate-hard	mid-June–October
Cathedral Lakes	4–5 hours	easy-moderate	mid-June–September
Waterwheel Falls	2 days	moderate	mid-June–October
Lyell Canyon	2 days	easy-moderate	July–September
Vogelsang	3 days	moderate	July–September
Mono Pass	3½–4½ hours	easy-moderate	mid-June–September
Mt Dana	6–7 hours	hard	July–mid-September
Wapama Falls	2½–3 hours	easy	May–November
Chilnualna Falls	4–5 hours	moderate	March–November
Sequoia & Kings Canyon National Parks			
Mist Falls	4–5 hours	easy	May–October

Fees & Permits	Transport	Features	Page
no permit	no	Day hike following chain of lakes to dramatic view-filled rocky pass	157
no permit	no	Short ascent to lake and meadow, with views of Yosemite's boundary peaks	159
no permit, NP fee $20	yes	Easiest day hike to top of one of Yosemite Valley's waterfalls	170
no permit, NP fee $20	yes	Day hike along Merced River to top of two Yosemite Valley waterfalls	171
no permit, NP fee $20	yes	Day hike to top of Yosemite's highest and world's fifth highest free-leaping waterfall	172
no permit, NP fee $20	yes	Near-loop hike on Yosemite Valley's south rim, with waterfalls and granite domes	174
free permit, $3 res fee, NP fee $20	yes	Ultimate hike to summit of Yosemite's most famous granite dome	176
no permit, NP fee $20	yes	Yosemite's most accessible dome, with panorama view and south rim viewpoint	179
no permit, NP fee $20	yes	Scenic Indian Ridge, leading to North Dome for in-your-face Half Dome views	182
no permit, NP fee $20	yes	More than 50 peaks visible from mountain-top at Yosemite's geographical center	186
no permit, NP fee $20	yes	Yosemite's largest expanse of granite; arguably its finest panoramic viewpoint	187
free permit, res fee $3, NP fee $20	yes	Traverses Clouds Rest and descends past two famous waterfalls to Yosemite Valley	189
no permit, NP fee $20	yes	Picturesque lakes, good swimming, beneath granite spires near Tuolumne Meadows	192
free permit, res fee $3, NP fee $20	yes	Near-continual cascades and waterfalls through Grand Canyon of Tuolumne River	193
free permit, res fee $3, NP fee $20	yes	Forested stroll to base of Yosemite's highest peak, with optional technical ascent	196
free permit, res fee $3, NP fee $20	yes	Loops over two passes through granite wonderland of Yosemite's Cathedral Range	198
no permit, NP fee $20	yes	A stroll through high meadows to historic pass on Yosemite's eastern boundary	202
no permit, NP fee $20	yes	Awesome views of Mono Lake from summit of Yosemite's second highest peak	204
no permit, NP fee $20	no	Day hike to base of two thundering waterfalls in Yosemite's quietest corner	206
no permit, NP fee $20	no	Uncrowded trail along cascading creek to top of waterfalls over Wawona Dome's shoulder	208
no permit, NP fee $10	no	Day hike to Kings Canyon's largest waterfall and great picnic spot	218

The Hikes	Duration	Standard	Season
Rae Lakes Loop	5 days	moderate	mid-June–September
Lake Reflection	4 days	moderate	mid-June–September
Congress Trail	1–1½ hours	easy	May–November
Trail of the Sequoias	2½–3 hours	easy	May–November
High Sierra Trail	8 days	hard	July–mid-September
Lower Monarch Lake	2 days	moderate	mid-June–September
Franklin & Sawtooth Passes	4 days	moderate-hard	mid-June–September
Eastern Sierra			
Minaret Lake	2 days	moderate	mid-June–October
Ediza Lake	2 days	easy-moderate	mid-June–October
Thousand Island Lake	2 days	easy-moderate	mid-June–October
Mammoth Crest	2 days	moderate	July–September
Duck Lake	2 days	easy-moderate	mid-June–September
Gem Lakes	2 days	easy	July–September
Fourth Recess Lake	2 days	moderate-hard	July–September
Humphreys & Evolution Basins	7 days	hard	July–September
Palisades	2 days	moderate	mid-June–mid-October
Sixty Lake Basin	5 days	moderate-hard	mid-June–September
Mt Whitney	3 days	hard	July–September
New Army & Cottonwood Passes	3 days	moderate	late June–mid-October
Long-Distance Trails			
Tahoe Rim Trail	10–17 days	moderate	June–September
Tahoe-Yosemite Trail	19–23 days	hard	July–mid-September
John Muir Trail	19–20 days	hard	mid-July–mid-September

Fees & Permits	Transport	Features	Page
free permit, res fee $10, NP fee $10	no	Gem-like lakes in Kings Canyon high country, crossing an alpine pass	219
free permit, res fee $10, NP fee $10	no	Secluded lake mirroring peaks of Kings-Kern Divide in its aqua waters	224
no permit, NP entry fee $10	no	Nature trail through world's finest groves of giant sequoia trees	227
no permit, NP entry fee $10	no	Tranquil loop along meadows and streams, visiting outstanding sequoia groves	229
free permit, res fee $15, NP fee $10	no	Quintessential traverse across Sequoia National Park to Mt Whitney, crossing two passes	229
free permit, res fee $10, NP fee $10	no	Sunsets beneath Great Western Divide on Mineral King's best overnight hike	233
free permit, res fee $10, NP fee $10	no	Two rugged passes in Sequoia National Park, on southern Sierra's Great Western Divide	235
free permit, res fee $5	yes	Rockbound indigo lake mirroring intimate views of towering Minarets	245
free permit, res fee $5	yes	Exquisite creekside hike to inviting lake beneath central Sierra's highest peaks	248
free permit, res fee $5	yes	View-filled loop hike to iconic granite-dotted lake beneath Banner Peak	250
free permit, res fee $5	no	Soaring continual ridgetop views for 100 miles, from Mono Divide to Yosemite	252
free permit, res fee $5	no	Chain of lakes leading to pass along Mammoth Crest and to expansive lake	254
free permit, res fee $5	no	A stroll along subalpine chain of picture-perfect lakes surrounded by alpine peaks	256
free permit, res fee $5	no	Crosses alpine pass on Sierra Crest to pristine waterfall-fed lake	258
free permit, res fee $5	no	Quintessential loop trip into northern Kings Canyon National Park, crossing three passes	263
free permit, res fee $5	no	Glacier-fed turquoise lakes beneath Sierra's greatest concentration of high peaks and glaciers	266
free permit, res fee $5	no	Remote lake-filled basin reached by two alpine passes in Kings Canyon high country	270
free permit, res fee $5	no	Rugged, steep trail to summit of highest peak in contiguous US	274
free permit, res fee $5	no	Loop through southern Sequoia National Park, visiting lakes and crossing two passes	277
free permit, res fee $5, max camping fee $10	no	Panoramic views from ridge tops of Lake Tahoe	283
free permit, res fee $5, max camping fee $10,	yes	Challenging route linking Lake Tahoe to Yosemite	286
NP fee $20, free permit, res fee $3, NP fee $20	start only	Renowned trail linking Mt Whitney and Yosemite National Park, crossing 11 hard passes	289

The Authors

John Mock & Kimberley O'Neil

John's summers as a youth were spent hiking along the Appalachian National Scenic Trail, and Kimberley's were spent exploring Wisconsin's Northwoods. After college, both migrated independently to California where they have been living and hiking ever since. Married in a Tibetan *gompa* in Kathmandu in 1991, today they divide their time between northern Pakistan and their northern California home. John's PhD in South Asian language and literature from the University of California at Berkeley and Kimberley's years of experience in the adventure travel industry have enabled them to also work as consultants on ecotourism in northern Pakistan for The World Conservation Union (IUCN), on the Khunjerab National Park for the WorldWide Fund for Nature (WWF), and with *National Geographic* magazine. John is currently a lecturer in Hindi and Urdu at the University of California at Santa Cruz. Avid cyclists and hikers, they've also coauthored Lonely Planet's *Trekking in the Karakoram & Hindukush* and contributed to *Hiking in the USA, Pakistan, Rocky Mountains, Lonely Planet Unpacked* and *Lonely Planet Unpacked Again*.

From the Authors

We are grateful for the extraordinary hospitality of friends – Kelly Rich, Mary Carlson, and Nigel and Charlayne Allan – who shared their perfectly situated homes in Yosemite, Carson City and Truckee, providing us with a base for our research and all-important hot showers. Thanks also to our friends at Marmot Mountain Ltd in Santa Rosa.

A highlight of our research was watching two endangered species in one afternoon, and we're thankful to George, the veteran Kings Canyon backcountry ranger, who alerted us on what to look for.

Finally, we'd like to acknowledge some unsung heros we met: the young girl and boy hiking with their parents who excitedly pointed to the summit of Mt Dana and announced, 'We spent the night up there!'; the Bubbs Creek trail crew, who made their 4.1mi, 1800ft daily commute each way seemingly without effort; and the 80-year-old woman making her regular hike along the Mono Pass trail toward Ruby Lake, ice axe in hand. These people whose names we do not know inspire us through their example, proving that hiking in the Sierra Nevada can be a lifelong pleasure. See you on the trail!

This Book

This 1st edition of *Hiking in the Sierra Nevada* was researched and written by the intrepid husband-and-wife team of John Mock and Kimberley O'Neil.

From the Publisher

Hiking in the Sierra Nevada was produced in Lonely Planet's Oakland, California office, with the helpful long-distance guidance of our colleagues in Melbourne, Australia.

Elaine Merrill edited the book under the skillful supervision of Maria Donohoe. Wade Fox contributed to the brief, and Ken DellaPenta created the index. Special thanks go to members of the On the Edge unit in Australia: hiking buffs Lindsay Browne, Sally Dillon, Glen van der Knijff and Nick Tapp, who contributed their formidable expertise with great grace and good humor.

John Culp was the lead cartographer, diligently mapping every contour on the 70-plus two-color hike maps. He was assisted by fellow cartographers Buck Cantwell, Lee Espinole, Patrick Phelan, Terence Philippe, Kat Smith, Herman So, Eric Thomsen and Rudie Watzig. Molly Green and Bart Wright were the cartographic technical experts. Tracey Croom supervised the project in the beginning, with Bart taking over as senior mapping honcho during edit and layout. Alex Guilbert oversaw all the cartographers.

Josh Schefers took time out from breaking his leg and making wedding plans to design the layout and put together the book's luscious color pages. Margaret Livingston also worked on layout. The cover was designed by Henia Miedzinski. Susan Rimerman, art director, led the design team.

Justin Marler coordinated the illustrations, as well as drawing a number of them, including the chapter end. Artists Hugh D'Andrade, Shelley Firth, Anthony Phelan and Lisa Summers also contributed to the illustrations.

Special thanks go to authors, John Mock and Kimberley O'Neil, whose physical stamina in doing all the hikes in the book was surpassed only by their commitment to writing and fine-tuning an excellent hiking guide.

Foreword

ABOUT LONELY PLANET GUIDEBOOKS

The story begins with a classic travel adventure: Tony and Maureen Wheeler's 1972 journey across Europe and Asia to Australia. Useful information about the overland trail did not exist at that time, so Tony and Maureen published the first Lonely Planet guidebook to meet a growing need.

From a kitchen table, then from a tiny office in Melbourne (Australia), Lonely Planet has become the largest independent travel publisher in the world, an international company with offices in Melbourne, Oakland (USA), London (UK) and Paris (France).

Today Lonely Planet guidebooks cover the globe. There is an ever-growing list of books, and there's information in a variety of forms and media. Some things haven't changed. The main aim is still to help make it possible for adventurous travelers to get out there – to explore and better understand the world.

At Lonely Planet we believe travelers can make a positive contribution to the countries they visit – if they respect their host communities and spend their money wisely. Since 1986 a percentage of the income from each book has been donated to aid projects and human-rights campaigns.

Updates Lonely Planet thoroughly updates each guidebook as often as possible. This usually means there are around two years between editions, although for more unusual or more stable destinations the gap can be longer. Check the imprint page (usually following the color map at the beginning of the book) for publication dates.

Between editions up-to-date information is available in two free newsletters – the paper *Planet Talk* and email *Comet* (to subscribe, contact any Lonely Planet office) – and on our Web site at www.lonelyplanet.com. The *Upgrades* section of the Web site covers a number of important and volatile destinations and is regularly updated by Lonely Planet authors. *Scoop* covers news and current affairs relevant to travelers. And, lastly, the *Thorn Tree* bulletin board and *Postcards* section of the site carry unverified, but fascinating, reports from travelers.

Correspondence The process of creating new editions begins with the letters, postcards and emails received from travelers. This correspondence often includes suggestions, criticisms and comments about the current editions. Interesting excerpts are immediately passed on via newsletters and the Web site, and everything goes to our authors to be verified when they're researching on the road. We're keen to get more feedback from organizations or individuals who represent communities visited by travelers.

Lonely Planet gathers information for everyone who's curious about the planet – and especially for those who explore it firsthand. Through guidebooks, phrasebooks, activity guides, maps, literature, newsletters, image library, TV series and Web site we act as an information exchange for a worldwide community of travelers.

Research Authors aim to gather sufficient practical information to enable travelers to make informed choices and to make the mechanics of a journey run smoothly. They also research historical and cultural background to help enrich the travel experience and allow travelers to understand and respond appropriately to cultural and environmental issues.

Authors don't stay in every hotel because that would mean spending a couple of months in each medium-size city and, no, they don't eat at every restaurant because that would mean stretching belts beyond capacity. They do visit hotels and restaurants to check standards and prices, but feedback based on readers' direct experiences can be very helpful.

Many of our authors work undercover; others aren't so secretive. None of them accept freebies in exchange for positive write-ups. And none of our guidebooks contain any advertising.

Production Authors submit their manuscripts and maps to offices in Australia, the USA, UK or France. Editors and cartographers – all experienced travelers themselves – then begin the process of assembling the pieces. When the book finally hits the shops, some things are already out of date, we start getting feedback from readers and the process begins again…

WARNING & REQUEST

Things change – prices go up, schedules change, good places go bad and bad places go bankrupt – nothing stays the same. So, if you find things better or worse, recently opened or long since closed, please tell us and help make the next edition even more accurate and useful. We genuinely value all the feedback we receive. A well-traveled team reads and acknowledges every letter, postcard and email and ensures that every morsel of information finds its way to the appropriate authors, editors and cartographers for verification.

Everyone who writes to us will find their name listed in the next edition of the appropriate guidebook. They will also receive the latest issue of *Planet Talk*, our quarterly printed newsletter, or *Comet*, our monthly email newsletter. Subscriptions to both newsletters are free. The very best contributions will be rewarded with a free guidebook.

We may edit, reproduce and incorporate your comments in all Lonely Planet products, such as guidebooks, Web sites and digital products, so let us know if you don't want your comments reproduced or your name acknowledged.

Send all correspondence to the Lonely Planet office closest to you:

Australia: Locked Bag 1, Footscray, Victoria 3011
USA: 150 Linden St, Oakland, CA 94607
UK: 10a Spring Place, London NW5 3BH
France: 1 rue du Dahomey, 75011 Paris

Or email us at: talk2us@lonelyplanet.com.au

For news, views and updates, see our Web site: www.lonelyplanet.com

HOW TO USE A LONELY PLANET GUIDEBOOK

The best way to use a Lonely Planet guidebook is any way you choose. At Lonely Planet, we believe the most memorable travel experiences are often those that are unexpected, and the finest discoveries are those you make yourself. Guidebooks are not intended to be used as if they provided a detailed set of infallible instructions!

Contents All Lonely Planet guidebooks follow roughly the same format. The Facts about the Destination chapters or sections give background information ranging from history to weather. Facts for the Visitor gives practical information on issues like visas and health. Getting There & Away gives a brief starting point for researching travel to and from the destination. Getting Around gives an overview of the transport options when you arrive.

The peculiar demands of each destination determine how subsequent chapters are broken up, but some things remain constant. We always start with background, then proceed to sights, places to stay, places to eat, entertainment, getting there and away, and getting around information – in that order.

Heading Hierarchy Lonely Planet headings are used in a strict hierarchical structure that can be visualized as a set of Russian dolls. Each heading (and its following text) is encompassed by any preceding heading that is higher on the hierarchical ladder.

Entry Points We do not assume guidebooks will be read from beginning to end, but that people will dip into them. The traditional entry points are the list of contents and the index. In addition, however, some books have a complete list of maps and an index map illustrating map coverage.

There may also be a color map that shows highlights. These highlights are dealt with in greater detail in the Facts for the Visitor chapter, along with planning questions and suggested itineraries. Each chapter covering a geographical region usually begins with a locator map and another list of highlights. Once you find something of interest in a list of highlights, turn to the index.

Maps Maps play a crucial role in Lonely Planet guidebooks and include a huge amount of information. A legend is printed on the back page. We seek to have complete consistency between maps and text and to have every important place in the text captured on a map. Map key numbers usually start in the top left corner.

Although inclusion in a guidebook usually implies a recommendation, we cannot list every good place. Exclusion does not necessarily imply criticism. In fact there are a number of reasons why we might exclude a place – sometimes it is simply inappropriate to encourage an influx of travelers.

Introduction

Walking in its rhythm and naturalness is the closest of all acts we choose to the acts we don't: breathing and the beating of our hearts, the other rhythms that direct the rhythm of walking. Of all the things we learn, it is the most natural, like birds learning to fly, and of all of them the act that becomes most unconscious. Walking is the only way to measure the rhythm of the body against the rhythm of the land.

> – **Rebecca Solnit** in *Savage Dreams*

The Sierra Nevada is a range of superlatives – the contiguous USA's longest continuous mountain range, highest peak, largest and deepest alpine lake, highest alpine lake, tallest waterfall, and what many call its finest mountain hiking. The distinctive glacier-polished granite landscape of the Sierra Nevada prompted naturalist and author John Muir to dub it the 'Range of Light,' a landscape that has inspired American poets, from Henry David Thoreau and Ralph Waldo Emerson to Gary Snyder, and drawn the focus of painters and photographers, from Albert Bierstadt to Ansel Adams.

The wealth of natural beauty is protected by three world-renowned national parks (Yosemite, Sequoia and Kings Canyon), eight national forests, 17 wilderness areas and 20 state parks and recreation areas, offering hikers stretches of wilderness unbroken by roads for more than 200mi. More than 500 peaks rise higher than 10,000ft above alpine wilderness, with sparkling lakes and streams, vast forests, groves of giant sequoia trees, spectacular waterfalls, and exposed granite domes, spires and canyons. Approachable from either its western or eastern side, and crossed by six

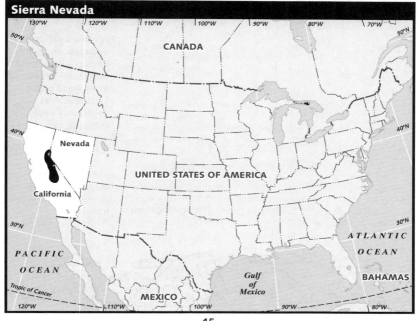

trans-Sierra highways, these mountains are easily accessible and inviting for a day, a weekend, a week or longer.

In addition to the famous Pacific Crest National Scenic Trail, three impressive trails ranging in length from 150mi to 218mi traverse key segments of the Sierra Nevada: The Tahoe Rim Trail encircles the Lake Tahoe basin; the Tahoe-Yosemite Trail links Lake Tahoe to Yosemite National Park; and the John Muir Trail links Yosemite National Park to Mt Whitney, the highest peak in the contiguous US.

Many of the hikes in this book cross or follow a segment of one of these renowned high mountain trails. Most hikes stay close to the crest of the Sierra Nevada – either following along it, across it, or doing a loop hike to it – and offer the most outstanding mountain vistas.

Facts about the Sierra Nevada

HISTORY

Native Americans have lived and traveled through the Sierra Nevada since at least 10,000 years ago. People living in the western foothills and those living in the eastern Sierra crossed the mountain passes in summer to trade, notably seashell beads and pinyon pine nuts. Arrowheads have even been found on Mt Whitney.

The Sierra Nevada received its name from 18th century Spanish missionaries, who called it 'una gran sierra nevada' and ventured infrequently into the mountains. *Sierra Nevada* means 'snowy mountain' in Spanish. Today, only the names of the range and of major rivers such as the San Joaquin and the now-anglicized Kings and Stanislaus bear witness to the Spanish presence. The first European to explore the high country was the trapper Jedediah Smith, in 1827. In the 1840s, Lieutenant John C Frémont of the US Army Topographical Engineers and his famous scout Christopher 'Kit' Carson explored the range. But it was the 1848 discovery of gold at Sutter's Mill in the western foothills near Coloma that brought a flood of gold seekers known as the forty-niners across the range. Settlers brought their wagons over the passes, following pioneer routes such as the Overland Trail, or Emigrant Trail, as the route was also called.

California achieved statehood in 1850. In 1863, the California Geological Survey, under the leadership of Harvard geology professor Josiah D Whitney, began the first systematic scientific exploration of the Sierra Nevada. Whitney, William H Brewer and topographer and artist Charles F Hoffmann visited Tuolumne Meadows, naming the first peak they climbed after Hoffmann. The next summer Brewer and Hoffmann, together with Clarence King and James Gardiner, explored the South Fork Kings River and named the highest peak they saw after their absent chief.

The latter part of the 19th century saw continued exploration by both the surveyors and by adventurers such as John Muir. These activities brought recognition to the Sierra Nevada, with two national parks established in 1890, and the Sierra Club formed in 1892. By the end of the 1930s, the entire Sierra had been explored and mapped, and the major peaks had all been climbed. In the 1950s and 1960s, a new generation of climbers turned their attention to the Sierra's big granite walls, and backpackers made high Sierra hiking one of California's most popular forms of recreation. Backpacking remains the mode of travel through which most people experience the Sierra Nevada today.

GEOGRAPHY

The Sierra Nevada, California's largest mountain range, extends 430mi through eastern California from the southern end of the Cascade Range near Lassen Peak to the Mojave Desert. The range is from 40mi to 80mi wide, and covers an area roughly equivalent to that of the French, Swiss and Italian Alps combined. It includes the headwaters of 24 major river basins and boasts 500 peaks higher than 10,000ft and 14 peaks above 14,000ft. Its characteristic rocky, lake-dotted wilderness above 9000ft, known as the High Sierra, is snow covered about eight months of the year. Structurally, the Sierra Nevada is a huge, tilted, asymmetrical range, with a gentle, rolling western side and a steep eastern side. Its eastern side drops down 10,000ft to the Great Basin, a 210,000 sq-mile region with no drainage to the ocean that encompasses most of Nevada and portions of the neighboring states of California, Utah, Idaho, Wyoming and Oregon.

CLIMATE

The Sierra Nevada has the mildest, sunniest climate of any major US mountain range. Prevailing westerly winds bring moist air from the Pacific Ocean over the mountains between October and April, when 80% of

Chronology of Sierra Nevada History

10,000 BC–AD 1820 – Native Americans inhabit and travel throughout the Sierra Nevada.
1000 BC – Ahwahneechee, also known as Sierra Miwok, settle in Yosemite Valley.
15th–16th centuries – Monache migrate from Owens Valley to the western Sierra foothills.
1805 – Spanish missionaries, led by Gabriel Moraga, discover the Kings River.
1833 – Joseph Reddeford Walker and a party of fur trappers glimpse Yosemite Valley.
1844 – John C Frémont reaches Carson Pass and reports seeing Lake Tahoe.
1844–46 – The infamous Donner party winters along the shores of Donner Lake.
1848 – Gold is discovered in the western foothills of the Sierra Nevada, starting the California gold rush.
1850 – John Ebbetts crosses Ebbetts Pass.
1851 – Mariposa Battalion, led by James D Savage, are the first non-native people to enter Yosemite Valley.
1855 – James Mason Hutchings leads the first tourist party to Yosemite Valley.
1860s – Mining settlements appear in the Owens Valley.
1863 – The California Geological Survey begins to systematically explore the Sierra Nevada.
1864 – The Yosemite Grant is signed by President Lincoln, creating Yosemite State Park.
1868 – John Muir first visits Yosemite.
1870s – The Wheeler Survey charts the region north of Tuolumne Meadows.
1884 – Theodore S Solomons conceives of a continuous trail along the Sierra Crest.
1890 – Sequoia, Yosemite and Grant Grove become national parks.
1891 – President Harrison establishes national forest reserves.
1892 – The Sierra Club is formed.
1893 – Sierra and Sequoia National Forest Reserves are established.
1892–97 – Solomons, over five journeys, travels from Lake Tahoe to the Kings River.
1897 – The Stanislaus National Forest Reserve is established.
1899 – The Tahoe National Forest Reserve is established.
1901 – Some 96 Sierra Club members make the first annual club outing.
1905 – The US Forest Service is established; national forest reserves become national forests.
1908 – Joseph N LeConte, William Hutchinson and Duncan McDuffie follow the Sierra Crest from Yosemite to Kings Canyon.
1914 – John Muir dies; the Tahoe-Yosemite Trail is conceived.
1915 – The California legislature appropriates funds, and work begins on the John Muir Trail.
1920 – The Sierra Nevada's last grizzly bear is destroyed near Kings Canyon.
1920–24 – US Forest Service policy of complete wildfire suppression evolves. Hydroelectric and urban water storage at Hetch Hetchy and Owens Valley come to national parks and forests.
mid-1920s – Solomons' dream comes true as the John Muir Trail is completed.
1926 – Kern Canyon and Mt Whitney become part of Sequoia National Park.
1940 – Kings Canyon becomes a national park, absorbing Grant Grove National Park.
1964 – The Wilderness Act is passed.
1965 – Kings Canyon itself and Tehipite Valley are added to Kings Canyon National Park.
1969 – The National Environmental Policy Act requires environmental impact statements.
1973 – The Endangered Species Act is passed.
1975 – The National Forest Management Act requires scientific planning for national forests.
1976 – Sequoia and Kings Canyon National Parks become a UNESCO biosphere reserve.
1979 – The California Wilderness Act is passed, and new wilderness areas are created in the Sierra Nevada.
1981 – The Tahoe Rim Trail is conceived.
1984 – Yosemite National Park becomes a UNESCO World Heritage Site.
2001 – The Tahoe Rim Trail is completed.

annual precipitation falls as snow. A 'rain shadow' effect leaves the eastern slopes comparatively dry. Snowfall also varies with elevation and latitude, with more snow falling between 6000ft and 8500ft and in the northern Sierra. Typically, 100 inches of snow falls at 5000ft and as much as 450 inches in the High Sierra. Snow, however, can fall during any month, and weather generally changes rapidly.

Summer temperatures can range from daytime highs of 80°F to nighttime lows of 50°F, but it can be 20°F cooler at high elevations. During the summer, California's Central Valley and the eastern deserts that surround the Sierra Nevada are hot, with daytime temperatures reaching from 90°F to more than 100°F. The warmest time in the mountains is from mid-July to mid-August when daytime high temperatures range from 70° to 90°F. Nighttime temperatures at the highest elevations drop to near freezing even in midsummer.

ECOLOGY & ENVIRONMENT

Humans have lived as an integral part of the Sierra Nevada's ecosystem for at least 10,000 years. Native American land management included hunting, burning, pruning and irrigation.

Starting in the early 19th century, non-Native American settlers began increasingly intensive resource use. Agriculture, mining, logging, grazing and settlements transformed the land and the rivers, and resource extraction and fire suppression became the management goals. In the early 20th century, wealthy elite began summering in mountain resorts, notably in the Lake Tahoe area.

After World War II, California's booming middle class flocked to the Sierra Nevada in their private automobiles, and the 1960 Squaw Valley Winter Olympic Games marked a paradigm shift from resource extraction to year-round recreational use. Population growth and development are now the greatest threats to the natural environment, degrading both its biodiversity and aesthetic quality. The Sierra Nevada is the main source of water for California, and water diversion for irrigation, power and

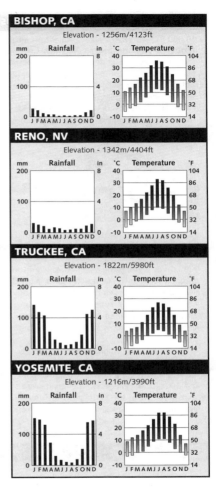

residential use has a significant impact on the ecosystem.

How the Sierra Nevada should be managed and who has jurisdiction over its resources is at the heart of the environmental issue. Should it be approached on a small scale taking into account the differences within the Sierra Nevada, or is it better to act from a single, unified vision for the entire bioregion? What seems clear is that

Sierra Nevada Geology

Where Does the Sierra Nevada Come From?

The Sierra Nevada is primarily **fault-block mountains (A)**, formed when, starting about 25 million years ago, an enormous block of the Earth's crust tilted westward along an eastern fault. The actual block formed slowly between 200 and 100 million years ago as molten

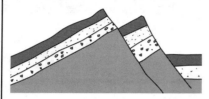

**Fault-block Mountains (A)
(eg, Sierra Nevada)**

magma cooled to form numerous granitic **plutons** far under the Earth's surface. Slowly, the surface rock eroded, exposing the granitic mass beneath. Relatively recent tilting and uplifting along the eastern fault line raised the granitic rock to near its present height and formed the steep eastern Sierra escarpment.

As the buried granite was uplifted, and the surrounding rock eroded, the pressures weighing down on the granite were released, causing the plutons to expand outward. The outermost parts of these solid granitic masses expanded more rapidly and separated to form huge sheets. Over time, the plutons became a series of shells. As the plutons reached the surface, the outermost sheets weathered and disintegrated, transforming angles into curves. Where the sheets paralleled the surface, they gradually evolved into the smooth rounded form of the Sierra Nevada's many **dome mountains (B)**, the most famous of which is Half Dome in Yosemite National Park.

Where the sheets ran perpendicular to the surface, they formed enormous smooth granite cliffs, the most famous of which is Yosemite's El Capitan.

**Progressive Rounding (B)
(eg, El Capitan)**

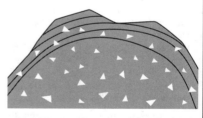

Many parts of the Sierra Nevada, especially in the north, show evidence of pronounced **volcanic activity (C)** that occurred between 40 and 10 million years ago. Molten material from deep within the Earth pushed through faults to form volcanoes, which deposited ash on the Earth's surface, filling valleys and

understanding the region as an ecosystem with multiple issues on different scales is preferable to short-run, factional actions that inadequately protect and conserve one of the world's great mountain ranges.

Next to loss of habitat, introduced non-native species present the greatest threat to the Sierra Nevada's ecosystem. With no natural enemies, they often crowd out native species, upsetting the balance in fragile habitats.

The brown-headed cowbird, introduced along with cattle grazing, lays its eggs in other birds' nests. This aggressive nest parasite has brought about a sharp decline in Sierra songbirds, especially the willow flycatcher, least Bell's Vireo, yellow warbler, chipping sparrow and song sparrow, and has driven Bell's Vireo to extinction.

Voracious lake trout, introduced into Lake Tahoe for sport fishing, have ravaged native Lahontan cutthroat trout. Non-

Sierra Nevada Geology

Volcanos (C) (eg, Cascades)

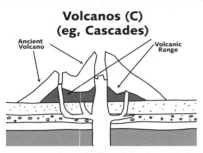

burying streams. In places where lava flowed, it remained behind after softer rock around it eroded away, leaving features such as the Dardanelles Cones and the Devils Postpile.

Glaciers & Glacial Landforms

As a glacier flows downhill under its weight of ice and snow, it creates a distinctive collection of landforms, many of which are preserved once the ice has retreated or vanished. Most of the Sierra Nevada's landscape has been substantially shaped by glaciers. Yosemite National Park provides one of the clearest and most dramatic examples on the face of the planet of glacial action.

The most obvious landform is the **U-shaped valley** gouged out by the glacier as it moves downhill, often with one or more bowl-shaped *cirques* at its head. Cirques are formed along high mountain ridges or at mountain passes or **cols,** Where an alpine glacier, which flows off the upper slopes and ridges of a mountain range, has joined a deeper, more substantial valley glacier, a dramatic **hanging valley** is often the result. In Yosemite, Bridalveil Fall and Yosemite Falls flow over the edge of hanging valleys. Hanging valleys and cirques commonly shelter hidden alpine lakes or **tarns**, such as those featured in many of the hikes in this book. The thin ridge that separates adjacent glacial valleys is known as an **arête**. Where a glacier flows over a knob of bedrock, it leaves a **roche moutonnée** or **sheepback**, elongated in the direction of the ice flow. Lembert Dome in Yosemite's Tuolumne Meadows is a good example of this.

As a glacier grinds its way forward, it usually leaves long, **lateral moraine** ridges along its course – mounds of debris either deposited along the flanks of the glacier or left by sub-ice streams within its heart (the latter, strictly, an **esker**). At the end or **snout** of a glacier is the **terminal moraine**, the point where the giant conveyor belt of ice drops its load of rock and grit. Both high up in the hanging valleys and in the surrounding valleys and plains, **moraine lakes** may form behind a dam of glacial rubble. Yosemite Valley was once filled by such a lake.

The plains that surround once-glaciated mountains may feature a confusing variety of moraine ridges, mounds and outwash fans – material left by rivers flowing from the glaciers. Perched here and there may be an **erratic**, a rock carried far from its origin by the moving ice and left stranded when the ice melted.

native trout introduced throughout the Sierra Nevada have impacted native yellow-legged frogs, wiping them out in some lakes. Introduced bullfrogs have completely replaced native red-legged and yellow-legged frogs in many locations; they also prey on perilously declining western pond turtles. Tumbleweed, almost a symbol of the American West, was actually introduced from Russia in the 19th century. Over 1200 sq miles of native oak woodlands in the western foothills, an area larger than Yosemite National Park, was converted to other vegetation and use within the last half of the 20th century, which shows that the most dangerous invader walks on two legs.

Conservation

The environmental and conservation movement in the US began in the Sierra Nevada, and the mountains have remained on center stage ever since. John Muir first focused attention on the Sierra, working to establish national parks (see 'John Muir,' below). Muir battled vigorously to protect the Tuolumne River in Yosemite National Park, but in 1923, the river was dammed. Hetch Hetchy Valley, which Muir called a second Yosemite Valley, was drowned to provide water for San Francisco. At the same time, most of the water of the Owens Valley in the eastern Sierra, including the 60 sq-mile Mono Lake, was diverted for Los Angeles. Activists still advocate restoring Hetch Hetchy. In the eastern Sierra, court rulings have forced Los Angeles to restrict water usage. As a result, Mono Lake is slowly recovering.

Excessive logging and associated road building have devastated old-growth forests. Water diversion and livestock grazing have impacted streams and riparian zones. Today, off-road vehicles pose a growing threat to the integrity of national

forests. The 1964 Wilderness Act and the 1973 Endangered Species Act provided conservationists with legal tools to counteract the relentless consumption of forests and rivers. In the 1990s, a national debate over the threatened extinction of the spotted owl focused attention on the crucial role of old-growth forests and the importance of intact habitat not only to the mountain ecosystem, but to the aesthetic and spiritual values of the entire nation.

Many organizations, including the US Forest Service (USFS) and key nongovernmental organizations, are actively working to protect the Sierra bioregion. The Sierra Club (☎ 415-977-5500, fax 977-5799, e information@sierraclub.org, w www .sierraclub.org), 85 Second St, 2nd Floor, San Francisco, CA 94105-3441, founded in 1892 by John Muir to preserve the Sierra Nevada, now addresses environmental issues nation-

John Muir (1838–1914)

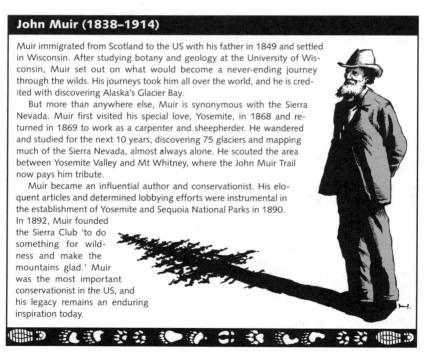

Muir immigrated from Scotland to the US with his father in 1849 and settled in Wisconsin. After studying botany and geology at the University of Wisconsin, Muir set out on what would become a never-ending journey through the wilds. His journeys took him all over the world, and he is credited with discovering Alaska's Glacier Bay.

But more than anywhere else, Muir is synonymous with the Sierra Nevada. Muir first visited his special love, Yosemite, in 1868 and returned in 1869 to work as a carpenter and sheepherder. He wandered and studied for the next 10 years, discovering 75 glaciers and mapping much of the Sierra Nevada, almost always alone. He scouted the area between Yosemite Valley and Mt Whitney, where the John Muir Trail now pays him tribute.

Muir became an influential author and conservationist. His eloquent articles and determined lobbying efforts were instrumental in the establishment of Yosemite and Sequoia National Parks in 1890. In 1892, Muir founded the Sierra Club 'to do something for wildness and make the mountains glad.' Muir was the most important conservationist in the US, and his legacy remains an enduring inspiration today.

wide. It has been instrumental in securing wilderness designation in California and in protecting the public forestlands in the bioregion through its Sierra Nevada Eco-Region Task Force, which serves as a forum for information sharing for activists.

The Sierra Nevada Alliance (☎ 530-542-4546, fax 542-4570, e sna@sierranevada alliance.org, w www.sierranevadaalliance .org), PO Box 7989, South Lake Tahoe, CA 96158, founded in 1993, is a regional coalition of grassroots and regional groups working to protect and restore the natural and community values. The Wilderness Society (☎ 415-561-6641, e ca@tws.org, w www.wilderness.org/ccc/california/range oflight.htm), Presidio Building 1016, POB 29241, San Francisco, CA 94129, founded in 1935, works to secure the preservation of wilderness nationwide. Its 'Range of Light' project in the Sierra Nevada promotes wildland conservation, protects the old-growth forest and encourages better management for national parks and wilderness areas. Also refer to Useful Organizations (p61) for more information.

PARKS & PROTECTED AREAS

More than 21,000 sq miles of the Sierra Nevada, encompassing two-thirds of the entire range, are protected under federal and state management. The US Department of the Interior and the US Department of Agriculture serve as custodians of national public lands. Within the Department of the Interior, the National Park Service (NPS) manages a significant amount of the Sierra Nevada, with the Bureau of Land Management (BLM) managing small scattered pockets. The overwhelming majority of the mountain region is managed by the Department of Agriculture through the United States Forest Service (USFS). Within California and Nevada, a handful of small state parks, mostly around Lake Tahoe, provide additional protection against highway construction and commercial development.

National Park Service

Established in 1916, the NPS manages three national parks in the Sierra Nevada;

Yosemite, Sequoia, and Kings Canyon, and two national monuments; Devils Postpile and Giant Sequoia. The NPS is also responsible for the Pacific Crest National Scenic Trail (PCT), coordinating and advising the various federal, state and private interests through whose land the PCT passes. The NPS protects the natural and historic features of the parks for future generations, while enabling recreation that supports preservation.

The NPS manages the heavily used parks in the interest of conservation, charging a fee for entrance and campgrounds and regulating through a quota system the number of people using backcountry trails and campsites. Many hikers appreciate the infrastructure (including well-marked trails, excellent interpretive materials and the presence of park rangers) that national parks offer. Visit the NPS website at w www.nps.gov for information about and links to NPS-managed areas.

National Forests

The USFS, established in 1905 under President Theodore Roosevelt, manages eight national forests in the Sierra Nevada; Plumas, Tahoe, Eldorado, Toiyabe, Stanislaus, Sierra, Inyo and Sequoia. National forests have less protection than national parks and wilderness areas, and surround them as a type of buffer. They are managed for 'multiple use,' which includes timber cutting, cattle grazing, mineral extraction, watershed management and recreation with and without vehicles. Hunting is also permitted in national forests. Within the Sierra Nevada's national forests are numerous USFS campgrounds that typically require a fee and operate on a first-come, first-served basis. USFS recreation areas, such as Whitney Portal, Big Pine Canyon, Bishop Creek, Rock Creek and Mammoth Lakes, offer picnic facilities and campgrounds. Visit the USFS website at w www.fs.fed.us or any of the numerous ranger stations for information.

Wilderness Areas

The US Congress enacted the Wilderness Act in 1964 to establish a National Wilderness Preservation System of federal lands 'where the Earth and its community of life are untrammeled by man, where man himself is a visitor who does not remain.' Wilderness status is reserved for the most pristine and intact wildlands and affords the highest degree of protection. Within a designated wilderness area, commercial activities, motorized access, roads, structures and facilities are generally prohibited. Although permits are required, camping is free. Roadless areas both within and adjacent to national parks are often designated as wilderness areas.

In addition to more than 2000 sq miles of wilderness within the Sierra Nevada's three national parks, the national forests encompass more than 3000 sq miles of wilderness in 17 designated wilderness areas. From north to south they are Bucks Lake, Mt Rose, Granite Chief, Desolation, Mokelumne, Carson-Iceberg, Emigrant, Hoover, Ansel Adams, John Muir, Kaiser, Dinkey Lakes, Monarch, Jennie Lakes, Golden Trout, South Sierra and Dome Land. Wilderness areas such as these offer what most hikers consider the finest hiking.

The concept of national parks and wilderness areas, which developed in the largely unpopulated American West, often strikes visitors from abroad as curiously American. Resonating deeply within the nation's collective soul, wilderness is linked to the wild frontier heritage and to an ideal of a spiritually pure promised land. It was John Muir himself who wrote,

In wilderness lies the hope of the world – the great, fresh, unblighted, unredeemed wilderness. The galling harness of civilization drops off, and the wounds heal ere we are aware.

Perhaps only in a country with such an enormous economic base and such substantial energy resources as the US could huge areas be set aside permanently as wilderness.

BLM Areas
The BLM manages public use of federal lands, from cattle ranges to 4WD vehicle roads. Very few activities are restricted on BLM lands, which means you can pretty much do as you please. This laissez-faire approach attracts offroad drivers and motorcyclists. Camping is free, although the BLM maintains some fee-based campgrounds. Little land in the Sierra Nevada is managed by the BLM.

State Parks
California and Nevada have their own state park systems. Within the Sierra Nevada, state parks are dwarfed by the massive federal system. The state parks, however, contain some surprisingly beautiful areas around Lake Tahoe with excellent, fee-based campgrounds.

POPULATION & PEOPLE
About 650,000 people live in the Sierra Nevada region, a population that doubled between 1970 and 1990 and is now growing at a rate faster than the rest of California. It is expected to triple again by 2040. Some people live in remote, isolated places, but many reside within easy commuting distance of rapidly growing metropolitan regions. Within 100mi of the Sierra's western foothills are San Francisco, Los Angeles, Sacramento, Fresno and Bakersfield, with Reno and Carson City nearby to the east.

Hikers traveling US 395 along the eastern Sierra will find Basque restaurants in most towns, run by descendants of 19th century immigrant Basque shepherds who grazed their flocks in the alpine meadows of the high Sierra.

SOCIETY & CONDUCT
Traditional Culture
As many as 300,000 Native Americans lived in California when the Spanish arrived in the 18th century. Washoe people's land centered on Lake Tahoe. The Nisenan Maidu lived in the heart of what became California's gold country. The Sierra Miwok traditional territory was in the central foothills, including Yosemite Valley. The Western Mono traditionally lived in the south-central foothills. The Northern Piute and Owens Valley Piute occupied the Sierra's eastern slopes. The Tubatulabal people occupied the Kern River Valley, from its headwaters near Mt Whitney to the southern Sierra.

By the end of the 19th century, native peoples in California were devastated by disease, military battles, poverty and cultural disruption. Forcibly removed from their traditional lands, and with their population depleted, a congressional act in 1906 began the establishment of reservations and rancherias (the Spanish term for a small•Indian settlement) for California's 'landless' Indians. Most Indian lands in the Sierra Nevada today are very small. Native people rely on federal lands for exercising their rights to access cultural resources and ceremonial sites, and to hunt, fish and gather plants.

About 300 Washoe live near Markleeville. Maidu and Miwok people live on small rancherias near their traditional homelands. About 400 Tubatulabal still live in the Kern River Valley. Around 2200 Owens Valley Piutes live on the Benton, Bishop, Big Pine, Lone Pine and Fort Independence reservations. Hikers traveling along US 395 can see some commercial activity from the tribe, such as casinos and stores. Visitors to the national parks find museums displaying artifacts and exhibits of Native American culture. Today it is largely through place names that hikers encounter remnants of Native American traditions.

Dos & Don'ts

During the busy summer months from June to August in the national parks and around Lake Tahoe, you find lots of people with whom you'll be sharing the scenery and the facilities. Most are generally well-behaved and polite, standing in line, obeying the rules and following instructions. In the backcountry, where people often go to commune with nature in solitude, talking loudly, littering, smoking, cutting vegetation, keeping a messy campsite and disregarding permit regulations are frowned upon. Hikers often make small talk when meeting and generally exchange brief greetings when passing on a trail. Most hikers stay to the right when passing other hikers.

Dress codes are practically nonexistent in the backcountry and it is definitely a place where you're likely to witness (or experience) public nudity. In heavy-use areas such as national parks, it's best to keep your clothes on, though men can hike bare-chested and women can hike in shorts and a sports bra. In the backcountry, most hikers eschew the use of swimming suits when taking a quick plunge into an inviting mountain lake. In towns and national park activity centers, shirt and shoes are required to enter most stores and all restaurants.

WATCHING WILDLIFE

The Sierra Nevada comprises a single, continuous ecosystem. About half of California's 7000 plant species grow in the Sierra Nevada, with more than 400 species growing only there. Some 300 animal species (mammals, birds, reptiles and amphibians) make their home in this mountain range, and another 100 species are occasional visitors.

The Sierra's summers are too dry and winters too cold for most deciduous trees, so it is the evergreen conifer (cone-bearing) trees that dominate throughout the mountain range and indeed, throughout California. The Sierra Nevada's forest relies heavily on fire to sustain itself as a healthy, functioning ecosystem.

Pines are the most common trees in the Sierra Nevada. It's easy to tell them from other conifers – firs, hemlocks, cedars, junipers and sequoias. Firs and hemlocks have single needles arranged along the twig. True firs have upright cones on their upper branches. Their needles grow in a row, with little smooth scars on the twigs where the old needles fell off. Douglas firs, which are halfway between true firs and hemlocks, have cones that hang down and 1-inch-long flat needles that grow all around the twig.

Hemlock cones hang down, and their half-inch long round needles – you can twirl them between thumb and forefinger – grow all around the twig. Cedars, junipers and sequoias all have scale-like needles. Cedar needles look like they were ironed flat, but junipers have round needles and distinctive, fragrant berries (the flavor in gin). Sequoias also have round, scale-like needles and are unmistakable giant trees, growing in isolated, well-identified groves.

The needles of pines grow in a bunch, bundled together on the twig. The key is to count the number of needles in the bundle. The only pine with a single needle is the pinyon pine. It has round 1½-inch-long needles and grows in the drier eastern and far southern Sierra. If the needles are two to a bundle, then you've probably got a lodgepole pine. If they're three to a bundle, you've got either a Jeffrey pine or a ponderosa pine. Jeffrey

Left: Coville's columbine grows in bright bunches.

pines have vanilla-scented bark and cones that are not prickly. Ponderosa pines have no smell and decidedly prickly cones – pick one up and see. If the pine has five needles in a bundle, you've got four possibilities.

Foxtail pines, found only at high elevations in the southern Sierra, have needles less than 1½ inches long, densely clustered on the twig like a fox's tail, and distinctively furrowed reddish bark. Sugar pines are very tall trees, with unmistakable cones more than 1ft long. Western white pines also grow tall, with 9-inch-long cones formed of thin scales. Whitebark pines are found only at very high elevation in the subalpine zone, so if you're near timberline, it's probably whitebark pine. *Pacific Coast Tree Finder,* by Tom Watts, is a handy pocket guide for identifying trees.

Each type of conifer grows in a specific elevation range, and as you hike upward, the trees are progressively more hardy for the colder, higher elevation climate. Hiking into the Sierra Nevada is actually like traveling north; as you ascend, you pass through four bands of vegetation, termed life zones – lower montane zone, upper montane zone, subalpine zone, and the highest, arctic-like alpine zone. Each band contains characteristic, easily recognizable plants and animals that demonstrate the remarkable diversity of life and habitat. On the drier, eastern side of the range, the life zones are higher than on the wetter, western side. Likewise, the cooler, north-facing slopes form a different habitat than the warmer, south-facing ones.

Plants and animals found predominantly in one zone typically also occupy the margins of adjacent zones. The boundaries of zones are variable, and slight differences in temperature or moisture can raise or lower the extent of a vegetation band. Animals, being mobile, have a wider range. Most can be found in several zones.

Two notable large mammals – coyotes *(Canis latrans)* and black bears *(Euarctos americanus)* – roam through every single Sierra life zone. Coyotes, stars of Native American legends and objects of ranchers' extermination campaigns, average from 20lb to 45lb and have pointed ears, a pointy nose and a 12-inch to 15-inch-long black-tipped tail. Black bears actually come in a variety of shades – light tan, dark brown, reddish brown – so their most recognizable feature is their short, rounded ears. While their traditional diet is wild plants, fish, insects and the inner bark of conifers, bears are great scavengers and known for their dexterity at opening anything containing food. Sadly, black bears have become campground pests at many national parks and wilderness areas (see Bears, p57).

Lower Montane Zone

Between 3500ft and 6000ft, evergreen conifer trees are the predominant vegetation. On arid southern slopes in the lower part of this zone, however, montane chaparral forms rough, dense, evergreen thickets of huckleberry oak *(Quercus dumosa)*, Sierra chinquapin *(Chrysolepis sempervirens)*, white ceanothus or buck brush *(Ceanothus cuneatus)* and manzanita *(Arctostaphylos manzanita)*. In shaded valleys you find montane hardwood habitat, with black oaks *(Q. kelloggii)*, evergreen canyon live oaks *(Q. chrysolepis)* and evergreen California laurels *(Umbellularia californica)*. Yosemite Valley is classic hardwood oak and conifer habitat. Warm, dry areas favor this zone's signature conifers, ponderosa pines *(Pinus ponderosa)*, along with incense cedars *(Calocedrus decurrens)* and sugar pines *(P. lambertiana)*, the world's tallest pine.

On the open ponderosa pine forest floor hikers may find carpets of mountain misery *(Chamaebatia foliolosa)*, and thickets of ceanothus and manzanita. Manzanitas produce lovely pink spring flowers and dry, russet autumn berries, a favorite food of black bears. Cool moist areas in this zone favor white firs *(Abies concolor)* and douglas firs *(Pseudotsuga menziesii)*. Along streams, look for pretty pink flowering currant bushes *(Ribes* sp.*)* and edible crimson thimbleberries *(Rubus parviflorus)*. In springtime, fleshy, bright red snow plants *(Sarcodes sanguinea)* emerge from the ground and broad-leafed white-flowering Pacific dogwoods *(Cornus nuttallii)* brighten the forest.

Fire is a common event in this zone, and the vegetation is well adapted to it. Natural, lightning-induced fires occur about every 10 years, burning the deadwood, brush and small trees while leaving mature trees intact. This favors ponderosa pines and black oaks. Where fire is suppressed,

Regal Redwoods

Giant redwoods *(Sequoiadendron giganteum)*, commonly called giant sequoia, are an ancient species more than 50 million years old. Once widespread, climatic changes have altered its distribution and it now survives only in 75 isolated groves in the western Sierra Nevada between 4500ft and 8000ft. These towering red giants are the largest living single organisms on Earth. A giant sequoia typically reaches between 250ft and 300ft in height and 40ft in diameter and lives as long as 3000 years (the oldest is estimated to be 3500 years old). The trees are impervious to fire and resistant to disease and insects; it is their immense mass that eventually causes them to topple when their shallow root system can no longer support their great weight. Protected groves of these majestic trees, which are related to the taller coast redwoods *(Sequoia sempervirens)* and dawn redwoods *(Metasequoia gylptostrobides)* of China, stand in Yosemite, Sequoia and Kings Canyon National Parks.

white firs and incense cedars proliferate. In Yosemite Valley, much to the consternation of park managers, these trees are replacing the more open pine and oak woodlands and obscuring once-famous views.

Unique giant sequoias (see 'Regal Redwoods,' p28) grow in isolated groves at the upper level of this zone and are all protected within three national parks and the Giant Sequoia National Monument.

Hikers passing through warm, dry oak or chaparral habitat may spot southern alligator lizards *(Elgaria multicarinata)* basking along the trail. Their yellow eyes and black back pattern on a mostly brown back and white underbelly distinguish them from smaller western fence lizards *(Sceloporus occidentalis),* which have a brown pattern on a mostly gray back, dark blue underbelly, and limbs that are orangish on the underside. Fence lizards, common along trails, prefer the ponderosa pine habitat. Another reptilian resident of this zone is the Gilbert's skink *(Eumeces gilberti)* with elastic, smooth-scaled skin and tiny legs. Its head and neck turn a bright pink when breeding in the spring. One resident of the warm, dry regions of this zone that hikers want to avoid is the western rattlesnake *(Crotalus viridus).* Although this venomous snake's warning rattle often signals its presence, hikers should be alert when hiking in this zone, especially mornings and late afternoons (see snake Warning, p206).

The abundant food supply in this zone supports many kinds of rodents. Brush mice *(Peromyscus boylii)* and very common white-footed deer mice *(P. maniculatus)* are active at night. It's easy to distinguish between very common squirrels and chipmunks; squirrels have a ring around their eyes and chipmunks have a face stripe that runs over their eyes. In open oak woodlands, bushy-tailed western gray squirrels *(Sciurus griseus)* build nests in trees, while smaller, brown California ground squirrels *(Spermophilus beecheyi)* burrow underground. Bushy-tailed Douglas squirrels *(Tamiasciurus douglasii)* thrive on pine cones and are active and readily seen, especially in sequoia groves. Small yellow-pine chipmunks *(Tamias amoenus),* with brightly patterned black and white stripes above and below their eyes and down their backs, burrow beneath brush in ponderosa and Jeffrey pine forests.

Among the nighttime predators hunting mice, insects and eggs are striped skunks *(Mephitis mephitis).* Easily identified by their white-crowned head and parallel white stripes along their black back, skunks can, if threatened, turn, raise their tail and in an instant emit a sulphurous spray for up to 15ft that stings the eyes and persists for hours. Solitary hunters in semi-arid canyons and forests, mountain lions *(Felis concolor)* grow up to 8ft in length. Although the cats are shy and rarely a threat to hikers, attacks have occurred. Mountain lions prefer deer, rabbits and small rodents.

Right: A mountain lion can weigh 200 lb.

Another nocturnal hunter in this zone, especially in the denser white fir habitat, is the great horned owl *(Bubo virginianus)*. Hikers may hear its call of five to eight hoots, with the second or third hoot rapid and doubled: hoooo, hoo-hoooo, hoooo, hoooo, hoooo. Old-growth douglas fir forests are the habitat for spotted owls *(Strix occidentalis)*. In daytime, ubiquitous red-tailed hawks *(Buteo jamaicensis)*, California's most common large hawk, soar in search of prey. Sharp-shinned hawks *(Accipiter striatus)*, half the size of their red-tailed cousins, are expert at catching small birds in flight. About the same size, but with pointed wings and black sideburns on a white face, American kestrels *(Falco sparverius)* are a common summer resident of this zone.

Hikers may hear the staccato tapping of acorn woodpeckers *(Melanerpes formicivorus)* in mixed oak and pine woodlands and of white-headed woodpeckers *(Picoides albolarvatus)* in ponderosa pine habitat. Small white-breasted nuthatches creep headfirst in all directions along tree bark, looking for bugs. The raucous voices of black-crested Steller's jays *(Cyanocitta stelleri)* as they boldly enter campsites in search of food make them the most readily noticed birds of the conifer forest.

As you reach the upper part of the lower montane zone, ponderosa pines yield to very similar Jeffrey pines *(P. jeffreyi)*, which grow well in dry, rocky soils. Especially prevalent in the drier, eastern parts of the Sierra Nevada, they are often accompanied by an understory of manzanitas. Lewis' woodpeckers *(Melanerpes lewis)*, mid-sized black birds with red cheeks, silver collar and pink belly, prefer the open Jeffrey pine forest. Black-tailed mule deers *(Odocolieus hemionus)* frequent this open habitat, as well as lower open oak and pine woodlands.

Upper Montane Zone

As hikers ascend from 6000ft to 8500ft, the conifers of the lower montane zone yield to their look-alikes in the upper montane zone. Ponderosa pines yield to Jeffrey pines, sugar pines yield to western white pines *(P. monticola)*, white firs yield to California red firs *(Abies magnifica)*, and incense cedars to red-barked western junipers *(Juniperus occidentalis)*, which favor exposed, south-facing granite slopes and ridges. Where the ground is moist and level, lodgepole pines *(P. contorta)* are the dominant conifers in the upper montane zone, which is sometimes

JOHN MOCK

Left: Lodgepole pine needles are cylindrical.

called the lodgepole pine zone. Where the ground is slightly sloped and dry, hikers stroll through strikingly colorful, open, red fir forest.

The drier red fir forest has fewer shrubs and flowers with less food for burrowing rodents than the wetter and more dense lodgepole pine forest of this zone. In the red fir forest, bright red snow plants are conspicuous in springtime, and sagebrush lizards *(Scleoporus graciosus)*, similar to but darker than fence lizards, bask in dry areas. Golden-mantled ground squirrels *(Spermophilus lateralis)*, with orange-colored heads and shoulders and black bordered white-striped backs, are easy to spot. More difficult to see are American martens *(Martes americana)*, about 2ft long with dense brown fur and a bushy tail, that prey on ground squirrels, often leaping from tree to tree as they seek their prey.

Western terrestrial garter snakes *(Thamnophis elegans)*, with a narrow yellow back stripe, prefer the moist lodgepole forest, where tiny deer mice and gray and black striped lodgepole chipmunks *(Tamias speciosus)* scurry about. Both long-tailed weasels *(Mustela frenata)* and short-tailed weasels, or ermines *(M. erminea)*, are active hunters here.

Mountain chickadees, with their black crown and throat and gray bodies, are perfectly camouflaged among the gray-barked lodgepole pines, where pine siskins *(Carduelis pinus)* and pine grosbeaks *(Pinicola enucleator)*, both finches, also thrive on seeds. Ground-dwelling blue grouse *(Dendragapus obscurus)* live in fir forests, where hikers may hear the drum-like reverberating hoot of the male. Woodpeckers, which fold their wings against their body as they fly, like lodgepole habitat. Look for medium-sized Williamson's sapsuckers *(Sphyrapicus thyroideus)*, with their two thin white head stripes, red throat and distinctive yellowish belly. Small red-breasted nuthatches *(Sitta canadensis)* creep head-down along tree trunks in search of insects.

In open areas, western wood pewees *(Contopus sordidulus)* and olive-sided flycatchers *(Contopus borealis)* catch flying insects, while olive-tinged golden-crowned kinglets *(Regulus satrapa)* and bright western tanagers *(Piranga ludoviciana)*, with their red head, yellow breast and black wings and tail, feed on flying insects in the treetops.

Streamside habitats offer the most open area in the upper montane zone. Willows *(Salix* spp.) line most streams, especially in the drier eastern Sierra. White-barked quaking aspens *(Populus tremuloides)* and gray-barked black cottonwoods *(P. balsamifera)*, whose leaves turn bright yellow in autumn, line streams and meadows, and are a favorite food of mountain beavers *(Aplodontia rufa)*, the Sierra Nevada's largest rodent. Along streams, American dippers *(Cinclus mexicanus)* make for interesting bird-watching. They bob as they perch on rocks, and their transparent eyelids enable them to walk underwater and feed on insect larvae. Lakes in this zone are often lined with lodgepole pines, where Pacific tree frogs *(Hyla regilla)* provide hikers with an evening serenade.

Right: Woodpeckers often nest in lodgepole pines.

Subalpine Zone

In the subalpine zone, between 8500ft and 10,500ft, trees are shorter and more widely spaced than at lower elevations and are often twisted by wind. Typically growing in small clusters, whitebark pines *(Pinus albicaulis)* prevail, with mountain hemlocks *(Tsuga mertensiana)* on moist north-facing slopes. In the southernmost Sierra, gnarled foxtail pines *(P. balfouriana)* thrive on dry, sandy or rocky slopes. Yellow-bellied marmots *(Marmota flaviventris)* abound everywhere in rocky areas and loud-voiced grey Clark's nutcrackers *(Nucifraga columbiana)*, with black wings and white tail feathers, are equally common.

Meadows, in addition to mosquitoes *(Culex* spp.), host a multitude of wildflowers, such as purple large-leaf lupines *(Lupinus polyphyllus)*, whorled penstemons *(Penstemon rydbergii)*, Sierra gentians *(Gentianopsis holopetala)*, pink swamp onions *(Allium validum)*, pine alpine shooting stars *(Dodecatheon alpinum)*, yellow alpine buttercups *(Ranunculus eschscholtzii)*, yellow seep-spring monkeyflowers *(Mimulus guttatus)* and tall, densely white-flowered corn lilies *(Veratrum californicum)*. Around lakes, pink mountain heather *(Phyllodoce breweri)* forms profuse carpets.

In open and rocky areas, look for short purple-and-white Brewer's lupines *(Lupinus breweri)* and timberline penstemons *(Penstemon davidsonii)*. You may also see pink rock fringes *(Epilobium obcordatum)*, Sierra primroses *(Primula suffrutescens)*, mountain pride penstemons *(Penstemon newberryi)* and spreading phlox *(Phlox diffusa)*. In sandy soil, look for pink pussy paws *(Calytridium umbellatum)*. Red-petaled wavy-leaved paintbrushes *(Castilleja applegatei)* and yellow-flowered mountain mule ears *(Wyethia mollis)*, with their large soft hairy leaves, grow on rocky slopes – often near trails.

Summer migrants to the subalpine zone include Rufus hummingbirds *(Selasphorus rufus)*, which feed on flowers, and white-throated swifts *(Aeronautes saxatilis)* and violet-green swallows *(Tachycineta thalassina)*, which feed on insects. Golden eagles *(Aquila chrysaetos)* soar overhead year-round.

Alpine Zone

Above tree line, higher than 10,000ft in the alpine zone, summer meadows are lush with grasses and wildflowers. Look for the purple petals and yellow disks of alpine asters *(Aster alpigenus)*, pink little elephant's heads *(Pedicularis attollens)*, yellow shrubby cinquefoil *(Potentilla fructicosa)* and alpine gentians *(Gentiana newberryi)*, with a white funnel-shaped flower with a dark purple strip on the outside of each petal. The bell-shaped tiny flowers of white heather *(Cassiope mertensiana)* and

Left: Lupine can grow to 3ft tall.

Top Left: Foxtail pines have a distinctive purple and resinous cone.
Top Right: Bright snow plants are rare and protected by law.
Bottom: Arrowleaf balsamroot provides color in the Sierra Nevada foothills.

JOHN MOCK

JOHN MOCK

WES WALKER

WAYNE BERNHARDSON

Clockwise from top left: Black bears ahead? They abound near Spooner Summit and throughout the Sierra. Sky pilot, able to grow at a high elevation, flourishes on Mt Dana, Yosemite National Park. Colorful Indian paintbrush grows creekside in the mountains. Yellow-bellied marmots are plentiful in rocky areas of the Sierra.

mats of four-inch-tall dwarf arctic willow *(Salix artica)* grow near lakes and streams. On dry and rocky places, hikers find white-petalled cut-leaved daisies *(Erigeron compositus)*, yellow cushion stenotus *(Stenotus acaulis)*, white- or yellow-petalled Coville's columbine *(Aquilegia pubescens)* and pale yellow alpine paintbrushes *(Castilleja nana)*. Here is also the aptly named alpine gold *(Hulsea algida)*, a favorite food of Sierra Nevada bighorn sheep (see 'Lambs to the Slaughter,' below). Growing higher than any other plant are purple clusters of sky pilot *(Polemonium eximium)*, amid granite rocks painted fluorescent orange by lichens.

In the open grasslands of the alpine tundra, rusty-brown Beldings ground squirrels *(Spermophilus beldingi)* and gray-crowned rosy finches are characteristic residents, as are horned larks *(Eremophila alpestris)*. On the rocky slopes live marmots and small, round-eared American pikas *(Ochotona princeps)*.

Endangered Species

Loss of habitat is the single greatest threat to wildlife in the Sierra Nevada. Throughout California, 30% of the fauna are considered at risk

Lambs to the Slaughter

Sierra Nevada bighorn sheep *(Ovis canadensis sierrae)* are unique to the steep, rugged crest and eastern escarpment of the Sierra Nevada. Historically, bighorn sheep were found from the Sonora Pass to the southern end of today's Sequoia National Park. Disease and competition from huge flocks of domestic sheep in the 19th and 20th centuries decimated the once abundant bighorn population.

In 1971, the USFS created two Bighorn Sheep Zoological Areas north and south of Kearsarge Pass to protect the sheep, and in 1972 California listed the bighorn as threatened. Bighorn were reintroduced to the Lee Vining canyon east of Yosemite National Park in 1985.

Since 1986, bighorn populations have dropped by two-thirds. The main factor driving the decline is predation by mountain lions and abandonment of low-elevation winter range due to mountain lion activity, leading to poor sheep nutrition in harsh late-winter and spring conditions. A California law protecting mountain lions from being hunted has increased the lion population, with the ironic consequence that bighorns are dying from poor nutrition.

California upgraded the bighorn's status from threatened to endangered in March 1999. In April 1999, the US Fish and Wildlife Service (USFWS) also listed the bighorn as endangered. The USFS plans to use prescribed burning to reduce hiding cover for mountain lions, which should improve bighorn habitat and their chance for survival.

by state or federal agencies, while only 17% of Sierra fauna are listed as endangered, threatened, of special concern, or sensitive. Still, this amounts to as many as 69 animal species. All management plans must conform to both state and federal laws to protect these species.

Endangered species include Sierra Nevada bighorn sheep, great gray owls *(Strix nebulosa)*, Peregrine falcons *(Falco peregrinus)*, willow flycatchers *(Empidonax trailii)* and mute mountain yellow-legged frogs *(Rana muscosa)*, one of the Sierra Nevada's few high-altitude amphibians.

Threatened species include California wolverines *(Gulo gulo luteus)*, Sierra Nevada red foxes *(Vulpes vulpes necator)*, bald eagles *(Haliaeetus leucocephalus)*, Lahontan cutthroat trout *(Oncorhynchus clarki henshawi)*, limestone salamanders *(Hydromantes brunus)* and California red-legged frogs *(Rana aurora draytonii)*.

Species not yet listed as endangered or threatened can be classified as species of concern, and include Yosemite toads *(Bufo canorus)*, northwestern pond turtles *(Clemmys marmorata marmorata)* and southwestern pond turtles *(C. marmorata pallida)*, California horned lizards *(Phrynosoma coronatum frontale)*, Mt Lyell salamanders *(Hydromantes platycephalus)*. Also on the species of concern list is California's state fish, the native golden trout *(Salmo aguabonita)*, the Piute cutthroat trout *(S. clarki seleniris)*, Pallid bats *(Antrozous pallidus)* and Townsend's big-eared bats *(Corynorhinus townsendii townsendii)*. Others include California spotted owls *(Strix occidentalis occidentalis)*, northern goshawks *(Accipter gentilis)*, olive-sided flycatchers *(Contopus cooperi)*, Pacific fishers *(Martes pennanti)*, American martens *(M. americana)* and the Sierra Nevada mountain beaver *(Aplodontia rufa californica)*.

Three animals once widely present throughout the range are now extinct in the Sierra Nevada: Bell's Vireo, the California condor and the grizzly bear. Bell's vireos were wiped out by nest-parasite cowbirds. California condors suffered from ingestion of lead rifle slugs in their prey, collision with power lines and indiscriminate shooting.

Although the state flag sports one, California's grizzly bears were exterminated by Euro-American settlers. Common throughout California in the mid-19th century, the last grizzly was shot near Kings Canyon in the 1920s. Grizzlies were especially common in the Yosemite region, where the Native American Ahwahneechee were known by the Miwok word *uzumati* (grizzly bear). This word, incorrectly pronounced by soldiers, was anglicized into 'yosemite.'

Left: A California condor.

Facts for the Hiker

The Sierra Nevada holds what may well be the finest hiking in the US. In addition to its spectacular scenery and near-perfect summer weather, hikers enjoy established, well-maintained and clearly marked trails. Signposts at trailheads and at trail junctions typically give distances and point the direction to destinations along the hike. Hikers, however, will not find signs marking the trail as they hike (other than rudimentary blazes on trees), except for on the Pacific Crest National Scenic Trail and the Tahoe Rim Trail, each of which has its own unique identifying emblem. Any cross-country travel is optional. All trailheads are accessible by a typical passenger automobile; a 4WD and/or high-clearance vehicle is not necessary for any of these hikes.

The mountains are still largely wilderness, with few visible signs of human presence other than the trails themselves. Bridges exist on some key river crossings, but hikers cross most smaller streams either via walking across a log, hopping rocks or by fording. These crossings can be difficult in early season, when water is high. Natural fire is a part of the landscape, and in late season when the lower elevation forests are dry, hikers may encounter smoke along the trail from wildfires. Because the available fuel is more scarce at higher elevation, hikers rarely encounter a wildfire in the high country. Lightning strikes are the main cause of fires. Storms can also bring snow or heavy rain, and hikers should be prepared for sudden changes in weather. Fortunately, most summer storms rarely last more than a few hours.

Human presence in the Sierra Nevada has, however, introduced two significant changes that all hikers must be prepared for: contaminated water and wildlife trying to get your food. That said, hiking in these mountains is a true pleasure. Most hikers in the Sierra Nevada consider their hikes in the mountains to be the finest times of their lives. To make the most of your hike, be it a

Highlights

Here are some hikes, listed thematically, to help you get started with selecting one that satisfies your craving for fun and adventure.

- **Best Day Hikes** Mt Tallac, Mt Rose, East Lake, Clouds Rest, North Dome, Four Mile & Panorama Trails, Trail of the Sequoias
- **Best Overnight Hikes** Half Dome, Tenaya Lake to Yosemite Valley, Lower Monarch Lake, Gem Lakes, Fourth Recess Lake
- **Ideal Picnic Spots** Mt Judah Loop, Winnemucca & Round Top Lakes, Nevada Fall, Sentinel Dome & Taft Point, Mist Falls
- **Hiking Peaks** Ellis Peak, Mt Tallac, Mt Rose, Half Dome, Mt Hoffmann, Mt Dana, Mt Whitney
- **Gentle Hikes** Rubicon Trail, Mono Pass, Congress Trail, Gem Lakes
- **Great Passes & Ridges** Dicks & Phipps Passes, St Marys Pass, Sawtooth Ridge, Vogelsang, Rae Lakes Loop, High Sierra Trail, Franklin & Sawtooth Passes, Mammoth Crest, Humphreys & Evolution Basins, Sixty Lake Basin, New Army & Cottonwood Passes
- **Alpine Lakes** Dicks & Phipps Passes, Virginia Lakes, Cathedral Lakes, Vogelsang, Lake Reflection, Minaret Lake, Thousand Island Lake, Palisades
- **Waterfalls** Grass Lake, Vernal Fall, Nevada Fall, Yosemite Falls, Four Mile & Panorama Trails, Sentinel Dome & Taft Point, Waterwheel Falls, Wapama Falls, Chilnualna Falls, Mist Falls
- **Early Season Hikes** Rubicon Trail, Wapama Falls, Chilnualna Falls
- **Wildflowers** Donner Summit to Squaw Valley, Echo Summit to Carson Pass, Winnemucca & Round Top Lakes, Cathedral Lakes, Lyell Canyon, Wapama Falls, Summit & Virginia Passes
- **Authors' Favorites** Tahoe Meadows to Spooner Summit, Falls Meadow, Summit & Virginia Passes, North Dome, Clouds Rest, Mammoth Crest, Sixty Lake Basin

day hike or a week-long backpacking trip, don't push yourself too hard starting out. Take breaks, stop for a swim, and spend time in meadows watching wildflowers, birds, butterflies and wildlife. Visit the top of a Sierra summit, no matter how high or low, for the reward of a true peak experience. The Sierra Nevada is a gentle wilderness, yet like all wilderness, it is a wild place. Treat it with respect and approach it with a clear understanding of your own abilities. No matter your age, no matter your abilities, there is more than enough here to fill a lifetime.

SUGGESTED ITINERARIES

Regardless of the length of your trip, combining several day hikes or short overnight or multiple-day trips enables you to see the most of the Sierra Nevada.

One Week

If you're planning a week-long trip, focus on a single geographical area. If this will be your only trip to the Sierra Nevada, then visiting Yosemite National Park is a must. The recommended approach is to do consecutive day hikes. You'll see the park's most spectacular features and also get in great shape. Start in Yosemite Valley with the Yosemite Falls, Vernal Fall and Nevada Fall hikes. Or, if you're more fit, you could do the Four Mile & Panorama Trails hike instead of the Vernal Fall and Nevada Fall hikes. Next head to Tuolumne and do the North Dome, Clouds Rest and Mt Dana hikes. If it's midsummer and too hot or too crowded in Yosemite Valley, you could start in Tuolumne with the Mt Dana or Mt Hoffmann hike, followed by the Tenaya Lake to Yosemite Valley hike with a side trip to Half Dome. A final day hike to Yosemite Falls would round out a week.

In the Lake Tahoe area, try combining several hikes. Start with one or more day hikes to the top of a peak, such as Mt Tallac and Mt Rose, for sweeping views over the lake. Ellis Peak is a shorter and easier (but still spectacular) alternative hike. Follow these day hikes with one or two overnight trips, such as the Tahoe Meadows to Spooner Summit hike and the Echo Summit to Carson Pass hike.

If you'd like to combine two geographical areas, drive to Tuolumne Meadows in Yosemite National Park for a day hike – North Dome, Cathedral Lakes or Mt Dana. Then continue on Hwy 120 to US 395 and head south for a series of day hikes in the eastern Sierra. First, do the Mammoth Crest hike from Mammoth Lakes; next, visit Gem Lakes in Little Lakes Valley as a day hike, and continue south on US 395 to finish up the week with a day hike in the Palisades.

For those wishing to spend their time in one place, the classic hike to the summit of Mt Whitney is the Sierra Nevada's most coveted hike, although it's only a three-day hike at most. Recommended week-long hikes are Humphreys & Evolution Basins or Sixty Lake Basin, both starting from the eastern Sierra, and the five-day Rae Lakes Loop in Kings Canyon National Park followed by a day trip to Sequoia National Park's Giant Forest.

Two Weeks

With two weeks, you have plenty of time to visit two geographical areas and include a few overnight or longer hikes.

Visit Yosemite National Park followed by the eastern Sierra for hiking amid the peaks of the High Sierra. Spend a few days in Yosemite Valley doing day hikes and include a trip to the top of Half Dome. Drive to Tuolumne and see the Cathedral Lakes and Mono Pass. Drive across Tioga Pass to the eastern Sierra and then south on US 395. There's plenty of time for hiking in the Mammoth area, followed by the Palisades and Little Lakes Valley.

Alternatively, visit Yosemite National Park and then, from US 395, do hikes in the Hoover Wilderness that access northeastern Yosemite. After Yosemite, drive toward Bridgeport and do the Virginia Lakes hike. Next drive to Green Creek and do the East Lake or Summit & Virginia Passes hike. Follow either of these hikes with the Sawtooth Ridge hike. If you're not too tired, drive west over Hwy 108 and make a quick trip to St Marys Pass.

If you're starting from southern California, drive north on US 395 and start with overnight hikes in the Palisades and Little Lakes Valley. Then tackle one of the longer hikes through Kings Canyon National Park – either Sixty Lake Basin or Humphreys & Evolution Basins. If you're up for it, check to see if any Mt Whitney day hike permits are available! (See the Mt Whitney hike, p274.)

Another strategy is to start in the Lake Tahoe area and make your way south. Start in Desolation Wilderness with the Dicks & Phipps Passes hike, possibly with an excursion to the top of Mt Tallac. Next, drive to Carson Pass on Hwy 88 for the Winnemucca & Round Top Lakes hike. Relax overnight at Grover Hot Springs State Park, then venture into Carson-Iceberg Wilderness on the Falls Meadow hike.

To focus on just one long hike, head to Sequoia National Park. First, allow a day to visit the Giant Forest and walk the Congress Trail and Trail of the Sequoias. Nearby is the trailhead for the High Sierra Trail, a classic trans-Sierra route that takes you across passes and to the summit of Mt Whitney. You'll finish in the eastern Sierra far away from where you started, but what a great hike it will have been!

One Month

The combination of hikes that you could do in a month is almost limitless. You can hike in Sequoia and Kings Canyon National Parks from the eastern Sierra, Yosemite's Tuolumne area, and continue north on US 395 to Lake Tahoe. But one month gives you the unique opportunity to indulge your hiking fantasies with a once-in-a-lifetime trip on one of the classic long-distance trails. To experience the almost uninterrupted wilderness that typifies the Sierra Nevada, try either the John Muir Trail or the Tahoe-Yosemite Trail.

WHEN TO HIKE

The hiking season, from June to October, has three parts. From June to July is early season, when snow remains in the high country, especially on north- and east-facing slopes. Rivers and streams are swollen, and mosquitoes flourish at lower elevations. Occasionally unstable weather brings rain, or

snow at higher elevations. In years with a light snowpack, the hiking season may start as early as April at lower elevations.

By midseason, from August to Labor Day, most snow has melted except on the north face of high-elevation passes. Days are warm and the weather is stable. Afternoon thunderstorms with lightning are common, though rarely lasting more than an hour or two. Still, it is a good idea to cross passes before noon. In late season, from Labor Day to mid-October, skies are generally clear and nights cold, often below freezing, and mosquitoes are gone. Pleasant days can be mixed with days of light rain or snow. The first major snowstorm, with more than a foot of snow accumulation higher than 10,000ft, usually arrives after mid-September, but typically melts off. By mid-October, snowfall no longer melts, and winter snow accumulation begins.

Hiking conditions depend upon the previous winter's accumulated snowpack and the rate of the annual spring thaw, which is determined by the amount of spring sunshine. The thaw begins in May, reaching the High Sierra in June and July. Hikers can contact ranger stations by April to ask if the year's snowpack is light, average or heavy. The California Department of Water Resources, with data provided by the California Cooperative Snow Surveys, reports the daily snowpack by river basin on their website at W http://cdec.water.ca.gov/snow/current/snow. This is a very useful planning tool for early season hikes.

The least crowded times are before Memorial Day and after Labor Day, when the backcountry is nearly deserted. A noticeable increase in activity starts on Memorial Day weekend. The busiest time is between Independence Day and Labor Day, with August being the peak month. Memorial Day, Independence Day and Labor Day weekends are the most crowded times, but the week and weekend before each of these holidays are comparatively quiet in the backcountry. See Public Holidays (p69) for details on when these holidays occur.

Summer days enjoy long hours of daylight. Sunrise is as early as 5:30am and the sun sets after 8pm. You can hike as long and far as you want, and still have plenty of daylight to settle into camp each evening and have dinner. Alternatively, you can hike all day and stop for your evening meal about 5 or 6pm, well before dusk, and hike again for another hour or two after dinner.

WHAT KIND OF HIKE?

Most hikers in the Sierra Nevada plan their own trip. A day hike is fairly easy to organize, requiring little more than packing a lunch and a few other essentials. Some day hikes also require you to register at the trailhead, which takes a few extra minutes to write your name and provide some information. Multiple-day backpacking trips, however, require more planning.

Almost all backpacking trips take you through national forests and wilderness areas where there are no places to get supplies and no shelters or huts. This means that a backpacking trip is always a camping trip, where you have to be self sufficient and start from the trailhead with everything you need. This includes the required permits (see Permits & Fees, p53) along with your shelter, bedding, camping and cooking equipment, and food and fuel for your entire trip. Independent backpacking is, therefore, physically and mentally exacting. It suits the patient and outgoing individual with a high degree of self reliance and enough physical conditioning to carry a full load and still do all the camp chores (eg, cooking, cleaning, hauling water, and setting up and striking camp).

You also need good trail sense and basic navigational skills. If you're considering tackling one of the long-distance trails, remember that your physical ability to carry food and fuel, usually no more than seven to ten days worth, requires you to resupply along the way. Of course, if you can do all this, backpacking is probably the most rewarding way to go, offering the greatest freedom to experience the backcountry at your own pace and interest. If you're not inclined to take on the challenge of an independent trip, you should either go on an organized hike or hire a guide.

If you decide on an independent backpacking trip, you can choose from two basic approaches to planning your itinerary. One approach is to hike along a trail each day, moving to a new campsite every night. With the advantage of moving progressively across new terrain daily, you avoid any backtracking. On long-distance trails this is usually the only option. If moving campsites every day seems like too much, you can always add a rest day. On such hikes, you either make a loop (circuit) or near loop that brings you back to the same starting point, or else follow a trail that starts in one place and finishes in another.

For hikes that start in one place and finish in another, you need to have a strategy to get between the two trailheads. This can mean having two vehicles and parking one at each trailhead, having someone drop you off and pick you up later, or (where possible) incorporating public transportation.

Another approach is to hike in from the trailhead one or two days and set up a base from which to do day hikes. This enables you to explore the surrounding backcountry with a light day-pack and maximize your hiking time since you don't have to strike and set up camp daily. It's a good approach if you only have a few nights, or if you haven't done much backpacking and are unaccustomed to carrying a heavy backpack. Such hikes, often called out-and-back hikes, are popular with anglers, rock climbers, peak baggers and photography enthusiasts.

ORGANIZED HIKES

Heading out into the wilderness can be intimidating for some people, but several companies market organized hikes to ease the hassles. They take care of getting a permit, planning meals, arranging supplies and equipment, and all you have to do is show up ready to hike. The level of service provided varies by company – some may require everyone to pitch in and help with cooking and camp chores and carry communal gear, while others may take care of these things for you.

These trips are perfect for hikes with complex logistics – for example, when you can't get a permit on your own for Mt Whitney, when attempting a peak such as Mt Lyell, or when doing longer trips like the High Sierra Trail or John Muir Trail, which require resupplying food along the way.

Organized trips, usually offered during the months with the best chance of good weather, range from $80 to $190 per day. Many companies also design custom trips. Contact the companies to request a brochure or inquire about dates, prices and itineraries:

Adventure 16 (☎ 619-283-2362 ext 139, e info@adventure16.com, w www.adventure16.com), 4620 Alvarado Canyon Rd, San Diego, CA 92120, offers High Sierra backpacking trips.

Call of the Wild (☎ 510-849-9292, fax 644-3811, e trips@callwild.com, w www.callwild.com), 2519 Cedar St, Berkeley, CA 94708, offers wilderness trips for women only.

Rainbow Expeditions II (☎ 303-239-9917, e info@rainbow2.com, w www.rainbow2.com), 7125 W 27th Ave, Wheat Ridge, CO 80215, offers hiking trips and wilderness backpacking retreats.

Sierra Club Outings (☎ 415-977-5522, w www.sierra club.org/outings/national), 85 Second St, 2nd floor, San Francisco, CA 94105, sponsors noncommercial volunteer-led hiking trips throughout the Sierra Nevada. The logistical support and experienced leadership makes these trips a good way to enjoy extended hikes. Discounts are available for teachers and students aged 18 to 25 years.

Sierra Wilderness Seminars (☎ 888-797-6867, e mail@swsmtns.com, w www.swsmtns.com), PO Box 988, Mt Shasta, CA 96067, offers backpacking trips, including Mt Whitney and some segments of the John Muir Trail.

Southern Yosemite Mountain Guides (☎ 800-231-4575, 559-877-8735, e symg@sierratel.com, w www.symg.com), PO Box 301, Bass Lake, CA 93604, offers backpacking trips to Mt Whitney, the High Sierra Trail and the John Muir Trail, as well as day hikes.

The World Outdoors (☎ 800-488-8483, 303-413-0938, fax 303-413-0926, e fun@theworldoutdoors.org, w www.theworldoutdoors.com), 2840 Wilderness Place, Suite F, Boulder, CO 80301, offers easy hiking trips in the national parks.

Yosemite Field Seminars (☎ 209-379-2321, w www.yosemite.org), PO Box 230, El Portal, CA 95318, are two- to five-day-long field seminars, sponsored by the nonprofit Yosemite Association. Topics range from wildflowers and geology to mammals and birds in Yosemite National Park; seminars involve daily hiking as far as 12mi.

Yosemite Mountaineering School & Guide Service (☎ 209-372-8344 at the Mountain Shop in Curry Village, ☎ 209-372-8435 at the gas station in Tuolumne Meadows, w www.yosemitepark.com /html/mountain.html), Yosemite National Park, Yosemite, CA 93589, offers backpacking trips and guided climbs.

GUIDES

A guide isn't necessary for backpacking in the Sierra Nevada, but qualified and experienced guides are available to accompany you. Guides either work independently or for a guide service. Specialized training is not required to become a guide, so ask any prospective guide what certification they have. If the guide works for a guide service, ask what in-house training they received and if the guide service is accredited. Guides operate under a special use permit issued by the USFS requiring bonded insurance. See Mountain Guides' Associations (p62), for a discussion of the types and levels of certifications and accreditation. In addition, ask if the guide has current wilderness first-aid certification with CPR for the professional rescuer.

The rates for hiring a guide, which are typically paid to the guide service, vary depending upon the number of people in your group. It can cost as much as $240 per person per day for one person or $150 per person per day for two people, and as little as $125 per person per day for four or more. The guides are responsible for all their own personal clothing and equipment.

Note that some guide services also act as outfitters, and may be listed under Organized Hikes (p38), in the previous section. Any national forest can supply a list of guides in their area. A list of authorized guide services includes the following:

Alpine Skills International (☎ 530-426-9108), PO Box 8, Norden, CA 95724

Mammoth Mountaineering School (☎ 800-549-7515), PO Box 7299, Mammoth Lakes, CA 93546

Nidever Mountain Guides (☎ 760-648-1122), PO Box 446, June Lake, CA 93529

Sierra Mountain Center (☎ 760-873-8526), PO Box 95, Bishop, CA 93515

Sierra Mountain Guides (☎ 775-852-4049), PO Box 33670, Reno, NV 89533

Sierra Mountaineering International (☎ 760-872-4929, ℮ info@sierramountaineering.com), PO Box 1011, Bishop, CA 93515-1011

Yosemite Guides (☎ 877-425-3366), PO Box 650, El Portal, CA 95318

ACCOMMODATIONS
Camping

Hikers usually stay in one of the many campgrounds throughout the Sierra Nevada before or after their hike or between hikes. Fees are usually per site as opposed to per tent or per person. USFS campgrounds (ranging from $6 to $15) usually have toilets, fire pits, picnic benches and potable water. Most operate on a first-come, first-served basis. The National Recreation Reservations Service (☎ 888-448-1474, 518-885-3639 from outside the US, Ⓦ reserve usa.com) handles reservations for many USFS campgrounds. They accept reservations up to eight months in advance, and charge a fee of $8.65 per reservation.

The USFS has a policy that allows and encourages 'dispersed camping,' which means you can pull your vehicle off the road and camp anywhere for free on USFS land unless it is posted otherwise (eg, with a 'No Camping Here' or equivalent sign). Campers must still comply with all other regulations, such as obtaining a campfire permit (see Permits & Fees, p53). One exception to the dispersed camping policy is in USFS recreation areas, particularly along the eastern Sierra, where camping is typically allowed only in designated campgrounds.

State park and national park campgrounds, which typically cost several dollars more per site than USFS campgrounds, often have hot showers and sometimes RV hookups (ie, sites with power). Many of them accept or require reservations. To make reservations at state park campgrounds in California, call ☎ 800-444-7245 from outside California, or ☎ 916-638-5883 within the state, or visit ReserveAmerica's website at Ⓦ www.parks.ca.gov/default.asp.

Alternatively, mail reservation requests to ReserveAmerica, PO Box 1510, Rancho Cordova, CA 95741-1510. The Sierra's only state park campgrounds, which are around Lake Tahoe, start at $15, plus a $7.50 reservation fee. The National Park Reservation Service (NPRS, ☎ 800-436-7275 Yosemite National Park only, 800-365-2267 all other national parks, 301-722-1257 outside the US, Ⓦ reservations.nps.gov), PO Box 1600, Cumberland, MD 21502, allows you to reserve campsites (starting at $16) up to five months in advance.

Many private campgrounds look like paved parking lots, but some have grassy, shaded sites for tents (usually starting at $14). RV sites cost more. Facilities include hot showers, coin laundry and often a swimming pool, game area, playground and convenience store. Kampgrounds of America (KOA, ☎ 406-248-7444, fax 248-7414), PO Box 30558, Billings, MT 59114-0558, is an international network of private campgrounds. Contact them to request their annual *Kampground Guide* or check their online campground listing at Ⓦ www.koa .com. Sites start at $15.

Occasionally, more than one party may be assigned to one campsite. If this is the case, be respectful of your neighbors. Don't pitch your tent right next to theirs and avoid spreading your gear out all over the campsite. Most importantly, don't stay up singing all night if they've gone to bed at 8pm (and if they stay up all night singing, you have every right to ask them, nicely, to quiet down). All campgrounds have quiet hours starting between 8 and 10pm and ending between 6 and 7am.

Backcountry campsites vary from being a flat piece of ground that you find for yourself to a clearing with logs set up as benches, and a wooden post giving the campsite's number. The type of campsite depends on where you are: Wilderness areas tend to have the former, and national parks the latter. Camping in the backcountry is always free.

Hostels

Hostelling International/American Youth Hostels (HI/AYH) are in or near most major cities. Although a hostel are is a good place to meet other hikers and find out about an area, there are only three hostels in the Sierra Nevada. Two hostels are near Yosemite National Park; one in Merced, 80mi from the park, and the other in Midpines 31mi from Yosemite Valley. The third hostel is in Independence in the eastern Sierra.

Hostels range from $14 to $18 for a dormitory bed ($2 or $3 more for nonmembers), and from $25 to $30 for a private room, if any are available. If your sleeping bag looks like it has been on the trail for a few weeks, you may have to rent bed linens for about $2. Independent hostels, often called backpackers hostels, are usually a few dollars cheaper and have a wide range of standards. Both types of hostel usually have kitchen and laundry facilities, information and bulletin boards, a TV room and a lounge. HI/AYH hostels are more likely to have a curfew and prohibit alcohol.

Get information from HI/AYH (☎ 202-783-6161, fax 783-6171, ⓔ hostels@hiayh.org, ⓦ www.hiayh.org), 733 15th St NW, Suite 840, Washington, DC 20005, or use the code-based reservation service at ☎ 800-909-4776 (to use this service you need the access code for the hostel, available from any HI/AYH office or listed in its handbook).

Hotels
Small towns in the mountains have a narrow range of accommodations, generally a few small motels where a double room costs less than $60. Motel and hotel chains are commonly clustered together near freeway exits near larger towns and cities. AAA (see Useful Organizations, p61) publishes an annual guide to accommodations.

FOOD
Local Food
Major fast food chains tend to be in high-traffic population centers, suited to the high-volume business style of such chains. In small towns, especially those in the eastern Sierra, hikers can find local family-owned fast food places serving their own take on burgers and shakes, often far better than the franchise clones. Mexican food is also widespread – this is California, after all – and the state's Pacific Rim location is evidenced by innumerable, generally low-cost Chinese restaurants.

Roadside produce stands along California's Central Valley highways leading to the mountains offer locally grown fruits, vegetables and nuts at a good value.

Backpackers' Cuisine

Here are some backpacking trip food ideas. *Wilderness Cuisine,* by Carole Latimer, offers recipes and cooking suggestions.

Breakfast
oatmeal or instant hot cereal
dry cereal or granola
powdered milk
powdered eggs
breakfast bars or granola bars
pop tarts
fresh or dried fruit (blueberries, raisins or currants)
brown sugar

Snack Lunch
bread or bagels
cheese and crackers
peanut butter and jelly sandwiches
hard-boiled eggs
fresh or dried fruit
fig bars
raisins, nuts or gorp
salami or jerky
energy bars

Dinner
packaged meals
bouillon cubes or instant soup
instant rice or noodles
instant stuffing or potatoes
quick-cooking whole grains
pasta
instant sauce packets
canned fish or meat
dried meat
dried mushrooms
sun-dried tomatoes
vegetables
Parmesan cheese
instant pudding

Eastern Sierra visitors will find Basque restaurants in many towns. Operated by descendants of 19th century Basque shepherds, they offer hearty all-you-can-eat family-style dinners in a colorful setting, which are a good value for a post-backpacking feast.

Nevada casinos offer super low-cost meal deals. The food is usually pretty good, because what casino operators really want is to get you into the casino so they can separate you from your money at the slot machines.

On the Hike

For a day hike, you can bring whatever food you like since you only have to carry it until lunchtime. Organizing food for a backpacking trip, however, requires advance planning. You need to plan menus with food that is easy to prepare, tastes good, provides enough calories to nourish you, isn't too heavy or bulky and is affordable.

Cooking One of the first decisions to make is whether you want to cook or not, because this affects what food you buy. On an overnight or two-night backpacking trip, you could consider keeping things simple and not cooking. A hot meal in the evening and a hot drink in the morning, however, are wonderfully satisfying. On longer trips, you're going to want to bring a stove and do some cooking. For a list of everything you need to bring, see Cooking Equipment (p48). Rather than taking the time in the middle of the day to prepare a hot lunch, it's easier to snack throughout the day – an art form called grazing.

Buying Food Before you can go food shopping, you need to plan a day-by-day menu. Consider eating the same meals every day and preparing quick-cooking one-pan meals to keep life on the trail simple and uncomplicated. The type of food you can buy falls into one of these general categories: fresh food; whole grains and pasta; prepared food; instant food; dehydrated food; and freeze-dried food. Each type of food has cost considerations too. Freeze-dried food is the most expensive,

costing from $4 to $7 per entrée. You may choose just one or two types of food or some combination of them all.

Fresh food can include vegetables that do not require any refrigeration, such as garlic, onions, carrots, potatoes and cabbage. Quick-cooking whole grain foods like couscous, polenta, grits and pasta are nutritious, inexpensive and are sold either prepackaged or in bulk. Prepared food can be anything from canned tuna to a can of tomato paste for pasta sauce. Instant food simply requires adding water. Many health food stores sell instant refried and black beans, humus, tabbouleh, chili and other soups in bulk.

Foods from breakfast rolls or scones to vegetarian and non-vegetarian dinner entrees and desserts like mousse are sold in dehydrated and freeze-dried forms. Dehydrated foods require soaking before cooking and take longer to cook than freeze-dried foods. Freeze-dried food is more flavorful than dehydrated food, and all you have to do is add boiling water and let your dish set for less than 10 minutes. Some packaging may claim a food is freeze-dried, when it's really a combination of freeze-dried and dehydrated food, so look for labeling that indicates that the package contains 100% freeze-dried food. Packages typically come in one-, two- and four-person serving sizes.

Bringing an assortment of your favorite spices can enhance the flavor of your meals. Try cinnamon, nutmeg and allspice on breakfast cereals, and salt and pepper, cayenne, roasted garlic, oregano, onion flakes or soy sauce with dinners.

Whatever your choice, you need to have enough of it. A typical backpacker burns up to 4500 calories per day. To replace that you need to consume the equivalent of 1.5lb to 2.5lb of food per day. The recommended serving sizes on packaged foods aren't enough for hiking, so double or triple the dry measurements printed on most packages when determining how much to buy. Those quantities may be enough for a meal at home, but you'll want a whole lot more after a day on the trail. Plan on buying and bringing one to two extra meals per week, just in case you get extra hungry or in case bad weather alters plans and you find yourself stuck unexpectedly. Forego buying foods in glass jars unless the contents can be transferred into a lighter weight nonbreakable container, and minimize the canned food you buy to avoid lugging empty cans around with you.

Some people say 'gorp' is an acronym for 'good old raisins and peanuts,' but the word first entered the American mainstream in the late 1960s when the popularity of backpacking began to increase. So what is gorp? It's basically a high-energy trail snack comprised of any combination of nuts, raisins, dried fruit and seeds. Gorp is sold both prepackaged and in bulk as 'trail mix' in many grocery stores. To make your own gorp, simply mix roughly equal amounts of each ingredient and put it in a sealable plastic bag, then munch it as you hike down the trail. Today, dozens of gorp recipes abound. Here are a few variations:

- granola, oats, raisins and (salted or dry roasted) peanuts
- Chex cereal, M&Ms, raisins and peanuts
- mixed nuts, dried fruit, M&Ms and sunflower seeds
- raisins, peanuts, M&Ms and sunflower seeds

Packing Food After buying your food, take time to organize and pack it. You want to have the correct quantity for your hike – neither too much nor too little. You also want to get rid of unnecessary packaging, which only adds weight and takes up space.

One approach is to measure ingredients and pack food into general breakfast, lunch and dinner bags. The other approach is to pack food into individual meals, each in its own sealable plastic bag. This really simplifies your camp routine because you don't have to measure food, all you do is grab the bag. You can easily combine dry ingredients too, like pre-mixing powdered milk and granola for breakfast. It helps to label each bag (eg, Breakfast Day 1, Dinner Day 2, etc). Jot down any specific cooking instructions you need right on the outside of the plastic bags.

Before you reach the trailhead, divide the food among the hikers in your party. Food is one of the heaviest items in a backpack, so share the burden of carrying it. In the event anyone gets separated, each person then has some food on hand.

When to Eat You can eat whenever you like. The only general rule is to reach camp each day in plenty of time to cook, eat and clean up your evening meal before dusk, when bears are especially active.

Storage Bears in the backcountry that are no longer afraid of humans make proper food storage mandatory. First, read the section on Bears (p57). This is a topic that national park and national forest rangers take seriously, so backpackers must understand what the laws are and what their options are.

Most backcountry campsites do not have bear boxes, so backpackers must protect their food by using one of two methods: bear-resistant food containers or the counterbalance method (see 'Counterbalance Method,' p44). The counterbalance method was the mainstay of backcountry food protection for decades. In many high-usage areas or in areas where known trouble-making bears roam, the counterbalance method is no longer effective. In many such areas, the law changed in the late 1990s so the counterbalance method is no longer allowed, and the use of bear-resistant food containers is mandatory. Penalties for violations can be high; one trailhead sign warns that if a bear gets your food, you can be fined $5000!

Backpackers can rent (for $3 per trip in national parks, but typically from $3 to $5 per day elsewhere, plus a refundable security deposit) or buy bear-resistant food canisters at many locations, including stores that sell equipment and most ranger stations that issue wilderness permits. Many national parks and national forests require the use of an approved bear-resistant food canister in areas with known bear problems or above specified elevations. The canister, although effective, has several drawbacks: It weighs between 2lb and 3lb; it costs between $75 and $95; bears can swat it around and even roll it into creeks or lakes; and it limits the distance of your backpacking trip since it holds only three to five days' worth of food. Most backpackers would opt for a shorter backpacking trip rather than carry two canisters. Larger canisters, designed for longer hikes, weigh even more and range in price from $140 to $170.

The following canisters have been either fully or conditionally approved by the Sierra InterAgency Black Bear Working Group for use in Yosemite and Sequoia & Kings Canyon National Parks as well as in Inyo National Forest: the 650-cubic-inch

Counterbalance Method

The counterbalance method was, until the late 1990s, the most widely used technique of backcountry storage to protect food and scented personal belongings from bears and other less intimidating critters. It's no guarantee, however, against persistent bears, and in a few areas it is totally ineffective. At best, it's a delaying tactic. In some areas of the Sierra Nevada, however, it is still a fine choice.

The idea is to hang two equally weighted stuff sacks, each over the branch of a tree. Locate an unobstructed tree branch at least 20ft above the ground that has a 5-inch diameter and extends at least 15ft away from the tree's trunk. It's important that the branch be sturdy enough to support your food, but not enough to support the weight of a bear cub.

Tie a rock to one end of an at least 50ft-long rope, which is from 1⅛ inches to 1¼ inches in diameter, and throw it over the branch at least 10ft away from the trunk. Divide your food equally into two sacks, each weighing not more than 10lb. Tie one sack to one end of the rope and hoist it to the branch. Tie the second bag as high on the rope as possible. Secure any excess rope to the second bag, leaving a loop out. Toss or push the second bag up until both bags hang at the same height, at least 12ft above the ground and 5ft below the branch. Retrieve the sacks by hooking the loop of rope with a long stick and pulling it slowly down.

Wild Ideas Bearikade, the lightest and most expensive (1lb 13oz, $195); the 588-cubic-inch Gio Enterprises Bear Can Backpacker (2lb 3oz, $95); and the 600-cubic-inch Garcia Machine's Backpacker Cache (2lb 11oz, $78). Look for further refinement and development in bear-resistant food containers as buyers strive to conform to the laws and manufacturers modify products that are deemed too heavy and too expensive.

Other innovative, lightweight containers are under development, but are not yet approved. One promising product is a bear-resistant food bag made of aramid fiber, the material used in manufacturing bulletproof vests and body armor, that attaches to trees with a sturdy cord. Sold under the name Ursack (☎ 866-232-7224, ⓦ www.ursack .com), Box 5002, Mill Valley, CA 94942, the 650-cubic-inch bag ($40) weighs 5oz and holds five to six days' worth of food. The 1200-cubic-inch bag ($60) weighs 7oz and holds nearly twice as much, and a double-strength 650-cubic-inch bag weighs 10oz.

Wild Food Living off the land may be a romantic concept, but in the Sierra Nevada you're likely to go hungry. Nibbling a few thimbleberries here and there isn't going to provide enough fuel to power you anywhere. The only abundant food source is fish, found in the many lakes and rivers (see Fishing, p59). Other edible foods include acorns, roots, berries, nuts, wild onions and watercress, all found at lower elevations. For a whimsical yet practical discussion about the topic of wild food, read *Stalking the Wild Asparagus,* a field guide by Euell Gibbons.

DRINKS
Alcoholic Drinks

Save these for after your hike. It's amazing how good a beer can taste after a day or three on the trail. Local microbrews are among the best.

California and Nevada require you to be 21 years or older to purchase beer, wine or liquor, which are sold in grocery stores and drugstores. You don't need to look for any special store. If you just want a drink, any bar and most restaurants will set you up.

On the Hike

To stay hydrated, you can bring any assortment of things to add to the water that you purify (see Water, p54) to drink. Instant coffee, tea bags, instant cocoa and powdered milk are great hot drinks, and powdered drink mixes and fruit juice are good during the day on the trail.

CLOTHING & EQUIPMENT

As you prepare for your hike, keep in mind that you have to carry everything you bring. A backpacking adage goes, 'The more you bring, the easier the camping. The less you bring the easier the walking.' The decision is yours to make. If your aim is to hike in for a day or two and hang out at a great backcountry campsite, then go for it. On the other hand, if your main purpose is to walk a long distance, then go as light as possible.

Clothing

Maintaining a comfortable body temperature while hiking, resting along the trail or relaxing at camp in the evenings is vital. To deal with the range of temperatures and weather conditions you can encounter in the outdoors, layering several thin garments affords the maximum flexibility. The concept is to have three main layers: a layer next to your skin that manages moisture; a middle layer for insulation; and an outer layer for protection from wind, rain or snow. Easily and quickly, you can peel layers off as you warm up and add them as you cool down.

The layer of clothing closest to your skin should be something other than cotton, which retains moisture and can leave you feeling chilled from sweat. Fabrics such as silk, wool or special synthetics are recommended, since they keep you warm and dry by wicking moisture away from the skin. The insulating layer of fleece, wool or down traps air, retaining heat next to your body. An outer breathable, waterproof shell layer – a jacket and pants – allows perspiration to evaporate, yet doesn't let wind or rain penetrate.

Footwear

What to wear on your feet is often the most important decision about what to bring. The first rule is that 1lb on your foot is like 10lb on your back! Basically, you want the lightest footwear suited to the hike you'll be doing. Consider the ruggedness of the terrain, the distance of the hike, how much weight you plan to carry, and whether it's going to be wet.

A boot's key features are what it's made from, how stiff the sole is, and if it is waterproof. Generally, a nonleather boot is adequate for most Sierra hikes. If you're going on day hikes or just backpacking to a base camp and going on day hikes from there, you can probably forego all-leather boots. The more rugged the terrain, however, the greater the need for an all-leather boot with a scree collar and stiffer sole. If you're carrying a heavy pack, you definitely need a stiffer sole and a more rugged boot. For hikes where it might be wet, muddy, or where snow might be present, a boot made with a breathable waterproof material like Gore-Tex is recommended.

Whenever you hike carrying a backpack, select boots with ankle support and skip the low-rise walking shoe-style models. Some minimalists, however, argue that wearing shoes as opposed to boots enables you to hike farther and faster, regardless of the increased risk of twisting an ankle. This may be true, but only for veteran hikers.

Make sure the boots fit your feet comfortably. When you go to a store to try on boots, wear the socks or combination of socks that you intend to wear while hiking. The salesperson should be able to help you get the right fit. You don't want boots that are too snug, which will give you blisters. And you don't want them too big so your foot can slip around. Break your boots in thoroughly before going hiking. On the hike, bring a pair of sandals with ankle straps or else training shoes to wear when fording rivers and when you reach camp.

Camping Equipment

Backpack The most comfortable type of backpack has an internal frame with a padded waistband that will take weight off your shoulders and sternum straps to stabilize the load. One with a zippered internal compartment to store valuables is helpful. Select the lightest weight backpack that's just large enough to meet your needs. A 5000-cubic-inch backpack is typically large enough to carry a week's worth of food, clothing and equipment. On short hikes bring a day-pack that's smaller than 2000 cubic inches.

How you load your backpack affects your comfort when hiking. With an internal frame pack, put the heaviest items closest to your back and higher up inside the pack. This keeps the weight distributed over your hips, which are best equipped to handle the most weight. Whenever you're walking on rough terrain or doing cross-country hiking, put the heaviest items lower in the pack. This lowers your center of gravity, increasing stability. Regardless of terrain, pack your sleeping bag in the very bottom of the backpack. If you have an external frame pack, load your gear into the main compartment keeping the heaviest items close to your back. They will

Clothing & Equipment Checklist

What you wear on a hike largely depends on the weather and time of year. It's essential, however, to bring the following equipment on all hikes.

- ❑ bandanna
- ❑ day-pack
- ❑ extra layer of clothing
- ❑ first-aid kit
- ❑ flashlight or headlamp
- ❑ hiking boots or shoes with extra laces
- ❑ hiking socks
- ❑ insect repellent
- ❑ jacket
- ❑ long-sleeved shirt or short-sleeved shirt

- ❑ map and navigational devices
- ❑ matches
- ❑ one-liter water bottle
- ❑ pants or shorts
- ❑ snack food
- ❑ sunglasses with retaining strap
- ❑ sunscreen
- ❑ swimsuit
- ❑ waterproof jacket or poncho
- ❑ wide-brimmed hat

For any overnight hike, though, add the following items to your must-have list.

- ❑ extra water bottle
- ❑ flashlight or head lamp with spare batteries and bulbs
- ❑ hand soap
- ❑ liner socks
- ❑ pocket knife

- ❑ small towel
- ❑ toilet paper, butane lighter and lightweight trowel
- ❑ toothbrush and toothpaste
- ❑ underwear

If you plan to hike either early or late in the season, here are some weather-specific items to include.

- ❑ gaiters
- ❑ lightweight gloves
- ❑ lightweight thermal underwear top and bottom

- ❑ pile or fleece jacket
- ❑ woolen or pile hat

ride higher up on your back than with an internal frame pack. Next, strap your sleeping bag onto the bottom of the frame.

Keep items you may need during the day easily accessible. Pack everything inside the backpack. Don't have items dangling on the outside where they may affect balance, fall off or get dirty. Keep compression straps tight so the load won't shift while you're walking.

Once you've loaded your backpack, a few simple steps can ease the task of getting it onto your back. Move one leg close to the upright backpack and grab its haul loop. With your knees bent and legs wide apart, slide the pack up your calf to your thigh. Steady the backpack with one hand and slide the other arm and shoulder through a shoulder strap. Then gently swing it onto your back and slip the other arm through the other strap. Buckle the waist belt and then adjust the shoulder and sternum straps. Make sure the weight of the pack is on your hips and not your waist. Adjust the straps during the day, tightening your shoulder straps when walking uphill and loosening them when going downhill.

Tent A lightweight tent is suitable for most hikes. Because the Sierra Nevada enjoys excellent summer weather, a tent is more for protection from mosquitoes than from rain. By August, when mosquitoes are mostly gone, a tent is optional if you don't mind sleeping under the stars. Many people just use a bivy sack or small free-standing mosquito screen over their head. A tent also protects you from the harmless, but plentiful ants on the ground. Select the lightest-weight tent that meets your needs, one with a waterproof fly sheet. A fully free-standing design, which allows you to erect and move the tent without stakes, makes setup easiest.

Sleeping Bag The primary choice in a sleeping bag is between down or synthetic insulating material. Down is warmer and lighter weight, but is useless when wet. Synthetic material is durable, less expensive, and insulates when wet, but is heavier and more bulky. A down bag with a water-resistant, breathable shell is best, but is the most expensive.

The Sierra Cup

Harking back to yesteryear, when mountain streams were chock-full of trout instead of parasites, hikers walked with the Sierra cup's aluminum handle hooked over their waist belt. When a stream beckoned, it was easy to dip the cup in for a refreshing sip of cool mountain water. Simplicity reigned supreme before Nalgene water bottles and water purifiers became necessities. The Sierra cup has withstood the test of time, and decades after its introduction, it's still more than just a cheap souvenir ($4). This lightweight, rugged multitasking cup, with its narrow bottom and wide mouth, serves as not only a drinking cup but as a bowl or even a small cookpot as well. Manufacturers have modernized its original aluminum construction by

making stainless steel and titanium versions and even super-sized ones, but its classic design has remained unchanged. As if by magic, the cup's handle and rim stay cool so as to not burn your hand or lips, but the hot chocolate, oatmeal breakfast or hearty soup inside stays just the right temperature long enough to drink or eat.

Sleeping bags are rated for temperature. The choice you make depends on your personal optimal sleeping temperature. When you're backpacking, also consider weight, because bags rated for colder temperatures are typically heavier than bags rated for warmer temperatures. A bag rated to 35°F is suitable for most hikes. On hikes that

Hiker's Checklist

CAMPING EQUIPMENT

- ❏ backpack or day-pack with waterproof pack cover
- ❏ bear-resistant food container or two stuff sacks and 50ft rope
- ❏ ground sheet for tent (optional)
- ❏ repair kit (needle, thread, tape, glue, cord)
- ❏ sleeping bag and insulating sleeping pad
- ❏ sleeping sheet (optional)
- ❏ tent with waterproof fly, tarp or bivy sack

COOKING EQUIPMENT

- ❏ cooking utensils
- ❏ dish towel, dish soap and scourer
- ❏ eating utensils (one spoon minimum), plate and insulated mug with lid
- ❏ food
- ❏ fuel and fuel containers
- ❏ mesh storage bag
- ❏ nesting cooking pots (1.5L or 2L) with lids
- ❏ pocket knife
- ❏ portable stove with windscreen, spare parts and cleaning wires
- ❏ pot grabber or hot pads
- ❏ waterproof matches and container or butane lighter

OPTIONAL COOKING EQUIPMENT

- ❏ collapsible polyethylene 2.5-gallon or 5-gallon water container
- ❏ collapsible wash basin(s)

MISCELLANEOUS

- ❏ altimeter, GPS and compass
- ❏ map(s) and guidebook
- ❏ photo ID and money
- ❏ whistle
- ❏ wilderness and/or campfire permit(s)

OPTIONAL

- ❏ bandanna
- ❏ binoculars
- ❏ camera and film
- ❏ fishing license and fishing gear
- ❏ hiking poles
- ❏ journal and pen/pencil
- ❏ plastic bags
- ❏ portable chair
- ❏ resealable plastic bags
- ❏ thermometer
- ❏ waterproof compression stuff sacks
- ❏ wristwatch

involve camping above tree line where it can frost anytime, you should consider a bag rated to 20°F.

An insulting foam mattress is indispensable. A self-inflating mattress is comfortable on rocky terrain. A closed-cell foam mattress is less expensive and lighter, but more bulky and less comfortable.

Cooking Equipment

When cooking for yourself, you need all the cooking equipment on the above checklist.

The choice of stove depends upon its durability, ease of use and fuel efficiency. Multi-fuel liquid stoves, in which the fuel container is connected to the stove by a fuel line, offer the greatest flexibility. The MSR WhisperLite Internationale stove is highly recommended because it's compact, rugged, burns almost anything and burns well at high altitude. Other recommendations include the MSR DragonFly, Optimus Explorer No 11 and Primus Multi-fuel. Cartridge stoves where the burner screws onto a butane or propane cartridge are also light-weight and easy to use, but create disposal problems. Hanging stove systems aren't necessary on the hikes in this book.

All fuel is widely available. White gas (also called white spirit or camp fuel) is the fuel of choice for most multi-fuel liquid stoves, but they burn anything from un-leaded gas to diesel and kerosene. Butane or propane cartridges (eg, Gaz, EPI Gas) sell for $3.95 for 110g and $4.30 for 215g.

Buying & Hiring Locally

An outdoor specialty store is the place to buy big-ticket items such as tents and sleeping bags and gear that must be highly reliable, such as a stove and raingear. You can save money on sleeping pads, cooking and eating utensils, flashlights and headlamps, pocket knives and batteries by buying them at a discount retailer. The local grocery or hardware stores in small towns often carry basic camping supplies. National parks also have specialty stores where you can buy almost all camping essentials. See the Access Town and Nearest Town sections in each hiking chapter for recommended outdoor supply stores.

Specialty stores usually also rent gear. Sample daily rental rates are $3 for a bear-resistant food container, $2 for an ensolite sleeping pad, $10 for a sleeping bag, $1 for day-pack, $8 for a backpack and $3 for gaiters. Climbing gear is also readily available for sale or rent.

MAPS & NAVIGATION

Bring a topographic map on all hikes except day hikes on known trails along which it's impossible to lose your way and that are heavily used by other hikers. Maps found in tourist and national park brochures do not provide adequate details for route-finding in the backcountry. Familiarize yourself with the map and the topographic features along your hike in advance of arriving at the trailhead.

Small-Scale Maps

DeLorme (☎ 207-865-4171, ⓦ www.delorme .com), PO Box 298, Freeport, ME 04032, publishes two atlases that cover the Sierra Nevada: the 1:150,000 *Northern California Atlas & Gazetteer,* which contains 104 topographic quadrangles, and the 1:150,000 *Southern & Central California Atlas & Gazetteer,* with 110 topographic quadrangles. These maps are useful for driving from all major cities and towns to the mountains, and they detail secondary roads, especially USFS roads to most trailheads. Many known trails are shown, which makes the maps useful for general trip planning. Benchmark Maps' *California Road & Recreation Atlas* includes landscape maps with excellent detailed roads and GPS grids.

Large-Scale Maps

The first step toward navigation in the mountains is knowing how to read a topographic map and buying the necessary maps that cover the hike.

The United States Geological Survey (USGS), an agency of the US Department of the Interior, publishes highly detailed topographic quadrangles, and private publishers produce equivalent maps that cover all Sierra Nevada trails and trailheads superbly.

USGS 1:125,000 maps ($8) with 200ft contour intervals and 1:100,000 maps ($7) with 150ft contour intervals are useful planning and backpacking maps. USGS 1:24,000 (7.5 minute) series ($4) with 40ft contour intervals offers excellent detail, but sometimes too much detail when a long hike covers multiple quadrangles. To order a USGS map index and price list, call ☎ 888-275-8747, fax 303-202-4693, visit the website at ⓦ www.usgs.gov, or write Western Distribution Branch, USGS Information Services, Box 25286, Denver, CO 80225. Maps are also available by mail or in person from the USGS (☎ 650-329-4390), 345 Middlefield Rd, Mail Stop 532, Menlo Park, CA 94025.

The USGS 1:62,500 (15 minute) series with 80ft contour intervals, the predecessor to the 1:24,000 (7.5 minute) series, has been discontinued, after being used from 1954 to the mid-1980s. Random 15 minute series quadrangles (ranging from $1 to $6) can occasionally be found in stores and at ranger stations.

Map Link (☎ 805-692-6777, fax 692-6788, ⒠ custserv@maplink.com), 30 S La Patera Lane, Unit 5, Santa Barbara, CA 93117, is the best source for reprints ($6) of many USGS 1:62,500 quadrangles. Wilderness Press (☎ 800-443-7227, 510-558-1666, fax 510-558-1696, ⒠ mail@wildernesspress.com, Ⓦ www.wildernesspress.com), 1200 Fifth St, Berkeley, CA 94710, has revised and also reprinted some USGS 1:62,500 quadrangles, and sells these and other maps (ranging from $5 to $7).

National Geographic Maps (Ⓦ maps .nationalgeographic.com/topo) sells high-quality scans of USGS 1:24,000 topographic maps that divide the Sierra Nevada into three regions, each on one CD-ROM ($49.95), from which you can customize and print your own trail maps: *Lake Tahoe & Surrounding Wilderness & Ski Areas; Yosemite, Mammoth & Central Sierra Wilderness Area;* and *Sequoia/Kings Canyon & Surrounding Wilderness Area.* Another useful CD-ROM is the *Yosemite National Park Map.*

USFS publishes nine maps of the Sierra's national forests ($4) and 14 1:63,360 topographic maps with 80ft contour intervals of its 17 wilderness areas (ranging from $4 to $8). To request a map list or order maps, contact and send payment to the USFS Pacific Southwest Region (☎ 707-562-8737), 1323 Club Drive, Vallejo, CA 94592.

Tom Harrison Maps (☎/fax 800-265-9090, 415-456-7940, Ⓦ www.tomharrisonmaps .com), 2 Falmouth Cove, San Rafael, CA 94901-4465, publishes excellent six-color shaded-relief topographic maps of various Sierra regions in scales ranging from 1:24,000 to 1:125,000. These waterproof plastic maps range from $8 to $9.

Buying Maps

Maps are readily available in stores that sell outdoor gear, at ranger stations, visitor centers and even some gas stations. Of course, you can order directly from the publishers, as noted in the previous sections.

Large specialty outdoor stores in some cities and the Wilderness Center in Yosemite Valley have map machine kiosks where you can print a custom 13-by-18-inch 1:24,000 map ($7.95) from CD-ROMs from National Geographic Maps on waterproof paperlike plastic in about four minutes. Visit the website (Ⓦ maps.nationalgeographic .com/topo) for locations of the kiosks.

GPS

Originally developed by the US Department of Defense, the Global Positioning System (GPS) is a network of more than 20 Earth-orbiting satellites that continually beam encoded signals back to Earth. Small, computer-driven devices (GPS receivers) can decode these signals to give users an extremely accurate reading of their location – to within 98.4ft, anywhere on the planet, at any time of day, in almost any weather.

The theoretical accuracy of the system increased at least tenfold in 2000 when a deliberate, in-built error, intended to fudge the readings for all but US military users, was removed. The cheapest hand-held GPS receivers now cost less than $100 (although these may not have a built-in averaging system that minimizes signal errors). Important factors to consider (other than price) when buying a GPS receiver are its weight and battery life.

It should be understood that a GPS receiver is of little good to hikers unless used with an accurate topographic map – the GPS receiver simply gives your position, which you must then locate on the map. GPS receivers will only work properly in the open. Directly below high cliffs, near large bodies of water or in dense tree cover, for example, the signals from a crucial satellite may be blocked (or bounce off the rock or water) and give inaccurate readings. GPS receivers are more vulnerable to breakdowns (including dead batteries) than the humble magnetic compass – a low-tech device that has served navigators faithfully for centuries – so don't rely on them entirely.

Using a Compass

Before you can navigate through the mountains, you need to be able to orient yourself. Often this is accomplished by taking a quick look around to locate a prominent peak or other visible feature or landmark that you can easily find on your map. If this doesn't work, a compass can help to determine your bearings. The simplest method is to place your map on a flat surface with the compass on top of the map. Align the edge of the compass with the edge of the map. Then rotate the map and compass together so the compass needle points to magnetic north as indicated on the map. Your line of sight to what you see around you now conforms directly to the bearings shown on your map.

A compass is optional for navigation on hikes in this book, because trails in the Sierra Nevada are well established and generally very well marked with signposts giving distances and pointing the direction to the next destination. If you're considering any cross-country hiking, however, bring a compass and know how to use it. Consider taking a course in navigation if you do not have these skills. The cheapest good-quality compasses, with a transparent base and a dial graduated in one- or two-degree increments, start at $9.

HIKES IN THIS BOOK
Route Descriptions

Route descriptions are described in actual walking days. An average hiker can comfortably complete each day, which starts or finishes at a campsite where you can pitch a tent and where water is available or else at a trailhead. When an intermediate campsite exists, it's indicated in the text. Hikers may choose to use intermediate campsites when going at a more leisurely pace or in case of illness. Some days have no alternative campsites because of terrain constraints or lack of water, and hikers must make it all the way.

Hike descriptions exclude segments on vehicle-carrying roads unless there's a high likelihood of walking on the road to find transport. When a hike starts or finishes at trailheads with facilities or near a town with accommodations, it's explained under Access Town at the beginning of the section or in the hike's Nearest Town section.

The hikes are named after the most prominent feature along the way, not necessarily in a point-to-point manner.

You can do many of the hikes in either direction. If there's a good reason for going one way or the other, the text explains it.

Level of Difficulty

As a guide to help you pick suitable hikes, each hike has a relative grading based on the authors' subjective impressions of its level of difficulty in relation to all other hikes in this book. The grading appears next to the heading 'Standard' in the Fact Box at the beginning of each hike:

Easy hikes present no navigational difficulties, don't require the use of all four limbs at any point and can be comfortably undertaken by a family with children aged 10 and older.

Moderate hikes can be done with a little exertion by someone of average fitness. The relative difficulty may reside in changes of elevation, length or route finding – or all three. These hikes assume that the hiker can use a compass, although it is not typically necessary to do so.

Hard hikes are just that: They're tough in terms of navigation, ascent and length.

Gradings of easy–moderate and moderate–hard are given to hikes that fall between categories. Of all the hikes in this book, 15% are easy, 29% are easy–moderate, 28% are moderate, 15% are moderate–hard, and 13% of all hikes are hard.

Factors considered in each hike's grading include the number of days, the maximum elevation, the total daily elevation gain and loss, whether the hike crosses any passes, the remoteness and isolation and the necessary fitness level. Adverse weather can make relatively easy hikes seem hard, and a hike done quickly can seem harder than one done slowly.

International rating systems used for climbing are somewhat useful for describing some hikes because they categorize terrain according to the techniques and equipment required to tackle them. No specific international standardized rating system for hiking, however, exists as it does for climbing. The Yosemite Decimal System (YDS), the rating system used in the US and the one referred to in this book, includes the following categories:

Class 1 – hiking with possible scrambling; hands generally not needed

Class 2 – off-trail scrambling through rough terrain (eg, talus); likely use of hands

Class 3 – simple climbing or scrambling, with moderate exposure possible, where beginners may want a rope; frequent use of handholds and footholds

Class 4 – intermediate climbing where use of rope (by beginners and average climbers) for belay is necessary because of exposure; a fall could be serious

Class 5 – climbing with rope and natural or artificial protection against a fall

Whenever a hike involves difficulties greater than YDS Class 1 or its equivalent, the hike description details the nature of the difficult section and gives a YDS class rating. See the boxed text below to see how the YDS corresponds with the French Union Internationale des Associations d'Alpinisme (UIAA), Welzenbach (German), Australian, and British rating systems.

Comparison of Rating Systems

YDS	UIAA	German	Australian	British
Class 1	I	1	1	E
Class 2	II	2	2	E
Class 3	II	3	3	MOD 1a,b,c
Class 4	-III	4	4	MOD 1a,b,c
Class 5	III	5	5	DIFF

Times & Distances

Each hike description details the number of days the hike takes and gives the approximate daily hiking time. The number of days doesn't include side trips or alternative routes, the details of which are listed separately. The daily hiking times are based on actual walking times, excluding stops for resting, eating, photographing or meandering.

Most hikers walk at a pace from 2 to 3 mph, or 6mi to 10mi per day. Most hiking days involve six to eight hours of walking; some days are longer, some shorter. The days are realistic for most reasonably fit hikers going at a moderate pace. Since everyone walks at their own pace, these times may not reflect your actual hiking time.

Distances, when given, are in miles and are based on data from available large-scale topographic maps compared with mileage posted on trail signs.

Maps in This Book

The maps in this book, which show the general route of individual hikes, are intended to be used in conjunction with the maps recommended in each hike's Planning section. At the start of each hiking chapter is a small-scale regional map with boxes showing the borders of the hikes mapped in greater detail. The scale and contour intervals, marked beneath the north arrow, vary from map to map. A wide line of green stipple shows the entire hike route, and a wide dashed line of green stipple shows any alternative routes. Boxes mark the start and finish points, and symbols indicate campsites and other features. A wide band of gray stipple shows land boundaries and borders, beyond which are notes about any adjoining or overlapping maps along with their page numbers.

Altitude Measurements

Altitudes measurements are taken mostly from USGS 1:24,000 topographic maps and some 1:62,500 maps, and are generally accurate to within 20ft.

Places Names & Terminology

The hike descriptions in this book use terms familiar to hikers in the US, which may not be common overseas. The glossary at the back of the book helps readers understand unfamiliar terms. Hike descriptions may use the directions 'right' or 'left.' For clarity, the compass direction is also given. The terms 'true right' and 'true left' refer to the two banks of a river as you face downstream. When facing downstream, 'true right' is on your right, and 'true left' is on your left.

How Far Is It?

It's the question on everyone's lips along the trail, and it's the question no one can really answer. For starters, few people ever include their destination in their question, assuming that everyone on the trail is heading to or from the same place they are. Furthermore, you have no idea how fast the person asking walks. What might take one person an hour to walk could take another person half or even double that time. Then there's the matter of trail signs or lack thereof.

Many trailheads have signs with a map giving the total mileage for hikes starting there. Signs at trail junctions usually give distances (in tenths of a mile) to or from the next destination. This is especially true for signs in national parks. National forests and wilderness areas have far fewer signs, whose detail is minimal by comparison and typically omits mileages. Additionally, many trail maps also include the mileage between trail junctions, some absurdly figured to a hundredth of a mile.

The careful observer, however, will note numerous discrepancies between these sources of information. Trail signs that were once accurate may now be wrong because the trailhead or original point of reference moved. Trails also may have been rerouted or regraded, changing the distance since the sign was made. Map makers may have relied on data from inaccurate trail signs, further spreading inconsistencies. Occasionally, trail signs are unclear and open to misinterpretation. The good news is that the differences are usually minor – just a few tenths of a mile and almost always less than a mile. It's never more than 10 or 20 minutes farther than you might have first thought, and sometimes the distance may even be shorter!

The best advice is to resist the urge to ask other hikers how long it's going to take you to get somewhere. Learn the rate at which you hike – the number of miles uphill and downhill that you can comfortably cover in an hour – and carry a trail map with you to gauge your whereabouts between trail junctions. An occasional glance at your wristwatch and a good map is all you need to figure out for yourself, 'How far is it?'

PERMITS & FEES
Wilderness Permits

The US has no national permit system, so the federal agency with jurisdiction over the area issues any required permits. Wilderness permits, also called wilderness use permits, backcountry use permits or visitor's permits are required for overnight trips in all national parks and most national forests and wilderness areas. Permits are generally not required for day hikes, although exceptions exist. When a hike crosses from one jurisdiction into another, it is not necessary to obtain another permit. The agency with jurisdiction over the area where a hike starts issues a permit for the entire route. The permits and regulations for each hike are detailed in the Planning section in the hiking chapters.

Many areas have a trailhead quota system that limits the number of day hikers and/or backpackers who start daily from each trailhead. This system prevents overcrowding and reduces the impact to wilderness areas. A varying percentage of the available permits may be allocated by advance reservations to guarantee the trailhead and entry date, with the remaining permits being issued on a daily first-come, first-served basis. Permits are usually free, although there may be a reservation fee or a per-night camping fee. Reservations are recommended at popular trailheads for all weekend entry dates and during August. Permits can be obtained at ranger stations, some information stations and visitor centers. Generally, non-quota trailheads in national forests and wilderness areas have self-issuing permits at the trailhead and in front of ranger stations.

Campfire Permits

Technically, a campfire permit is required above 7000ft on all USFS land and BLM land, but not in national parks, for anyone making wood or charcoal fires, and cooking on portable stoves fueled by gas, jellied petroleum or pressurized liquid fuel.

A free annual campfire permit valid throughout California is available at any USFS ranger station. In areas where a wilderness permit is required, the wilderness permit acts as a campfire permit and you do not have to get a separate campfire permit. In essence, this regulation applies only to areas outside national parks that do not require wilderness permits. The elevation above which fires are prohibited varies between jurisdictions, so generally backpackers need to carry their own stove and fuel if they want to cook hot meals.

National Park Fees

The cost of entry into a national park ranges from $10 to $20 per vehicle, and from $5 to $10 for pedestrians and cyclists. The fee is payable upon entry. Cash and travelers checks are the only accepted payment methods.

When you visit more than one federal fee-based area (eg, national parks, national monuments, national wildlife refuges, national recreation areas and national historic sites), it's cheaper to buy either of two types of passes. The National Parks Pass ($50) and the Golden Eagle Pass ($65), which also includes entry to BLM and Corps of Engineers fee-based areas, admit the passholder and any accompanying passengers in a private vehicle and are valid for one year from the date of purchase. You can purchase these passes at any entrance station on site, or by contacting the National Parks Foundation (☎ 888-467-2757, ⓦ www .nationalparks.org). You can also get a National Parks Pass by mailing your request to 27540 Ave Mentry, Valencia, CA 91355.

RESPONSIBLE HIKING

In many parts of the world, tourists, tour operators and host communities follow voluntary codes of conduct. Guidelines are readily available to implement ecohiking principles.

Ask yourself what you can do to lessen the negative impact your hike might have on the environment. Taking responsibility for yourself and your actions is a basic obligation of all hikers. Perhaps the most important single action you can take is to reduce the size of your hiking party, which minimizes your overall impact. Avoid overvisited hiking areas by selecting a less-known destination and traveling during the off-peak season when possible.

Fires

Campfires are generally not allowed above tree line (where there is no fuel anyway). Each national park and national forest has its own rules banning fires above fixed elevations, which are detailed in the hiking chapters. Cooking on a gas stove and foregoing campfires is the environmentally preferred way to be in the backcountry. During the hiking season, the temperatures are never so cold that a campfire is necessary for warmth. Never throw cigarettes and matches where they could cause a wildfire.

Water

Water contamination occurs when human waste and other contaminants enter open water sources. This spreads diseases and poses a health risk for residents, hikers and wildlife. Be careful when washing, bathing and when going to the toilet. Wash yourself, your dishes and your clothes in a basin and discard soapy water and food residue at least 100ft from open water sources. Use soap sparingly and don't put soaps, even biodegradable soaps or toothpastes, into water sources.

Toilets

Toilets exist on some popular hiking routes and at some backcountry campsites. When no facilities exist, find a discreet location at least 100ft from any open water source to relieve yourself. How to best deal with human feces depends on where you are. Below tree line, bury it in a six-inch-deep hole with other organic matter where soil microbes and worms will decompose it.

Zen & the Art of Dishwashing

'Zen,' wrote the teacher Shunryu Suzuki, 'is concentration on our usual everyday routine.' Hiking and camping in the Sierra Nevada may seem like anything but your usual everyday routine, but the art of making it easy and natural is just that – establish and follow a daily routine. Dishwashing is part of it. One simple practice I learned at a California Zen center is when you are finished eating, pour a little water or tea onto your plate or into your bowl or cup, and use your spoon to work any little bits of food off the surface. Drink the liquid, and do it again, until the bowl is clean. Zen tea. No waste, no pollution, easy cleanup.

– John Mock

Above tree line, spread feces out thinly on rocks to dry it in the sun where the sun's ultra-violet (UV) rays kill bacteria and microorganisms. Burn toilet paper rather than burying it in a hole, taking care to not start a wildfire, or pack it out.

Garbage

Garbage disposal systems don't exist along hiking routes, so be sure no one in your party pollutes. Separate rubbish on hike into organic, burnable and nonburnable. Dispose of organic trash, such as food scraps, by burying it or packing it out. Above 13,000ft organic waste can easily take decades to decay, so carry it to lower elevations for disposal. Collect burnable rubbish and organize a camp routine to burn it, preferably where a fire scar already exists.

Candy wrappers and cigarette butts should not be discarded along the trail. Nonburnable rubbish, such as tin cans, bottles, aluminum foil and plastics, should not be buried because it doesn't decompose, and wildlife may dig it up and scatter it. Aluminum foil, foil-lined packages and plastics release toxic ozone-depleting gases when burned, so pack nonburnable rubbish out and dispose of it in

the nearest town or facility. If you find rubbish at a backcountry campsite, you should pack it out. Pick up others' rubbish when you see it along the trail.

You can minimize the rubbish you produce while hiking by removing packaging from foods before your hike and repacking them into sturdy reusable containers. Don't buy or drink beverages in unrecycleable plastic containers or tin cans. None of this is difficult or time consuming, but it makes a substantial difference.

Access

Hikes in this book do not cross private property unless the owners have given clearance for all hikers to pass through without prior notification. Any exceptions are noted in the hike descriptions. People who own property in scenic areas are often protective of their land, so respect this right and avoid trespassing on private property. These areas usually have clearly visible 'private property' or 'no trespassing' signs.

Dogs

Dogs are allowed in most areas in the Sierra Nevada except in the wilderness of national parks. Some exceptions may apply to USFS-administered wilderness areas. Ask at the ranger station that issues your wilderness permit about any special regulations pertaining to pets. Keep dogs leashed at all times – it protects wildlife from your dog and vice versa, and prevents your dog from intimidating other hikers or disrupting their wilderness experience. Ignoring leash laws can result in a fine.

Other Considerations

Using established campsites and places for cooking, sleeping and relieving yourself concentrates the environmental impact and minimizes overall disturbance. Select a level site at least 100ft from open water sources and the trail. Avoid camping in fragile meadows. Don't clear vegetation or cut trees, limbs or brush to make camp improvements. Making trenches around tents leaves soil prone to wind and rain erosion. Before leaving a campsite, naturalize the area and replace rocks, wood or anything else you moved.

Anywhere in the mountains, it's possible to come across something of historic significance – remnants of a log cabin, a ranger's cabin, obsidian chips or arrowheads, arborglyphs, or even a grave – do not disturb it. Vandalism destroys the human history of these mountains.

Remember that wildlife is wild. Do not harass or feed any wild animal.

WOMEN HIKERS
Attitudes Toward Women

Despite legal equality and enlightened public policies, it's fair to say that sexist attitudes toward women are still widespread. Gender equality, however, is valued in the outdoors community. Anyone in pursuit of fresh air in wide-open spaces is generally perceived to be as good as anyone else and capable of accomplishing the task at hand – like reaching the summit of Mt Whitney or hiking the John Muir Trail.

Female hikers are most likely to encounter sexism on the trail when passing cowboys who lead pack trips (see Pack Trips, p61). The easiest strategy is to ignore them, regardless of what they say, and just keep walking.

Safety Precautions

Women are probably safer on backcountry trails than in many cities and towns. It's common to see women hiking and backpacking alone and in groups in national parks. In wilderness areas and especially in national forests, female hikers are fairly uncommon. Many women feel comfortable alone on day hikes, but not on overnight backpacking trips. To increase their sense of safety, many women hike with dogs anywhere outside national parks, where dogs are not allowed.

If you're unaccustomed to hiking alone, you may feel safer sticking to busy trails and campsites where you will meet other people. Or, you may want to look for a traveling companion before hitting the trail – check for notices on bulletin boards at visitor centers and ranger stations. Alternatively, you may want to join an organized hike (see p38).

Organizations

Maiden Voyages (W www.maiden-voyages .com) is an online magazine with a database of hundreds of travel services, including hiking and backpacking companies, owned, run by and/or geared toward women. Other good websites for women are W www.journey woman.com and *Backpacker* magazine's women's page at W www.backpacker.com /womenspage.

A Journey of One's Own, by Thalia Zepatos, contains travel tips, anecdotes and a long list of sources and resources for the independent female traveler. *Adventures in Good Company,* also by Zepatos, covers a huge range of adventure, outdoor and special interest tours and activities for women.

Women's bookstores are very good places to find out about upcoming gatherings and readings, and often have bulletin boards where you can find or place travel notices.

HIKING WITH CHILDREN

Backpacking with Babies & Small Children, by Goldie Silverman, is a valuable resource for anyone planning to hike with children. Parents need to know their children's needs and abilities well and to select their hikes carefully. Most parents would be best advised to choose easier hikes with reasonable elevation changes that avoid crossing more difficult passes.

DISABLED HIKERS

For disabled visitors, the national parks have accessibility brochures and a services coordinator that offer park information and ranger-led activities. When arrangements need to be made in advance, contact any park visitor center, or contact the coordinator prior to your arrival. *Easy Access to National Parks: The Sierra Club Guide for People With Disabilities,* by Wendy Roth and Michael Tompane, is a carefully researched guide for intrepid travelers with physical limitations.

The Golden Access Pass for year-round entry to all federal fee-based areas, including national parks, is free for blind or permanently disabled US citizens or permanent residents. The pass is available at park entrance stations to visitors showing proof of disability.

DANGERS & ANNOYANCES
Bears

Black bears are active day and night throughout the Sierra Nevada. Regardless of their color, only black bears live in the area. Two kinds of black bears roam the mountains: wild bears and nonwild (or tame) bears. Wild bears are intimidated by people and flee when they encounter humans. The nonwild bears do the opposite and are notorious for regularly breaking into vehicles in parking lots and raiding campgrounds and backcountry campsites in search of food. Although these bears rarely threaten your physical safety, losing your

food will leave you unnerved and probably end your hike.

Everyone must take precautions at all times to protect their food and scented personal belongings (eg, toothpaste, soap) and even rubbish, which attract bears. Use bear boxes, which are large metal food storage lockers cemented, bolted or chained into position, where provided at parking lots, campgrounds and a few backcountry campsites. Bear boxes are at national park trailheads, but only at the most troublesome USFS trailheads. Current national park policies, however, advocate the removal of existing bear boxes from the backcountry, claiming they violate the wilderness act that prohibits the building of structures. For other storage techniques at backcountry

Bearanoia

Bears seem like every hiker's nightmare. Don't give a bear any reason to come near you and ruin your trip. Bears prowl in many areas, because they know an easy meal is often found where people are. Keep your camp clean! Cook your evening meal well before dusk and wash your dishes immediately after eating. Store your food, rubbish and scented toiletries in a bear-resistant food container and put it at least 20ft away from where you sleep.

If a bear visits your campsite, immediately yell, clap your hands, throw stones or sticks, bang pots and try to look big. Raise your arms, open your jacket and make lots of noise. When there's more than one person, stand close together to appear more intimidating. You may need to do this more than once, but the more racket you make the first time, the less likely the bear is to make another visit. Whatever you do, don't surround the bear – give it room to escape. Never, ever, get between a mother bear and her cubs, which may be up a nearby tree.

If a bear huffs at you and shows its profile, it may be about to bluff-charge you. Stand your ground, or step back very slowly. Make yourself look big, and make a big noise. Don't stare, but keep eye contact. As the bear backs away, you should too. Never drop your backpack – that may be just what the bear wants. Never run from a bear. You only trigger its instinct to chase, and you cannot outrun a bear.

You can and should fight back if a black bear attacks you. Use any means available – throw rocks, hit it with your gear or a big stick. Fortunately, no black bear has ever made such an unprovoked attack on a human in Yosemite, Sequoia or Kings Canyon National Parks.

campsites, see On the Hike (p42), under Food for a detailed discussion of your options for dealing with bears.

Mosquitoes

The Sierra is teeming with annoying mosquitoes, especially in June and July. Bring lots of insect repellent and wear long-sleeved shirts and long pants, if necessary. Even though temperatures are moderate, bring a lightweight tent or mosquito screen for protection.

Don't forget the repellant!

Pack Strings

Conflict can arise between hikers and stock users not only because of the inherently different philosophy of these two modes of backcountry travel, but also because the trails just aren't big enough for both hikers and horses. (See Pack Trips, p61, for an overview of this activity.) To minimize conflict, try to understand the philosophical differences. When hiking, remember that horses and pack animals have right of way. Hikers must yield by stepping at least 10ft off the trail, preferably on the downhill side, to allow the pack string to pass by. Stock users can help hikers who are not familiar

with stock by being patient and suggesting the best place for them to pass.

Despite good intentions on the part of all, hikers invariably find the experience of shared trails to be somewhat unpleasant. The steel-shod hooves of pack animals gouge trails, often turning them into dusty troughs. The excrement of pack animals not only smells bad, but also draws swarms of flies that bite and annoy hikers. Furthermore, some of the cowboys who lead the pack trips may exhibit a macho 'Marlboro man' attitude that smacks of sexism. Hikers are likely to find themselves going to lengths to avoid pack strings and may even develop equinophobia, distaste for horses and mules.

At the Trailhead

A few precautions can reduce the chance of any theft from your vehicle parked at trailheads. First, ask at the nearest ranger station about any known problems at your trailhead. Carry your money and valuables with you in your backpack and don't leave valuables inside the vehicle. Leave any front seat console and glove box open, so would-be thieves can see there's nothing there. (Make sure your glove box doesn't have a light that stays on when it's open, otherwise it'll drain your battery.) Be somewhat organized before you get to the trailhead, so you don't spend an hour displaying everything you've got and what you're leaving behind. When you get to the parking area, grab your gear and head out.

Don't leave miscellaneous things inside the vehicle. If you leave anything, put it in the trunk or other enclosed area so bears can't look inside and mistake it for a cooler or food. Leave any scented items or food in bear boxes where available, or discard them before reaching the trailhead. Try to avoid leaving your vehicle at an isolated trailhead. Consider parking farther away and walking to the trailhead if another, more heavily used parking area is within a reasonable distance. Use shuttle buses whenever possible, and where shuttles don't exist, carpool. Park your vehicle facing in, so the trunk or rear access door points toward the most exposed part of the parking area. Be sure your vehicle has a locking gas cap so you don't return to find an empty tank. If your vehicle has a trunk release inside, lock it so thieves wouldn't be able to access the contents of the trunk if they broke into the vehicle through a window. It's unlikely thieves would attempt to steal the vehicle itself, but you could consider temporarily disabling it if you know what you're doing. Never hide or bury your vehicle's keys in, under or near the vehicle.

OTHER ACTIVITIES
Rock Climbing
Clean Sierra Nevada granite offers some of the world's finest climbing. If you're tempted to go climb a rock, here are some ideas.

The Lake Tahoe region's two best climbing areas are Lovers Leap and Donner Pass. Lovers Leap, near the town of Strawberry on US 50, west of Echo Summit, has incredible multipitch climbs on near-vertical granite. Routes are made easier by numerous thin horizontal dikes that in places offer almost a ladder up the cliff. The best climbing is from mid-June to October. Detailed route descriptions are in *Rock Climbing Lake Tahoe,* by Carville and Clelland. Donner Pass, on US 40 just south of and parallel to I-80, has many fine single and multipitch climbs. The climbing season is from July to October.

Yosemite National Park is synonymous with high-quality climbing, and Yosemite Valley is the planet's mecca for rock climbers. From bouldering to big walls, Yosemite Valley has it all. Although climbing is possible year-round, the main climbing season is from March to November, avoiding the hottest summer months. Read *Yosemite Climbs: Free Climbs,* by Don Reid and George Meyers, and *Rock Climbing Yosemite's Select,* by Reid, for detailed route descriptions. Tuolumne Meadows has unparalleled clean climbing on high-elevation granite domes, and is very popular from July to September, when most routes in Yosemite Valley are too hot. *Rock Climbs of Tuolumne Meadows,* by Reid, details the routes.

The entire Sierra Nevada offers a nearly unlimited number of superb climbs on a multitude of peaks. The Sawtooth Ridge, the Minarets, the Mono Divide, the Palisades and the Mt Whitney area offer easy access and a high concentration of climbs. *The High Sierra: Peaks, Passes and Trails,* by RJ Secor, and *Sierra Classics: 100 Best Climbs in the High Sierra,* by John Moynier and Claude Fiddler, detail the routes.

Mountaineering
For all routes Class 4 or lower, the Sierra offers unlimited scope. Hikers who enjoy peak bagging will find full information in *The High Sierra: Peaks, Passes and Trails,* by RJ Secor. The Mountaineer's Route on Mt Whitney, which was John Muir's ascent route in 1873, is a famous Class 3. The Palisades, near Big Pine, have the most alpine character and the largest glaciers. The Cathedral Range in Yosemite National Park offers incredibly scenic, easily accessible routes from Tuolumne Meadows.

Fishing
Thousands of lakes and hundreds of rivers make trout fishing a popular pastime. Native rainbow, cutthroat and golden trout still live in a few places, but introduced brown and brook trout are far more abundant. Many lakes and rivers on USFS land are stocked annually, although those in national parks are not. With so many great fishing spots, hikers can contemplate not only where to fish but what kind of trout they want to land. Some legendary rivers are the West Walker and the East Fork Carson, with Markleeville as a center for these. The eastern Sierra streams near Bishop are also renowned.

A state fishing license is required if you're aged 16 years or older and must be in plain sight attached to your outer clothing above the waist. Licenses are readily available at stores, resorts and ranger stations near trailheads.

Ask locally what regulations apply. Anglers need to be able to identify species, because maximum daily limits on the number of fish by species may be in effect. In some areas, only catch-and-release fishing is permitted. Bait fishing may be prohibited in favor of using artificial lures or flies with barbless hooks. *Sierra Trout Guide,* by Ralph and Lisa Cutter, is the most complete guidebook for enthusiasts who want to combine fishing with hiking.

White-Water Rafting

Rivers coursing down the western slopes of the Sierra Nevada provide a playground for white-water enthusiasts of all ages and experience levels. The rafting season varies from river to river, as does the level of difficulty. Each river is rated according to difficulty using the European Rapid Rating System, which assigns a class from I (very easy) through VI (very difficult, beyond limits of navigation). Runoff from typical early-season snowmelt creates massive flows and lots of big rapids. Later in the season, lower flows and river levels often create more technical rapids.

Nearest to Sacramento are the American and Stanislaus Rivers. The South Fork American River (Class II-III, April to October) is ideal for beginners and families. The neighboring North Fork American River (Class IV, April to June) and Middle Fork American River (Class IV, June to October) are more challenging. The North Fork Stanislaus River (Class IV, May to September) offers the most continuous white water of any river in California.

Two rivers descend from Yosemite National Park. The Merced River (Class III-IV, April to July) is the Sierra's best one-day intermediate trip. The Tuolumne River (Class IV, March to October) is considered the best all-around white-water trip. From the highest reaches of the Kings-Kern Divide flows the Kern River, which cuts a deep canyon through Sequoia National Park. Trips on the Lower Kern River (Class III, April to September) and Upper Kern River (Class III, April to July), both staged from near Bakersfield, have the best white water in the southern Sierra.

Several companies run commercial rafting trips, ranging in length from half-day to one, two and three days. Many companies offer daily departures on the most popular and accessible rivers. Trips range from $100 to $150 per person per day, depending on logistics. The companies provide everything you need; all you have to do is show up ready to paddle. Contact OARS (☎ 800-346-6277, ☎ 209-736-4677, fax 209-736-2902, reservations@oars.com, Ⓦ www.oars.com), PO Box 67, Angels Camp, CA 95222.

Cycling

Cycling on highways through the Sierra Nevada is a popular way to explore the range. Cycling on hiking trails is not allowed in national parks or wilderness areas, but is permissible on national forest or BLM land. In national parks, cycling is allowed only on paved roadways. Bicycles are available for rent in some national parks.

Mountain biking is very popular, with the Mammoth area being a real hot spot. Mammoth Mountain has more than 70mi of single-track trails with lift access. Those more interested in solitude than downhill will also find lots of off-road trails in the area; pick up the free *Mammoth Lakes Area Off-Highway Vehicle and Mountain Biking Map* at the visitor center in Mammoth Lakes. Rock Creek Lake, north of Bishop, has both fun rides and seriously insane highly popular rides. Some sections of the Tahoe Rim Trail (see p283) are open to mountain bikers. Contact the Tahoe Rim Trail Association for details.

Dogwood Mountain Bike Adventures (☎ 916-966-6777, Ⓔ mtbiketour@aol.com, Ⓦ www.adventuresports.com/mtnbike/river_rat /dogwood.htm), 9840 Fair Oaks Blvd, Fair Oaks, CA 95628, offers professionally led, scenic, low-traffic trips through varied terrain for all mountain bikers.

Pack Trips

A 100-year-old tradition of transporting hikers into the backcountry remains popular. These are high-impact outings where hikers ride horses and have their gear and food put onto pack animals (typically mules), and the whole show, called a pack string, is led along the trail by real-life cowboys. Outfitters are licensed to run pack trips from specific trailheads following specific trails. Most of these are in the eastern Sierra, where the steeper and higher elevation approaches to the backcountry make pack trips attractive.

Pack trips take several forms. On a full-service pack trip, packers supply all the gear and food and accompany you throughout the trip. One variation on this theme is for you to hike rather than ride a horse. On a spot trip, you ride with the stock to a specified backcountry location and get dropped off and then picked up later, on a specified date. On a dunnage trip, you hike to a pre-arranged destination, and your equipment and supplies or resupplies are carried there by pack stock. The trails frequented by these pack strings are more dusty and rutted, but better graded and more gradual than those trails limited exclusively to backpackers.

Because of the heavy impact of using steel-shod pack stock for backcountry travel, the USFS has concluded that there is a need to encourage the use of alternative, low-impact stock such as llamas. Such non-traditional stock not only leaves less impact, but also helps relieve the conflict between hikers and stock users. One non-traditional pack-stock operator is Lee Lin Llama Treks (☎ 800-526-2725, e leelin@llamatreks.com, w www.llamatreks.com), PO Box 2363, Julian, CA 92036.

USEFUL ORGANIZATIONS
Government Departments

The three national parks in the Sierra Nevada – Yosemite, Kings Canyon and Sequoia – provide endless information about hiking and backcountry travel (see those hiking chapters).

The USFS (w www.fs.fed.us) provides trail information for national forests and wilderness areas, which may overlap one or more national forests, and also issues wilderness permits. These offices can also direct hikers and campers to ranger stations that are close to trailheads. The national forests in the Sierra Nevada and the wilderness areas they manage (except for the Toiyabe National Forest) are all administered as part of the US Forest Service Pacific Southwest Region 5. They include the following:

Eldorado National Forest
100 Forni Rd, Placerville, CA 95667 (☎ 530-622-5061)Carson-Iceberg, Desolation and Mokelumne Wilderness Areas

Inyo National Forest
873 N Main St, Bishop, CA 93514 (☎ 760-873-2400) Ansel Adams, Golden Trout, Hoover and John Muir Wilderness Areas

Plumas National Forest
159 Lawrence St, Quincy, CA 95971 (☎ 530-283-2050) Bucks Lake Wilderness Area

Sequoia National Forest
900 W Grand Ave, Porterville, CA 93257 (☎ 209-784-1500) Dome Land, Golden Trout, Monarch and Jennie Lakes Wilderness Areas

Sierra National Forest
1600 Tollhouse Rd, Clovis, CA 93611 (☎ 559-297-0706) Ansel Adams, Dinkey Lakes, John Muir, Kaiser, Monarch and Jennie Lakes Wilderness Areas

Stanislaus National Forest
19777 Greenley Rd, Sonora, CA 95370 (☎ 209-532-3671) Carson-Iceberg, Emigrant and Mokelumne Wilderness Areas

Tahoe National Forest
631 Coyote St, Nevada City, CA 95959 (☎ 530-265-4531) Granite Chief Wilderness Area

Toiyabe National Forest
1200 Franklin Way, Sparks, NV 89431 (☎ 775-331-6444) Carson-Iceberg, Hoover, Mokelumne and Mt Rose Wilderness Areas

For information on state parks in California, visit the state's website at w cal-parks.ca.gov. An annual day-use parking pass ($35) is advantageous when visiting several parks.

Hiking Clubs

Hiking clubs offer a great introduction to the mountains, an opportunity to meet and exchange information with other hikers, and a way to share planning and transportation. Often associated with a large employer or a university, these clubs can be hard to find. Start at a local outdoors store, which may have club members on staff or an informative bulletin board. Some clubs are listed in the Yellow Pages under 'Clubs – Hiking.' Most clubs allow visitors to participate on most hikes free of charge, but it's essential to contact the trip leader in advance. For college or university clubs, contact the recreation department, often found at the main gymnasium.

The largest and most active hiking club is the Sierra Club (☎ 415-977-5500, Ⓦ calif ornia.sierraclub.org), 85 Second St, San Francisco, CA 94105. Its 13 California chapters and numerous local groups have a busy schedule of chapter and local outings. Call, visit the website or look in the White Pages under 'Sierra Club' to find the nearest chapter. They usually have no membership requirement, are free or have minimal expense sharing, are volunteer lead, and are a great way to learn about the parent organization. Also see Sierra Club Outings, p39.

Mountain Guides Associations

The American Mountain Guides Association (AMGA), the only organization in the US that is a member of the International Federation of Mountain Guides Association (IFMGA, also known as UIAGM), certifies professional mountain guides, who typically lead guided climbs.

The three categories of certification are alpine guide, rock guide and ski mountaineering guide. When a guide earns all three certifications, they are classified as a certified IFMGA guide.

Few guides have formal training other than perhaps in-house training at a guide service, so the purpose of AMGA is to raise the guide's technical and professional standards to a higher, worldwide level. The AMGA also gives accredited status to guide services and schools. Visit the AMGA website at Ⓦ www.amga.com for more information or to look for a certified guide or an accredited guide service.

Other Organizations

The High Sierra Hikers Association (Ⓔ HSHAhike@aol.com, Ⓦ www.highsierra hikers.org), PO Box 8920, South Lake Tahoe, CA 96158, is a nonprofit association that addresses issues affecting hikers in the High Sierra. It offers information, research papers, essays and resource links.

The Sierra Nevada Hikers Webring (Ⓦ nav.webring.yahoo.com/hub?ring=sierra &list) is an interesting and worthwhile online collection of websites about the Sierra Nevada, from the informative to the eclectic.

Members in the American Automobile Association (AAA, pronounced 'triple-ay') are entitled to travel information, free road maps and guidebooks and the purchase of American Express travelers checks without commission. The AAA membership card often entitles you to discounts for accommodations and car rentals. All major cities and towns have a AAA office (Ⓦ www.aaa.com). AAA also provides emergency roadside service (☎ 800-222-4357) in the event of an accident or breakdown or if you lock your keys in the car. Members of other national and state motoring associations – such as the UK Automobile Association or the NRMA and its counterparts in Australia – can use AAA service if they carry a membership card and letter of introduction from their home country's organization.

TOURIST OFFICES

The US does not have national tourist offices in other countries. Tourism promotion in the US is done at the state and local level. Each state has an office that sends material on request. Many cities have a convention and visitors bureau, and smaller towns have a chamber of commerce, an organization of local businesses, that promotes tourism. Most chamber offices can come up with a list of accommodations, restaurants and services provided by its members, but few provide hiking information. When making an inquiry specify that you're interested in hiking, camping and recreation-related information, but for more reliable information, be prepared to go to outdoor stores and to ask the NPS or

USFS. Information USA has a website (W www.information-usa.com) with links to state and city tourist organizations, consulates, maps and weather information.

DOCUMENTS

All visitors should carry their driver's license and any health, automobile or travel-insurance cards. Youth cards are not that helpful in the Sierra Nevada.

Before leaving home, you should photocopy all important documents (passport data page and visa page, credit cards, travel insurance policy, air/bus/train tickets, driver's license, etc). Leave one copy with someone at home and keep another with you, separate from the originals.

Travel Insurance

It's worth taking out travel insurance to cover medical care, emergency evacuation, personal property and trip interruption. Consider insuring yourself for the worst possible scenario – an accident requiring helicopter evacuation or ambulances and hospitalization. For an extended trip, insurance may seem very expensive, but if you cannot afford the insurance premiums, you probably cannot afford a medical emergency either. Some policies pay only for a medical emergency and exclude non-emergency care. You may prefer a policy that pays doctors or hospitals directly rather than requiring your paying on the spot and filing a claim later. If you file a claim later, ensure that you keep all documentation. Some policies require you to make a collect call to the insuror at a center in your home country to authorize treatment or to assess your situation. Others may require you to get a second opinion before receiving any medical care.

Personal property insurance covers loss or theft of your belongings. Remember to report any incident to the nearest police and obtain any police report that you may need to file a claim. If you have prepaid for any travel arrangements, trip interruption or cancellation insurance covers any unreimbursed expenses if you cannot complete your trip due to illness, an accident or the illness or death of family members.

Before you purchase travel insurance, check any existing policy you may own to see what it covers abroad. Some policies may refuse to pay claims when you engage in certain 'dangerous' activities; verify that hiking and backpacking is a covered activity.

Travel insurance is available from private companies; you can also ask any travel agency for recommendations. The international student travel policies handled by STA Travel and other student travel organizations are a good value. They frequently include major medical and emergency evacuation coverage in the cost of a student travel ID card.

MONEY

Hikers do not need any money on the trail. However, carry cash and travelers checks along with an ATM card and/or credit card for food and accommodations in cities, towns, national parks and campgrounds. Long-distance hikers will want to carry some cash for resupplying and buying snacks at stores near trailheads. If you need cash while traveling, ATM machines are ubiquitous and are even found at small town grocery stores, gas stations and in national parks.

Most campgrounds only accept exact change in cash or personal checks, so plan on carrying a checkbook or plenty of small denomination notes like $1 and $5 to avoid overpaying for lack of correct change. Some national park campgrounds accept credit cards, but not all do. National parks do not accept credit cards for entrance fees or passes.

On the Hike

Thankfully, there are some places in the world where there is nothing to buy. These include the wilderness of the Sierra Nevada. Once you leave the last town or national park concession stand nearest the trailhead, there is no place to buy snacks, drinks, supplies or souvenirs. Backcountry camping is free.

Security

Using common sense prevents most theft. As a general rule, keep your valuables in the backpack you carry and in your line of sight, and never flash large wads of cash. The backpack's top pocket isn't recommended; an interior zippered pocket is better. Put all money in a resealable plastic bag or other waterproof pouch. Keep all your gear inside your tent at night.

Costs

Budget $45 per person per day when staying in hotels and using public transport. This includes daily per-person accommodations (double rooms) costing $30, and $15 each for food. Hotels, particularly those around Lake Tahoe, can be from 10% to 15% less expensive Sunday through Thursday than on Friday and Saturday. The cost of staying in campgrounds between hikes ranges from $8 to $18 per night per site.

On the trails, per-person daily costs vary significantly, depending on the kind of hike you choose. Backpacking expenses range from $10 to $15 per day when you carry your own pack, buy food locally, provide your own equipment and use public transportation to trailheads. The cost of transport to trailheads is listed under each hike. Organized hikes range in price from $80 to $190 per day.

POST & COMMUNICATIONS
eKno Communication Service

Lonely Planet's eKno global communication service provides low-cost international calls – for local calls you're usually better off with a local phone card. eKno also offers free messaging services, email, travel information and an online travel vault, where you can securely store all your important documents. You can join online at w www.ekno.lonelyplanet.com, where you will find the local-access numbers for the 24-hour customer-service center. Once you have joined, always check the eKno website for the latest access numbers for each country and updates on new features.

Post

The US Postal Service (USPS), the busiest postal system in the world, is reliable, fast and inexpensive. Rates for 1st-class mail within the US are $0.34 for letters up to 1oz, $0.23 for each additional ounce up to 13oz,

and $0.21 for postcards. Packages over 13oz go as priority mail. Rates are $3.50 up to 1lb, $3.95 up to 2lb, $5.15 up to 3lb, $6.35 up to 4lb and $7.55 up to 5lb. Rates over 5lb are based on the destination.

The cost of parcels mailed anywhere in the US is $2.72 for 2lb or less. For heavier items, rates differ according to destination – the maximum weight is 70lb. Parcel post is the lowest rate but the slowest service.

International airmail rates (except to Canada and Mexico) are $0.80 for a 1oz letter and $0.80 for each additional ounce. International postcard rates are $0.70. Letters to Canada and Mexico are $0.60 for a 1oz, and $0.50 for a postcard. Aerograms cost $0.70.

If you have correct postage, just drop your letters or postcards into any mailbox. If you need to buy postage, weigh your mail, or send a package heavier than 1lb, go to a post office, usually open 8am to 5pm weekdays and 8am to 2pm Saturday.

General delivery mail can be sent to you c/o General Delivery at any post office that has its own zip code. Mail is usually held for 10 days before it's returned to the sender. If you are planning a long-distance hike and want to mail supplies to yourself, be sure to write 'Hold For Arrival' on the package, along with the date you expect to arrive. You need photo identification to collect general delivery mail.

For 24-hour postal information, call ☎ 800-275-8777 or check the website at w www.usps.com. Both give zip (postal) codes for a given address, the rules about parcel sizes, and the location and phone number of any post office.

Telephone

The US telephone system, comprising numerous regional phone companies, long-distance carriers and mobile phone companies, is still evolving. Technically it's highly efficient, but is more oriented to the needs of local users than to foreign visitors. Carrying a phone card – either from your home phone company or from a calling-card service that offers low rates between the US and wherever you want to call – is almost always a better option than using US pay

Top: Fragrant wild sage blooms in the scenic Sierra Nevada wilderness.
Bottom: Campers on the Whitney Portal Trail wake up to breathtaking scenery.

Top: A hiker crosses a wooden suspension bridge over Woods Creek, Kings Canyon National Park.
Bottom Left: Horsepackers follow the trail near Barney Lake, Mammoth Lakes Basin.
Bottom Right: A hiker meets the challenge of wilderness camping in Sequoia National Park.

phones. The Lonely Planet eKno service is one to consider.

If you're calling from abroad, the international country code for the US is ☎ 001. All phone numbers within the US have a three-digit area code, followed by a seven-digit local number. From within the same area code, just dial the seven-digit number. If you're calling outside the area code, dial ☎ 1 first, then the area code and the seven-digit number. The three-digit prefixes ☎ 800 and ☎ 888 are for toll-free numbers. The ☎ 900 prefix is for premium-rate high-cost calls (horoscopes, phone sex, jokes, etc).

For local directory assistance dial ☎ 411. For directory assistance outside the area code, dial ☎ 1 plus the area code and 555-1212. Directory assistance is not free – charges can be significant – so consider using a telephone directory if possible.

To make an international direct call, dial ☎ 011, then the country code (which is in the front of any telephone directory), followed by the area or local code and the number.

Fax

Fax machines are easy to find in large towns and cities at photocopy stores and shipping companies like Mail Boxes Etc. Hikers can use fax machines for making wilderness permit reservations and for booking accommodations.

Email

Traveling with a portable computer is a great way to stay in touch with life back home, but unless you know what you're doing it's fraught with potential problems. If you plan to carry your notebook or palmtop computer with you, remember that the power supply voltage in the US may vary from that at home, and you risk damage to your equipment. The best investment is a universal AC adaptor for your appliance, which will enable you to plug it in anywhere without frying the innards. You'll also need a plug adaptor – often it's easiest to buy these two items before you leave home.

Also, your PC-card modem may or may not work once you leave your home country – and you won't know for sure until you try. The safest option is to buy a reputable 'global' modem before you leave home, or buy a local PC-card modem. Keep in mind that the telephone socket will probably be different from the one you have at home, so ensure that you have at least a US RJ-11 telephone adaptor that works with your modem. You can almost always find an adaptor that will convert from RJ-11 to the local variety for you. For more information on traveling with a portable computer, see ⓦ www.teleadapt .com or ⓦ www.warrior.com.

Major Internet service providers such as AOL (ⓦ www.aol.com), CompuServe (ⓦ www.compuserve.com) and IBM Net (ⓦ www.ibm.net) have dial-in nodes throughout the US; it's best to download a list of the dial-in numbers before you leave home. If you access your Internet email account at home through a smaller ISP or your office or school network, your best option is either to open an account with a global ISP, like those mentioned above, or to rely on cybercafes and other public access points to collect your mail.

If you do intend to rely on cybercafes, you'll need to carry three pieces of information with you to access your Internet mail account: your incoming (POP or IMAP) mail server name, your account name and your password. Your ISP or network supervisor will be able to give you these. Armed with this information, you should be able to access your Internet mail account from any net-connected machine in the world, provided it runs some kind of email software (remember that Netscape and Internet Explorer both have mail modules). It pays to become familiar with the process for doing this before you leave home.

To find cybercafes throughout the US, visit ⓦ www.netcafeguide.com for an up-to-date list. You may also find public net access in post offices, libraries, hostels, hotels, universities and so on. The nearest place to Yosemite National Park to check email is Sierra Tel in Mariposa, on Hwy 140 about 43mi west of Yosemite Valley. Around the Lake Tahoe area, any of the many chamber of commerce offices offer email and Internet access.

INTERNET RESOURCES

The World Wide Web is a rich resource for travelers. You can research your trip, hunt down bargain airfares, make hotel and campground reservations, reserve wilderness permits, check on weather conditions or chat with locals and other travelers about the best places to visit (or avoid!).

There's no better place to start your Web explorations than the Lonely Planet website (W www.lonelyplanet.com). Here, you'll find succinct summaries on traveling to most places on earth; postcards from other travelers; and the Thorn Tree bulletin board, where you can ask questions before you go or dispense advice when you get back. You can also find travel news and updates to many of our most popular guidebooks, and the subWWWay section links you to the most useful travel resources elsewhere on the Web.

Most government organizations, national parks and conservation organizations have websites, which are listed throughout this book. Some focus on hiking. The Great Outdoor Recreation Pages (W www.gorp.com) has interesting articles that are constantly updated to reflect the seasons. Life on the Trail (W www .lifeonthetrail.com) reviews backpacking gear, recipes and women's issues, with a knowledgeable staff who answer queries on these subjects. For hiking and packing tips, as well as information on lightweight backpacking gear and backpacking skills, visit W www.backpacking.net/contents.html.

BOOKS
Lonely Planet

For more detailed information on the Sierra Nevada area, look to Lonely Planet's *California & Nevada* guidebook. To plan hikes in the Pacific Northwest, the Rocky Mountains or other parts of the country, pick up Lonely Planet's *Hiking in the USA,* or *Hiking in the Rockies*.

Travel & Exploration

My First Summer in the Sierra, by John Muir, is the inspirational diary Muir kept while tending sheep in 1869, when he recognized his life calling. *Gentle Wilderness: The Sierra Nevada,* by John Muir, updates the famous naturalist's writings with modern photographs.

Yosemite and the High Sierra, by Ansel Adams, the Sierra's most renowned photographer, offers a compilation of his finest images and most exuberant writings. *History of the Sierra Nevada,* by Francis P Farquhar, is the classic history of the Sierra Nevada from the time Spaniards first saw it to 1965. *The Destruction of California Indians,* by Robert Fleming, is a powerful and chilling account of California history. *Sierra Crossing – First Roads to California,* by Thomas Frederick Howard, is also highly recommended.

Natural History

Sierra Nevada Natural History, written by Tracy I Storer and Robert L Usinger, is thorough, usable and the best guide to the Sierra's natural species. *A Sierra Nevada Flora,* by Norman Weeden, provides outdoors enthusiasts with in-depth coverage of wildflowers, ferns, shrubs, trees and plant life. *A Sierra Club Naturalist's Guide to the Sierra Nevada,* by Stephen Whitney, is a condensed, comprehensive guide to a huge subject. *Sierra Nevada Wildflowers,* by Karen Wiese, is a field guide with photos and easy-to-understand descriptions of more than 230 wildflowers, arranged for quick identification. *Sierra Nevada Tree Identifier,* by Jim Paruk, is one of the best small books for recognizing Sierra Nevada trees. *Conifers of California,* by Ronald M Lanner, is a beautifully illustrated and researched reference manual.

Sierra Nevada Field Card Set – Birds, Flowers, Mammals, and Trees of the Sierra Nevada, drawings by Elizabeth Morales, are handy, unbreakable, waterproof field identification cards depicting the most commonly seen flora and fauna.

Place Names of the Sierra Nevada, by Peter Browning, gives the derivation and lore of each name given to the rivers, valleys, mountain peaks, lakes and passes of the High Sierra.

Buying Books

Bookstores in Yosemite, Sequoia and King Canyon National Parks, run by each park's natural history association, carry the widest selection and are great places to make a purchase (see the Books section in those chapters for details). Local bookstores in Sierra towns also carry a specialized selection. The following stores are worth a try.

Bookshelf at Hooligan Rocks (☎ 530-582-0515), 11310 Donner Pass Rd, Truckee

Truckee Books (☎ 530-582-8302), W River St at Hwy 267, Truckee

Bookshelf at the Boatworks (☎ 530-581-1900), 760 N Lake Blvd, Tahoe City

Mountain Bookshop (☎ 209-532-6117), 13769-I Mono Way, Sonora

Mountain High Books & Video (☎ 760-872-2665), 621 West Line St, Bishop

Spellbinder Books & Coffee Bar (☎ 760-873-4511), 124 S Main St, Bishop

FILMS
The John Muir Trail is a 75-minute-long VHS video of the 211mi journey along the most majestic mountain path in the US (see the John Muir Trail hike, p289).

CD-ROMS
Two multimedia CD-ROM trail guides ($39.95 each) cover 5000 sq miles of the Sierra Nevada with 3000mi of trail descriptions and 275 predefined trips. *Sierra Nevada North* covers Tahoe to the southern border of Yosemite National Park and *Sierra Nevada South* covers from the southern border of Yosemite National Park to Golden Trout Wilderness south of Sequoia National Park. To order the CD-ROMs, contact the publisher Mountain Images, Inc (☎ 800-788-8908, 805-969-3139, fax 253-595-8322, e sierra@mtnimages.com, w www.silcom.com/~mtnimages/), 149 Rametto Blvd, Santa Barbara, CA 93108.

Some maps are available on CD-ROM (see Maps & Navigation, p49).

NEWSPAPERS & MAGAZINES
National newspapers, such as *USA Today,* offer national weather reports that are usually too general to be of much use to hikers. Better are local newspapers whose weather forecasts are not only more specific, but also often feature informative articles about local mountain areas. The leading outdoors-oriented magazine, *Outside,* can be found in airports and supermarkets. Its online version (w www.outsideonline.com) is updated daily and has current news on gear, destinations and personalities. Specifically for hikers is *Backpacker: The Magazine of Wilderness Travel,* found in some general bookstores, the occasional supermarket and most outdoor stores. It, too, has an excellent website (w www.backpacker.com), with a Trail Talk Forum, links to Sierra wilderness area information and more.

RADIO & TV
The major networks blanket California with television and radio broadcasts through local affiliate stations. National and some international coverage is given on network news programs, but hikers will find local news and weather far more pertinent to their plans. Several AM radio stations have an all-news format, on which you can catch a brief local weather report every 10 minutes.

WEATHER INFORMATION
Unpredictable and changeable weather, a given in the mountains, also presents a small yet inherent risk in wilderness travel. Before starting your hike, it's sensible to find out what the weather forecast is. Often the easiest place to do that is at ranger stations and visitor centers, which post daily weather reports on bulletin boards.

The National Weather Service (w www.wrh.noaa.gov) announces a three-day weather forecast twice daily, at 4am and 4pm (Pacific Daylight Time). Regardless of the forecast, carry rain gear at all times and be prepared for the worst. *Reading Weather – Where Will You Be When the Storm Hits,* by meteorologist Jim Woodmency, explains how to anticipate storms by understanding clouds and weather patterns, which is important general knowledge for anyone heading into the backcountry.

PHOTOGRAPHY
Film & Equipment
Color print film is more widely available than slide film. Prices are high in the national

parks and nearby small towns, so no matter what film you prefer, stock up before heading into the mountains. Drugstore chains offer reasonable prices, followed by supermarkets, pharmacies, small grocery stores, outdoor stores and hardware stores, in that order. B&W film is rarely sold outside major cities. Advance Photo System (APS) film, such as Kodak's Advantix, is becoming popular, but is hard to find in smaller towns.

Drugstores are a good place to get your film processed cheaply – starting at $6 for a 24 exposure roll. One-hour processing is more expensive, usually about $11.

Excessive heat can damage film, so don't leave your camera or film in the top compartment of your pack or in your car on a hot day. Don't forget a spare battery for your camera, and a sealable bag to store exposed film. Putting a clear plastic bag over your camera to protect it from dust lets you carry it over your shoulder while hiking.

Choice of equipment is a personal matter, but an SLR camera with a mid-range zoom (eg, 35mm to 135mm) covers a wide range of situations. A good second lens to carry might be a 24mm or 28mm for panoramas. A 'skylite' filter protects the lens and cuts down on high-altitude UV glare, and a polarizing filter darkens the sky to avoid underexposing the landscape.

Technique

The best light for photography is around dawn and dusk. The high contrast of midday light tends to emphasize shadows when photographing. Cloudy days offer diffuse, soft light that gives surprisingly good results. A shaft of sunlight breaking through clouds and highlighting a mountain or lake makes a dramatic image. In unusual lighting situations, taking several different exposures helps ensure you get at least one good picture. To photograph elusive wildlife, plant yourself in a meadow or near a water source before dawn or after dusk and be prepared to wait at least an hour. A tripod enables you to work even in dim light.

Long or medium range shots of people are usually no problem, but if you want a close shot, you should always ask. Pay attention to the background when photographing people. Most built-in light meters underexpose a person's face if the background is bright sky or reflective granite.

Airport Security

All passengers have to pass their carry-on baggage through X-ray machines at airports. In the US, since the terrorist attacks of September 11, 2001, the strength of these X-rays has been stepped up. One or two passes will probably not jeopardize most slower film (ISO 200 and lower), but faster film can become fogged by only one or two passes. You may want to carry your film spools loose in a clear plastic container or bag and ask the X-ray inspector to visually check the film. There is still a chance that someone may insist you pass your film through the X-ray.

Undeveloped film, unexposed or exposed, is much more vulnerable to fogging than developed film, so one way to protect your images is to buy film after you reach your destination and have it processed before you leave. Another way to avoid problems with fogging is to avoid film altogether by taking a digital camera on your trip. It is generally agreed that digital memory is not affected by X-ray, and as an added bonus, you won't have to carry around multiple rolls of film. Just make sure you take the usual precautions to keep your camera dry, and that you take an extra set of batteries.

TIME

California and Nevada have a single time zone, Pacific time, which is eight hours behind Universal time (UT), also called Greenwich mean time. Daylight saving time is observed.

LAUNDRY

Self-service coin-operated laundromats are in most sizable towns and some high-end private campgrounds. To find one, check the telephone directory under 'Laundries.'

BUSINESS HOURS

Generally businesses open at 9 or 10am and close at 5 or 6pm, but there are no hard-and-fast rules. In large cities, a few supermarkets, restaurants and convenience stores stay open 24 hours. Some stores are open until 9pm, especially those in shopping malls, and many open for shorter hours on Sunday (typically noon to 5pm).

Ranger stations and national park visitor centers are generally open daily 8 or 9am to 6 or 7pm from Memorial Day to Labor Day. After Labor Day they open later, close earlier and may close for an hour in the middle of the day. During winter, many are closed or only open on weekends.

PUBLIC HOLIDAYS

Banks, post offices and government offices are closed on public holidays. Many stores, however, remain open. The holidays during the hiking season are Memorial Day, observed the last Monday in May; Independence Day, July 4; and Labor Day, observed the first Monday in September. These days and the weekends preceding these holidays are busy times in the mountains. Allow extra driving time because freeways are typically clogged with picnickers and outdoor enthusiasts getting away from urban areas for the long holiday weekend. The terms Memorial Day and Labor Day are used in the text because these holidays define some opening and closing dates for parks, roads, campgrounds and other facilities.

Health & Safety

The Sierra Nevada is generally a very healthy place to visit, with no prevalent diseases. Both California and Nevada are very well served by hospitals, medical centers, walk-in clinics and referral services, which are easily found in cities, towns and even in national parks. In an emergency call ☎ 911 for an ambulance to take you to the nearest hospital emergency room.

Keeping healthy while traveling and hiking depends on your predeparture preparations, your daily health care while traveling and how you handle any medical problem that does develop. The sections that follow aren't intended to alarm, but they are worth a skim before you go.

PREDEPARTURE PLANNING
Health Insurance
Due to the high cost of health care, international visitors should have adequate health insurance. See Travel Insurance, p63, under Documents.

Physical Preparations
How much physical preparation you need, of course, depends on your current level of conditioning and the kind of hike(s) you're planning. If you exercise regularly and are planning day hikes or an easy overnight backpacking trip, you may not need any additional conditioning. If you're not in shape or are planning a longer or more difficult backpacking trip, establishing a training routine will make your trip more enjoyable.

Try to do something for a minimum of 30 minutes at least three times a week. The best preparation is that which resembles what you will be doing on the trail – working your leg muscles and increasing your aerobic capacity. Get out for short hikes and carry a light backpack. Gradually increase the length of your training hikes and the weight you carry. If hiking outdoors isn't possible, head for the gym for an aerobics class, the stair-stepping and climbing machines and weightlifting. Make walking a part of your daily life. Climb stairs instead of taking the elevator, and park your vehicle farther away from your destination than normal and walk the rest of the way. Cycling and swimming are excellent choices for aerobic conditioning and increasing endurance.

Immunizations
No immunizations are required for visiting the US, but before any trip it's a good idea to make sure you are up to date with routine vaccinations such as diphtheria, polio and tetanus. It's particularly important that your tetanus is up to date – the initial course of three injections, usually given in childhood, is followed by boosters every 10 years.

First Aid
It's essential to know the appropriate responses in the event of a major accident or illness, especially when hiking in remote areas. Consider taking a recognized course in basic first aid before you go, and carrying a first-aid manual. Although detailed first-aid instruction is beyond this book's scope, some basic points and tips for prevention are listed under Traumatic Injuries, see p77, and Safety on the Hike, p79.

Other Preparations
If you have any known medical problems or are concerned about your health in any way, it's a good idea to have a full checkup before you go. It's far better to have any problems recognized and treated at home than to find out about them halfway up a trail. It's also sensible to have had a recent dental checkup, since toothache on the trail can be a miserable experience. If you wear glasses, take a spare pair and your prescription.

If you need a particular medicine, take enough with you to last the trip. Be sure you know the generic name, rather than the brand name, as this will make getting replacements easier. To avoid any problems, it's also a good idea to have a legible prescription or letter from your doctor to prove that you legally use the medication.

Health Guides
If you are planning to be away or hiking in remote areas for some time, you might consider taking a more detailed health guide such as: *Medicine for Mountaineering & Other Wilderness Activities,* by James A Wilkerson; *The Outward Bound Wilderness First-Aid Handbook,* by Jeff Isaac; *Mountaineering Medicine and Backcountry Medical Guide,* by Fred T Darvill Jr; or *Medicine for the Backcountry,* by Tilton and Hubbell.

Travel with Children from Lonely Planet also includes advice on travel health for younger children.

Online Resources
Several excellent travel health sites are on the Internet. From the Lonely Planet home page there are links at W www.lonely planet.com/weblinks/wlprep.htmlheal to the World Health Organization and the US Centers for Disease Control & Prevention plus many other sites.

STAYING HEALTHY
Hygiene
To reduce the chances of contracting an illness, you should wash your hands frequently, particularly before handling or eating food. Keeping your feet clean minimizes the chance of blisters or fungal infections. When hiking, put on clean underwear and socks daily. Change sweaty clothes, including socks, immediately when you get into camp. Wear shoes at all times. Avoid insect bites by covering bare skin when insects are around, sleeping in a tent or under a mosquito net, and by using insect repellents.

Water
Water that is contaminated with bacteria, cysts and viruses transmits many diseases. Tap water is generally fine to drink throughout the US. At campgrounds, however, ask the campground host or at the nearest ranger station if the water is safe to drink. Often, if it isn't safe, a sign is posted. Open

Medical Kit Checklist

General guide, hiker's first-aid kit:

First aid supplies

❑ **sterile adhesive bandages** (for minor cuts, abrasions and puncture wounds)

❑ **sterile and nonsterile bandages** (for dressing wounds)

❑ **waterproof butterfly closures** (to hold wound edges together)

❑ **rolled gauze** (to hold dressings)

❑ **high-compression elastic bandage with Velcro closure**

❑ **waterproof adhesive tape**

❑ **bandage scissors**

❑ **blister treatment** (adhesive pads such as mole foam)

❑ **thermometer**

❑ **tweezers**

❑ **knee or ankle brace**

❑ **antiseptic swabs or liquid** (to cleanse minor wounds)

❑ **topical antibiotic ointment**

Medications

❑ **analgesics for pain and fever** (aspirin, acetaminophen)

❑ **antihistamines for allergic reactions, itchiness** (eg, diphenhydramine)

❑ **anti-inflammatory** (ibuprofen, naproxen)

❑ **antibiotics** (for bacterial infections; consult your physician)

Miscellaneous

❑ **skin applications for irritations** (sunburn, bites, sore muscles)

❑ **eye drops** (for washing out dust)

❑ **water purification tablets** or **iodine** or **water filter**

❑ **waterproof sunscreen**

❑ **lip salve** with **sunblock**

❑ **insect repellent**

❑ **matches**

water sources – lakes, rivers, streams and springs – in the Sierra Nevada are known to be contaminated with the pathogen *Giardia lamblia*. When you don't know for certain that the water is uncontaminated, it's necessary to purify drinking water.

Water Purification Boiling, treating chemically and filtering are three practical ways to purify water.

The best way of purifying water is to bring it to a rolling boil for at least one minute, which kills all intestinal-disease-causing organisms. At higher elevation, water boils at a lower temperature, but still gets hot enough for disinfection. When you can't boil water, treat it chemically or filter it.

When used correctly, iodine is an effective chemical treatment to purify water. It's available in three forms: tablets, tincture and crystals. Iodine products are lightweight and easy to use, although their effectiveness depends on concentration, exposure time, temperature, pH and turbidity of the water. After treating water with any form of iodine, let treated water stand for at least 20 minutes before drinking. If the water is particularly cold, let it warm up in the sun before treating it. Otherwise, allow treated water to stand longer.

Iodine in tablet form is marketed under various brand names (eg, Potable Aqua). Tablets are easy to carry and use and dissolve quickly. If the tablets get wet, however, they become ineffective. Tincture of iodine is a liquid form typically sold in a glass bottle (eg, Lugol's solution, Povidone or Betadine). The recommended dosage is two to three drops per 1L of water.

Iodine crystals are also sold in glass bottles. Prepare a saturated iodine solution by filling the bottle with water. After this solution stands for one hour, it's ready to use. Remember to protect glass bottles from breaking. Add flavored drinking powder, rehydration salts or herbal tea bags only after the water is completely disinfected. Vitamin C binds with any excess iodine and also improves the taste.

Chlorine tablets, sold under various brand names, don't kill all pathogens

(Giardia lamblia and amoebic cysts) and aren't recommended.

Filtration works by straining out chemicals, microorganisms and suspended solids. The size of the pores in a water filter determines its effectiveness. All filters remove *Giardia lamblia,* some remove smaller bacteria, but none remove viruses. To kill viruses, chemical disinfection or boiling is necessary. Only filters that combine filtration with disinfection produce water safe to drink.

Food
Hikers will find food throughout the Sierra Nevada region to be safe and healthy. California grows most of the nation's produce, and the abundance and variety of fresh food in grocery stores often astounds visitors to the region. The food supply throughout the US is regulated and inspected by the US Department of Agriculture (USDA) and the Food and Drug Administration (FDA) to ensure quality and safety. However, the mechanized agricultural and livestock industries operate on such an enormous scale that it is impossible to ensure that all food is 100% safe.

Meat, particularly ground beef used in burgers, is occasionally contaminated during processing by coliform bacteria from the intestines of the slaughtered animals. These organisms contaminate undercooked meat, and can cause food poisoning and diarrhea if eaten. Be sure that any meat or poultry you eat is thoroughly cooked and freshly served. Fast food chains take great care to ensure that their burgers are properly cooked, so hikers should not be overly concerned about grabbing a double cheeseburger on the road. More serious problems, such as bovine spongiform encephalitis, or mad cow disease, have so far not been reported in the US meat supply.

USDA and FDA testing has not shown demonstrable proof that genetically modified food is unsafe, and US regulations do not require such food to be labeled. Hikers who want to avoid eating any 'frankenfood,' however, should stick to food labeled 'organic.' California certifies food as organic, which means it is not genetically modified and no chemical pesticides or fertilizers have been used in growing the food. Dairy products are labeled if they come from milk from cows that have not been given any hormones. Eggs are labeled if they are organic, hormone-free, antibiotic free – or all of the above. You'll find a wide variety of organic food in all major grocery stores in California and Nevada and in most smaller stores as well.

When backpacking, you need to eat between 3000 and 4500 calories per day or from 1.5lb to 2lb per day. It's hard to hike when you're not eating enough. Make sure your diet is well balanced. You need extra calories, especially carbohydrates. Consider taking vitamin supplements if your intake of vitamin-rich foods is insufficient, or when traveling for an extended time.

Common Ailments

Blisters Your socks and boots should fit comfortably, with enough room to move your toes; boots that are too big or too small cause blisters. Be sure your hiking boots are well worn in before your trip. At the very least, wear them on a few short hikes before tackling longer outings.

Wet or dirty socks also cause blisters, so carry a spare pair and change them regularly. Keep your toenails clipped, but not too short. As soon as you feel a hot spot coming on, put tape or an adhesive foam pad on it to act as a second skin. If a blister develops, don't pop it. Pad it, wait for it to burst and keep the new skin clean. Blisters eventually turn into calluses.

Fatigue More injuries happen toward the end of the day when you're tired. Never set out on a hike that's beyond your capabilities that day. To reduce the risk, don't push yourself too hard and do take regular rest breaks. Toward the end of the day, relax your pace and increase your concentration. Eat energy-giving snacks throughout the day to replenish depleted reserves.

Knee Pain Swelling of the knee from pounding descents can be incapacitating. If you are prone to this, take anti-

Everyday Health

Normal body temperature is up to 98.6°F; more than 4°F higher indicates a high fever. The normal adult pulse rate ranges from 60 to 100 per minute (children from 80 to 100, and babies from 100 to 140). As a general rule the pulse increases about 20 beats per minute for each 2°F rise in fever.

Respiration (breathing) rate at rest is also an indicator of illness. Count the number of breaths per minute: between 12 and 20 is normal for adults and older children (up to 30 for younger children, and 40 for babies). People with a high fever or serious respiratory illness breathe more quickly than normal. More than 40 shallow breaths a minute may indicate pneumonia.

inflammatory medications before you start hiking. A brace may also help. Minimize the pounding by carrying less weight and by taking small steps with slightly bent knees, making sure that your heels hit the ground before the rest of your foot. Hiking poles are effective in taking some of the weight off the knees.

MEDICAL PROBLEMS & TREATMENT

The following sections are meant to prepare hikers for possible medication situations, although most hikers get nothing worse than a blister or small scrape.

Environmental Hazards

Hikers are at more risk than most groups from environmental hazards. The risk, however, can be significantly reduced by using common sense.

Altitude Acute Mountain Sickness (AMS) occurs from a failure of the body to adapt to high elevations, resulting in a buildup of intercellular fluid, which accumulates in the lungs (high altitude pulmonary edema or HAPE) and/or in the brain (high altitude cerebral edema or HACE). HAPE and HACE are both progressive, life-threatening conditions, which may occur simultaneously.

Ignoring progressive symptoms may lead to unconsciousness and death within hours. AMS is easily preventable and should never be fatal.

Watch for symptoms at intermediate altitudes between 5000ft and 8000ft, as AMS is known to occur as low as 6000ft. 'High altitude' is an arbitrary descriptive term, but for medical purposes could be understood to mean elevations above 8000ft. These categories help gauge the range of higher elevations where AMS generally occurs and is more severe: high altitudes between 8000ft and 11,500ft; and very high altitudes over 11,500ft. The Sierra Nevada's highest elevation is just below 14,500ft.

The key to preventing AMS is to ascend slowly so acclimatization can take place. When hiking higher than 10,000ft, limit your daily increase in sleeping elevation to 1000ft. Keep your fluid intake high and avoid diuretics, such as caffeine and alcohol. Since the body takes in less oxygen while sleeping, avoid taking sleeping sedatives, which lower your breathing rate and decrease oxygen levels in your blood.

Hikers need to understand and recognize the symptoms of AMS, be aware of its risks and know how to respond to symptoms. Be alert for symptoms in yourself and those hiking with you. AMS progresses slowly but steadily over 24 to 48 hours. Early signs of AMS are headache, persistent yawning, hyperventilation, shortness of breath, loss of appetite, poor sleep and waking up at night gasping for breath (ie, Cheyne-Stokes breathing). It's not uncommon to experi-ence these symptoms when ascending. They indicate you have reached your limit of acclimatization and that you need to stop and rest in order to acclimatize further.

When you continue to ascend, symptoms will steadily worsen. As fluid accumulates in the lungs, the person with HAPE becomes progressively more breathless, at first while walking and eventually even at rest. Breathlessness is accompanied by a cough, dry at first, and a discernable rattling or gurgling in the lungs, which progresses to production of pink, frothy sputum, then bloody. Death from drowning results. As fluid collects in the brain, a person with HACE experiences headache, loss of appetite, nausea, and becomes lethargic and tired. As the severity increases, disorientation and loss of coordination develop. A hiker with HACE has difficulty doing simple tasks such as lacing boots or tying knots. With increasing lethargy comes a desire to lie down, followed by lapsing into a coma. Without immediate descent, death is inevitable.

Treatment of AMS is simple. When you experience any symptoms, especially headache and/or breathlessness, stop and rest until they go away. Symptoms may be confused with a cold or an upset stomach or being out of shape. Do not ascend when you have any symptoms. If the symptoms don't go away, or get worse, descend immediately to the last elevation where you were symptom-free regardless of the time of day. A person suffering from AMS may not think clearly and may have to be forced to descend. Even if the diagnosis of AMS is uncertain, descend when you suspect AMS, as a prompt descent always relieves symptoms. You can always re-ascend later.

Prophylaxis is not recommended to prevent AMS. It's safer to rely on planned, slow ascent. Some medications, however, have proven effective to treat AMS. Acetazolamide 250mg (Diamox) can be taken before ascent to prevent or to relieve mild AMS symptoms, such as headache and nausea, and promote sleep at high altitudes. Recent studies indicate that 125mg is just as effective and causes fewer side

Warning

Self-diagnosis and treatment can be risky, so you should always seek medical help. Although this section includes drug dosages, they are for emergency use only. Correct diagnosis is vital.

Note that generic names rather than brand names for drugs are listed throughout this section. Consult a pharmacist for locally available brand names.

Warning

Eastern Sierra and trans-Sierra trailheads near mountain passes typically are at elevations higher than 8000ft and often above 9000ft. Hikers starting at these elevations must be careful to practice proper acclimatization. For example, when driving from sea level in the Los Angeles or San Francisco areas, spend at least one night at a lower elevation in a nearby town or campground before camping or hiking at high altitudes in the backcountry.

effects. Dexamethasone 0.5mg (Decadron and Oradexon), a steroid drug thought to reduce brain swelling, is useful for HACE. Don't take it to prevent the onset of AMS. Nifedipine 10mg (Procardia and Adalat) lowers pulmonary artery pressure and is useful for HAPE. Don't take it as a prophylaxis.

Sun You can get sunburnt quickly, even on hazy, cloudy, or overcast days and even when it snows. Use a high quality sunblock or sunscreen and lip moisturizer with a Sun Protection Factor (SPF) of 30 or 50 with UV-A and UV-B protection and reapply throughout the day. Remember to cover areas such as under your nose and chin that don't normally see sun. Wear protective clothing for your face, ears and neck. Wearing a wide-brimmed hat and putting a bandanna around your neck offer added protection. Use zinc oxide or another cream or physical barrier for your nose if traveling across snow for extended periods. If, despite these precautions, you get burnt, calamine lotion, aloe vera or other commercial sunburn relief preparations are soothing.

Heat Dehydration, a condition caused by excessive fluid loss, occurs in cold as well as hot conditions and because of diarrhea and vomiting. The body expends fluids in saliva, urine and sweat that need to be replenished. Make sure you drink enough and don't wait until you feel thirsty to drink. Always carry water when you hike. Urine is normally pale

yellow, and darkening urine and decreased urination are symptoms of dehydration. Drink more fluid and avoid diuretics, such as caffeine; a minimum intake of 3 quarts per day is recommended. Oral rehydration salts (ORS) and powdered electrolyte mixes can be added to drinking water to replace essential salts lost through diarrhea or sweating.

Overexposure to heat and sun, dehydration or deficiency of salts can cause heat exhaustion. Symptoms include faintness, a weak and rapid pulse, shallow breathing, cold or clammy skin and profuse perspiration. Lay a victim down in a cool, shaded area. Elevate their feet and massage their legs toward the heart. Give them a drink of cool, salty water (ie, 1½ teaspoon of salt in a glass of water) or a sweet drink. Allow them to rest and don't let them sit up too soon.

Heatstroke, a life-threatening emergency condition, is the onset of a high fever caused by exposure to high temperatures in which the body's heat-regulating mechanism breaks down. Symptoms are extremely high body temperature (102°F to 106°F), rapid pulse, profusion followed by a cessation of sweating, and then dry, red, hot skin. Severe, throbbing headaches and lack of coordination may also occur, and a victim may be confused or aggressive. Eventually a victim convulses and becomes unconscious. Hospitalization is essential, but meanwhile it's imperative to lower the body temperature by getting the victim out of the sun, cooling them in water, sponging briskly with a cool cloth, or wrapping in cold clothes or a wet sheet or towel and then fanning continually. Give fluids if they're conscious, but avoid caffeinated ones.

Cold When hiking and camping at higher altitudes be prepared for cold, wet or windy conditions, even when just out for a few days.

Hypothermia occurs when the body loses heat faster than it produces it, lowering the core body temperature. Even when the air temperature is above freezing, the combination of wind, wet clothing, fatigue and hunger can lead to hypothermia. Dress in insulating layers and wear a hat, as much heat is lost through the head. On the trail, keep fluid intake high and carry food containing simple sugars to generate heat quickly.

Symptoms of hypothermia are shivering, loss of coordination (slurred speech) and disorientation or confusion. These can be accompanied by exhaustion, numb skin (particularly toes and fingers), irrational or violent behavior, lethargy, dizzy spells, muscle cramps and violent bursts of energy. To treat the early stages of hypothermia, first get the victim out of the elements like wind, rain or snow. Then prevent heat loss by replacing any wet clothes with layers of dry, warm ones. Next have the victim drink warm liquids, avoiding alcohol, and eat high-caloric food with sugars or carbohydrates. Don't rub the victim, but place them near a fire or gently bathe with warm, not hot, water. It may be necessary to place the victim, naked, in sleeping bags and get in with them. Early recognition and treatment of mild hypothermia is the only way to prevent severe hypothermia, a critical condition.

Frostbite occurs when extremities freeze. Signs include crystals on the skin, a whitish or waxy skin accompanied by itching, numbness and pain. Warm affected areas by immersing in warm water or covering with clothing or sleeping bags. When skin becomes flushed, stop warming, elevate, and expect pain and swelling. Exercise the area if possible, but don't break blisters or rub affected areas. Apply dressings only if the victim must be moved. When fingers or toes are affected, separate the digits with sterile pads. Seek medical attention.

Infectious Diseases

Diarrhea Simple things like a change of water, food or climate can all cause a mild bout of diarrhea, but a few rushed toilet trips with no other symptoms is not indicative of a major problem. Diarrhea that results from ingesting toxins produced by bacteria growing on food is called food poisoning. Most diarrhea, however, results from infection caused by consuming fecally contaminated food or water. Paying particular attention to personal hygiene, drinking purified water and taking care of what you

eat are important measures to take to avoid getting diarrhea while hiking and traveling.

Diarrhea leaves you miserable and possibly unable to hike. The good news is that almost all travelers' diarrhea can be effectively treated with antibiotics. Fluid replacement remains the mainstay of management. Taking frequent sips of liquid is the best approach. Although a stool test is necessary to identify which pathogen is causing diarrhea, the nature of the onset of symptoms is a useful diagnostic as to its cause.

Bacterial diarrhea is self-limiting and will usually go away within one week. Bacterial diarrhea is characterized by its sudden onset, and is often accompanied by vomiting, fever and blood in the stool. You will probably be able to recall just what time of day your diarrhea began, and the symptoms will be uncomfortable from the start. Treat with either 400mg norfloxacin or 500mg ciprofloxacin twice daily for three days.

Giardia lamblia, the parasite responsible for giardiasis, resides in the upper intestine and moves from host to host as nonactive cysts that exit the body with feces. The cysts survive in streams and dust, and the parasite is a known resident in the Sierra Nevada's streams and lakes. This infection is characterized by a slow onset, and a grumbly, gassy gut. Symptoms occur one to two weeks after ingesting the parasite. The symptoms may disappear for a few days and then return. This often goes on for several weeks before travelers decide to seek treatment.

The best antibiotic treatment for giardiasis is 100mg quinacrine three times daily for five to seven days. This drug, however, is often hard to get. The more common treatment is metronidazole in a 250mg dose three times daily for seven days. Both drugs produce mild nausea, fatigue and a metallic taste in the mouth. Neither can be taken with alcohol.

Fungal Infections Sweating liberally, bathing less than usual and going longer without a change of clothes all mean that hikers risk picking up a fungal infection, which, while an unpleasant irritant, presents no danger. Fungal infections are encouraged by moisture, so wear loose, comfortable clothing, avoid artificial fibers, wash frequently and dry thoroughly. If you get an infection, wash and dry the infected area daily. Apply a topical antifungal powder or cream with 1% tolnaftate. Try to expose the infected area to air or sunlight as much as possible. Wash all socks and underwear in hot water and change them regularly.

HIV & AIDS Human Immunodeficiency Virus (HIV) attacks the body's cells that protect against infections. A person infected with HIV may be asymptomatic, may have symptoms, or may have Acquired Immune Deficiency Syndrome (AIDS), a fatal disease. It's impossible to know if an otherwise healthy looking person is infected with HIV or has AIDS without doing a blood test.

Any exposure to blood, blood products or bodily fluids may put an individual at risk of transmission. HIV/AIDS can also be spread by transfusions with infected blood. HIV/AIDS can also be spread by use of dirty needles. Immunizations, acupuncture, tattooing, and body piercing can potentially be as dangerous as intravenous drug use if the equipment isn't sterilized.

Rabies This fatal viral infection is caused by a bite or scratch from an infected animal. Dogs are noted carriers as are bats, monkeys, wolves, foxes and cats. It's their saliva that is infectious. Any bite, scratch or even lick from a warm-blooded, furry animal needs to be cleaned immediately with soap and water, and then with an alcohol disinfectant and antibiotic ointment. If any possibility exists that the animal is rabid, seek medical help immediately to receive a series of booster injections administered over a few weeks that prevent symptoms and death. Treatment can be difficult to get and is expensive, but be conservative in your judgment.

Tetanus Tetanus, a potentially fatal infection also known as lockjaw, occurs when a wound becomes infected by a bacteria that lives in soil and animal feces, so clean all cuts, punctures or animal bites. Tetanus can

be prevented by vaccination, so make sure your vaccination is current.

Traumatic Injuries
Ankle and knee sprains are common hiking injuries. To help prevent ankle sprains, wear a sturdy boot that has adequate ankle support. If you do suffer a sprain, immobilize the joint with a firm bandage, and relieve pain and swelling by keeping the joint elevated for the first 24 hours and, where possible, by using ice or snow on the swollen joint. Take analgesic or anti-inflammatory medication to ease discomfort. If the sprain is mild, you may be able to continue your hike after a couple of days. For more severe sprains, seek medical attention, as an X-ray to rule out the possibility of a broken bone may be necessary.

For large wounds with gaping skin, irrigate the wound with disinfected water to wash out any debris and with an iodine solution to kill any bacteria. Tape the wound shut and bandage. For serious head wounds, open fractures and penetrating wounds, no treatment you can administer while hiking is effective. Give antibiotics (250mg penicillin or erythromycin four times a day for five days) and evacuate the victim as quickly as possible. Treat for shock and use pressure to control bleeding. For extensive trauma, when bones or tendons are visible, treat the victim for shock, use pressure to control bleeding, administer antibiotics and evacuate.

Cuts & Scratches
Cleanse small wounds with soap and an antiseptic solution (Povidone or iodine). Apply a topical antibiotic ointment (bacitracin, neosporin, polysporin or mycolog) to disinfect wounds and prevent infection, and bandage to clean the wound clean. Keep the wound dry, and watch for swelling or redness around the wound, indicative of infection.

Bites & Stings
Bees & Wasps Stings from bees or wasps are usually painful rather than dangerous. Calamine lotion or a commercial sting relief spray may ease discomfort and ice packs reduce any pain and swelling. People who

are allergic to stings, however, may experience severe breathing difficulties and require urgent medical care.

Snakes Snakes are not common in the Sierra Nevada above 5000ft, although they are occasionally found higher. The only venomous snake found here is the western rattlesnake *(Crotalus viridis)*. To minimize your chances of being bitten by a snake, look where you're going, wear socks and boots and don't put your hands into holes and crevices or below boulders. Rattlesnakes usually give a warning of their presence, and backing away from them slowly usually prevents confrontation. Remember that their bite is seldom fatal and that only one in three adult rattlesnakes actually injects venom when it bites. Snakes usually only bite in self-defense, so don't provoke them.

Antivenims are readily available at hospitals. Immediately wrap the bitten limb tightly, the same way you would a sprained ankle, and then attach a splint to immobilize it. Keep the victim still and seek medical help, if possible taking the dead snake for identification. Don't attempt to catch the snake if there is a possibility of being bitten again. Using tourniquets and sucking out the poison are now comprehensively discredited.

Ticks These pests live in the western foothills of the northern Sierra Nevada, but are rarely found above 5000ft. Of the 48 species in the area, the western black-legged tick *(Ixodes pacificus)* is the only tick known to transmit Lyme disease. Ticks climb on grasses and vegetation, and usually get onto people when they inadvertently brush up against the greenery when walking. Ticks do not fly, jump or drop from trees.

The easiest method to avoid ticks is to wear long-sleeved shirts and long pants, despite temperatures, when hiking in known tick areas. Wearing light-colored clothes makes spotting any freeloaders much easier. Tuck your shirt into your pants and your pants into your socks, and use an insect repellent registered for use against ticks. Check all over your clothing and body daily for ticks.

If you find a tick attached to your skin, remove the tick promptly using tweezers rather than your fingers. Press down around the tick's head with the tweezers, grab the head and tick's mouth parts as close to the skin as possible. Gently pull the tick straight out. Avoid crushing or squeezing the attached tick, because exposure to its body fluids can transmit Lyme and other diseases. Wash your hands and put an antiseptic on the bite area. If you develop a skin rash or flu-like symptoms – fever and body aches – consult a physician. Lyme disease can be treated with antibiotics, but left untreated it can cause chronic health problems.

Poison Oak

Western poison oak *(Toxicodendron diversilobum)* flourishes in the canyons, chaparral and oak woodlands of the Sierra Nevada below 5000ft. This shrub is most easily identifiable by its shiny triple-lobed reddish-green leaves, which turn crimson in autumn. Touching the plant or even inadvertently brushing up against it along the trail can contaminate you and your clothes with a

nearly invisible oily resin, which contains a toxic chemical called urushiol. This produces a miserable progressive skin rash that develops into itchy blisters; swelling may also be present. The rash can appear as soon as 30 minutes after exposure and last as long as two weeks. If you're exposed to poison oak, wash the affected area quickly with soap and water. Remove any contaminated pieces of clothing, being careful not to place them in your tent against your sleeping bag or other clothing. An antihistamine may offer symptomatic relief.

Women's Health

Women often find that their menstrual cycles become irregular or even cease while they travel, due to the change in diet, routine and environment. This is not uncommon when traveling or engaging in strenuous activities like hiking. Remember that a missed period in these circumstances doesn't necessarily suggest pregnancy. Your cycle should return to normal when you return to a more regular lifestyle. You can always seek advice and get a pregnancy test at family planning clinics in towns and cities.

Poor diet, lowered resistance due to the use of antibiotics for minor illness and even taking contraceptive pills can lead to vaginal infections, particularly in hot weather. Maintaining good personal hygiene and wearing loose-fitting pants and cotton underwear helps prevent infections, but keeping clean is not always easy when camping. Antibacterial hand gel or premoistened wipes can be useful if you don't have access to soap and water.

If you think you might be or know you are pregnant and decide to go hiking, you may require extra time for acclimatization. It may be prudent to limit your hiking to a few days or a week, keeping in mind the distance you are from transport and medical care if complications arise. Miscarriage is not uncommon, and most miscarriages occur during the first three months of pregnancy, so this is the most risky time to travel as far as your own health is concerned. Even normal pregnancies can make a woman feel nauseated and tired for the first trimester,

and have food cravings that can't be satisfied by the diet available on the trail. During the second trimester, the general feelings often improve, but fatigue can still be a constant factor. In the third trimester, the size of the baby can make walking difficult or uncomfortable. Pregnant women generally should avoid all unnecessary medication. Consult your physician.

SAFETY ON THE HIKE

Hiking and backpacking in mountain areas has inherent risks and uncertainties. To help make your hike a safe one, plan to be self-sufficient. Obtain the best available maps. Be prepared for changeable weather by carrying adequate clothing and equipment. Choose a hike that is within your range of physical ability and commitment.

Always seek local advice on trails, equipment and weather before heading out. Be aware of your hike's objective dangers and pay attention on the trail. A minor injury, a twisted ankle or a fall down a hillside can be life-threatening if you're alone. Promote mountain safety by following a few basic rules: Don't hike alone, don't hike too high too fast, be law-abiding and don't hike without the required permits.

Hike Safety – Basic Rules

Taking a few simple precautions reduces the odds of getting into trouble on the trail.

- Allow plenty of time to finish your day hike or reach your backcountry destination before dark, particularly when daylight hours are shorter.
- Don't overestimate your capabilities. If the going gets too tough, give up and head back.
- If possible, don't hike on your own. Always leave details of your intended itinerary and route, including expected return time, with someone responsible before you set off.
- Before setting off, make sure you have a relevant map, compass, whistle, and that you know the weather forecast for the area for the next 24 hours.

Bears

Black bears inhabit the Sierra Nevada, yet pose almost no threat to your physical safety. No bear has ever made a predatory attack on a human in Yosemite, Sequoia or

Kings Canyon National Parks. Bears are a major nuisance, however, so read the discussion of Bears, p57, for more information.

Crossing Rivers

When footbridges and natural bridges such as fallen logs or a series of rocks are absent, you may have to ford a river or stream swollen with snowmelt. Look for the widest and most shallow place to ford, because high water can be fast flowing enough to be a potential risk. Never ford above a waterfall, rapids or a gorge, where a slip could prove disastrous.

Before stepping out from the bank, ease one arm out of the shoulder strap of your pack and unclip the belt buckle. In this way, should you lose your balance and be swept downstream, it's easier to slip out of your backpack instead of being dragged under or flailing helplessly. If linking hands with others, grasp at the wrist; this gives a tighter grip than a handhold. If you're fording alone, plant a stick or your hiking poles upstream to give you greater stability and help you to lean against the current. Use these supports to feel the way forward and walk side-on to the direction of flow so that your body presents less of an obstacle to the rushing water.

Lightning

Lightning strikes occur in the Sierra Nevada during every month of the year. Lightning tends to strike prominent topographic features, so when a storm brews, act quickly and descend from exposed areas such as ridgelines, rock domes and peaks. Stay away from open meadows and lone trees, and move away from water or wet ground.

A dense forest of trees of equal or similar height, preferably in a low-lying area, is the best place to take shelter. The next-best area for protection is in a wide depression in an open meadow. Shallow caves and overhangs are not safe places. Avoid small depressions and gullies too.

Once you find a suitable spot, move any metal or graphite objects – external frame backpacks, hiking poles, crampons or ice axes – away from you. Next, insulate yourself from the ground by sitting on your sleeping pad or internal frame backpack. If you don't have these items, crouch with your feet close together and curl up as tightly as possible to minimize the contact your body has with the ground. Do not lie down. If several hikers are in the same area, disperse to 25ft or more apart.

You can tell whether the storm is coming closer to you by timing the interval between the lightning flash and the sound of thunder. Thunder takes five seconds to travel a mile. If the interval gets shorter, the storm is nearing. If someone is struck by lightning and stops breathing, start CPR immediately.

Hunting Season

Hunting is not allowed in national parks and wilderness areas, but is allowed in national forests, on BLM lands and in other areas. The hunting season is usually late September to March but varies according to the game and from area to area, so check at the nearest ranger station to your trailhead to find out what areas are currently getting the most use by hunters. Wear brightly colored clothes when hiking to alert hunters of your presence. You can buy a plastic orange vest, often worn by hunters, at most grocery stores and hardware stores in popular hunting areas. Hunting doesn't just mean shooting guns, as bow hunting is also prevalent and equally as dangerous for nonhunters.

Rescue & Evacuation

When rescue and evacuation become necessary, assess your situation and don't panic. Rescue doesn't always imply someone else coming to 'rescue' you. Be resourceful and do not rely on others to get you out of trouble.

Evacuation can mean shortening a backpacking trip because of a minor illness or injury, or responding immediately to a serious illness or injury. For minor illness or injury, a victim may be able to walk with assistance. When a victim can't walk, perhaps they can be carried on a mule or horse. Helicopter evacuation can't be guaranteed and is to be considered only for life-threatening medical emergencies such as a serious trauma caused by falling, rock fall, avalanche, frostbite, serious illness or advanced AMS.

When someone in your party is injured or falls ill and can't move, leave somebody with them while another person goes for help. If there are only two of you, leave the injured person with as much warm clothing, food and water as it's sensible to spare, plus a whistle and flashlight. Mark the position with something conspicuous – a brightly colored piece of clothing or equipment, or perhaps a large stone cross on the ground.

If you need to call for help, use these internationally recognized emergency signals. Give six short signals, such as a whistle, a yell or the flash of a light, at 10-second intervals, followed by a minute of rest. Repeat the sequence until you get a response. If the responder knows the signals, this will be three signals at 20-second intervals, followed by a minute's pause and a repetition of the sequence.

Search & Rescue Organizations Search and Rescue (S&R) and Mountain Search and Rescue (MSR) organizations are run by county sheriff's departments. The best thing to do in an emergency is call ☎ 911; then the dispatcher will contact the relevant parties. If you have a non life-threatening emergency but you need a search and rescue operation, contact the nearest police or sheriff (listed in the front of the telephone directory and on most public telephones) or the NPS, if relevant.

Helicopter Rescue & Evacuation Helicopter evacuation may fail to save a life because of lack of details. Assess the need

for a physician to accompany the helicopter and communicate this clearly with whomever is sent to request a helicopter. Detail the number of victims, the nature of the injuries and the current condition of the victim(s), and the degree of urgency of the evacuation (eg, Is someone unconscious?). This critical information may alter a pilot's decision on whether to fly in marginal weather. Be explicit about where you are and stay put for two days once you send a message.

In order for the helicopter to land, there must be a cleared space of 75ft x 75ft, with a flat landing pad area of 20ft x 20ft. Don't mark the center of the landing spot with materials or objects that can get caught in and damage the helicopter's rotors. Secure all gear. Erect a streamer or make smoke downwind of the pad to indicate wind direction (helicopters fly into the wind when landing). In cases of emergency, when no landing area is available, a person or harness might be lowered. Take extreme care to avoid the rotors when approaching a landed helicopter. When you see a helicopter and haven't sent for one, don't wave at it. This keeps pilots from making unnecessary landings and minimizes their risk.

If a helicopter arrives on the scene, there are a couple of conventions you should be familiar with. Standing face on to the chopper:

• Arms up in the shape of a letter 'V' means 'I/We need help.

• Arms in a straight diagonal line (like one diagonal of the letter 'X') means 'All OK.'

Getting There & Away

AIR
Airports & Airlines

The cities with major international airports nearest the Sierra Nevada are Los Angeles, Oakland, San Francisco and San Jose in California; and Reno and Las Vegas in Nevada. Other international airports include Sacramento and Fresno in California's Central Valley. Most international flights are likely to arrive in either the Los Angeles or San Francisco area airports, since other international airports only have a few flights from neighboring countries such as Mexico and Canada. If you want to fly to a smaller regional or municipal airport, connections are available to Stockton, Modesto, Merced and Bakersfield. These airports are all in California's Central Valley, west of the Sierra Nevada. Reno and Las Vegas are the airports nearest the eastern side of the Sierra Nevada.

Buying Tickets

World aviation has never been so competitive, making air travel a better value than ever. But you have to research the options carefully to make sure you get the best deal. The Internet is an increasingly useful resource for checking airfares.

Full-time students and people under the age of 26 (under 30 in some countries) have access to better deals than other travelers. You have to show documentation proving your date of birth or a valid International Student Identity Card (ISIC) when buying your ticket and boarding the plane.

Generally, there is nothing to be gained by buying a ticket directly from the airline. Discounted tickets are released to selected travel agents and specialist discount agencies, and these are usually the cheapest deals going.

One exception to this rule is the expanding number of 'no-frills' carriers, which mostly sell only directly to travelers. Unlike the 'full-service' airlines, 'no-frills' carriers often make one-way tickets available at around half the round-trip fare, meaning that it is easy to put together an open-jaw ticket when you fly to one place but leave from another.

The other exception is booking on the Internet. Many airlines, full-service and 'no-frills,' offer some excellent fares to Web surfers. These companies may sell seats by auction or simply cut prices to reflect the reduced cost of electronic selling.

Many travel agencies around the world have websites, which can make the Internet a quick and easy way to compare prices. There are also an increasing number of online agents that operate only on the Internet.

Online ticket sales work well if you are doing a simple one way or round trip on specified dates. However, online super fast fare generators are no substitute for a travel agent who knows all about special deals, has strategies for avoiding layovers and can offer advice on everything from which airline has the best vegetarian food to the best travel insurance to bundle with your ticket.

You may find that the cheapest flights are advertised by obscure agencies. Most such firms are honest and solvent, but there are some unreliable, rogue outfits around. Paying by credit card generally offers protection, as most card issuers provide refunds if you can prove you didn't get what you paid for. Similar protection can be obtained by buying a ticket from a bonded agent, such as one covered by the Air Travel Organiser's License (ATOL) scheme in the UK (more details are available at Ⓦ www.atol.org.uk). Agents who accept only cash should hand over the tickets right away and not tell you to 'come back tomorrow.' After you've made a booking or paid your deposit, call the airline and confirm that the booking was made. It's generally not advisable to send money (even checks) through the mail unless the agent is very well established – some travelers have reported being ripped off by fly-by-night mail-order ticket agents.

If you purchase a ticket and later want to make changes to your route or get a refund, you need to contact the original travel agent. Airlines issue refunds only to the purchaser of a ticket – usually the travel agent who bought the ticket on your behalf. Many travelers change their routes halfway through their trips, so think carefully before you buy a ticket that is not easily refunded. Any taxes for US airports are normally included in the cost of the ticket.

Frequent Fliers Most airlines offer frequent-flier deals that can earn you a free air ticket or other goodies. To qualify, you have to accumulate sufficient mileage with the same airline or airline alliance. Many airlines have 'blackout' periods, or times when you cannot fly for free on your frequent-flier points (Christmas and Chinese New Year, for example). The worst thing about frequent-flier programs is that they tend to lock you into one airline, and that airline may not always have the cheapest fares or most convenient flight schedule.

Courier Flights Courier flights are occasionally advertised in the newspapers, or you can contact the air-freight companies listed in the phone book. You may even have to go to the air-freight company to get an answer – the companies aren't always keen to give out information over the phone. For more information, you should contact the International Association of Air Travel Couriers (IAATC; ☎ 1-561-582-8320) in the US or visit its website at Ⓦ www.courier.org. Joining this organization does not necessarily guarantee that you'll get a courier flight.

Second-hand Tickets You'll occasionally see advertisements on youth hostel bulletin boards and sometimes in newspapers for 'second-hand tickets.' That is, somebody purchased a round-trip ticket or a ticket with multiple stopovers and now wants to sell the unused portion of the ticket.

The prices offered look very attractive indeed. Unfortunately, these tickets, if used for international travel, are usually worthless, as the name on the ticket must match the name on the passport of the person checking in. Some people reason that the seller of the ticket can check you in with his or her passport, and then give you the boarding pass – wrong again! Usually the immigration people want to see your boarding pass, and if it doesn't match the name in your passport, then you won't be able to board your flight.

What happens if you purchase a ticket and then change your name? It can happen – some people change their name

---

WARNING

The information in this chapter is particularly vulnerable to change: Prices for international travel are volatile, routes are introduced and canceled, schedules change, special deals come and go, and rules and visa requirements are amended. Airlines and governments seem to take a perverse pleasure in making price structures and regulations as complicated as possible. You should check directly with the airline or with a travel agent to make sure you understand how a fare (and ticket you may buy) works. In addition, the travel industry is highly competitive, and there are many lurks and perks.

The upshot of this is that you should get opinions, quotes and advice from as many airlines and travel agents as possible before you part with your hard-earned cash. The details given in this chapter should be regarded as pointers and are not a substitute for your own careful, up-to-date research.

when they get married or divorced and some people change their name because they feel like it. If the name on the ticket doesn't match the name in your passport, you could have problems. In this case, be sure you have documents such as your old passport to prove that the old you and the new you are the same person.

Ticketless Travel Ticketless travel, whereby all your reservation details are contained within an airline computer, is becoming more common. On simple round-trip journeys the absence of a ticket can be a benefit – it's one less thing to worry about; however, if you are planning a complicated itinerary which you may wish to amend en route, there is no substitute for the good old paper version.

Travelers with Specific Needs

If they're warned early enough, airlines can often make special arrangements for travelers, such as wheelchair assistance at airports or vegetarian meals on the flight. Children under the age of two travel for 10% of the standard fare (or free on some airlines) as long as they don't occupy a seat (but they don't get a baggage allowance). 'Skycots,' baby food and diapers should be provided by the airline if requested in advance. Children aged between two and 12 can usually occupy a seat for half to two-thirds of the full fare and do get a baggage allowance.

The disability-friendly website www .everybody.co.uk has an airline directory that provides information on the facilities offered by various airlines.

The UK

Discount air travel is big business in London. Advertisements for many travel agencies appear in the travel pages of the weekend broadsheet newspapers, in *Time Out,* in the *Evening Standard* and in the free magazine *TNT.*

For students or travelers under the age of 26, one popular travel agency in the UK is STA Travel (☎ 020-7361 6262, W www.sta travel.co.uk), which has an office at 86 Old

Brompton Rd, London SW7, and branches across the country. This agency sells tickets to all travelers but cater especially to young people and students.

British Airways offers special round-trip fares to Los Angeles valid for one month for as low as UK£239. Air France has round-trip fares to Los Angeles via Paris in July and August for UK£420. In September, fares are lower when Air France round-trip fares to Los Angeles cost UK£350.

KLM and Northwest Airline have round-trip fares to San Francisco in June and July for UK£250. In August, high season round-trip fares with Air France via Paris cost UK£420.

Continental Europe

Recommended agencies in the Netherlands include NBBS Reizen (☎ 020-620 5071, W www.nbbs.nl), 66 Rokin, Amsterdam, plus branches in most cities; and Budget Air (☎ 020-627 1251, W www.nbbs.nl), 34 Rokin, Amsterdam. Another agency, Holland International (☎ 070-307 6307), has offices in most cities.

Recommended agencies in Germany include STA Travel (☎ 030-311 0950), Goethestrasse 73, 10625 Berlin, plus branches in major cities across the country.

Recommended travel agencies in France include OTU Voyages (☎ 01 40 29 12 12, W www.otu.fr), 39 ave Georges-Bernanos, 75005 Paris, with branches across the country. The company specializes in student and youth travel. Other recommendations include Voyageurs du Monde (☎ 01 42 86 16 00), 55 rue Ste-Anne, 75002 Paris; and Nouvelles Frontières (nationwide number ☎ 08 25 00 08 25, Paris ☎ 01 45 68 70 00, W www.nouvelles-frontieres.fr), 87 blvd de Grenelle, 75015 Paris, which has branches across the country.

Recommended travel agencies in Italy include CTS Viaggi (06-462 0431), 16 Via Genova, Rome, a student and youth specialist with branches in major cities; and Passagi (☎ 06-474 0923), Stazione Termini FS, Galleria Di Tesla, Rome.

Recommended agencies in Spain include Barcelo Viajes (☎ 91-559 1819), Princesa 3,

28008 Madrid, which also has branches in major cities. Nouvelles Frontières (☎ 91-547 42 00, W www.nouvelles-frontieres.es), has an office at Plaza de España 18, 28008 Madrid, as well as branches in major cities.

Recommended agencies in Switzerland include SSR (☎ 022-818 02 02, www.ssr.ch), 8 rue de la Rive, Geneva, a business with branches throughout the country; and Nouvelles Frontières (☎ 022-906 80 80), 10 rue Chante Poulet, Geneva.

From Paris to either San Francisco or Los Angeles expect to pay 3300FF for a round-trip fare between June and September and 3100FF at other times of the year. Round-trip fares from Brussels cost 3700FF year-round and from Geneva 4000FF.

The USA

Discount travel agents in the US are known as consolidators (although you won't see a sign on the door saying 'Consolidator'). San Francisco is the ticket consolidator capital of the US, although some good deals can be found in Los Angeles, New York and other major cities.

Council Travel, America's largest student-travel organization, has around 60 offices in the US; its head office (☎ 800-226-8624) is at 205 E 42 St, New York, NY 10017. Call Council for the office nearest you or visit its website at W www.ciee.org. STA Travel (☎ 800-777-0112) has offices in Boston, Chicago, Miami, New York, Philadelphia, San Francisco and other major cities. Call for office locations or visit the website at W www.statravel.com.

Ticket Planet is a leading ticket consolidator in the US and is recommended. Visit its website at W www.ticketplanet.com.

Canada

Canadian discount air-ticket sellers are also known as consolidators, and their airfares tend to be about 10% higher than those sold in the US.

Travel CUTS (☎ 800-667-2887) is Canada's national student-travel agency and it has offices in all major cities. Its website is W www.travelcuts.com.

Australia

For flights between Australia and North America, there are a lot of competing airlines and a wide variety of airfares. Round-the-World (RTW) tickets are often real bargains, and since Australia is pretty much on the other side of the world from Europe or North America, it can sometimes work out cheaper to keep going right around the world on a RTW ticket than to do a U-turn on a round-trip ticket.

Quite a few travel offices specialize in discount air tickets. Some travel agencies, particularly smaller ones, advertise cheap airfares in the travel sections of weekend newspapers.

Two well-known agents for cheap fares are STA Travel and Flight Centre. STA Travel (☎ 03-9349 2411) has its main office at 224 Faraday St, Carlton, in Melbourne, with offices in all major cities and on many university campuses. Call ☎ 131 776 Australiawide for the location of your nearest branch, or visit its website at W www.statravel.com.au. Flight Centre (☎ 131 600 Australia wide) has a central office at 82 Elizabeth St, Sydney, and there are dozens of offices throughout Australia. The Flight Centre website is W www.flightcentre.com.au.

The high season for travel to the US lasts for a month, from mid-June to mid-July, when a round-trip fare to Los Angeles or San Francisco costs A$2099. Fares during the shoulder season, from mid-July through October, cost A$1799. It's worth shopping around, since there are always good fare deals to the US.

New Zealand

Round-the-World (RTW) and Circle Pacific fares for travel to or from New Zealand are usually the best value – often cheaper than a round-trip ticket. Depending on which airline you choose, you may fly across Asia, with possible stopovers in India, Bangkok or Singapore, or across the US, with possible stopovers in Honolulu, Australia or one of the Pacific Islands.

Flight Centre (☎ 09-309 6171) has a large central office in Auckland at National Bank Towers, on the corner of Queen and

Darby Sts, and many branches throughout the country. STA Travel (☎ 09-309 0458) has its main office at 10 High St, Auckland, and has other offices in Auckland, as well as in Hamilton, Palmerston North, Wellington, Christchurch and Dunedin. Its website is ⓦ www.sta.travel.com.au. Round-trip fares to Los Angeles or San Francisco start at NZ$2089 for travel from June to October.

Asia

Most Asian countries offer fairly competitive airfare deals. Bangkok, Singapore and Hong Kong are the best places to shop around for discount tickets. Hong Kong's travel market can be unpredictable, but some excellent bargains are available if you are lucky.

Khao San Rd, in Bangkok, is the budget traveler's headquarters. Bangkok has a number of excellent travel agents, but there are also some suspect ones; ask the advice of other travelers before handing over your cash. STA Travel (☎ 02-236 0262), 33 Surawong Rd, is a good and reliable place to start.

In Singapore, STA Travel (65-737 7188) is located at 35a Cuppage Road, Cuppage Terrace. Check its website at ⓦ www.sta travel.com.sg. STA offers competitive discount fares for Asian destinations and beyond. Singapore, like Bangkok, has hundreds of travel agents, so you can compare prices on flights. Chinatown Point shopping center, on New Bridge Rd, has a good selection of travel agents.

Hong Kong has a number of excellent, reliable travel agencies and some not-so-reliable ones. A good way to check on a travel agent is to look it up in the phone book: Fly-by-night operators don't usually stay around long enough to get listed. Phoenix Services (☎ 2722 7378, fax 2369 8884), Room B, 6th floor, Milton Mansion, 96 Nathan Rd, Tsimshatsui, is recommended. Other agencies to try are Shoestring Travel (☎ 2723 2306), Flat A, 4th floor, Alpha House, 27-33 Nathan Rd, Tsimshatsui; and Traveller Services (☎ 2375 2222), Room 1012, Silvercord Tower 1, 30 Canton Rd, Tsimshatsui.

From Bangkok expect to pay US$684 for a round-trip fare, from Hong Kong US$657, and from Tokyo US$625.

LAND
Bus

Greyhound (☎ 800-231-2222) has a network of bus routes covering most of the US and is the major long-distance bus company in California and Nevada. Complete schedule and fare information is also available at ⓦ www.greyhound.com. If you don't have your own vehicle, Greyhound is about the cheapest way to get most anywhere.

Within California, Greyhound has many connections to destinations near the Sierra Nevada. These bus stops are along the western side of the Sierra and around Lake Tahoe. Information about service to and from specific towns is detailed in the hiking chapters of this book. Greyhound has no service in the eastern Sierra.

One route that accesses the length of the western side of the Sierra Nevada travels along Hwy 99 through the Central Valley, stopping at Sacramento, Stockton, Merced, Fresno and Bakersfield, among other cities. Merced is the closest city to Yosemite National Park that is served by Greyhound from San Francisco ($26 one way, five hours) and Los Angeles ($29, seven hours). Similarly, Fresno is the closest city to Sequoia and Kings Canyon National Parks that is served by Greyhound from San Francisco ($31, six hours) and Los Angeles ($22, six hours), although there is no public transportation between Fresno and Sequoia and Kings Canyon National Parks.

Train

Amtrak (☎ 800-872-7245) has an extensive rail network throughout the US. Complete schedule and fare information is also available at ⓦ www.amtrak.com. The trains are comfortable with dining and lounge cars on long-distance routes. It's a good idea to make advance reservations since seating is limited.

Amtrak has several daily round-trip train routes serving the Central Valley city of Merced, where you can transfer to public transportation to Yosemite Valley, and Fresno, where you can rent a vehicle to get to Sequoia and Kings Canyon National Parks.

Amtrak also has a train route across the Sierra Nevada between the San Francisco Bay Area and Reno. The train stops in Truckee, the nearest town to Lake Tahoe with any train service. There is no train service along the eastern Sierra.

From major international airports, the first leg of Amtrak service is by bus to the nearest train station. From San Francisco, the bus goes to Emeryville, where you board the train. The fare from San Francisco costs $30/54 one way/round trip, including the bus service to Merced, and $34/65 to Fresno. From Los Angeles ($29/55), the bus goes to Bakersfield, where you board the train. The fare from Los Angeles costs $23/44 to Fresno and $29/55 to Merced. From Reno, the bus goes to Sacramento, where you board the train ($29/55) to Merced.

The train usually takes longer because of the mandatory bus transfers, so it's more convenient to ride Greyhound instead.

Car & Motorcycle
Driving is undoubtedly the most convenient way for hikers to get to and from the Sierra Nevada. Driving through the mountains is a cultural and sensual experience in and of itself. Rent a car if you need it. The obvious frustration hikers encounter is the thought of how much money they're spending to let the rental car sit at the trailhead.

If you're doing a long hike that's near a town, investigate the cost of hiring a taxi or shuttle service to drop you off and pick you up from the trailhead instead of renting a car. For young travelers (aged under 25 and especially under 21), car travel is scarcely an option. Car rentals are expensive, or unavailable at times, and insurance can be prohibitive.

Car rental prices vary widely from place to place, company to company, car to car, and day to day. Fortunately, California is a comparatively inexpensive place to rent a car. As a general guideline, a weeklong subcompact economy rental with unlimited mileage starts at $150. If you're arranging a rental before you arrive in California, check with a travel agency, online service, or directly with the car rental agency. If you get a fly-drive package, local taxes may be an extra charge. Otherwise once you're in a city, check the established agencies (call them on their toll free numbers), but also check with local companies. An unlimited mileage plan is usually a better value than a cost-per-mile plan when you're driving long distances in the mountains.

Camper Vans
Traveling in a camper van or RV can be a surprisingly economical option for budget travelers, as it can take care of eating, sleeping and traveling in one convenient package. Rental rates start at $1025 per week in low season (late August to May) and at $1420 per week in high season (June to late August). Several good websites direct you to rental locations and include listings of vehicles for sale. Cruise America RV Rental & Sales (W www.cruiseamerica.com) is popular, and their RVs are conspicuous on many highways. Also visit these websites: W www.rv rentals.net, W www.rvusa.com, W www.camp americarv.com and the RV Rental Association at W www.rvamerica.net.

Passport America (☎ 800-681-6810, fax 228-831-4616), 18315A Landon Rd, Gulfport, MS 39503, sells a discount RV travel card, which gives discounts at many campgrounds, for an annual fee of $44.

Driver's License
Visitors can legally drive in the US for up to 12 months with their home driver's license. An International Driving Permit (IDP) is a very useful adjunct and may have more credibility with US traffic police, especially if your home license doesn't have a photo or is in a foreign language. Your automobile association at home can issue an IDP, valid for one year, for a small fee. You must carry your home license together with the IDP.

Bicycle
Cycling is a cheap, convenient, healthy, environmentally sound and above all fun way

of traveling. One note of caution: Before you leave home, be sure you can get parts for your bike in the US. Some European threads and specifications may be different. The Sierra Nevada and most cities in California have lots of bike shops where skilled mechanics can help you.

Bicycles can travel by air. You can take them apart and put them in a bike bag or box, but it's much easier simply to wheel your bike to the check-in desk, where it should be treated as a piece of baggage. You may have to remove the pedals and turn the handlebars sideways so that the bike takes up less space in the aircraft's hold; check all this with the airline well in advance, preferably before you pay for your ticket. Deflating the bicycle tires prevents the tubes from bursting.

HIKE OPERATORS ABROAD

Organized hiking holidays are not prevalent in the Sierra Nevada. To organize a trip, contact a local company for suggestions (see Organized Hikes, p38, and Guides, p39).

Getting Around

Road travel is the only way to get around the Sierra Nevada, since there are no airports and no train services in the mountains. Having your own vehicle is by far the most convenient form of transportation, although it's possible to get between a few destinations using public transport.

BUS

Bus service is limited in the Sierra Nevada, operating primarily in the Lake Tahoe Area, on primary roads to Yosemite National Park, and between a few towns in the eastern Sierra.

Tahoe Area Regional Transit

Tahoe Area Regional Transit (TART, ☎ 800-736-6365, 530-550-1212) has year-round bus service ($1.25) along 30mi of the west and north shore of Lake Tahoe: from Tahoe City south on Hwy 89 along the west shore to Sugar Pine Point State Park near Tahoma; east on Hwy 28 along the north shore to Incline Village; and north on Hwy 89 to Truckee. The TART route to Truckee connects with Amtrak and Greyhound service.

Three seasonal trolleys operate around Lake Tahoe from late June to early September. The Tahoe Trolley (☎ 530-581-6365) operates from 10:30am to 10:30pm daily between Squaw Valley and Emerald Bay ($1.25). The Truckee Trolley (☎ 530-587-7451) operates from 9:15am to 5:15pm daily in the town of Truckee between Donner Lake and Commercial Row ($1). The Nifty 50 Trolley (☎ 530-541-7548) operates from 10am to 10pm daily between Zephyr Cove in Nevada and Emerald Bay in California through the town of South Lake Tahoe ($3 all day).

Yosemite Area Regional Transportation System

Yosemite Area Regional Transportation System (YARTS, ☎ 877-989-2787, W www .yarts.com) operates two bus routes to Yosemite Valley; daily year-round service from Merced ($20/40 one way/round trip)

along Hwy 140, and summer-only weekend service from Coulterville ($10/20) along Hwys 132 and 120. The YARTS Merced service has connections to Amtrak and Greyhound. Obtain your ticket before boarding the bus; contact any of the numerous local ticket sellers, to be found at various tourist centers and commercial businesses. Verify schedules and the location of ticket sellers directly with YARTS.

Mammoth YARTS operates a round-trip bus ($15/20 one way/round trip) between Mammoth Lakes and Yosemite Valley, which stops in Tuolumne Meadows, once a day on weekends in June and September and once daily in June and July. For information on schedules or to make a reservation call Mammoth California Vacations (☎ 800-626-6684), which handles Mammoth YARTS bookings.

Inyo Mono Transit

Inyo Mono Transit (☎ 800-922-1930) operates two bus routes along US 395 between Bridgeport and Lone Pine. The Bishop-Bridgeport route, which has stops in the town of Mammoth Lakes ($2.50 Bridgeport-Mammoth Lakes and $3.50 Mammoth Lakes-Bishop), operates buses ($6) twice weekly, on Monday and Wednesday. The Bishop-Lone Pine route operates two daily round-trip buses ($4) weekdays.

CAR & MOTORCYCLE

It's a good idea to check road conditions before driving into the mountains. The California Department of Transportation (Caltrans) reports road conditions via the Caltrans Highway Information Network. Call ☎ 800-427-7623 from anywhere in California or visit the website at W www .dot.ca.gov. To hear California road conditions from Nevada, call ☎ 916-445-7623 for northern California road conditions or ☎ 213-628-7623 for southern California road conditions. Be ready to enter on the phone pad the number of the highway about which you want information. When you're on the Nevada side of the state line around Lake Tahoe, call road information in Reno at ☎ 775-793-1313 for Nevada road conditions. In winter-like conditions when heavy snowfall is likely, you may be required to carry tire chains in your vehicle or to fix them onto your vehicle's tires before proceeding.

Road Rules

The maximum speed limit on most highways is 65mph, although some rural highways may have a maximum speed limit of 70mph. Some two-lane undivided highways only have a maximum of 55mph. Many two-lane trans-Sierra and secondary mountain roads have substantially slower maximum speed limits, so allow ample driving time.

Driving faster than the maximum speed limit, which is posted on all roads, is against the law. Similarly, when you drive too slowly and block the normal flow of traffic, you may receive a ticket. If you're on a winding, two-lane mountain road where passing is unsafe and you see more than five vehicles behind you, etiquette and the law dictate that you pull off the road to let the other vehicles pass. Designated turnout areas are posted along many highways, especially along curvy sections and steep hills.

Many mountain roads are steep, with grades between 5% and 8%. Save your brakes when going downhill by downshifting, and in hot summer weather avoid overheating when going uphill by turning off the air-conditioning and ensuring your vehicle has sufficient coolant. For safety, turn your headlights on during the daytime when driving at high speed on two-lane roads. Vehicles always drive to the right in the US.

The law requires motorists to yield to all pedestrians. The law as well as common sense require everyone in the vehicle to use safety belts.

Penalties are severe for driving under the influence of drugs or alcohol (DUI). It's illegal to drive in California with a blood alcohol concentration of 0.08% or higher. Just two drinks can take you over this threshold. The police, sheriff and highway patrol officers can give roadside sobriety tests. On holiday weekends, they may set up roadblocks to deter drunk drivers. Refusing to take the sobriety test is treated the same as failing it. Carrying open containers of alcohol inside a vehicle is illegal.

BICYCLE

Cyclists have the same rights and responsibilities as motorists, and ride in the same direction as other traffic. Generally, cyclists are not allowed to ride on freeways.

HITCHHIKING

Hitchhiking is never entirely safe, and it's not recommended. Hikers who hitchhike should know that they are taking a potentially serious risk. It's safer to hitchhike in pairs. Hitchhiking on US 395 in the eastern Sierra, where there's less traffic and people are likely to stop, is easier than on the western side. Having an easily readable destination sign also helps. Hitchhiking along small roads to trailheads is usually not too difficult. A good approach is to ask other hikers at trailheads for a ride.

Government employees, such as rangers, are prohibited by law from giving non-government employees a ride in government vehicles. Remember that they're just doing their job, which can be frustrating when that ranger is the only person you're likely to encounter on some remote backroads.

LOCAL TRANSPORTATION

Only sizable towns have local bus systems, which provide service within the town. Any service that connects several towns in the region is mentioned under the Access Town(s) or Access Facilities section in the hiking chapters. None of the towns have local train service, and the only Amtrak service actually on a train (as opposed to a bus) is between Reno and Truckee. Taxis are available in most towns, but not in small towns. Check the telephone directory for local telephone numbers. Taxis, which are metered, are a comparatively expensive form of transportation, and come in handy every now and then. Private trailhead shuttle companies transport hikers to many eastern Sierra trailheads (see the Eastern Sierra chapter for details).

Lake Tahoe

Brilliantly blue and surrounded by mountains, Lake Tahoe sits like a jewel along the California-Nevada state line; the western shore is in California, the eastern in Nevada. On the Sierra Nevada's western side, the well-watered forests extend down through California's gold country to the grasslands and towns of the Central Valley.

On the eastern side, the Carson Range drops off to the Nevada desert. The Truckee River, whose headwaters are north of Carson Pass, flows into the lake's southern end and out from its northwest end. In the mountains encircling the lake are three national forests – Eldorado, Tahoe and Toiyabe – and three wilderness areas – Desolation, Granite Chief and Mt Rose – offering a plenitude of trails. On a warm day the vanilla-like fragrance from the bark of Jeffrey pines drifts by hikers walking through Tahoe's eastern forests.

HISTORY

Native American Washoe lived in the Carson Valley in winter and migrated to Tahoe in summer. They revered the lake and called it Da Ow A Ga, meaning 'the edge of the lake.' Early explorers mispronounced 'Da Ow' as 'tahoe,' and the name stuck. John C Frémont was the first person to record seeing Lake Tahoe in 1844, when he reached the summit of Red Lake Peak north of Carson Pass. In the same year came the first wagon train guided by a Piute known as Captain Truckee, after whom the emigrants named the river they followed.

The pass over the Sierra Nevada along this route is named for the infamous Donner Party (see p97). Deposits of gold and silver drew miners to Tahoe in the 1850s and 1860s, where they made roads and logged the hillsides surrounding the lake to supply the Comstock Lode mines of Nevada's Virginia City. The Central Pacific Railroad, built by Mark Hopkins and Leland Stanford in the 1860s, used Truckee as the main town on the transcontinental

railroad between Sacramento and Ogden, Utah. By the beginning of the 20th century, the mining and timber industries had diminished, and the unique beauty of the lake and mountains shifted the area's economic emphasis to recreation.

The Tahoe Basin formed during a major Sierra Nevada uplift period about 65 million years ago. The lake itself began to

Lake Tahoe

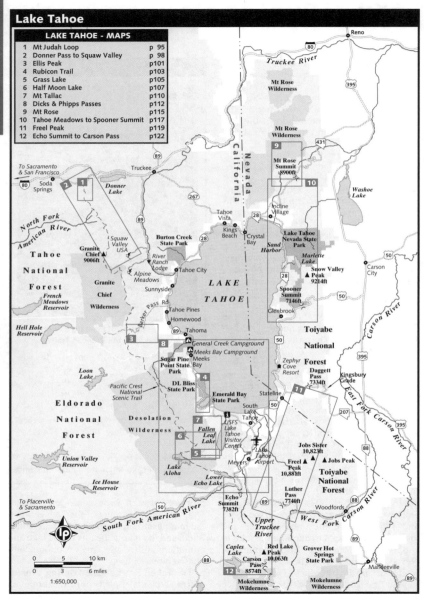

form about 2.3 million years ago, when lava produced a volcanic dam that blocked the basin's outflow. At least seven major lava flows over the next million years raised the elevation of the lake higher than 7000ft, but the Truckee River has eroded through the lava to bring the lake to its present elevation of 6225ft. Relatively recent glaciation (glaciers retreated only 13,000 years ago) left moraine such as that forming the sides of Emerald Bay and of Fallen Leaf Lake.

Lake Tahoe is the Sierra Nevada's largest lake, North America's third deepest and the world's tenth deepest. The lake, fed by 63 streams and two hot springs, is 22mi long and 12mi wide, with 72mi of shoreline. Its greatest depth is 1645ft, while its average depth is 1000ft. The lake's bottom, at an elevation of 4580ft, is lower than the Carson Valley at the eastern base of the Carson Range.

INFORMATION
Maps
Tom Harrison Maps 1:71,280 *Recreation Map of Lake Tahoe,* which depicts almost the entire Tahoe Basin, is the most useful overall planning map.

Books
Lingering in Tahoe's Wild Gardens, by Julie Stauffer Carville, offers a refreshing look at many trails. *Tahoe: From Timber Barons to Ecologists,* by Douglas Hillman Strong, explains the environmental history of Lake Tahoe and current issues confronting the lake. *Plants of the Tahoe Basin: Flowering Plants, Trees and Ferns,* by Michael Graf, is a comprehensive illustrated guide to the area's flora.

Information Sources
For general trail information and wilderness information, visit the USFS website at W www.r5.fs.fed.us to look at the area's national forests. Visit W www.tahoesbest.com /hiking for further information. For public transportation schedules, visit W www.lake tahoetransit.com. A 24-hour weather forecast is available by calling the National Weather Service at ☎ 531-546-5253.

Permits
A free wilderness permit is required for any day hike or overnight trip in Desolation Wilderness. Wilderness permits are not required for overnight trips in Granite Chief Wilderness or Mt Rose Wilderness. In cases where a permit is required, details are given in the Planning section for each individual hike.

North Lake Tahoe

Lake Tahoe's only outlet, the Truckee River, flows from its northwest shore, forming a corridor for Hwy 89 between Tahoe City and Truckee. World-famous ski resorts flank the slopes above the lake and its outlet, and above the resorts are rocky peaks and ridge tops, including Granite Chief Wilderness. With comparatively fewer visitors, hikes along these ridges offer vistas of Lake Tahoe and Donner Lake, abundant wildflowers and a sense of solitude. Most hikers visit the area on a day hike from one of its readily accessible trailheads.

ACCESS TOWNS
Tahoe City
Information The North Lake Tahoe chamber of commerce (☎ 530-581-6900), 245 N Lake Blvd, at the Hwy 28/Hwy 89 intersection, has a useful visitor information center. The center's Cyber Station offers email and Internet access for $6 for 30 minutes. The USFS William Kent visitor information station, 2mi south of Tahoe City on the west side of Hwy 89, offers national forest information and issues wilderness permits. Hwy 28 is called N Lake Blvd and Hwy 89 South is called W Lake Blvd.

Supplies & Equipment Alpenglow (☎ 530-583-6917), 415 N Lake Blvd, sells maps and outdoor gear.

Places to Stay & Eat *William Kent Campground* ($15) is adjacent to the William Kent information station. *Tahoe City Inn* (☎ 800-800-8246, 530-581-3333, fax 530-583-5030, e tahoe.city.inn@juno.com,

LAKE TAHOE

www.tahoecityinn.com, 790 N Lake Blvd) has all nonsmoking rooms starting at $33 and a spa.

Izzy's Burger Spa, along the east side of Hwy 89 on the north side of Fanny Bridge, has tasty burgers, fries, shakes, as well as some vegetarian options. *Tahoe House Bakery & Gourmet (☎ 530-583-1377, 625 W Lake Blvd)*, about a mile south of town, serves Swiss and California cuisine and sells European-style breads and pastries along with sandwiches and gourmet foods in its deli.

Getting There & Away Tahoe City, at 6253ft, is along Lake Tahoe's northwestern shore at the Hwy 89/Hwy 28 intersection, 13mi south of Truckee and 29mi northwest of South Lake Tahoe.

Tahoe Area Regional Transit, or TART (☎ 800-736-6365, 530-550-1212), has year-round bus service ($1.25) from Tahoe City south on Hwy 89 along the west shore to Sugar Pine Point State Park near Tahoma, east on Hwy 28 along the north shore to Incline Village, and north on Hwy 89 to Truckee. Southbound buses on Hwy 89 and eastbound buses on Hwy 28 depart Tahoe City every hour on the half hour. North-bound buses on Hwy 89 depart at 7:30, 9:30 and 11:30am and 1:30 and 3:45pm.

The Tahoe Trolley (☎ 530-581-6365), a shuttle bus ($1.25) between Squaw Valley and Emerald Bay, operates 10:30am to 10:30pm from late June to early September.

Truckee

Information The Truckee-Donner chamber of commerce (☎ 530-587-2757, fax 530-587-2439, **e** info@truckee.com, **w** www.truckee .com), 10065 Donner Pass Rd, is in the train depot along Commercial Row. The chamber of commerce offers email and In-ternet access, charging $1 for five minutes. Tahoe National Forest's Truckee ranger station (☎ 530-587-3558), 10342 Hwy 89 North, is at the east end of town at the I-80 intersection. Donner Pass Rd (also called Commercial Row), north of and parallel to the railroad tracks, is lined with restaurants and stores.

Supplies & Equipment Granite Chief, on Donner Pass Rd at the northwest corner of its intersection with Hwy 89 South, sells and rents gear. Next door to it is Truckee Mountain Sports.

Places to Stay & Eat The USFS *Granite Flat Campground* ($12) is just south of town on Hwy 89. *Donner Memorial State Park (☎ 800-444-7275 reservations, a $7.50 fee applies)*, 3mi west of downtown along Donner Pass Rd, has campgrounds ($14) along the southeast shore of Donner Lake.

Cottage Hotel (☎ 530-587-3108, 10178 Donner Pass Rd), at the west end of Com-mercial Row, lacks frills and phones, but rooms with a shared bathroom only cost $40. *The Truckee Hotel (☎ 800-659-6921, 530-587-4444, fax 530-587-1599, **w** www.truckeehotel .com, 10007 Bridge St)* is an historic Victorian with an excellent restaurant and rooms with shared bathrooms starting at $60.

Earthly Delights (☎ 530-587-7873, 10087 W River St), a deli and bakery, has gourmet takeout and rustic breads. *Squeeze In (10060 Donner Pass Rd)* serves an almost endless variety of omelettes (boasting 57 types) and sandwiches. *Pacific Crest (10042 Donner Pass Rd)* is a California-style bistro specializing in seafood, pasta, salads and wood-fired pizzas.

Getting There & Around Truckee, which straddles I-80 and Hwy 89, is 13mi north of Lake Tahoe via Hwy 89 from Tahoe City or Hwy 267 from Kings Beach, and 35mi west of Reno, which has the area's only interna-tional airport.

Amtrak trains depart eastbound for Reno ($15/30 one way/round trip) at 3:11pm, and westbound for San Francisco via Emeryville ($31/62) at 11:36am. It's hardly worth taking a train toward San Francisco, because you have to ride a bus anyway between Truckee and Sacramento, where you board the train and ride to Emeryville, where once again you must transfer to a bus for the final leg of the trip to San Francisco. Greyhound buses for Reno ($10/19 one way/round trip, 50 minutes) depart at 6, 8:10am and 1:10, 4:15

and 8pm. Buses for San Francisco ($35/72, 5½ hours) depart three times daily. The Truckee bus stop is at the train depot.

TART (☎ 800-736-6365, 530-550-1212) has year-round bus service to Tahoe City, with connections from there east to Incline Village and south to Sugar Pine State Park near Tahoma. Buses ($1.25) depart Truckee's train depot at 8:30 and 10:30am, and 12:45, 2:45 and 4:45pm.

Truckee Trolley (☎ 530-587-7451), a shuttle bus ($1), operates in town between Donner Lake and Commercial Row from 9:15am to 5:15pm during summer only.

Mt Judah Loop

Duration	3–3½ hours
Distance	4.5mi (7.24km)
Standard	easy
Start/Finish	Donner Pass
Public Transport	no

Summary The accessible summit of Mt Judah, west of Truckee, affords fabulous views of Donner Lake as well as peaks in and surrounding Tahoe National Forest.

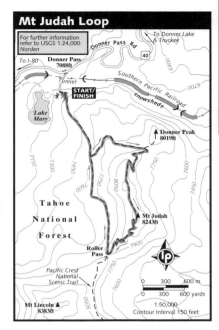

The very popular Mt Judah Loop is a well-used trail that follows gradual contours as it rises 1153ft from the trailhead to the summit of Mt Judah at 8243ft. The hike doesn't take long and is easily reached from I-80, making it an excellent short excursion for those driving between Tahoe and the San Francisco Bay Area. The views from the summit are some of the most expansive anywhere in the northern Sierra. During July, numerous varieties of pink and purple penstemons, perhaps Tahoe's best display, and bright red-purple rock fringe flowers dot Mt Judah's eastern slopes.

The nearest campground is at Donner Memorial State Park along Donner Lake, but there's no place to camp along the trail. The Mt Judah Loop hike can easily be extended into a longer day hike or backpacking trip by continuing south on the Pacific Crest National Scenic Trail (PCT) to Squaw Valley (see the Donner Pass to Squaw Valley hike, p96).

PLANNING
When to Hike
The hiking season is from mid-June to mid-October.

Maps
The USGS 1:24,000 *Norden* quadrangle covers the hike.

Permits & Regulations
A permit is not required for this day hike.

GETTING TO/FROM THE HIKE
From I-80 west of Truckee, take the Soda Springs exit east a few miles or take the Donner Pass Rd exit west 6.7mi to Donner Pass (7088ft) on US 40. At the pass, turn south onto a poorly maintained, unpaved road marked only by small 'Pacific Crest Trail' and 'Overland Emigrant Trail' emblems, and follow it 0.2mi and park along the narrow roadway. The signed trailhead (7090ft) is 30 steps east of the road.

THE HIKE

Ascend rocky switchbacks, following the PCT southbound, to the junction with the Mt Judah Loop trail. About a mile from the trailhead, turn east (left), before the chairlifts, and ascend gently along a forested trail toward Donner Peak (8019ft) whose rocky summit offers excellent views of Donner Lake below.

The trail turns south and climbs gently along the ridge to the broad summit of **Mt Judah** (8243ft), a perfect picnic spot. Descend south through hemlock forest to rejoin the PCT. A worthwhile five-minute detour south (left) leads to historic **Roller Pass**, where the Overland Trail crossed the Sierra. Follow the gentle trail north (right) back to the trailhead.

Donner Pass to Squaw Valley

Duration	7½–8½ hours
Distance	15.5mi (24.9km)
Standard	moderate-hard
Start	Donner Pass
Finish	Granite Chief Trail Trailhead
Public Transport	finish only

Summary This ridge-crest hike with miles of wildflowers and expansive vistas skirts the base of four prominent peaks northwest of Lake Tahoe.

The hike between Donner Pass and Squaw Valley combines segments of two trails, the PCT and the Granite Chief Trail. Following a view-filled ridgeline for 8mi, the hike skirts Mt Judah, Mt Lincoln, Anderson Peak and Tinker Knob, traverses a meadowy bowl and drops down the Granite Chief Trail to Squaw Valley, site of the 1960 winter Olympics.

With a total elevation gain and loss of over 6030ft – 2590ft ascent and 3440ft descent – covering 15.5mi, it is an ambitious day hike. It's possible to do this hike as an overnight trip, but most of the route lacks water. The first and only feasible campsite with water along the entire trail is almost 12mi from Donner

Pass, by which point you may as well continue to the trailhead at the finish.

You need to have two vehicles or to arrange for someone to drop you off or pick you up, since the trailheads are 17.5mi apart by road. Alternatively, if you only have one vehicle, you can use it along with a combination of public transportation and a taxi to get between the trailheads.

PLANNING
When to Hike

The hiking season is from mid-June to mid-October, with wildflowers blooming from late June to September.

Maps

The USGS 1:24,000 *Norden, Granite Chief* and *Tahoe City* quadrangles cover the hike. The trail is not marked on these quadrangles between Donner Pass and Tinker Knob. The trail between Tinker Knob and the Granite Chief Trail junction has been rerouted and does not pass by Mountain Meadow Lake as indicated on the *Granite Chief* quadrangle, but rather goes west of and above the lake. The junction of the PCT and Granite Chief Trail is on the ridge north of the peak marked 8436ft south of the lake. Similarly, the trail is not accurately shown near the Granite Chief Trail Trailhead and fire station; the map incorrectly indicates the trail dropping down to the Olympic Village Inn.

Permits & Regulations

A wilderness permit is not required for day hikes or overnight trips in Granite Chief Wilderness.

GETTING TO/FROM THE HIKE
To the Start

From I-80 west of Truckee, take the Soda Springs exit east a few miles or take the Donner Pass Rd exit west 6.7mi to Donner Pass (7088ft) on US 40. At the pass, turn south onto a poorly maintained, unpaved road marked only by small 'Pacific Crest Trail' and 'Overland Emigrant Trail' emblems, and follow it 0.2mi and park. The signed PCT Trailhead, at an elevation of 7090ft, is 30 steps east of the road.

From the Finish

The signed Granite Chief Trail trailhead is at the fire station on Chamonix Place at Squaw Valley Rd, 2.2mi west of the junction of Squaw Valley Rd and Hwy 89. Squaw Valley Rd meets Hwy 89 just 5mi north of the Hwy 89/Hwy 28 intersection in Tahoe City and 8.4mi south of the Hwy 89/I-80 intersection in Truckee.

The TART bus stop, referred to as the Squaw Valley Inn stop, is across from the fire station on Squaw Valley Rd before the

The Donner Party

In the 19th century, more than 40,000 people traveled west along the Overland Trail in search of a better life in California. Among them was the ill-fated Donner Party, whose story is a tragic and morbid tale in the history of westward migration.

The Donner Party departed Springfield, Illinois, in April 1846. With six wagons and a herd of livestock, the families of George and Jacob Donner and James Reed intended to make the trip as comfortable as possible. In Independence, Missouri, a large group of emigrants joined them, making the party about 87 people. From here on it was slow going and by the time they reached Fort Bridger in July, they were running well behind schedule. Eager to save 350mi, most of the party elected to try the Hastings Cutoff, unaware that it had never been used by wagons.

It was soon apparent that the shortcut wasn't saving any time. There was no road for the wagons in the Wasatch Mountains, and most of the livestock died crossing the Great Salt Desert. Several wagons had to be abandoned. Arguments and fights broke out among members of the party. James Reed killed a man and was banished in the middle of the desert. By the time the party reached the eastern foot of the Sierra Nevada, near present-day Reno, in October, they were exhausted and tempers were short.

Snowstorms came early that year, and the party tried and failed three times in November to cross Truckee (now Donner) Pass. Hoping that a break in the weather would reopen the pass, they settled in for the winter at Truckee (now Donner) Lake. Half of the party camped at Truckee Lake, while George Donner and most of the others were at Alder Creek, 6mi away. The 10 members of the Irish-Catholic Breen family stayed in a cabin built two years before by another emigrant party. They had food to last a month and felt certain that the weather would clear by then. It didn't.

Snow fell for weeks, reaching a depth of more than 20ft. Hunting and fishing became impossible, and people were surviving on boiled hides and bones from the livestock that had become buried under the snow. In late December, 15 people made a desperate attempt to cross the pass. They became lost and had to sit out a Christmas storm that killed two of them. With no food left, the rest ate their bodies. One month later, seven of the original 15 reached Sutter's Fort in California.

The first rescue party reached the Donner Party in late February and took 21 survivors back with them. By the time the second rescue party arrived in March, led by the once banished James Reed who had made it to Sutter's Fort in mid-October and was now rescuing his family, evidence of cannibalism was everywhere. Journals and reports tell of 'half-crazed people living in absolute filth, with naked, half-eaten bodies strewn about the cabins.' Most were too weak to travel. By mid-April, when a final rescue party arrived, the only person remaining at the camp was Lewis Keseberg. The rescuers found George Donner's body cleansed and wrapped in a sheet, but no sign of Tamsen Donner, George's wife. Keseberg admitted to surviving on her flesh.

Altogether 47 of the 89 members survived. They succeeded in crossing the country and settled in California, but their lives were irrevocably changed by the harrowing events of that winter near Donner Lake. The most definitive histories of the tragedy are *Ordeal by Hunger,* by George R Stewart, and *Winter of Entrapment: A New Look at the Donner Party,* by Joseph A King.

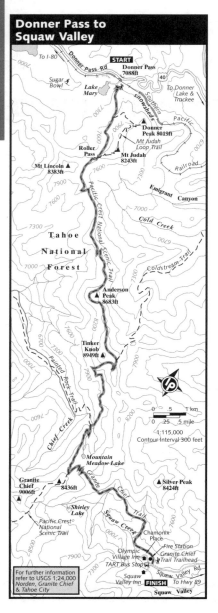

Donner Pass to Squaw Valley

bridge over the creek. If doing this hike in the reverse direction, the trailhead sign is visible from the TART bus stop, but only if you know where to look. Stand facing the fire station and walk up the driveway. A small 'trail' sign is on the wall to the right (east). The trailhead sign is around the corner of the building on its east side between the building and the adjacent condominiums.

If you're relying on only one vehicle, park it at the Donner Pass trailhead. Then from Squaw Valley after the hike, ride the TART bus ($1.25) northbound to Truckee and get off at the Bank of America on Donner Pass Rd. Get a transfer slip before getting off the bus and walk across the street to the trolley stop. Ride the Truckee Trolley (☎ 530-587-7451) westbound along the north shore of Donner Lake toward the end of the line at West End Beach on Donner Lake Rd at the intersection of Donner Pass Rd. There's no pay phone at West End Beach, so get off a stop or two before at a hotel or store where there's a pay phone. A convenient trolley stop is at the Donner Lake Village Resort. From the pay phone, call a local taxi (☎ 888-881-8294) for a pick-up. The 3½mi taxi ride up to Donner Pass from here costs about $12. The only glitch is that the last daily bus leaves Squaw Valley at 4pm. In order to finish the hike by then, you need to start hiking by 7 or 8am at the very latest. Expect to take at least one hour to get back to Donner Pass this way. It's a bit of a hassle, but the hike is definitely worth the extra effort.

THE HIKE

The trail departs Donner Pass (7088ft), heading south in a 10-minute flurry of switchbacks up a rocky talus slope. It then calms down and traverses south, with views of Mt Lincoln ahead and small Lake Mary below. Purple lupines, pink penstemons and yellow mountain mule ears brighten the trail, and pale lavender pennyroyals add a minty fragrance. After a few more gentle, well-graded switchbacks, the trail traverses the west-facing hillside through open red-fir forest. Entering an open area that is a winter ski run, the trail comes to a signed junction with the northern end of the Mt Judah Trail 30 minutes from the trailhead.

Continue straight, passing under a chairlift and crossing an unpaved road that leads up into the forest five minutes from the junction. Be careful not to inadvertently stray onto the road. The trail enters fir forest and passes west of and below Mt Judah (8243ft) for 20 to 25 minutes, and then reaches a junction with the southern end of the Mt Judah Trail. Two large white pines stand just west of this junction. Two minutes farther south is the historic **Roller Pass** (7860ft), 2.5mi from the trailhead. In use from 1846, it was a key crossing on the Emigrant Trail Truckee River Route. The trail ascends briefly through forest to the ridge crest, offering views east over Emigrant Canyon and Coldstream Valley and back north to the rounded summit of Mt Judah. At the boundary of a ski area, a faded sign says Anderson Peak is 4mi and Tinker Knob 6mi ahead.

A few minutes beyond that sign, next to a seasonal trickle (8060ft), is another sign on a tree, which reads 'Mt Lincoln.' This sign doesn't indicate a spur trail to the top of Mt Lincoln, rather it just indicates that the peak visible from here is Mt Lincoln. Other peaks along this trail are similarly marked.

The 4mi between Mt Lincoln and Anderson Peak have some of the hike's best views and wildflowers. Along the east side of ski-lift crowned **Mt Lincoln** (8383ft), the trail emerges on an open ridge just south of the summit. Mt Lincoln's grassy summit is easily attained from its south side. The views on either side of the ridge offer the first glimpses south and west into Granite Chief Wilderness. Wildflowers bloom all around as the trail rolls south along the spectacular wind-swept crest for over 1½ hours. Nearing rocky **Anderson Peak**, the trail works up and around a rock outcrop (8210ft).

At the base of the squared-off Anderson Peak, a hand-lettered PCT sign keeps you from ascending the slope toward the peak. The trail curves southwest 15 minutes to circle the peak in a counterclockwise direction, first traversing its forested northern side and then the talus-draped western flanks, crossing a few short sections of stable

scree and talus. Along the northwest flank of Anderson Peak (8683ft), where there are excellent views north to Mt Lincoln and Mt Judah, you pass a sign at 8480ft pointing to Anderson Peak (this does not indicate a trail to the summit) and another saying Tinker Knob is 2mi ahead. The trail then ascends southeast and regains the grassy ridge crest.

Continuing one hour and 2mi south along the spectacular, open, wind-swept ridge, the trail rises gradually yet steadily toward the prominent outcrop of exfoliating granite called **Tinker Knob** (8949ft). Passing over its shoulder (8760ft), the trail moves to the east side of the ridge. This vantage point has the hike's best views, including a distant look at Lake Tahoe and the Carson Range above its east shore.

For the next hour, the trail plunges 2mi to reach the Painted Rock Trail junction.

Descending from Tinker Knob for 10 minutes on a sandy slope filled with mountain mule ears, the trail comes to a signed junction with the Coldstream Trail, which leads to Donner Lake. Continue south along the ridge a short distance. Look for a PCT emblem on a wooden post to point you in the right direction. The trail drops down the west side of the rocky ridge, south of Tinker Knob, and winds down into forest of firs and pines, contouring the southern flank of Tinker Knob. Turning southeast, the trail descends through meadows of mule ears, lupines and pennyroyals, with the rocky ramparts of the ridge crest above to the east.

About 30 minutes from the Coldstream Trail junction, the trail crosses a willow-lined stream, and continues down into the lush valley. A granite slope gleams across the valley. Traversing through granite outcrops, after 20 minutes the trail comes to a larger stream. Across the stream and above its southern bank a stand of firs and white pines shades a level open area, the only suitable *campsite* (7770ft) along the entire hike. Twenty minutes farther, cross a creek (ignoring the broken trail sign) and come to the well-signed junction (7560ft) with the Painted Rock Trail. A sign declares Squaw Valley to be just 4mi ahead, but it's an old sign posted before the longer rerouting of the trail, which now continues for more like 5mi, to avoid privately owned land.

The mile-long ascent to the Granite Chief Trail junction can take as long as 45 minutes. From the Painted Rock Trail junction, ascend south through forest along a granite ridge. Soon the ridge opens, offering inspiring views looking back at Tinker Knob and the rocky escarpment to its southeast. The PCT reaches the signed junction (8160ft) with the Granite Chief Trail along the ridge just north of a low but distinctive rise (marked as point 8436ft on some maps).

The final segment of this hike is a 4mi descent on the Granite Chief Trail to Squaw Valley, which offers views of Lake Tahoe most of the way. Turning left and away from the southbound PCT, head down the Granite Chief Trail on switchbacks through red-fir forest. The trail levels out as it nears a small creek, then drops down to the southeast amid granite outcrops above Squaw Valley, crossing the stream several times. The Squaw Valley tram cables run between huge towers on the rocky peaks ahead. The trail traverses granite slabs adjacent to moderate cliffs along the valley's northern side. Contouring around, it descends to the valley floor. For the last few minutes as you near the trailhead, parts of the trail are overgrown, and multiple use trails make it confusing. Going downhill, it's hard to get lost, and eventually the trail crosses an unpaved road and goes a very short distance farther to the trailhead at the Squaw Valley fire station (6240ft).

Ellis Peak

Duration	3–3½ hours
Distance	6mi (9.7km)
Standard	easy-moderate
Start/Finish	Ellis Peak Trailhead
Public Transport	no

Summary Hike along a panoramic ridge, ascending 1390ft, to a scenic peak above Lake Tahoe's west shore with sweeping 360-degree views.

Ellis Peak (8740ft) offers remarkable views of Desolation Wilderness, Granite Chief

Wilderness and Lake Tahoe from high above its west shore – views surpassed only by those attained on the much more strenuous hike to Mt Tallac. The hike has a total of 3640ft of elevation gain and loss, in equal amounts of ascent and descent, with two steep sections – one of 491ft from the trailhead to get onto the ridgeline, and a final two-part ascent of 520ft to the summit of Ellis Peak.

PLANNING
When to Hike
The hiking season is from July to mid-October.

Maps
The USGS 1:24,000 *Homewood* quadrangle covers the hike.

Permits & Regulations
A wilderness permit is not required for this day hike.

GETTING TO/FROM THE HIKE
From Hwy 89 along Tahoe's west shore, 4.2mi south of the Hwy 89/Hwy 28 intersection in Tahoe City and 2.2mi north of Homewood, turn west onto Barker Pass Rd (USFS Rd 03). The roadside sign along Hwy 89 reads 'Blackwood Canyon.' Early in the season, a locked gate keeps the road off-limits. It usually opens by July. Contact the Tahoe National Forest ranger station in Truckee to find out if the road is open. Follow Barker Pass Rd up Blackwood Canyon 6.9mi to the signed trailhead on the south side of the road, where the pavement ends; the unpaved road continues beyond the trailhead to Barker Pass itself.

THE HIKE
From the trailhead (7780ft), marked by a large Ellis Peak Trail sign, the wide trail makes an initial 30-minute ascent of 491ft through fir forest to emerge onto a spectacular windswept ridge. Tahoe's north shore comes into view on your left, but even more impressive is the austere granite beauty of Desolation Wilderness, to your right. Loon Lake Reservoir is the large lake at the

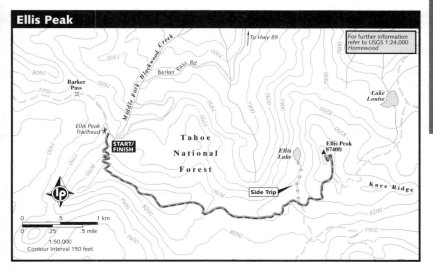

lower end of Rockbound Valley. A few gnarled pines cling to the ridge, and on its sandy slopes blooms a veritable garden of scarlet Indian paintbrush, delicate white and lavender spreading phlox and velvet-leaved yellow mountain mule ears. Continue along the gradually ascending ridgeline, delighting in the incredible views, for 10 minutes to the highest point on the ridge (8500ft).

The trail descends 15 minutes through fir forest to a low point of 8100ft, then ascends slightly, passing through open stands of large, lichen-coated red fir to reach a trail junction (8220ft) with an unpaved road, 15 minutes from the low point and 2.5mi from the trailhead.

A side trip to **Ellis Lake** (8170ft) takes 15 minutes round-trip. Turn left (north) onto the unpaved road, pass a small shallow pond and continue on the level road a few minutes to the small, pretty lake, nestled among firs beneath the rocky ramparts of Ellis Peak.

To reach Ellis Peak, cross the unpaved road and continue on the trail, steeply at first, 30 minutes (1/2 mile) to the summit. Ellis Peak has two summits. The **south**

summit is 50ft lower than the **north summit** (8740ft), which is five minutes farther and rewards with a marvelous panorama encompassing Granite Chief Wilderness and Twin Peaks (8878ft) to the north, all of azure Lake Tahoe, and drop-dead gorgeous Desolation Wilderness to the south. Retrace your steps back to the trailhead in 1½ hours.

South Lake Tahoe Basin

Desolation Wilderness, the Sierra Nevada's most popular wilderness, is a compact 100-sq-mile area about 8mi wide by 12.5mi long. Although the granite summits of its Crystal Range average only 9500ft, and trail elevations average just 8000ft, the 130 lakes and the polished granite landscape give Desolation a true 'High Sierra' feel. Easy access makes it possible to traverse the wilderness area in a day. Most hikers enjoy one of the outstanding day hikes or embark on a two- or three-night backpacking trip.

ACCESS TOWN
South Lake Tahoe
Information Hwy 89 is Emerald Bay Rd and US 50 is Lake Tahoe Blvd in South Lake Tahoe (6252ft). The USFS Lake Tahoe visitor center (☎ 530-573-2674) is on Hwy 89, 3mi northwest of the Hwy 89/US 50 intersection, about a mile west of Camp Richardson. The center has trail information, issues wilderness permits (☎ 530-573-2736), and sells books and maps. USFS Lake Tahoe Basin headquarters & visitor information (☎ 530-573-2600 information) is at 870 Emerald Bay Rd (Hwy 89) near the US 50 intersection.

The Interagency visitor information station on US 50/Hwy 89 near Meyers is useful for orientation, but has limited information. The Lake Tahoe Visitors Authority (☎ 800-288-2463, 530-544-5050, ltva@virtualtahoe.com, Ⓦ www.virtualtahoe.com), 1156 Ski Run Blvd, runs a free reservation service for South Lake Tahoe lodging. The South Lake Tahoe chamber of commerce (☎ 530-541-5255, Ⓦ www.tahoeinfo.com), 3066 Lake Tahoe Blvd, is another resource with a helpful visitor center.

Supplies & Equipment Tahoe Sports Ltd, which sells gear and maps, has two stores: 4008 Lake Tahoe Blvd (☎ 530-542-4000), in the Crescent V Fashion Center; and 1032 Emerald Bay Rd (☎ 530-544-2284), in the South Y Center.

Places to Stay & Eat *Doug's Mellow Mountain Retreat (☎ 530-544-8065, ⒺⒷ hostel guy@hotmail.com, 3787 Forest Rd),* a hostel four blocks off US 50, has beds for less than $20. The *Campground by the Lake (☎ 530-542-6096, 1150 Rufus Allen Blvd off Lake Tahoe Boulevard),* facing the lakeshore, costs $18 and has shower facilities. Its spectacular setting and views belie its central location. South Lake Tahoe has plenty of motels, mostly along US 50, the least expensive of which start at about $50. It is easiest to contact the Lake Tahoe Visitors Authority (see above) for availability and rates.

Red Hut Waffle Shop (☎ 530-541-9024, 2723 Lake Tahoe Blvd) is a popular breakfast-only spot. *Sprouts Cafe (☎ 530-541-6969, 3123 Harrison Ave),* facing Lake Tahoe Blvd, across from the chamber of commerce, serves inspired, healthy choices and tasty smoothies. *Freshies (☎ 530-542-3630, 3330 Lake Tahoe Blvd),* just east of the Campground by the Lake, has a casual rooftop setting with lake views. Freshies serves salads and grilled sandwiches and has good vegetarian choices. Casinos in nearby Stateline, Nevada, offer the biggest bang for the buck.

Getting There & Away South Lake Tahoe, as its name implies, wraps itself along the southern lakeshore on US 50. At the time of writing, all scheduled flights to the regional Lake Tahoe Airport, south of town on US 50, had been suspended indefinitely due to high fuel costs.

The nearest airport is the Reno/Tahoe International Airport, in Reno. The Tahoe Casino Express (☎ 800-446-6128, 775-785-2424) has 14 daily scheduled shuttle buses ($17/30 one way/round-trip, 1¾ hours) between the airport and several South Lake Tahoe hotels and casinos.

Greyhound buses depart for San Francisco ($35 one way, six hours) at 3:25 and 11am and 6:30pm from 1000 Emerald Bay Rd at the US 50/Hwy 89 intersection.

The Nifty 50 Trolley (☎ 530-541-7548), a shuttle bus ($3 all day), plies the shoreline between Zephyr Cove and Emerald Bay from 10am to 10pm daily from late June to early September.

Rubicon Trail

Duration	2–2½ hours
Distance	5mi (8km)
Standard	easy
Start	Rubicon Trail Trailhead
Finish	Vikingsholm parking lot
Public Transport	finish only

Summary This scenic lakeside stroll passes through two spectacular state parks and offers endless breathtaking views of Lake Tahoe's azure waters.

The Rubicon Trail passes through two of the three state parks along Lake Tahoe's quieter and more secluded western shore and is the only hiking trail to actually access the lakeshore. The picturesque trail meanders the southwest shoreline from Rubicon Point to Emerald Point through DL Bliss State Park, and then follows the northwest shore of Emerald Bay through Emerald Bay State Park to an historic mansion. The DL Bliss State Park section of Tahoe's lakeshore was preserved when Duane Leroy Bliss and his wife Elisabeth Tobey Bliss donated more than 700 acres to the state in 1929.

The gentle trail has a total elevation change of slightly more than 1000ft, mostly as short uphill and downhill sections just south of Rubicon Point. The longest descent, 350ft, is in the middle of the hike, while the biggest ascent of 400ft comes at the very end.

The trailheads are 4.1mi apart by road, so you need either to have two vehicles for a shuttle, arrange for someone to drop you off or pick you up, or plan to walk back to where you parked your vehicle. Campgrounds are available in both DL Bliss State Park ($16) and Emerald Bay State Park ($15).

PLANNING
When to Hike
The state parks are open from mid-May to mid-September.

Maps
The USGS 1:24,000 *Emerald Bay* quadrangle covers the hike. The *DL Bliss/Emerald Bay State Parks* sketch map is available at the state park visitor center for $0.50.

Permits & Regulations
A wilderness permit is not required for this day hike. DL Bliss State Park charges a $2 per-vehicle day-use fee. Emerald Bay State Park does not charge a fee for using the Vikingsholm parking lot.

GETTING TO/FROM THE HIKE
To the Start
The Rubicon Trailhead (6290ft) is located in DL Bliss State Park off Hwy 89. From South Lake Tahoe, follow Hwy 89 around

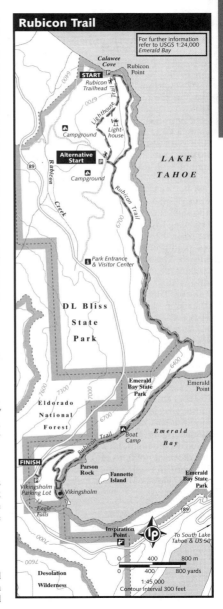

Emerald Bay. The park entrance is 1.9mi north of the Vikingsholm parking lot, and 12.5mi north of the Hwy 89/US 50 intersection in South Lake Tahoe, or 17.2mi south of the Hwy 89/Hwy 28 intersection in Tahoe City.

Driving from the south, turn right (east) into the park, passing the visitor center, and drive 1mi to where you pay the park fee. Continue 0.7mi beyond it to a stop sign where a sign reads '1½mi to Rubicon Trail.' Turn right and reach the signed trailhead parking lot in 0.5mi. Parking is very limited, so it's advisable to arrive early in the morning.

If the parking lot is full when you arrive, don't despair. Drive back 1/2 mile to the stop sign, turn left and go another 0.5mi to a parking area on the west (right) side of the road, 0.2mi before you return to where you paid the park fee. On the road's east side are two small trailhead signs at knee height. One says 'Rubicon Trail,' but if you follow this direct path, you miss the Rubicon Trail's most scenic segment. The other sign says 'Lighthouse Trail,' which leads 1mi (about 30 minutes) to the start of the Rubicon Trail near Rubicon Point. For this alternative start to the hike, follow the Lighthouse Trail northeast 0.7mi as it ascends 150ft through burned forest to a signed junction.

A side trip heads right out from the junction 0.1mi to a small wooden lighthouse. Erected in 1916 by the US Coast Guard, it was in use only until 1919, when another lighthouse was built farther north at Sugar Pine Point. Turn left at the junction and descend 440ft over 0.3mi to join the Rubicon Trail near Rubicon Point, enjoying the good views of Rubicon Bay through the open canopy.

From the Finish

The Vikingsholm parking lot (6630ft), in Emerald Bay State Park, is along Hwy 89 1.9mi south of DL Bliss State Park.

If you don't have a vehicle, the Nifty 50 Trolley stops at Vikingsholm every hour just after the hour (see p102 for more information).

THE HIKE

Heading east from the Rubicon Trailhead (6290ft), the trail stays high above the waters of Calawee Cove. After a few minutes it bends southward, passing above **Rubicon Point** (6237ft). You can detour on many small use trails down to the point itself. The trail stays from 200ft to 300ft above the rugged lakeshore for the next 30 minutes. In places where it skirts the rocky bluffs above the deep blue lake, a chain railing protects you from the edge. The views over Tahoe are stunning, but most impressive is the visibility – up to 70ft – into Tahoe's depths. Remarkable as this is, it has been reduced about 30% in recent decades by algae growth. Along the trail grow pinemat manzanitas, alpine prickly currants and tobacco brushes, and in moist areas are stands of aspen, mountain alder and creek dogwood. Look for osprey that nest in the tops of trees.

An unsigned junction, 1.4mi from the start of the Rubicon Trail, marked only by a wooden post, indicates the shortcut back to the alternative starting trailhead (6580ft). Beyond this junction, the Rubicon Trail is less rocky, broader and basically level. After 20 minutes strolling through forest, you descend two gentle switchbacks, and, following the shore for another 20 minutes, cross a small creek and come to a sandy swimming beach (6230ft) facing **Bonnie Bay** – a good spot if you relish a dip in Tahoe's chilly waters.

From the beach, a lesser-used trail skirts Emerald Point, rejoining the Rubicon Trail a few minutes ahead. The main trail, also called the Bypass Trail, leaves the water's edge and heads southwest into a rich forest of incense cedars, Jeffrey pines, sugar pines and white firs, emerging after five minutes along the shore of Emerald Bay, with Mt Tallac rising overhead. The trail to Vikingsholm takes only 30 minutes to walk from here. It hugs the shore and passes through **Boat Camp** ($10), a campground open to boaters and hikers alike. Don't stray to the right onto the paved road in the campground. Instead, follow the footpath that stays along the bayshore and crosses several wooden footbridges. Just after passing **Parson Rock** on your left, you reach the Vikingsholm area. The first building you see is the **Gardener's Cottage**, where a link trail heads right to the service road that leads up to the parking lot. Continue straight ahead past the dock near the swimming beach to the Vikingsholm **castle** (6230ft), a replica of a 9th century Norse fortress. This developed area is called the Harvey West Unit of Emerald Bay State Park. The 0.7mi from the castle to the parking lot, a 400ft ascent on a well-graded and mostly paved service road, is the most strenuous part of the entire hike and takes at least 15 minutes.

cliffs above the lake's northwest shore, and the summertime water is just right for a dip.

Grass Lake is not recommended for an overnight trip, since the popular lake has no feasible campsites. Other lakes in Desolation Wilderness are a better choice for camping trips (see the Half Moon Lake hike, p106, and the Dicks & Phipps Passes hike, p111).

PLANNING
When to Hike
The hiking season is from July to mid-October.

Maps
The USGS 1:24,000 *Emerald Bay* and *Echo Lake* quadrangles cover the hike, but Tom Harrison Maps 1:42,240 *Desolation Wilderness Trail Map* does it on one sheet. The USFS 1:31,680 topographic map *A Guide to the Desolation Wilderness* ($3) is excellent.

Permits & Regulations
A free day-use permit that day hikers get by self-registering at the trailhead is required to enter Desolation Wilderness.

GETTING TO/FROM THE HIKE
From the US 50/Hwy 89 intersection in South Lake Tahoe, head west 3mi on Hwy 89 to Fallen Leaf Rd, beyond Camp Richardson and directly opposite the entrance to the Tallac Historic Site. Turn left (south) onto Fallen Leaf Rd, pass the USFS *Fallen Leaf Campground* and go 4.8mi on this paved, bumpy single-lane road to a junction at the south end of Fallen Leaf Lake.

Grass Lake

Duration	2½ hours
Distance	5.6mi (9km)
Standard	easy
Start/Finish	Glen Alpine Trailhead
Public Transport	no

Summary A gradual trail rises 675ft to a rockbound lake fed by a dramatic waterfall in a quiet yet easily accessible corner of Desolation Wilderness.

Glen Alpine Creek, lined with pink flowering currants and manzanitas, splashes along the mostly shaded trail to sizeable Grass Lake at the head of an intimate valley. Tiny pine-dotted granitic islands in the lake create a picturesque foreground to the rocky peaks above. A large waterfall cascades over red

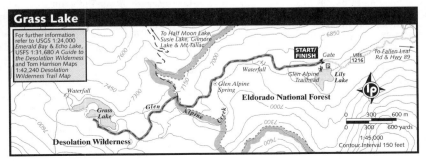

Turn left onto USFS Rd 1216 just beyond the fire station, following the sign with an arrow, which reads 'Lily Lake, Glen Alpine Falls, Desolation Wilderness Trailhead.' This equally narrow road follows Glen Alpine Creek heading steeply up and away from the lake 0.6mi and across a bridge to a paved parking lot at the end of the road. The Glen Alpine Trailhead (6560ft) is at the locked green metal gate.

THE HIKE

From the locked gate (6560ft), walk west along a broad gravel road. After five minutes the gravel ends as you ascend northwest (right) above cascading Glen Alpine Creek. A few signs reading 'Trail' keep you from inadvertently wandering onto pockets of private property along the way until, 20 minutes from the trailhead, you reach **Glen Alpine Springs**.

The buildings here are remnants of Glen Alpine Camp, a resort built in 1884. During its heyday in the late 19th and early 20th centuries it was very fashionable, but by WWII it had slipped into decline, and it closed in 1966. In 1977 the resort was privately purchased in conjunction with the USFS, and in 1987 a nonprofit organization for its historical preservation was established. A joint restoration project is now underway. Just beyond the barn, where guests' stagecoaches were housed, is **Soda Spring**. The spring, in a protected wooden enclosure, was discovered in 1863 by entrepreneur Nathan Gilmore, who by 1883 had begun bottling and shipping the naturally carbonated spring water.

Beyond the spring, the broad path narrows to a footpath and ascends west in a leisurely way, passing a boundary sign for Desolation Wilderness after 15 minutes. Two minutes beyond, in a cluster of trees, is a signed trail junction (6860ft), 1.7mi from the trailhead. The trail to Mt Tallac goes straight. Turn left onto the trail to Grass Lake.

Heading southwest, the trail crosses the outflow creek from Grass Lake twice in close succession, via logs early in the season or by hopping rocks later when the water is low. Lodgepole pines and firs shade the trail, which continues up over granite 30 minutes to the southern shore of Grass Lake (7235ft), 1.1mi from the trail junction.

The hike saves its best views for last, and the trail along the lakeshore takes you to several nice viewpoints before petering out in dense willow shrub beneath the jagged cliffs of **Keiths Dome** (8646ft). Jacks Peak (9856ft) dominates the view to the northwest with **Dicks Peak** (9974ft) just over its shoulder. In the distance to the east are the peaks of the Carson Range. To the northwest a dramatic cascade, which comes from Susie Lake, pours over ochre cliffs into Grass Lake. After soaking in the view over lunch, retrace your steps to the trailhead in one hour.

Half Moon Lake

Duration	2 days
Distance	11mi (17.7km)
Standard	easy-moderate
Start/Finish	Glen Alpine Trailhead
Public Transport	no

Summary Secluded and scenic Half Moon Lake, hemmed in on three sides by rock walls more than 1300ft above the lakeshore, is tucked into the largest and deepest cirque in Desolation Wilderness.

Desolation Wilderness teems with inviting lakes, ideal for overnight camping trips. Easily accessible but comfortably removed from the main trails, picturesque Half Moon Lake lies in an enormous granite cirque, offering a dramatic and secluded site.

PLANNING
When to Hike

The hiking season is from July to September.

Maps

The USGS 1:24,000 *Emerald Bay, Echo Lake* and *Rockbound Valley* quadrangles cover the hike, but Tom Harrison Maps 1:42,240 *Desolation Wilderness Trail Map* does it on one sheet. The USFS 1:31,680 topographic map *A Guide to the Desolation Wilderness* ($3) is excellent.

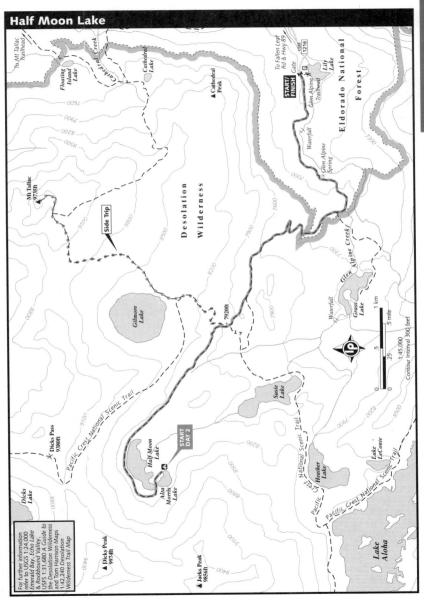

Half Moon Lake

To Mt Tallac Trailhead

Floating Island Lake

Cathedral Creek

Cathedral Lake

▲ Cathedral Peak

7600
7900
8200
8500
8800

▲ Mt Tallac 9735ft

9100

Side Trip

Desolation Wilderness

7600

7900

8200

8500

Gilmore Lake

9700

7920ft

7900

7900

Pacific Crest National Scenic Trail

Dicks Pass 9380ft

9100

Dicks Lake

8800

▲ Dicks Peak 9974ft

9100

▲ Jacks Peak 9856ft

9400

Half Moon Lake

START DAY 2

Alta Morris Lake

8200

8500

8800

9100

Susie Lake

8200

Pacific Crest National Scenic Trail

Heather Lake

Lake LeConte

7900

8200

8500

Lake Aloha

9100

To Fallen Leaf Rd & Hwy 89

1216

Lily Lake

START/ FINISH

Glen Alpine Trailhead

Gate

Waterfall

Glen Alpine Spring

7000

Eldorado   National   Forest

7300

Glen Alpine Creek

Waterfall

Grass Lake

7300

7600

1 km

.5 mile

.5

.25

0

1:45,000

Contour Interval 300 feet

For further information refer to USGS 1:24,000 Emerald Bay, Echo Lake & Rockbound Valley; USFS 1-31,680 A Guide to the Desolation Wilderness and Tom Harrison Maps 1:42,240 Desolation Wilderness Trail Map

Permits & Regulations

Free wilderness permits are required for day hikers and backpackers. A trailhead quota system operates from June 15 to Labor Day due to the popularity of Desolation Wilderness. The USFS accepts reservations no more than 90 days in advance and only during the quota period. They issue 50% of available permits by reservation, and 50% on a first-come, first-served basis. To make a reservation, mail or fax the request with a $5 reservation fee to Eldorado National Forest (☎ 530-644-6048, fax 644-3034), 3070 Camino Heights Drive, Camino, CA 95709.

Everyone must pick up their permit in person at the Eldorado National Forest office mentioned above (5mi east of Placerville off US 50) or at the USFS Lake Tahoe visitor center (see p102). Backpackers who have a reservation and have previously made arrangements may also pick up their permit at the USFS William Kent visitor information station (see p102). A camping fee of $5 per person for one night or a maximum of $10 per person for two or more nights is also payable when picking up the permit.

Wood fires are not allowed in Desolation Wilderness.

GETTING TO/FROM THE HIKE

From the US 50/Hwy 89 intersection in South Lake Tahoe, head west 3mi on Hwy 89 to Fallen Leaf Rd, beyond Camp Richardson and directly opposite the entrance to the Tallac Historic Site. Turn left (south) onto Fallen Leaf Rd and go 4.8mi on this paved, bumpy single-lane road to a junction at the south end of Fallen Leaf Lake. Turn left onto USFS Rd 1216 just beyond the fire station, following the sign with an arrow that reads 'Lily Lake, Glen Alpine Falls, Desolation Wilderness Trailhead.' This equally narrow road follows Glen Alpine Creek, heading steeply up and away from the lake 0.6mi and across a bridge to a paved parking lot which is at the end of the road. The Glen Alpine Trailhead (6560ft) is located at the locked green metal gate.

THE HIKE

Day 1: Glen Alpine Trailhead to Half Moon Lake

3–3½ hours, 5.5mi (8.9km), 1580ft (474m) ascent

Follow the trail west 45 minutes from the Glen Alpine Trailhead (6560ft) to a signed junction, 1.7mi from the trailhead, where a trail to Grass Lake turns left (see the Grass Lake hike, p105). Continue straight at this junction, heading north on switchbacks up open granite slopes. The trail bends west and parallels the outlet stream from Gilmore Lake, then fords the stream and comes almost immediately to a signed junction, 1.6mi from the Grass Lake junction. Take the right fork (the left fork heads to Susie Lake), and ascend past a shallow pond to meet the combined PCT and Tahoe-Yosemite Trail after 0.3mi. Cross the PCT and head straight, contouring northwest toward Half Moon Lake.

The trail rises and falls, passing several small ponds as it enters the enormous cirque, Desolation's largest and deepest, beneath Jacks Peak (9856ft) and Dicks Peak (9974ft). Follow the trail over talus and pockets of meadow as it curves around the north shore of the crescent-shaped **Half Moon Lake** (8140ft). Cross the lake's inlet stream and reach good **_campsites_** amid trees above the northwest shore of dramatically situated Alta Morris Lake, 1.9mi from the PCT junction.

Day 2: Half Moon Lake to Glen Alpine Trailhead

2–3 hours, 5.5mi(8.9km), 1580ft (474m) descent

Retrace your steps back to the trailhead.

Side Trip: Mt Tallac

2½–3 hours, 5mi (8km), 1815ft (545m) ascent, 1815ft (545m) descent

The side trip to Mt Tallac (9735ft) starts 1.9mi from Half Moon Lake at the signed trail junction (7920ft) with the PCT. At the junction, head east 0.6mi to the junction with the trail to Dicks Pass. Pass the junction, continuing 0.1mi east along the outlet from Gilmore Lake (8310ft). The trail to Mt

Tallac crosses the lake's outlet to its east side and ascends steeply northeast through forest, then turns north through more open forest. Emerging onto the open hillside as it nears a saddle, the trail turns east toward rocky Mt Tallac (9735ft) and rises to meet the Mt Tallac Trail coming from Cathedral Lake (see the Mt Tallac hike for a description of this trail). Continue up to the summit for sweeping views of Desolation Wilderness, Fallen Leaf Lake and Lake Tahoe, 1.8mi beyond Gilmore Lake. Return from the summit the same way.

Mt Tallac

Duration	6–7 hours
Distance	9mi (14.5km)
Standard	hard
Start/Finish	Mt Tallac Trailhead
Public Transport	no

Summary Hiking to the top of Mt Tallac, above Tahoe's southwestern lakeshore, rewards a steep ascent of 3255ft with majestic views of Fallen Leaf Lake, Desolation Wilderness and Lake Tahoe.

The rocky summit of Mt Tallac (9735ft) is a popular destination for serious day hikers. No other high peak is so close to Lake Tahoe, and therefore so easily accessible, with its incomparable views of the vast lake and adjacent granite landscape of Desolation Wilderness. Tallac, the only peak around Tahoe with a Washoe name, means 'great mountain.' Its greatness is evident once you're at the commanding summit. The trail to the summit, however, is steep in places, gaining 3255ft over 4.5mi, with an equally knee-pounding descent to return to the trailhead.

It's also possible to visit Mt Tallac on a side trip from two other hikes described in this section: from Day 2 of the Half Moon Lake hike, p108; and from Day 2 of the Dicks & Phipps Passes hike, p113. An alternative and leisurely day hike to Cathedral Lake, 2.1mi from the Mt Tallac Trailhead, provides excellent views of Fallen Leaf Lake and Lake Tahoe.

PLANNING
When to Hike
The hiking season is from July to September.

What to Bring
The summit of Mt Tallac is often windy, so carry a jacket even if it's warm at the start, and beware of thunderstorms. Carry extra drinking water.

Maps
The USGS 1:24,000 *Emerald Bay* quadrangle covers the hike. Tom Harrison Maps 1:42,240 *Desolation Wilderness Trail Map* also covers the hike. The USFS 1:31,680 topographic map *A Guide to the Desolation Wilderness* ($3) is excellent.

Permits & Regulations
A free day use permit is required to enter Desolation Wilderness. Day hikers can simply get a permit by self-registering at the trailhead.

GETTING TO/FROM THE HIKE
The Mt Tallac Trailhead parking area (6480ft) is at the end of a paved road 1mi south of and directly opposite the entrance to Baldwin Beach, 0.7mi west of the USFS Lake Tahoe visitor center.

When driving northbound on Hwy 89, you'll see a sign reading 'Mt Tallac Trailhead,' whereas the sign when coming southbound reads 'Mt Tallac, City Camps.' When you turn onto this road, a sign reads 'Camp Shelly.' The road makes a few jogs – a left-turn, then a right – both of which are clearly signed.

If you don't have a vehicle, the Nifty 50 Trolley can drop you at the visitor center on Hwy 89 (see South Lake Tahoe, p102, for more information), and you can walk to the trailhead from there.

THE HIKE
The trail rises moderately through open forest 30 to 45 minutes to level off along the top of an ancient glacial moraine ridge high above the west shore of large Fallen Leaf Lake. Offering striking views of this beautiful lake, the gradual trail follows the ridge

LAKE TAHOE

Mt Tallac

For further information
refer to USGS 1:24,000
Emerald Bay, USFS 1:31,680
*A Guide to the Desolation
Wilderness* and Tom
Harrison Maps 1:42,240
*Desolation Wilderness
Trail Map*

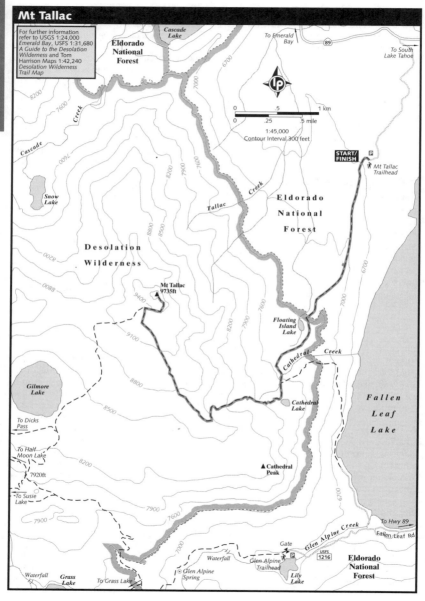

1:45,000
Contour Interval 300 feet

30 to 45 minutes, then moves off it into forest and enters Desolation Wilderness near the north end of tiny **Floating Island Lake**, 1½ miles from the trailhead. The lake's name comes from floating mats of vegetation that periodically slough off the shore into its shallow waters.

Beyond the lake's inlet, the trail rises past a panoramic viewpoint, then crosses Cathedral Creek and passes a junction with a trail coming from Fallen Leaf Lake. Small, clear Cathedral Lake lies 0.5mi ahead.

Beyond Cathedral Lake, the trail steepens significantly, ascending along a creek that is the last reliable water, to emerge in a rocky bowl. Cross the bowl and make a steep but short ascent to the ridgeline. The trail's steepness eases, and it turns northeast to follow near the ridge crest, with spectacular views over Desolation Wilderness all the way to the rocky summit. The afternoon views of Lake Tahoe from the summit are unsurpassed. Retrace your steps back to the trailhead.

Dicks & Phipps Passes

Duration	4 days
Distance	31.2mi (50.2km)
Standard	moderate
Start	Echo Lake Trailhead
Finish	Meeks Bay Trailhead
Public Transport	finish only

Summary A traverse of the granitoid, lake-filled landscape of Desolation Wilderness has abundant forested campsites and great swimming, and crosses two passes en route to Lake Tahoe's western shore.

The glacier-polished granite landscape of the 100-sq-mile Desolation Wilderness holds more than 100 lakes and numerous streams. With its dramatic, almost lunar appearance, splendid vistas, subalpine forest, flower-filled meadows, renowned fishing, good trails, easy access and close proximity to Lake Tahoe's southwestern shores, it is one of the most frequently visited wilderness areas in the US. This hike, part of the Tahoe-Yosemite Trail, also includes a segment of the combined PCT

and Tahoe Rim Trail. This is the quintessential traverse of Desolation Wilderness, crossing two passes and camping at beautiful lakes.

You must have two vehicles or have someone to drop you off or pick you up, since the trailheads are miles apart and public transport only serves the finishing trailhead.

PLANNING
When to Hike
The hiking season is from July to September. The hike is better in mid or late season, because the Crystal Range receives comparatively more snowfall than other areas around Lake Tahoe.

Maps
The USGS 1:24,000 *Echo Lake, Pyramid Peak, Rockbound Valley, Emerald Bay* and *Homewood* quadrangles cover the hike. Three maps cover Desolation Wilderness on one sheet: Tom Harrison Maps 1:42,240 *Desolation Wilderness Trail Map,* Wilderness Press' 1:62,500 *Fallen Leaf Lake,* revised from the USGS quadrangle of the same name; and the USFS 1:63,360 *Desolation Wilderness* map. The USFS 1:31,680 topographic map *A Guide to the Desolation Wilderness* ($3) is also excellent.

Permits & Regulations
A free wilderness permit is required for this hike. A trailhead quota system operates from June 15 to Labor Day, due to the popularity of Desolation Wilderness. The USFS accepts reservations no more than 90 days in advance and only during the quota period. They issue 50% of available permits by reservation, and 50% on a first-come, first-served basis. To make a reservation, mail or fax the request with a $5 reservation fee to Eldorado National Forest (☎ 530-644-6048, fax 644-3034), 3070 Camino Heights Drive, Camino, CA 95709.

Everyone must pick up their permit in person at the Eldorado National Forest office mentioned above (5mi east of Placerville off US 50) or at the USFS Lake Tahoe visitor center (see p102). Backpackers who have a reservation and have previously made arrangements may also pick up their permit

LAKE TAHOE

Dicks & Phipps Passes

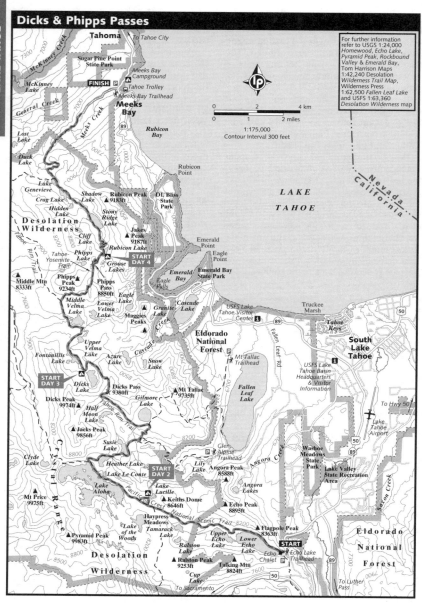

For further information refer to USGS 1:24,000 *Homewood, Echo Lake, Pyramid Peak, Rockbound Valley & Emerald Bay,* Tom Harrison Maps 1:42,240 *Desolation Wilderness Trail Map,* Wilderness Press 1:62,500 *Fallen Leaf Lake* and USFS 1:63,360 *Desolation Wilderness map*

1:175,000
Contour Interval 300 feet

0   2   4 km
0   1   2 miles

Tahoma
To Tahoe City

McKinney Creek

Sugar Pine Point State Park

McKinney Lake

Meeks Bay Campground
FINISH   P
Tahoe Trolley
Meeks Bay Trailhead

General Creek

Meeks Creek

Meeks Bay

Rubicon Bay

LAKE TAHOE

Lost Lake

Duck Lake

Lake Genevieve

Shadow Lake
Rubicon Peak 9183ft
DL Bliss State Park

Rubicon Point

Crag Lake

Hidden Lake

Stony Ridge Lake

Desolation Wilderness

Cliff Lake

Jakes Peak 9187ft

Rubicon Lake

Tahoe-Yosemite Trail

Phipps Lake

Grouse Lakes

START DAY 4

Emerald Point

Eagle Point

Middle Mtn 8333ft

Phipps Peak 9234ft

Phipps Pass 8850ft

Eagle Lake

Emerald Bay

Emerald Bay State Park

Eagle Falls

Middle Velma Lake

Lower Velma Lake

Maggies Peaks

Cascade Lake

Granite Lake

Cascade Creek

USFS Lake Tahoe Visitor Center

Truckee Marsh

Tahoe Keys

50

Fontanillis Lake

Upper Velma Lake

Azure Lake

Snow Lake

Eldorado National Forest

Mt Tallac Trailhead

South Lake Tahoe

START DAY 3

Dicks Lake

Dicks Pass 9380ft

Cascade Creek

Mt Tallac 9735ft

Fallen Leaf Lake

USFS Lake Tahoe Basin Headquarters & Visitor Information

89

To Hwy 50

Dicks Peak 9974ft

Half Moon Lake

Gilmore Lake

Tahoe Rim Trail

Lake Tahoe Airport

Jacks Peak 9856ft

Susie Lake

50

Clyde Lake

Crystal Range

Heather Lake
Lake Le Conte

START DAY 2

Glen Alpine Trailhead

Lily Lake

Angora Peak 8588ft

Washoe Meadows State Park

Lake Valley State Recreation Area

Mt Price 9975ft

Lake Aloha

Pacific Crest

Lake Lucille

Keiths Dome 8646ft

Angora Lakes

89

Saxton Creek

Pyramid Peak 9983ft

Lake of the Woods

Haypress Meadows

Tamarack Lake

Echo Peak 8895ft

Flagpole Peak 8363ft

Eldorado

Ralston Lake

National Scenic Trail

Upper Echo Lake

Lower Echo Lake

START

National

Desolation

Ralston Peak 9253ft

Talking Mtn 8824ft

Echo Lake Chalet

Echo Lake Trailhead

Forest

Wilderness

Cup Lake

50

89

To Sacramento

To Luther Pass

Nevada
California

at the USFS William Kent visitor information station (see p102). A camping fee of $5 per person for one night or a maximum of $10 per person for two or more nights is also payable when picking up the permit.

Wood fires are not allowed in Desolation Wilderness.

GETTING TO/FROM THE HIKE
To the Start
A mile west of Echo Summit on US 50 is a paved road that heads east and then north 1.5mi to the southeast end of Lower Echo Lake. A water taxi can shuttle visitors from the trailhead to Upper Echo Lake, eliminating the first 2.9mi of walking.

From the Finish
Meeks Bay, between Sugar Pine Point and DL Bliss State Parks, is on Hwy 89 along Lake Tahoe's western shore, 19mi northwest of South Lake Tahoe and 11mi south of Tahoe City. The signed trailhead is west of the highway, north of Meeks Creek, across from the USFS *Meeks Bay Campground* ($15).

If you don't have your own vehicle, you can ride the Tahoe Trolley (☎ 530-581-6365), a shuttle bus ($1.25) between Emerald Bay and Tahoe City that operates 10:30am to 10:30pm, late June to early September.

THE HIKE
Day 1: Lower Echo Lake to Lake Lucille
3½–4 hours, 6.5mi (10.5km), 936ft (281m) ascent, 170ft (51m) descent
From Echo Chalet (7414ft), a summer-only resort, the trail crosses the dam at Lower Echo Lake's outlet and turns west to follow the lake's rocky northern shore beneath Flagpole Peak (8363ft). It goes through forest along Upper Echo Lake, beyond which it ascends rocky switchbacks, passing a junction with a trail leading left to Tamarack Lake and reaching **Haypress Meadows** (8350ft) after 4.2mi. The trail levels and crosses a saddle, then passes a junction with a trail that goes left to Lake of the Woods. A short distance beyond, a side trail (8300ft) turns right and descends to *campsites* along the northwest shore of pretty **Lake Lucille**

(8180ft), beneath Keiths Dome (8646ft) with beautiful views north of Mt Tallac (9735ft) and Dicks Peak (9974ft).

Day 2: Lake Lucille to Dicks Lake
5–6 hours, 9.8mi (15.8km), 1720ft (516m) ascent, 1480ft (444m) descent
Return to the main trail and turn right onto the Tahoe-Yosemite Trail, which descends to artificially made **Lake Aloha** (8116ft). The trail follows the rocky northeast shore of this large lake, which has many small granite islands. Pyramid Peak (9983ft) and Mt Price (9975ft) rise dramatically above its southwest shore. At a junction near the lake's northeast end, the trail turns right and goes east to pass by *campsites* on the northern shore of pretty **Heather Lake** (7900ft) and continues down to popular Susie Lake (7780ft). After skirting the southern shore of the latter, the trail turns north, crosses the lake's outlet, and bending eastward, winds down to the valley floor, passing a trail that descends to the Glen Alpine Trailhead near Fallen Leaf Lake.

The trail turns north and begins to ascend through forest, passing a second right turn to the Glen Alpine Trailhead and also a trail turning northwest (left) to Half Moon Lake. The trail to Dicks Pass makes switchbacks up open slopes and enters forest, working up along the outlet stream from Gilmore Lake. Shortly before reaching Gilmore Lake, the trail turns northwest (left) and begins a steady ascent toward Dicks Pass. A detour to and *camping* at Gilmore Lake (8310ft) allows for a 3.6mi round-trip excursion to the summit of Mt Tallac (see the Half Moon Lake hike, p106, for a description of this side trip).

With views of the impressive cliffs above Gilmore Lake to the right and inviting Half Moon Lake below to the left, the trail traverses open slopes and small meadows to reach **Dicks Pass** (9380ft) on the ridge between Dicks Peak and Mt Tallac. The actual pass is not the low point, but is a few hundred yards east of it and higher along the ridge. From the broad grassy pass, the trail descends through forest to a junction. The trail to the right leads to Eagle Lake and Emerald Bay. Follow the trail to the left, which angles south back to the abundant *campsites* along Dicks Lake's north shore (8420ft).

Day 3: Dicks Lake to Rubicon Lake

3½–4½ hours, 6.8mi (10.9km), 950ft (285m) ascent, 1070ft (321m) descent

The trail heads north, passing east of shallow Fontanillis Lake, then descends through forest west of Upper Velma Lake. The trail turns left, passing south of **Middle Velma Lake** (7900ft), then turns north and descends into a marshy area west of that lake. Heading north, it rises through forest to a junction where it leaves the combined PCT and Tahoe Rim Trail and turns right, following the Tahoe-Yosemite Trail toward Phipps Pass.

The trail rises steadily through forest, then switchbacks up open slopes to a hairpin turn, which offers sweeping views over Rockbound Valley, through which flows the Rubicon River. The trail turns back sharply southeast and begins a steadily rising traverse of the southern slopes of Phipps Peak (9234ft). Passing south of the peak, with views back down to the Velma Lakes, the trail bends northeast to reach **Phipps Pass** (8850ft) on the peak's shoulder. It traverses down steep, rocky slopes, passing high above the tiny Grouse Lakes, and descends in switchbacks into forest to Rubicon Lake (8300ft), which has *campsites* along its western shore and under hemlocks at the southern end.

Day 4: Rubicon Lake to Meeks Bay

4 hours, 8.1mi (13km), 2070ft (621m) descent

A short ascent takes you to a slight saddle above the northwest shore of Rubicon Lake. You then follow switchbacks down through forest, crossing Meeks Creek and passing *campsites* along the western shore of Stony Ridge Lake. The trail follows the tumbling creek as it flows out of the lake, then passes above Shadow Lake and descends through forest to recross the creek and reach the eastern shore of Crag Lake. The trail rolls down beneath Rubicon Peak (9183ft) to shallow, heavily used *campsites* at Lake Genevieve, at the northern end of

which it passes a junction with a trail leading to General Creek.

Descend steadily along the well-shaded Meeks Creek, swinging east, then back west, to reach a crossing of the creek. From here, the sandy trail rolls through meadows and open forest, and leaves Desolation Wilderness as it drops down to meet the unpaved, closed road that leads to Meeks Bay (6230ft).

Carson Range

The north-south Carson Range extends above the eastern shore of Lake Tahoe from Mt Rose Wilderness as far south as Red Lake Peak at Carson Pass. Lake Tahoe's highest peaks, Freel Peak (10,881ft), Jobs Sister (10,823ft) and Mt Rose (10,776ft), are in this range, and hikers reach all of them for unparalleled Tahoe views. Drier than the mountains above Tahoe's western shore, the Carson Range has a longer hiking season, with autumn aspen colors that are delightful. Hwy 431 and US 50 cross the range and provide quick access to the crest line. Many hikers enjoy day hikes along the crest, and superb overnight hikes are possible if you seek a peaceful stay above Tahoe's blue expanse.

ACCESS TOWN

See Tahoe City, p93, and South Lake Tahoe, p102.

Mt Rose

Duration	6–8 hours
Distance	11.8mi (19km)
Standard	moderate
Start/Finish	near Mt Rose Summit
Public Transport	no

Summary This day hike to the summit of Tahoe's third-highest peak involves a steady 1876ft ascent along a trail with abundant wildflowers and incomparable views.

Mt Rose (10,776ft), in the Carson Range northeast of Lake Tahoe, is the third-highest peak in the Tahoe area and the only peak higher than 10,000ft with an official trail to its summit. This popular day hike ascends 1876ft over 5.9mi (and descends the same amount over the same distance), offering a visual feast with dramatic views and spectacular wildflowers. Blue and white lupines, bright yellow mountain mule ears and purple pen-stemons are common. Close to the dry ground look for the broad, coconut-scented yellow flowers of the unusual woody-fruited evening primrose, and on sunny midsummer days, inhale the minty fragrances of sage-brush and mountain pennyroyal.

PLANNING
When to Hike
The hiking season is July to mid-October, although snow lingers along many north-facing aspects through early July.

What to Bring
The summit is notoriously windy and often very cold, so bring a jacket, even on a hot sunny day.

Maps
The USGS 1:24,000 *Mt Rose* quadrangle covers the hike. Toiyabe National Forest's Carson ranger station (☎ 775-882-2766), 1536 S Carson St (US 395), Carson City, provides trail information and sells maps.

Permits & Regulations
A wilderness permit is not required, even if one is inspired to spend the night on the summit or anywhere else in Mt Rose Wilderness.

GETTING TO/FROM THE HIKE
The trail starts at a locked gated on an unpaved service road on the north side of Hwy 431, 0.3mi west of Mt Rose Summit (8900ft) and 7.7mi northeast of Incline Village. Parking is along the wide shoulder on Hwy 431. Additional parking in a paved lot with toilets is at the Tahoe Meadows trailhead on the south side of Hwy 431, 0.4mi west of the Mt Rose trailhead. At Mt Rose Summit is the attractive USFS *Mt Rose Campground* ($7). Mt Rose Summit

refers to the highest point along Hwy 431 and not to the top of Mt Rose itself.

THE HIKE
Contour gently upward along the service road through stands of lodgepole pine on the slopes above **Tahoe Meadows**. Lake Tahoe and the Crystal Range soon come into view, as does small Incline Lake in the forest beyond the southwest edge of Tahoe Meadows. The road bends north, with Third Creek below to the west and, after a fairly level 2.3mi, comes to a small seasonal pond. Flowery meadows surround this pond, which is home to quite vocal tree frogs.

The Mt Rose Trail leaves the road here, turning northeast (right) over a gentle saddle into broad meadows at the head of **Galena Creek**, and follows an old dirt road across the head of the meadows. Passing among some trees at the meadow's far edge, the trail turns northeast and passes a gushing spring, the source of Galena Creek.

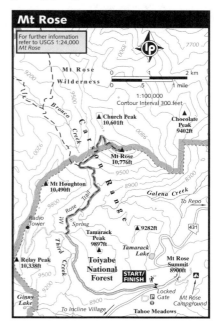

The trail rejoins the dirt road and follows power lines. Descending mostly open slopes, it narrows to become a trail again and reaches another stream, the last year-round water source. It crosses the stream and traverses mostly north across open slopes where lupines bloom profusely.

The trail rounds a corner to enter a gully, dry by mid-August, and ascends it heading northwest. The trail ascends steadily, with some steep sections, entering Mt Rose Wilderness, then reaching a saddle and trail junction northwest of Mt Rose. The left fork continues to Davis and Big Meadows. The trail to the summit of Mt Rose, still 1.4mi away, follows the right fork up switchbacks on the west-facing slope, ascending above tree line to the summit ridge. The trail follows the ridge south to the summit, from where Lake Tahoe, Truckee Meadows and Reno are visible. To the distant south, Freel Peak and Jobs Sister, the only points higher than Mt Rose in the Tahoe area, stand out clearly. Far to the north, volcanic Lassen Peak (10,457ft) in the Cascade Range is visible on a clear day. Retrace your steps back to the trailhead.

Tahoe Meadows to Spooner Summit

Duration	2 days
Distance	22mi (35.4km)
Standard	easy-moderate
Start	Tahoe Meadows Trailhead
Finish	Spooner Summit North
Public Transport	no

Summary Continuous breathtaking panoramas of Lake Tahoe and the surrounding peaks make this hike along the 8000- to 9000-foot crest of the Carson Range a delight.

Hiking the crest of the Carson Range, high above Tahoe's eastern lakeshore, offers probably the finest vistas of the entire Tahoe area. This well-signed segment of the Tahoe Rim Trail is best as a leisurely overnight trip, but can be done as a strenuous day hike. The trail crosses several unpaved service roads inside the Lake Tahoe Nevada State Park, which offer shorter, alternative ways to Hwy 28, which runs along the lakeshore.

You need to have two vehicles or to arrange for someone to drop you off or pick you up, since the trailheads are many miles apart by road. If you cannot make these arrangements, an alternative day hike with outstanding views starts from Spooner Summit North and goes to Snow Valley Peak and then returns to Spooner Summit North.

PLANNING
When to Hike
The hiking season is mid-June to October. Weekdays have negligible mountain bike traffic (which is allowed only between Hwy 431 and Snow Valley Peak Rd) compared with weekends.

Maps
The USGS 1:24,000 *Mt Rose, Marlette Lake* and *Glenbrook* quadrangles cover the hike.

Permits & Regulations
A wilderness permit is not required for this hike, and no permit is necessary to camp in the state park.

GETTING TO/FROM THE HIKE
To the Start
The unsigned Ophir Creek Trailhead (8540ft) is at the southern edge of Tahoe Meadows on the southeast side of Hwy 431, 6.5mi northeast of Incline Village opposite the private road that leads west going to Incline Lake.

Parking is limited along the gravel shoulder of Hwy 431. A larger, paved parking area is 0.8mi farther east on Hwy 431.

From the Finish
A Tahoe Rim Trail sign at Spooner Summit, on US 50 0.8mi east of the US 50/Hwy 28 intersection on Lake Tahoe's eastern shore and 9mi west of the US 50/US 395 intersection in Carson City, easily identifies the trailhead. An unpaved parking area is along the road's north shoulder.

THE HIKE
Day 1: Tahoe Meadows to Marlette Peak

7–8 hours, 13mi (21km), 1300ft (390m) ascent, 1560ft (468m) descent

The Tahoe Rim Trail follows the Ophir Creek Trail (8540ft), an abandoned dirt road, along the edge of **Tahoe Meadows** for 10 minutes and then turns south (right) at a junction. The trail rises slightly through forest and crosses a dirt road after another 30 minutes, bringing the first views of Lake Tahoe. It narrows and contours gently through open forest, coming to a small year-round stream 2.5mi from the trailhead. (The next water is at Lower Twin Lake, 6mi ahead.)

The trail traverses a ridge through Toiyabe National Forest with superlative views west of Lake Tahoe and east of **Washoe Lake**. About 2.5mi from the stream, it skirts the edge of Diamond Peak ski area, with simultaneous views east and west. It traverses the west side of the ridge, then descends the eastern slope on two long, moderate switchbacks to reach a long saddle across the ridge, coming back to the west side and to additional remarkable Tahoe views. Here the trail enters the **Lake Tahoe Nevada State Park**.

The trail drops to meet the unpaved Tunnel Creek Rd, which is 3.5mi from the ski area and descends to Incline Village. The trail turns east (left) onto Tunnel Creek Rd for five minutes, and then turns right onto another dirt road for five more minutes to a junction with another dirt road leading to Upper Twin Lake. The trail turns left off the road and, 50yd farther, forks left and drops slightly to skirt the east shore of small, shallow, grass-fringed Lower Twin Lake.

South of Lower Twin Lake, in the only serious ascent on the hike, the trail ascends 750ft on long switchbacks through open forest, offering glimpses of Tahoe, Crystal Bay and Washoe Lake. From the top, the trail drops to a level area and soon comes to the junction (8540ft) with the **Sand Harbor Overlook Trail**, 2.5mi from Tunnel Creek Rd. This spur trail (0.6mi one way) crosses an 8840ft ridge to a viewpoint that is not to

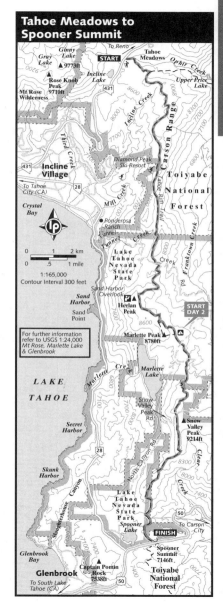

Tahoe Meadows to Spooner Summit

Look for the small, rust-colored red fox in
meadows and forests.

be missed, directly overlooking Sand
Harbor, 2600ft below, and all of Lake Tahoe.

Continuing south through forest 15
minutes to an open, meadowy ridge overlooking pretty Marlette Lake (7823ft), the
trail works down to a junction with the Marlette Peak Trail, which turns right and
rejoins the Tahoe Rim Trail farther ahead.
Contouring around the eastern slopes of
Marlette Peak (8780ft) through forest and
crossing a small snowmelt stream, the trail
soon arrives at the primitive, free *Marlette
Peak Campground* (8280ft).

Day 2: Marlette Peak
to Spooner Summit North

5–6 hours, 9mi (14.5km), 860ft (258m)
ascent, 1976ft (593m) descent

Water is scarce between the campground
and Spooner Summit. The Tahoe Rim Trail
passes the southern end of the Marlette
Peak Trail within five minutes, and in five
more crosses unpaved North Canyon Rd,
which descends 5.8mi via **Marlette Lake** to
Spooner Lake on Hwy 28. The trail continues south and, after 20 minutes, turns right
and follows a set of jeep tracks for a few
minutes. It then turns left at a signpost and
winds up through forest to emerge into an
open meadow of sage and lupine. As it

ascends this ridge, the views open to the
north including Mt Rose, **Slide Mountain**
and a distant Reno. Meandering up
through flower-filled meadows high above
Marlette Lake with truly exceptional views
of all Lake Tahoe and beyond, the trail
crosses a ridge above Marlette Lake and
drops gently to a junction with unpaved
Snow Valley Peak Rd, which goes 0.3mi
southeast to the antenna-infested top of
Snow Valley Peak (9214ft) and west down
to North Canyon Rd.

After crossing Snow Valley Peak Rd, the
trail narrows and traverses downward
across Snow Valley Peak's western slope
through sage and lupine with outstanding,
continuous Tahoe vistas. Contouring down,
with North Canyon Rd visible below, the
sagebrush yields to manzanita, and the trail
enters forest about 45 minutes after crossing
Snow Valley Peak Rd. It descends through
forest with glimpses east and west to reach a
trail junction, 4.2mi from Spooner Summit.
Passing this trail, which descends to North
Canyon Rd, the Tahoe Rim Trail rolls down
steadily through forest, passing several
wooden signposts advertising nearby vista
points. US 50 road noise indicates arrival at
Spooner Summit (7146ft).

Freel Peak

Duration	2 days
Distance	22.6mi (36.3km)
Standard	easy–moderate
Start	Kingsbury South
Finish	Big Meadow North
Public Transport	no

Summary A spectacular segment of the Tahoe
Rim Trail crosses two passes and includes a
beautiful lakeside campsite and an optional, but
highly desirable, visit to Tahoe's highest peak.

The Tahoe Rim Trail between Daggett Pass
and Big Meadow hugs the crest of the
Carson Range, offering outstanding views
over both the Carson Valley to the east and
of scintillating Lake Tahoe to the west and
north. **Star Lake**, directly below the steep

face of Jobs Sister, is one of Tahoe's loveliest lakes. The hike passes below Freel Peak (10,881ft), the Tahoe Basin's highest summit, named for James Freel, a 19th century miner and rancher from Illinois who settled nearby. The peak itself, crowned by a microwave tower, lies a strenuous 1mi and 1151ft above the Tahoe Rim Trail and is reached by an unmaintained use trail.

You need to have two vehicles or to arrange for someone to drop you off or pick you up, since the trailheads are about 21mi apart by road. If you cannot make these arrangements, an alternative 8.8mi round-trip day hike to Freel Peak is possible only if you have a 4WD vehicle. For this alternative trip, from Hwy 89, 1.8mi north of the Hwy 88/Hwy 89 intersection and 0.8mi east of Luther Pass (7740ft), turn north onto USFS Rd 051, marked only by a tiny sign along the left-hand side of this unpaved 4WD road. Drive along Willow Creek to the road's end, veering left onto USFS Rd 051F, and the alternative trailhead. Ascend to Armstrong Pass, and go north to the saddle where the cross-country route to Freel Peak leaves the Tahoe Rim Trail.

PLANNING
When to Hike
The hiking season is from July to mid-October.

Maps
The USGS 1:24,000 *Freel Peak* and *South Lake Tahoe* quadrangles cover the hike.

Permits & Regulations
A wilderness permit is not required for this overnight trip.

NEAREST TOWN
See South Lake Tahoe, p102.

GETTING TO/FROM THE HIKE
To the Start
From the US 50/Hwy 207 intersection a few miles north of South Lake Tahoe, drive 3.2mi east on Hwy 207, which is called Kingsbury Grade, to Daggett Pass. Turn south (right) on Tramway Drive and go 1.3mi to a fork, bear

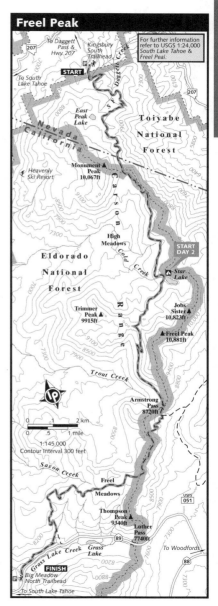

left on Quaking Aspen Lane to the trailhead at the south end of the Heavenly ski area's Stagecoach parking lot (7600ft).

From the Finish
Big Meadow North is on the north side of Hwy 89, 3.2mi west of Luther Pass (7740ft) and 5.2mi southeast of the Hwy 89/US 50 intersection, 8mi south of South Lake Tahoe.

THE HIKE
Day 1: Kingsbury South to Star Lake
4½–5 hours, 8.5mi (13.7km), 2140ft (642m) ascent, 640ft (192m) descent
Water is unreliable between the trailhead and Star Lake, so carry all the water you need for the day. From the trailhead (7600ft), ascend beneath Heavenly's Stagecoach ski lift. At the top of this short but steep ascent, the trail joins a short stretch of unpaved service road, then turns east, leaving the road, and ascends gently to a point overlooking Carson Valley to the east. Turning sharply west, continue up and, as the trail turns south to a saddle, you will catch glimpses of Lake Tahoe.

From the saddle (8200ft), the trail descends slightly, heading southeast to cross **South Fork Daggett Creek** (8080ft), 1.8mi from the trailhead. Passing near granite boulders, the trail crosses a broad ridge with good views over Carson Valley, and turns south to climb amid red firs and white pines to another ridge. The trail turns west and continues amid fragrant Jeffrey pines toward massive, granite-crowned Monument Peak.

Turning south, the trail crosses a saddle (8600ft) and dips steeply to cross Mott Canyon Creek (8320ft) and pass beneath a ski lift. Traversing out of Mott Canyon Creek, it heads south across the east flank of Monument Peak (10,067ft) and crosses the state boundary. Entering California, the trail continues its steady traverse upward to **Monument Pass** (8840ft), just southeast of the granite peak. Here you leave Toiyabe National Forest and the ridge's east side and cross over to the western side of the Carson Range, entering Eldorado National Forest. The trail contours south, descending slightly well above a branch of Cold Creek, passing

above High Meadows, with fine views of Freel Peak ahead. Crossing another branch of Cold Creek (8600ft), the trail begins a gentle steady climb south until it nears Cold Creek and turns east to follow it a short distance to its source, **Star Lake** (9100ft). *Campsites* are along the north shore, with excellent views of the rocky north face of Jobs Sister (10,823ft) towering above the turbid lake.

Day 2: Star Lake to Big Meadow North
7–8 hours, 14.1mi (22.7km), 1270ft (381m) ascent, 3090ft (927m) descent
Cross the outlet from Star Lake and head south, ascending the ridge that descends from Jobs Sister. Turning southwest toward Freel Peak, traverse high above Cold Creek and come to a stream (9360ft) descending from Freel Peak. Across the stream, the trail passes a small pond directly beneath Freel Peak and ascends to a **saddle** on Freel Peak's northwest ridge (9730ft).

To detour to the top of Freel Peak itself, a 2mi round trip from this saddle, head southeast from the windswept ridge to the base of a steeper section and follow a use trail up the ridgeline, staying on its west side. As the angle eases, work east across the stony slope high above the bowl below, following the track up easier slopes to the summit. The loose, stony slope makes for a tiresome slog, but the 3**60-degree panorama** from Tahoe's highest peak (10,881ft) is spectacular. A few clumps of dwarfed whitebark pine offer little shelter from the constant wind. Return via the same route to rejoin the Tahoe Rim Trail.

Descend from the saddle, traversing south. Then turn north, toward the cliffs called Fountain Face, and continue the descent a short distance to another sharp turn back to the south. The trail descends amid sagebrush and scattered trees and crosses several streams that offer the last reliable water until Freel Meadows, more than 5mi ahead. The trail continues its descent, bending southeast, with views of the meadows of Fountain Place and of distant Desolation Wilderness, and reaching **Armstrong Pass** (8720ft). A spur trail leads 0.4mi from the pass to an alternative trailhead at the end of USFS Rd 051F, which is used by people doing day hikes to the top of Freel Peak.

From the junction, continue southwest on the Tahoe Rim Trail along the ridgeline, ascending to a slight saddle (9200ft). Turning south, cross to the ridge's east side and head southeast, ascending to pass east of a small summit. The trail turns west and soon arrives at a spectacular viewpoint (9360ft) overlooking Lake Tahoe above Hell Hole Meadows. From here, the trail traverses southwest and then west into expansive **Freel Meadows**, the headwaters of Saxon Creek.

Descend westward, ascending briefly northward before resuming a westward course through Tucker Flat and passing south of a small summit. The views in this segment are excellent. Beyond the summit, the trail jogs north, then southwest and descends steadily, bearing south, to a trail junction above Hwy 89. A spur trail branches left (south) here, descending 0.6mi to the Grass Lake trailhead (7300ft), on Hwy 89, 1.6mi east of the Big Meadow North trailhead. This spur trail offers the shortest approach, by about 3.6mi, when doing a day hike to Freel Meadows from Hwy 89. Continue southwest from this junction, still staying on the Tahoe Rim Trail, and make a steep descent west, paralleling the highway, to the Big Meadow North trailhead (7280ft).

Echo Summit to Carson Pass

Duration	2 days
Distance	12.7mi (20.4km)
Standard	easy-moderate
Start	Echo Summit
Finish	Meiss Lake Trailhead
Public Transport	no

Summary Easy walking, beautiful wildflower gardens and remarkable solitude characterize this hike between two trans-Sierra highways, making it one of the best overnight trips close to Lake Tahoe.

The superb hike between Echo Summit and Carson Pass follows a lightly used segment of the combined PCT and Tahoe-Yosemite Trail and visits the scenic headwaters of the Truckee.

You must have two vehicles or arrange for someone to drop you off or pick you up, since the trailheads are miles apart by road. If you cannot do this, try an alternative 8.8mi round-trip day hike or overnight outing to Showers Lake starting and finishing at the Meiss Lake trailhead. It's possible to lengthen this hike by continuing south on the Carson Pass to Ebbetts Pass hike (see p131).

PLANNING
When to Hike
The hiking season is from mid-June to October.

Maps
The USGS 1:24,000 *Echo Lake, Caples Lake* and *Carson Pass* quadrangles cover the hike. The USFS 1:63,360 *Eldorado National Forest* map also does, but without topographic detail.

Permits & Regulations
A wilderness permit is not required for this overnight hike.

GETTING TO/FROM THE HIKE
To the Start
The trailhead is at the Echo Summit Sno-Park (7382ft) at the end of a short road that turns south off US 50, 0.3mi west of Echo Summit.

From the Finish
The Meiss Lake Trailhead parking lot is along the north side of Hwy 88, 0.1mi west of Carson Pass (8574ft). Parking costs $3 per day between June 1 and October 1.

Carson Pass is 8.8mi west of the Hwy 88/Hwy 89 intersection, which is 19mi from South Lake Tahoe and 13mi from Markleeville.

THE HIKE
Day 1: Echo Summit to Showers Lake
5–6 hours, 8.3mi (13.4km), 1178ft (354m) ascent
Heading south a mile to Benwood Meadow, the trail ascends southwest, crossing a

forested ridge to reach the head of **Bryan Meadow**. Turn south (left) at the trail junction, following the forested ridge between Sayles Canyon and the Upper Truckee River. Then turn southeast to skirt Little Round Top (9590ft), where patches of snow lie late in the season. Passing through a gated fence, descend into beautiful meadows of wildflowers. As you near **Showers Lake** (8650ft), turn east, onto a trail that circles its north shore, to picturesque ***campsites*** near the lake's outlet. Nearby, across the open basin of the Upper Truckee Meadows, Round Lake, Dardanelles Lake and Four Lakes are inviting.

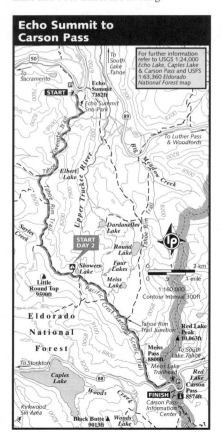

Day 2: Showers Lake to Meiss Lake Trailhead

2½–3 hours, 4.4mi (4.7km), 150ft (45m) ascent, 227ft (68m) descent

Circle the lake's south shore and rejoin the trail, which rises slightly to the south, then turns southeast and descends into Upper Truckee Meadows. It crosses several small streams and comes to a junction with the Round Lake Trail in 2.2mi, where the Tahoe Rim Trail turns northeast (left). Continuing south on the PCT, the trail rolls upward through beautiful meadows, crossing the nascent Truckee River and its feeders several times, with striking Red Lake Peak to the east providing a wildly colorful backdrop to the lush meadows. From **Meiss Pass** (8800ft), the saddle at the head of the meadows that separates the Truckee and American River Basins, are views south to Round Top and back north to Freel Peak. The trail descends a steep open slope, then passes under trees, crossing a small stream, and turns southeast to the trailhead, which is just west of Carson Pass (8574ft).

Other Hikes

Five Lakes

Nestled beneath the Sierra Crest in Granite Chief Wilderness is a forested basin with five timberline lakes. The 5mi (8.1km) round-trip hike to the lakes takes 2½ hours, ascending about 1000ft and descending an equal amount. The easy and wide trail makes for a good family outing, perfect for picnicking or fishing. The lakes, however, are too shallow and grassy for swimming. The USGS 1:24,000 *Tahoe City* and *Granite Chief* quadrangles cover the hike. A wilderness permit is not required for this hike.

From the Hwy 89/Hwy 28 junction in Tahoe City, drive 3.7mi north on Hwy 89 to Alpine Meadows Rd. Turn west (left) onto Alpine Meadows Rd and go 2.1mi to the signed trailhead (on the right), which is opposite the second intersection with Deer Park Drive (on the left).

The Five Lakes Trail crosses private property, so stay on the designated trail. Head southwest from the trailhead (6560ft) and begin a steady ascent on switchbacks. As the trail turns west, it ascends more gradually and enters forest. More switchbacks lead to a traverse northwest on open slopes, with views overlooking Alpine Meadows and west to Squaw Peak (8885ft). At the Granite Chief Wilderness boundary sign (7520ft), the trail heads into dense red-fir forest, providing welcome shade from the sun-drenched ascent. Turning southwest, you reach a signed trail junction (7560ft) in a few minutes. Turn left (south), following the sign to 'Five Lakes.' The lakes are barely visible through the trees to the left of the trail. In two or three minutes, the trail reaches the largest and lowest-elevation lake (7520ft). To find the other lakes, head southeast along the east end of the largest lake.

Eagle Lake

The sound of rushing water fills the air as an aspen-lined trail leads you up a narrow canyon to the placid water of the rockbound Eagle Lake. Tucked into the most easily accessible corner of Desolation Wilderness, the 2mi (3.2km) round-trip hike to Eagle Lake only takes an hour. The 400ft ascent from the trailhead to the lake may get your heart pumping, but the broad and heavily used trail is easy to follow, with several scenic overlooks along the way. The USGS 1:24,000 *Emerald Bay* quadrangle covers the hike.

From Hwy 89, high above Emerald Bay along Lake Tahoe's southwest shore, look for the USFS Eagle Falls Picnic Area and the signed Eagle Falls Trailhead. It costs $3 to park in the lot, but parking along the highway or at Vikingsholm is free. Take a minute at the trailhead to self-register; a free day-use permit is required on all hikes in Desolation Wilderness.

The trail starts out with a climb of 100 granite stairs to reach the Eagle Falls footbridge in 10 minutes. Cross the footbridge and soon pass the Desolation Wilderness boundary sign, beyond which is a beautiful overlook of Emerald Bay. Ten minutes farther is a trail junction. Turn right (southwest) to Eagle Lake; the left fork goes to Velma Lake. The lakeshore is just a few minutes ahead. Granite cliffs and peaks rise high above the lake on all sides, with forest dotting the rocky shores of this enclosed basin.

Jones Creek & Whites Creek Loop

Jones Creek and Whites Creek are parallel creeks draining the northeastern flanks of Mt Rose. An easy-moderate 9.2mi (14.8km) loop hike crossing the watershed between them goes through a rarely visited part of Mt Rose Wilderness and takes four hours. The trail is at its finest in the autumn, when its many aspen groves dazzle hikers with an array of fall colors. Other times of the

Many birds, including the raucous Steller's jay, make their home in the Sierra.

year, it's delightful for an exercise hike or a picnic. The USGS 1:24,000 *Washoe City, Mt Rose, Mt Rose NW* and *Mt Rose NE* quadrangles cover the hike.

The trailhead (6000ft) is at the north entrance to Galena Creek State Park off Hwy 431, the Mt Rose Hwy, southwest of Reno. Head west, starting a steady ascent, and cross Jones Creek 15 minutes from the trailhead. Turn left (west) at the trail junction on the opposite bank of the creek and ascend more steeply through ponderosa pine forest to reach the Mt Rose Wilderness boundary sign.

The valley opens up and the gradient eases as you reach a beautiful bowl. Six long, gentle switchbacks lead up from the head of the bowl and away from Jones Creek to the trail's highest point (8066ft), on a ridge with views of the Truckee Meadows and Reno. This ridge separates Jones Creek to the south from Whites Creek to its north. A spur trail leads from the ridge to nearby Church's Pond (8290ft).

The loop continues west and descends a forested hillside through aspen groves to the head of scenic Whites Canyon. Cross to Whites Creek's true left bank and follow the gentle trail as it curves east and heads downvalley, where you cross to the creek's true right bank. Shortly beyond the crossing, the footpath widens where it meets an old road popular with mountain bikers. Follow the road downvalley to a junction, where a small sign indicates the place to turn right, and head southeast 10 minutes, up the forested slope to a low rise. From the top of this rise, the trail traverses through open forest and back to the trail junction at Jones Creek, offering pleasant views over Reno's southwest foothills the whole way. Make a left turn at the trail junction and return to the trailhead in 10 minutes.

Tahoe to Yosemite

Four wilderness areas in the northern and central Sierra – Mokelumne, Carson-Iceberg, Emigrant and Hoover – stretch between the Sierra Nevada's two most popular recreation spots, Lake Tahoe and Yosemite National Park. Ancient lava once covered much of the area, but subsequent erosion exposed the underlying granite, leaving black basaltic and reddish volcanic summits in sharp contrast with white and gray granite outcrops. The dark volcanic peaks rise above deep forested canyons and river valleys in these wilderness areas, providing a sharp contrast to the classic lake-filled granite landscape of other areas in the Sierra Nevada. Open ridge-top meadows and a relatively heavier forest cover further heighten the contrast, giving the region a colorful and distinctive flavor.

Most visitors to these areas gravitate toward places along one of the three trans-Sierra highways that transect the area, like Silver and Caples Lakes on Hwy 88, Lake Alpine on Hwy 4, or Spicer Meadow Reservoir and Pinecrest Lake along Hwy 108. Once away from trailheads, however, hikers find delightfully surprising solitude in this vast wilderness.

HISTORY

Native American Maidu and Miwok of the western Sierra and Washoe and Piute of the eastern Sierra traversed the region's passes to hunt and trade. Spanish missionaries entered the area at the beginning of the 19th century, and one of the major rivers here, the Stanislaus, was named after Estanislao, a Native American who refused to stay at the mission.

In 1844, John C Frémont and his scout Kit Carson surveyed the region. A river, a pass, a mountain range, and the Nevada state capitol were later named in honor of this famous scout. During the gold rush, the Overland Trail served as the main route through the region, and traces of that original trail are still found along Hwy 88.

Ebbetts Pass on Hwy 4 was named for John Ebbetts, who led a party over the pass in 1850 and recommended it as a railroad route!

INFORMATION

The USFS publishes 1:63,360 topographic maps of each wilderness area that are useful

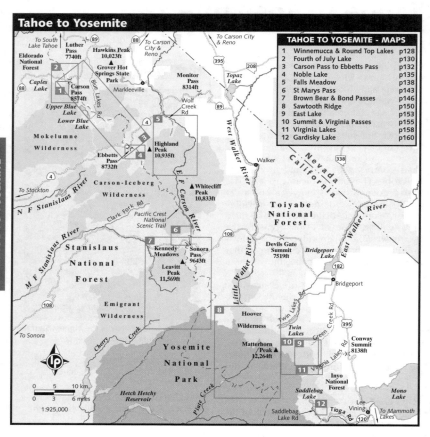

Tahoe to Yosemite

for planning as well as for hiking: *Mokelumne Wilderness; Carson-Iceberg Wilderness; Emigrant Wilderness;* and *Hoover Wilderness.*

For general wilderness information, visit the USFS website at Ⓦ www.r5.fs.fed.us to look at the national forests that manage each wilderness area.

A free wilderness permit is required for any overnight hike in the Mokelumne, Carson-Iceberg, Emigrant and Hoover Wilderness Areas. Permits are available at trailheads and ranger stations, which are identified in the individual hike's Planning section.

Toiyabe National Forest also issues free wilderness permits for all hikes in the Hoover Wilderness section of this chapter (see Permits & Regulations, p147.)

Mokelumne Wilderness

Nestled between Hwy 88 and Hwy 4, Mokelumne Wilderness spans three national forests – Eldorado, Toiyabe and Stanislaus. Its deep, glacially carved and forested canyons at elevations as low as 4000ft yield to dark, rocky ridges and summits of volcanic rock. Round Top (10,381ft) is its highest peak. Several other 10,000ft peaks are visible from most hikes in this section and from vantage points along the Pacific Crest National Scenic Trail (PCT). Compared with other parts of the Sierra Nevada, Mokelumne Wilderness has uncrowded trails, expansive scenery, verdant, rolling, rock-crowned ridges and plenty of lakes for swimming and fishing.

ACCESS TOWN
Markleeville
Markleeville, settled by Jacob Marklee in 1861, is the seat of remote Alpine County, California's least densely populated county.

The USFS and Alpine County chamber of commerce (☎ 530-694-2475, fax 694-2478, [e] alpinecounty@alpinecounty.com, [w] www .alpinecounty.com) jointly run the visitor information center at the north end of town, where hikers can self-issue free wilderness permits for the Mokelumne and Carson-Iceberg Wilderness Areas.

Grover's Corner and the *Markleeville General Store* sell groceries, and the latter also sells some basic gear.

J Marklee Town Station (☎ 530-694-2507), the town's only motel, costs $50/55 for singles/doubles. *Alpine Hotel/Cutthroat Saloon (☎ 530-694-2150)* is the best place for hearty, inexpensive meals and a beer. *M's Coffee House (☎ 530-694-9337)*, behind the saloon, is a fine place for espresso and bagels.

The USFS *Markleeville campground* ($10; 5500ft), open May to September, is 0.8mi south of town on the east side of Hwy 89 along Mokelumne Creek. Year-round Grover Hot Springs State Park (☎ 530-694-2249) is 4mi west of town on Hot Springs Rd. The pleasant, forested state park *campground* ($16) has shower facilities. Call ☎ 800-444-7275 for reservations; a $7.50 fee applies. Across the adjacent meadow is a well-known **hot spring** with two large pools ($4 entrance fee, $1 bathing suit and towel rental).

Markleeville (5501ft) is on Hwy 89 between Hwy 88 and Hwy 4, 30mi southeast of South Lake Tahoe via Luther Pass

(7740ft), and 63mi northwest of Bridgeport via spectacular Monitor Pass (8314ft).

Winnemucca & Round Top Lakes

Duration	2–2½ hours
Distance	4.5mi (7.2km)
Standard	easy-moderate
Start	Winnemucca Trailhead
Finish	Lost Cabin Mine Trailhead
Public Transport	no

Summary Hike along splashing streams to two subalpine tarns separated by a wonderfully scenic ridge beneath the jagged summit of Round Top.

The open, rolling country along the Sierra Crest just southwest of Carson Pass offers expansive views, scenic lakes, lovely streams and rolling ridges topped by dramatic volcanic outcrops in Mokelumne Wilderness. A rewarding and relatively easy day hike, especially worthwhile in early summer when wildflowers are at their peak, traverses this terrain. The hike has a total elevation gain and loss of 2380ft, with roughly equal amounts of ascent and descent. This loop hike is best done as a day hike, because camping is prohibited at both lakes. For an overnight trip in the area see the Fourth of July hike, p129.

PLANNING
When to Hike
The hiking season is from mid-June to October.

Maps
The USGS 1:24,000 *Caples Lake* and *Carson Pass* quadrangles cover the hike, as does the USFS 1:63,360 *Mokelumne Wilderness* map.

Permits & Regulations
A wilderness permit is not required for this day hike, but is required for any overnight trip in Mokelumne Wilderness. Free self-issuing permits are available at both trailheads.

GETTING TO/FROM THE HIKE

Both trailheads are in the USFS Woods Lake Recreation Area. The signed turnoff is on Hwy 88, 1.8mi west of Carson Pass, which is 8.8mi west of the Hwy 88/Hwy 89 junction, 19mi from South Lake Tahoe and 13mi from Markleeville.

To get to the start, go south on the narrow road 1.3mi to the Winnemucca Trailhead; parking is limited.

The Lost Cabin Mine Trailhead, 0.2mi from the Winnemucca Trailhead, is in the USFS **Woods Lake Campground** between sites 12 and 13, where a sign reads, 'Lost Cabin Mine

Trail, follow this road to trailhead.' From this sign turn right and walk through the campground to return to the parking area near the Winnemucca Trailhead or turn left and walk 0.4mi to the overflow parking area. Parking is not allowed at this trailhead.

THE HIKE

Cross a wooden footbridge over the outlet from Woods Lake to reach the signed Winnemucca Trailhead (8220ft). Go straight for a few minutes then turn south as the Winnemucca Trail ascends along the true right bank of Winnemucca Lake's lodgepole pine-

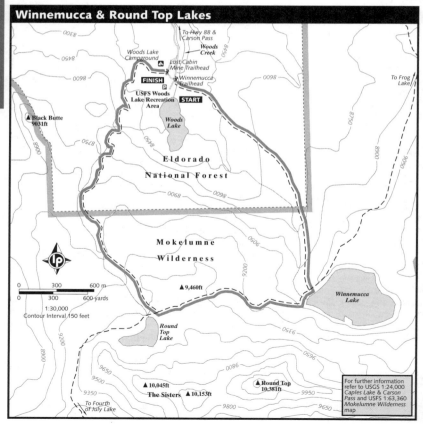

Winnemucca & Round Top Lakes

lined outlet stream amid granite outcrops. Some large firs stand on the slopes above the trail. After 20 minutes of shaded hiking, pass an interpretive sign for an **Arrasta**, a large granite circle in the ground, used by 19th century Mexican miners for crushing ore. The trail heads up along the creek, amid some large lodgepole pines, then moves away from the creek and onto the base of the open meadowy slope descending from a verdant spur above and to the left. Several species of paintbrush abound on the slope as the trail continues upward, reaching the Mokelumne Wilderness boundary sign in 10 minutes.

Now touching the splashing creek as it tumbles over granite boulders, the soft, gentle trail passes scattered stands of whitebark pines and, 1.6mi and 45 minutes from the trailhead, reaches a signed junction near the edge of large **Winnemucca Lake** (8980ft). A classic tarn, the lake is beautifully situated beneath imposing **Round Top** (10,381ft). To the east is the gray bulk of **Elephants Back** (9585ft) and to the north is the grassy, rounded **Red Lake Peak**, from whose summit Kit Carson was the first non-native to see Lake Tahoe. Along the level northern shore of the lake are a few deep green hemlocks and clusters of wind-warped whitebark pines.

From the trail junction at Winnemucca Lake, head west (left) and cross its outlet. The ascending trail crosses two small streams cascading down the rocky slope from snowbanks at the base of Round Top. You gain perspective as you ascend gradually and the view of Winnemucca Lake and Elephants Back opens. Red heather blooming amid the granite outcrops adds a splash of color to the subalpine landscape. In 30 minutes, you reach a saddle (9420ft), the lowest point on the north-south ridge separating Winnemucca and Round Top Lakes and their outlet streams. Phlox, sage and paintbrush flourish between scattered stands of whitebark pines beneath the dramatic summits of Round Top and **The Sisters** (10,153ft and 10,045ft) to its west. The ridge you are on is actually a spur extending northwest from the ridge connecting Round Top and The Sisters.

To get the hike's best views, walk north (right) of the trail two minutes from the saddle to the top of the granite outcrop (9460ft). The expansive vista sweeps northwest from **Caples Lake**, northeast to Red Top Peak and east to **Hawkins Peak** (10,023ft) rising behind Elephants Back. Distant Lake Tahoe and the upper Truckee Meadows are visible above Meiss Pass, a perspective similar to (but more easily attained than) that of Kit Carson more than 150 years ago.

A strenuous side trip to climb Round Top for 360-degree views also starts from the saddle. Head southeast on the spur ridge, on a faint use trail to the main scree-covered ridge and thence to the tricky summit.

From the saddle, the trail descends for two minutes to **Round Top Lake** (9340ft), 0.9mi from Winnemucca Lake, with dramatic views north to distant peaks and west to **Squaw Ridge** and Caples Lake. The expansive views continue as the trail descends along the true right bank of the outlet from Round Top Lake. Pass the wilderness boundary sign in 15 minutes, after which the descent steepens for another 15 minutes.

Descending past an old mine shack and an old rusted car chassis and passing below the buildings of the **Lost Cabin Mine**, the trail arrives at a sign for the Round Top Trail and Lost Cabin Mine Trailhead (8240ft). Here, the footpath widens and joins an old private unpaved road. Continue down the road, passing a metal gate that spans the road. Two minutes below the gate reach the Woods Lake campground, one hour and 2mi from Round Top Lake.

Fourth of July Lake

Duration	2 days
Distance	15.1mi (24.3km)
Standard	moderate
Start/Finish	Carson Pass Trailhead
Public Transport	no

Summary Hiking this clockwise loop around an ancient ochre-colored volcanic peak includes spending the night at a sparkling alpine lake.

The popular overnight circumambulation of volcanic Round Top (10,381ft), the highest summit in Mokelumne Wilderness, crosses the Sierra Crest at one of its lowest points and camps at beautiful Fourth of July Lake.

PLANNING
When to Hike
The hiking season is from mid-June to September.

Maps
The USGS 1:24,000 *Carson Pass* and *Caples Lake* quadrangles cover the hike, as does the USFS 1:63,360 *Mokelumne Wilderness* map.

Permits & Regulations
The Eldorado, Stanislaus and Toiyabe National Forests all issue free wilderness permits for the Mokelumne Wilderness. The easiest place for you to get a permit is at the USFS Carson Pass Information Center (☎ 209-258-8606), at Carson Pass

on Hwy 88. Campfires are not allowed above 8000ft.

GETTING TO/FROM THE HIKE
Carson Pass is 8.8mi west of the Hwy 88/Hwy 89 junction, which is 19mi from South Lake Tahoe and 13mi from Markleeville. The trailhead is adjacent to the Carson Pass Information Center on the south side of Hwy 88 at Carson Pass (8574ft).

Parking costs $3 per day between June 1 and October 1. An overflow fee-based parking lot is 0.1mi east of the pass along a paved dead-end road with great views overlooking Red Lake.

THE HIKE
Day 1: Carson Pass to Fourth of July Lake
6–7 hours, 9.5mi (15.3km), 1186ft (356m) ascent, 1596ft (479m) descent
The trail ascends along a ridge from the Carson Pass Trailhead (8574ft) south into

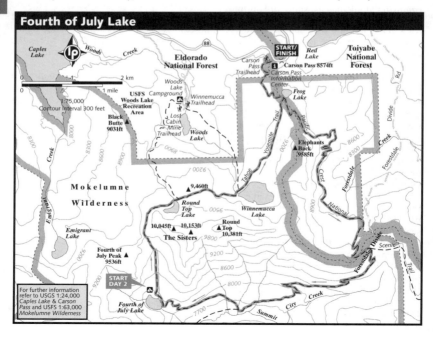

Mokelumne Wilderness 1.2mi to **Frog Lake,** a popular destination for day hikers. At a junction beyond the lake, the trail forks. Follow the PCT, the left fork, and ascend southeast then east to pass north of old, volcanic **Elephants Back** (9585ft). On this part of the trail you get fine views both east and west. Snow patches linger late in the season along this ridge (9080ft) as the trail descends to a northeast spur, then turns and descends south to traverse the upper **Forestdale Creek Basin** (8320ft), high above Faith Valley.

Ascending out of the basin, the trail passes above some small lakes and zigzags to **Forestdale Divide** (9000ft), which is 4.5mi from Carson Pass. Leaving the PCT, which forks left, follow the Summit City Trail, which turns right and descends to Summit City Creek. Turn north (right) onto the Tahoe-Yosemite Trail, leaving the Summit City Trail, 3.5mi from Forestdale Divide and ascend 1.5mi to spectacular *campsites* along the east shore of **Fourth of July Lake** (8164ft).

Day 2: Fourth of July Lake to Carson Pass

3–4 hours, 5.6mi (9km), 1296ft (389m) ascent, 886ft (266m) descent

Follow the trail north along Fourth of July Lake's inlet and then east 2.3mi to **Round Top Lake** (9340ft) and the junction with the Round Top Trail to Woods Lake. Turn right (east) and cross the view-filled saddle (9460ft) between Round Top and Winnemucca Lakes. Descend gently to **Winnemucca Lake** (8980ft) and the junction with the Winnemucca Trail to Woods Lake, which is 0.9mi from Round Top Lake. See the Winnemucca & Round Top Lakes hike, p127 for a more detailed description of this segment.

Continue along the northwest shore of Winnemucca Lake and ascend north out of the lake basin, passing to the west of Elephants Back. Turn left at the junction with the PCT at Frog Lake, which is 1.2mi from Winnemucca Lake. Retrace your steps from here 1.2mi back to the Carson Pass Trailhead.

Carson Pass to Ebbetts Pass

Duration	4 days
Distance	23mi (37km)
Standard	moderate
Start	Carson Pass Trailhead
Finish	Ebbetts Pass Trailhead
Public Transport	no

Summary Traverse Mokelumne Wilderness from north to south on a view-filled hike that rolls along ridges, skirts dramatic rocky peaks and spends every night at scenic lakes.

The segment of the PCT between Carson Pass (8574ft) and Ebbetts Pass (8732ft) runs through two portions of Mokelumne Wilderness, in the middle of which are the **Blue Lakes**, a popular recreation area. Beyond Blue Lakes, the trail skirts dramatic **Raymond Peak** (10,014ft), one of the highest summits in Mokelumne Wilderness.

You need to have two vehicles or to arrange for someone to drop you off or pick you up, since the trailheads are nearly 31mi apart by road. If you cannot make these arrangements, you have three alternative overnight hike possibilities that cover portions of this hike: from Carson Pass to Fourth of July Lake (see Fourth of July Lake, p129); from Ebbetts Pass to Raymond Lake (see Day 4 of this hike, p133); and from Upper Blue Lake to Grouse Lake (see Other Hikes, p160). Alternatively, if you're already in the Lake Tahoe area, you can combine this hike with the two-day Echo Summit to Carson Pass hike (see p121).

PLANNING
When to Hike

The hiking season is from mid-June to September. Exercise caution after mid-August, when bow hunting season begins near Blue Lakes.

Maps

The USFS 1:63,360 *Mokelumne Wilderness* map covers the hike, as do the USGS

1:24,000 *Carson Pass, Pacific Valley* and *Ebbetts Pass* quadrangles.

Permits & Regulations

A free wilderness permit is required for this hike. The Eldorado, Stanislaus and Toiyabe National Forests issue free wilderness permits for Mokelumne Wilderness. The easiest place to get a permit is at the USFS Carson Pass Information Center (☎ 209-258-8606) at Carson Pass on Hwy 88. Campfires are prohibited above 8000ft in Mokelumne Wilderness.

GETTING TO/FROM THE HIKE
To the Start

Carson Pass is 8.8mi west of the Hwy 88/Hwy 89 junction, which is 19 mi from South Lake Tahoe and 13mi from Markleeville. The trailhead is adjacent to the Carson Pass Information Center, on the south side of Hwy 88 at Carson Pass (8574ft). Parking costs $3 per day between June 1 and October 1. An overflow fee-based parking lot is 0.1mi east of the pass along a paved dead-end road with great views overlooking Red Lake.

From the Finish

Ebbetts Pass (8732ft), 50mi northeast of Angels Camp and 17.9mi southwest of Markleeville, is on Hwy 4, the least-traveled and narrowest trans-Sierra highway. The highway has a 24% grade approaching the pass. The dotted line that usually runs down the middle of the road disappears on the highway's steepest sections, but don't worry, the road doesn't. Along the southeast side of Hwy 4, just 0.4mi northeast of Ebbetts Pass, look for a sign reading 'Pacific Crest Trailhead Parking.' The trailhead parking lot is 0.1mi from this turnoff.

THE HIKE
Day 1: Carson Pass to Forestdale Divide

4 hours, 4.5mi (7.2km), 820ft (246m) ascent, 760ft (228m) descent

See Day 1 of the Fourth of July Lake hike, p130, for a description of the hike from Carson Pass south toward Forestdale

TAHOE TO YOSEMITE

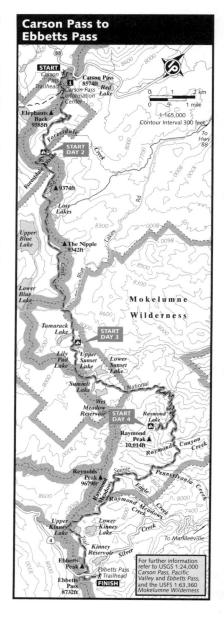

Carson Pass to Ebbetts Pass

Divide. Before you reach Forestdale Divide, on the north side of this pleasant valley, cross the outlet stream of **two small lakes**. Leave the PCT and go a few minutes farther to *campsites* (8660ft) along the larger, upper lake.

Day 2: Forestdale Divide to Lake Camp

5–5½ hours, 5mi (8km), 560ft (168m) ascent, 1400ft (420m) descent

Continue on the PCT, passing the junction with the trail leading southwest along Summit City Creek. Here, the PCT leaves Mokelumne Wilderness and crosses an unpaved road, which it then parallels southeast well above it. You continue along the ridge crest to a high point of 8960ft and traverse east and south of Peak 9374. Soon you descend to a slight saddle (8660ft) west of Lost Lakes.

Passing south of the lakes, you traverse the open western slopes of anatomically named **The Nipple** (9342ft), high above Upper Blue Lake (8131ft). Descend through forest to cross Blue Lakes Rd, which comes from Hope Valley. Continue southeast, crossing Pleasant Valley Creek and the outlet of Tamarack Lake. A few minutes beyond is a small unnamed lake with an island in it and pleasant *campsites* (7820ft) along its northwest shore.

Day 3: Lake Camp to Raymond Lake

4–4½ hours, 6.5mi (10.5km), 1494ft (448m) ascent, 320ft (96m) descent

The PCT continues its southeast course, passing **Lily Pad Lake**, then turns east and passes south of Upper and Lower Sunset Lakes and north of Wet Meadows Reservoir. Beyond these lakes, the trail goes over a saddle (8120ft) south of a small knob where it re-enters Mokelumne Wilderness.

Cross a stream (7800ft) and zigzag up a ridge to the junction with the short spur trail to Raymond Lake. Turn right (south) and follow the spur trail to *campsites* along the south shore of lovely **Raymond Lake** (8994ft), beneath the dramatic rocky summit of Raymond Peak (10,014ft).

Day 4: Raymond Lake to Ebbetts Pass

5½–6 hours, 7mi (11.3km), 1180ft (354m) ascent, 1442ft (433m) descent

Return to the junction and follow the PCT southeast (right), crossing several meadows and streams. The trail bears south and then east around Reynolds Peak (9679ft), crossing Pennsylvania Creek, Eagle Creek and Raymond Meadows Creek. It then goes over a saddle to reach **Upper Kinney Lake** (8700ft). Swinging south of the lake, the trail rises over a ridge and descends past small **Sherrold Lake** to reach Hwy 4. The PCT crosses Hwy 4 in an almost unnoticeable and unsigned spot in the forest 0.1mi east of Ebbetts Pass. Cross the road and soon turn left onto a spur trail that takes you to the trailhead parking lot in five minutes.

Carson-Iceberg Wilderness

Bordered by Hwy 4 on the north and Hwy 108 on the south, Carson-Iceberg Wilderness straddles the Sierra Crest within the Stanislaus and Toiyabe National Forests. Water along its west slope flows into the Stanislaus River, while its east slope drains into the Carson River, whose protected headwaters are the home of threatened native Lahontan and Piute cutthroat trout. The rugged landscape is dominated by volcanic peaks and ridges, with deep granite canyons. Prominent peaks include Sonora Peak (11,459ft), near St Marys Pass, and Highland Peak (10,935ft), visible on the Noble Lake and Falls Meadow hikes. It is a wilderness of streams, meadows and forests, with relatively few lakes. It retains a wild character unexcelled by any other part of the Sierra Nevada and holds nearly 200mi of view-filled hiking trails.

ACCESS TOWN

See the description of goods and services in Markleeville, p127.

Noble Lake

Duration	3½–4½ hours
Distance	7.6mi (12.2km)
Standard	easy-moderate
Start/Finish	Ebbetts Pass Trailhead
Public Transport	no

Summary Traverse a segment of the Pacific Crest National Scenic Trail (PCT) above forested Noble Canyon to a subalpine lake with good fishing and sweeping views of rugged volcanic peaks.

Noble Canyon in Carson-Iceberg Wilderness is wilder and more rugged than Mokelumne Wilderness and the Lake Tahoe area to the north, offering more solitude and more open, broader vistas for those who make the drive up scenic Hwy 4. The fairly gentle trail has 890ft of ascent and 700ft of descent, for a total of 3180ft of elevation gain and loss round trip, as it contours south above the deep and forested Noble Canyon between Ebbetts Pass and scenic Noble Lake. The mountains visible along the way may not be the Sierra Nevada's highest, but the striking volcanic peaks and pleasant flower-lined trail and cascading streams delight most any hiker.

Camping at Noble Lake serves as a base for a day hike over the ridge to the east to picturesque Bull Lake. You can also make a short, easy ascent of nearby Tryon Peak (9970ft) or head northeast along a ridge route to make your way to the rocky summit of Highland Peak (10,935ft).

PLANNING
When to Hike
The hiking season is from June to October.

Maps
The USGS 1:24,000 *Ebbetts Pass* quadrangle covers the hike, as does the USFS 1:63,360 *Carson-Iceberg Wilderness* map.

Permits & Regulations
A permit is not required for this day hike. A free wilderness permit is required for any overnight trip in the Carson-Iceberg Wilderness. You can self-issue permits at the trailhead.

GETTING TO/FROM THE HIKE
Along the southeast side of Hwy 4, just 0.4mi northeast of Ebbetts Pass, look for a sign reading 'Pacific Crest Trailhead Parking.' Ebbetts Pass (8732ft), 50mi northeast of Angels Camp and 17.9mi southwest of Markleeville, is on Hwy 4, the least-traveled and narrowest trans-Sierra highway. The highway has a 24% grade approaching the pass. The dotted line in the middle of the road disappears on the highway's steepest sections, but don't worry, the road doesn't. From Markleeville, go 4.9mi southeast on Hwy 89 to its junction with Hwy 4. Then follow Hwy 4 13mi southwest of the Hwy 4/Hwy 89 junction to the turnoff. Drive 0.1mi to the trailhead parking lot.

The PCT actually crosses Hwy 4 just 0.1mi east of Ebbetts Pass, but there are no signs on either side of the road marking the trail. The narrow dirt path heads into the forest on both sides of the road, but you'll see it only if you know where to look. A minimal amount of parking along the roadside nearby offers an alternative start, but the USFS clearly wants hikers to park in the parking lot 0.3mi farther to the northeast.

The USFS *Silver Creek campground* ($10) is on Hwy 4, 5.2mi northeast of the trailhead parking lot turnoff.

THE HIKE
A spur trail leads southwest five minutes from the parking lot (8670ft) to a signed junction (8760ft) with the PCT. Turn left (east) and follow the southbound PCT for five minutes, as it rises over an open spur ridge (8860ft) where yellow mule ears, purple lupines and scarlet paintbrushes bloom in early summer. You have sweeping views of **Highland** and **Silver Peaks** above the eastern slopes of Noble Canyon, and rocky **Raymond Peak** to the north in Mokelumne Wilderness.

Traversing south through open, flower-filled meadows, the trail soon enters stands of fir and pine and turns southeast beneath the base of dark volcanic cliffs that form the western ramparts of Noble Canyon. Crossing several streams that descend from snow at the base of the cliffs, you find blue-bells along the streams and blue forget-me-nots, yellow western wallflowers and pink mallows along the trail.

Rising through red firs and lodgepole pines, the trail passes a small, seasonal grassy pond and comes to a granite-topped forested ridge (8820ft). Turning briefly north to descend the ridge, the trail swings around granite outcrops amid large red firs and soon heads southward. The open gravel and manzanita speckled slope offers fine views across the canyon as you begin a steady southeast traverse, descending gradually into dramatic upper Noble Canyon.

The trail continues along the open slope, with Highland Peak prominent across the canyon. Granite outcrops above the trail are topped by the dark, volcanically formed ridge crest. Occasional large junipers cling to the granite, and the trail crosses several small willow and flower-lined streams descending from the ridge.

Nearing the head of Noble Canyon, one hour from the trailhead, the trail crosses a willow-lined side stream that splashes down in leaps and jumps from the dark brown cliffs above. Swinging east, the trail crosses the main stream (8280ft) after another 10 minutes. In the streambed are large masses of composite rock that have broken and fallen from the cliffs above. Turning almost 180° at the canyon's head, the trail runs north, rising past several very large, very old juniper trees to a ridge. Turning southeast again, it soon meets the Noble Canyon Trail at a signed junction (8400ft), 1½ hours from the trailhead. .

Traversing steadily upward to the south and then southeast through open forest of large red firs, the trail turns north as it crosses a small stream and climbs switchbacks up a rocky but flower-strewn slope. The views north to Raymond Peak and the distant

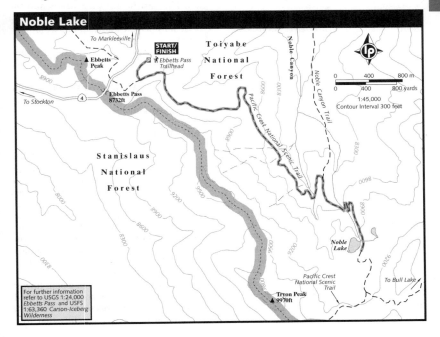

Noble Lake

Carson Range are excellent. Passing through a stand of junipers, the trail turns south again. Rock turrets point skyward along the ridge to the west as the trail ascends this dramatic, open, flower-filled area.

Soon you arrive near the willow-lined inlet and shore of **Noble Lake** (8860ft), which seems small and not so noble. Above its south shore, pine trees offer shade and a possible *campsite* (8900ft).

To the west, flat-topped **Tryon Peak** makes a tempting destination for those seeking higher views. Easy, open slopes lead to its summit, from where a traverse of the ridge crest heading north leads to easy grassy slopes that descend back to Noble Lake in a two-to-three-hour loop. From Noble Lake, retrace your steps back to the trailhead.

Falls Meadow

Duration	2 days
Distance	22.4mi (36km)
Standard	moderate
Start	Wolf Creek Trailhead
Finish	High Trail/River Trail Trailhead
Public Transport	no

Summary Hiking along the deepest canyon east of the Sierra Crest takes you into a true wilderness, with ample wildlife watching opportunities, where few others venture to go.

The East Fork Carson River forms the longest, deepest canyon east of Sierra Crest, and is one of the wildest places in the entire Sierra Nevada. Off the main trans-Sierra trails, the East Fork Carson River winds through a rarely visited and uniquely beautiful part of Carson-Iceberg Wilderness. Even on a summer weekend, you may not see another person. The river makes a long descent between high ridges, forming a deep, beautiful forested canyon with numerous broad and verdant meadows.

The river itself is home to endangered Lahontan cutthroat trout, and fishing is prohibited along the upper reaches, which are truly wild and scenic. Birds are everywhere

and trout are in all the streams. Observant hikers can see plentiful signs of large mammals and may even spot a bear. Bears here are wild and typically flee from human presence, a behavior that, unfortunately for both bears and humans, is increasingly rare in the Sierra Nevada.

The rocky summits and ridges, green grassy meadows, forested hills and open sagebrush slopes in this montane zone give this hike a unique quality. With its outstanding scenic features, infrequent visitation, good trails and remarkable wildlife, this near-loop hike is not to be missed.

PLANNING
When to Hike
The hiking season is from mid-May to October. The relatively low elevations make this a hot midsummer hike, so the best months are from mid-May to June, when wildflowers bloom, and from September to October, when aspen colors are at their peak. The two fords of East Fork Carson River can be difficult in May and early June.

Maps
The USGS 1:24,000 *Wolf Creek* and *Disaster Peak* quadrangles cover the hike, as does the USFS 1:63,360 *Carson-Iceberg Wilderness* map. Vandals have damaged several wooden trail signs. You can still read them, but if they're damaged further or missing it might be tricky to know where to go. This is a hike where carrying a topographic map and compass may come in handy.

The trail in use along the East Fork Carson River is not the same one marked on maps that were published before a flood damaged the trail and caused it to be rerouted in some places.

Permits & Regulations
A free wilderness permit is required for this hike. You can self-register at the trailhead or get a permit at the ranger station in Markleeville or Carson City. To protect the endangered Lahontan cutthroat trout, fishing is prohibited in Murray Canyon and upstream from Falls Meadow on the East Fork Carson River.

GETTING TO/FROM THE HIKE

From the junction of Hwy 4/Hwy 89, 4.9mi southeast of Markleeville, continue south on Hwy 4 2.4mi to Wolf Creek Rd (also USFS Rd 032). Turn left (southeast) onto Wolf Creek Rd, which is signed 'Wolf Creek' and 'East Carson River.' Follow USFS Rd 032 3.4mi to a signed junction; the first 1.9mi are paved, but beyond that it is an unpaved road. The roads are broad and well-graded, yet bumpy with washboards. The roads to both well-signed trailheads diverge at this junction.

To reach the Wolf Creek Trailhead, the start of the hike, stay on USFS Rd 032, bearing right (south) at the junction with USFS Rd 090. Go 1.6mi to the signed trailhead, a total of 5mi from Hwy 4. Park your vehicle here unless you have two vehicles and can leave one at each trailhead. To get an early start to the hike, you may want to camp at the Wolf Creek trailhead, where there is a no-fee undeveloped *camping area*. Water comes from the nearby creek.

To reach the High Trail/River Trail Trailhead, where the hike finishes, turn left (northeast) at the junction onto USFS Rd 090. Follow USFS Rd 090 along the east end of Wolf Creek Meadow and up a steep switchback. At the top of the switchback, leave USFS Rd 090 and turn right at a signed junction to the trailhead, 0.8mi from the junction with USFS Rd 032. The trailhead is 4.2mi from Hwy 4.

When you finish the hike and arrive at the High Trail/River Trail Trailhead, walk back along the broad, level USFS Rd 090 and USFS Rd 032 to reach the Wolf Creek Trailhead where you parked your vehicle when you started. It is 2.4mi by road between the trailheads. By taking a shortcut that starts at the southwest end of the parking lot, you can shorten the distance by 0.3mi.

The pleasant walk along the length of Wolf Creek Meadow takes 45 minutes to an hour. You cannot rely on getting a ride, because you'll find few vehicles travel these roads. Keep Markleeville's Grover Hot Springs in mind for a post-hike soak.

THE HIKE
Day 1: Wolf Creek Trailhead to Falls Meadow

6 hours, 11.1mi (17.9km), 2320ft (696m) ascent, 1900ft (570m) descent

The locked metal gate at the trailhead (6480ft) marks the Carson-Iceberg Wilderness boundary. The wide trail, once a jeep track, heads south amid ponderosa pines, along **Wolf Creek's** true left bank. The trail crosses occasional outcrops of yellow-tinged granite and ascends gently. Cottonwoods and a few aspens flourish along the creek and in moist meadows. The trail continues gradually upward, passing through some dense, shady stands of white firs to reach a barbed-wire gate on top of a small granite rise, 1¼ hours from the trailhead.

As the trail bends west and descends from the rise, **Arnot Peak** (10,054ft) at the head of the valley comes into view. Passing through forest beneath the bulk of **Patterson Peak**, the trail reaches another barbed-wire gate, one hour from the last gate, where you have open views upvalley of Arnot Peak. To the west, a low rocky ridge descends from Patterson Peak to meet the trail, which passes through fir forest near the base of the ridge. You soon reach the signed junction with the **Bull Canyon Trail**, 4.8mi from the trailhead.

The Bull Canyon Trail turns right (southwest), but continue straight (south) on the Wolf Creek Trail. Cross a small stream one minute beyond the junction and 10 minutes farther cross Bull Canyon Creek, which descends from Bull Lake. The trail turns west and briefly ascends the hillside spur between Bull Canyon Creek and Wolf Creek, then turns south and reaches another barbed-wire gate near a solitary large juniper five minutes from Bull Canyon Creek.

Traversing an open slope, where mule ears and lupines bloom amid scattered junipers, the trail passes above Wolf Creek, which tumbles over a small waterfall through a channel cut into volcanic rock. As the trail again nears the creek, a few lodgepole pines appear, indicating the transition between the lower and upper montane zones. Along the trailside, pretty pink saucers of white-veined

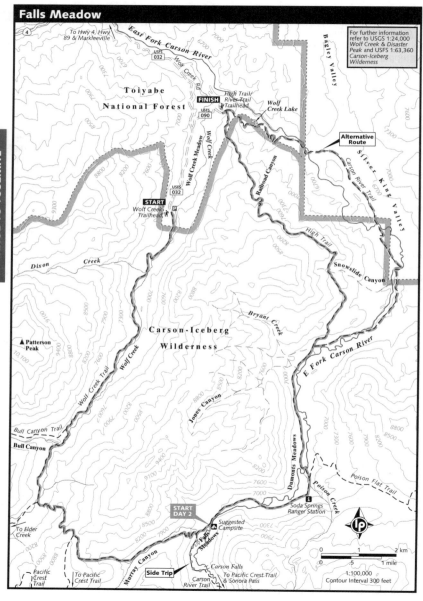

Falls Meadow

mallow and creamy white mariposa lily cups bloom in early summer.

Continuing through open country with good views of the peaks and ridges enclosing upper Wolf Creek, you near the creek and pass a spur trail once used by cattle ranchers that leads left to a meadow. Stay to the right, still heading south, as the trail ascends slightly, heading straight toward the prominent lava butte (9578ft) whose columnar face culminates in a level summit.

Continuing through lodgepole pine forest and bending back southward, the trail crosses a swath, cleared of tall trees by snow avalanches from the lava butte, and comes to a crossing of Wolf Creek, 20 minutes beyond the unsigned spur trail. Cross to the true right bank, staying along the stream near the willows, and avoid straying off into the meadow. Go along the creek for two minutes south, to a signed junction, 1.6mi from the Bull Canyon Trail junction. At this junction, which marks the end of the Wolf Creek Trail, a trail to **Elder Creek** turns right (southwest). Turn left (southeast) following the sign for **Murray Canyon.**

The trail to Murray Canyon heads directly east into forest away from the butte, and does not veer south into the meadow. Follow the signs pointing east for Murray Canyon and pass a side trail that goes off to the right. Soon enter a pine forest and pass through a gap in a barbed-wire fence. In a series of switchbacks up an open sagebrush-dotted slope, the trail ascends amid an early summer display of lupines, mariposa lilies, mallows, mule ears and paintbrushes. Some blazes on trees show the way.

As you ascend, the views grow ever more impressive of the lava butte and the **Highland Peak** massif, which, together with Patterson Peak, separate Wolf Creek from Noble Canyon to its west. After 30 minutes of well-graded switchbacks, the ascent eases and the trail nears a small creek. Large aspens southwest of the trail show carvings, called **arborglyphs** (see p141) that were likely made by late 19th century Basque shepherds.

Switchbacks resume up a juniper-dotted, wildflower-strewn slope, and you continue southeast 30 minutes to the **ridge top** (8800ft). The saddle, which is in a forest, is obscured from view from below. A signpost that reads 'Connects to PCT' marks the turnoff for the trail to **Golden Canyon**, one hour and 1.6mi from the Elder Creek junction. This signpost has been severely mutilated in an apparent attempt to obliterate it. The trail to Golden Canyon heads right (south), but head straight (southeast) and begin the descent into Murray Canyon.

As you descend, views open to the southeast of **Whitecliff Peak** (10,833ft) above the White Canyon of the East Fork Carson River. The flower-lined trail descends northeast for 1¼ hours through mixed lodgepole pines and red firs along aspen-lined Murray Creek, crossing back and forth across the creek and crossing numerous small side streams. In a short and level grassy area where the trail is overgrown, look for blazes on trees.

Finally, cross to the true right bank of Murray Canyon Creek and, two or three minutes beyond the crossing, pass through a gap in a fence. Here you get a good view of the lush grass and braided river in Falls Meadow below and the granite ridge at the meadow's head where Carson Falls tumble hidden from view. The trail descends on steep but well-graded switchbacks of pulverized granite 20 minutes to the forested valley floor and a signed junction with the 'Carson River Trail,' 3.1mi from the ridge top. Turn left (east) at the junction and immediately cross Murray Canyon Creek. Walk five minutes through open woodlands of large ponderosa pines to *campsites* (6900ft) under pines at the north end of **Falls Meadow**, along the East Fork Carson River's true left bank where the river narrows to pass a granite outcrop. Bears are very active in this area, and camping as far downvalley and downwind as possible is preferable to camping along Murray Canyon Creek, a route along which bears travel.

Side Trip: Carson Falls
45 minutes–1 hour, 2mi (3.2km), 300ft (90m) ascent, 300ft (90m) descent
From the campsite in Falls Meadow, walk five minutes upvalley, cross Murray Canyon

Creek and reach the signed junction of the trail descending from Murray Canyon. Turn left (southeast) at the junction and follow the obvious trail along the west side of Falls Meadow. After 20 minutes, cross a side stream. Once on the opposite bank, the trail goes 20ft on a raised constructed bed to keep it above high water.

The trail then zigzags five minutes up a granite rib and traverses east between two parallel ribs. At the end of these ribs, as you again near the East Fork Carson River, you reach a signpost where the Carson River Trail turns right, heading up-valley parallel to the river. From the signpost, turn left and head two minutes toward the river, which flows over cascades carved in the granite. The 80ft high **Carson Falls** (7200ft) are hidden in a gorge above the south end of Falls Meadow. You can clamber down the granite boulders along the river to catch a glimpse of the falls. Return downvalley via the Carson River Trail to your campsite.

Day 2: Falls Meadow to High Trail/River Trail Trailhead

5–6 hours, 11.3mi (18.2km), 1280ft (384m) ascent, 1620ft (486m) descent

It's an easy walk through open ponderosa-pine forest along the true left bank of the East Fork Carson River, 30 minutes to the first of two river crossings. Ford the river to its true right bank and walk through sagebrush east, across the western end of **Dumonts Meadow**. Then head into ponderosa-pine forest and continue 15 minutes to the Soda Springs ranger station (6800ft), 2.2mi from Falls Meadow. The ranger station is sporadically occupied during summer, and camping is not permitted. Mountain lions frequent this area in addition to bears.

Ten minutes farther, reach the signed junction with the Poison Flat Trail, which heads east (right). Go north (left), staying on the Carson River Trail, through the grassy, sagebrush-lined eastern end of Dumonts Meadow. In seven or eight minutes, come to the second river crossing and ford the river to its true left bank. Beyond this point, the trail leaves the beau-

tiful meadows along the broad and level river valley and heads into more forested areas away from the river.

Go north on a sandy trail through fragrant sage and purple lupines into an open, park-like, needle-carpeted ponderosa pine forest. As you leave the lush tall grasses of Dumonts Meadow, the river narrows to pass a granite outcrop and churns over rock through clear pools below. The trail traverses the hillside above the river, then passes a small meadow where the river meanders peacefully before it speeds up to pass another granite outcrop.

Cross **Jones Canyon Creek** and reach the signed junction (6560ft) with the High Trail, 2.5mi from Soda Springs and one hour from the second ford. Here the High Trail goes left (north) and the River Trail goes right (northeast). Both the High Trail and River Trail lead to the same trailhead. The High Trail is 0.8mi shorter than the alternative River Trail (see Alternative Day 2), but with 1000ft more ascent. The trade-off for lots of big views is no water along the trail and no campsites. In early season the High Trail is a better choice, because the numerous river crossings on the River Trail can be difficult. The creeks near this junction offer the last reliable water until reaching the finishing trailhead.

Follow the High Trail, which forks left and heads north, quickly crossing **Bryant Creek**. Ascending steadily, the trail commences a series of switchbacks that take you up the steep hillside amid granite boulders and outcrops, with good views south over Dumonts Meadow and the **East Fork Carson River**. The unnamed granite peak (8615ft) above and west of Soda Springs is prominent. Reach the top of the switchbacks beneath a granite cliff after 30 minutes.

The trail descends slightly, passing between two higher points, and heads north, away from a dry streambed which flows northeast. The trail then bends northwest and begins a steady gradual ascent, traversing up and around the folds in the ridges that descend from the west. The trail alternates between the forested northern aspect and the manzanita shrub-covered southern aspect of these folds, with views over **Silver King Valley** to the east. Mountain mahogany and manzanita line the slopes.

Passing the dry gully of **Snowslide Canyon**, the trail rises up to a spur with excellent views of Silver King Valley. Turning east, the trail briefly ascends the spur's crest before heading northwest through forest to a juniper-crowned **knoll** (7840ft), with views north of **Hawkins Peak** and **Bagley Valley** with **Heenan Lake** at its head. The knoll marks the highest point along the High Trail, two hours after leaving the East Fork Carson River. A piece of Hwy 89 is visible above the far shore of Heenan Lake. In the distance to the north are Freel Peak and the Carson Range.

Descend through forest heading west and cross a small stream flowing over mossy rock where yellow seep-spring mon-keyflowers bloom. The trail continues down switchbacks and passes through aspens above Railroad Canyon Meadow, 45 minutes below the knoll. Descending north another 45 minutes along a ridge through forest, you drop down a rocky open area to the signed junction of the High Trail with the River Trail, 6.6mi from where they split. Turn left (southeast), immediately pass the Carson-Iceberg Wilderness boundary sign and reach the parking area at the trailhead (6560ft) in three minutes.

Alternative Route: Falls Meadow to High Trail/River Trail Trailhead

Alternatively, follow the River Trail down the East Fork Carson River to the trailhead. The River Trail is a better option in late season, when water in the river is low and easy to cross.

Arborglyphs

The bark of aspens is the canvas and the tip of a pocketknife the brush. The lone Basque sheep-herder who roamed the mountains of the American West is the artist. In Europe, the Basque were

whalers and sailors, accomplished at navigation. When they joined the immigration to the American West during the gold rush in the mid-19th century, they were fortune seekers like everyone else. By the turn of the 20th century, however, the Basques had become synonymous with sheepherding.

To while away their time in the mountains, the sheep-herders carved their story onto tree trunks. The history of who the shepherds were and when and where they grazed their livestock was documented only in remote and isolated aspen groves in 10 western states. Much of the writing is in the Basque language, Euskara, but it is the intimate pictures that reveal details about their lives. These arborglyphs include self-portraits as well as whim-sical and erotic images.

An aspen's life spans fewer than 100 years, so these carvings are fast disappearing. To see one in the Sierra is a truly unique experience. *Speaking Through the Aspens: Basque Tree Carvings in California and Nevada,* by Jose

Mallea-Olaetxe, PhD, presents a passionate portrayal of this little known part of Basque history. Dr Mallea, who can be contacted at the University of Nevada at Reno (e mallea@scs.unr.edu), guides trips to view carvings.

Alternative Day 2: Falls Meadow to High Trail/River Trail Trailhead

6–7 hours, 12.1mi (19.5km), 240ft (72m) ascent, 580ft (174m) descent

See Day 2, p140, for a description of the hike from Falls Meadow to the junction of the High Trail and River Trail, 4.7mi from Falls Meadow. Head right (northeast), staying on the River Trail 7.4mi to the trailhead. The River Trail has as many as five additional fords of the Carson River between this junction and the trailhead, for a total of seven fords from Falls Meadow. The River Trail is 0.8mi longer than the High Trail, with 1000ft less ascent. Beyond Grays Crossing, near the lowest point (6320ft) along the River Trail, start a short final ascent to the trailhead (6560ft).

St Marys Pass

Duration	1–1½ hours
Distance	2.6mi (4.2km)
Standard	easy
Start/Finish	St Marys Pass Trailhead
Public Transport	no

Summary An outstanding short day hike to St Marys Pass offers inspirational views and beautiful wildflowers, with an opportunity for even more fabulous side trips.

St Marys Pass (10,400ft), on the Sierra Crest, lies just 1.3mi north of and 950ft above Hwy 108 on the southern boundary of Carson-Iceberg Wilderness. With views not only of the wilderness to the north, but of nearby Leavitt Peak and the more distant northern Yosemite high country to the south, the pass is one of the Sierra Nevada's most scenic. Wildflowers only add to your enjoyment. From the pass, you can hike to the top of nearby Sonora Peak (11,459ft) for even more views, or drop down into the beautiful Clark Fork Meadow to spend the night in a granite-encircled meadow.

PLANNING
When to Hike

The hiking season for St Marys Pass is from July to September.

Maps

The USGS 1:24,000 *Sonora Pass* quadrangle covers the hike, as do the USFS 1:63,360 *Carson-Iceberg Wilderness* and 1:63,360 *Stanislaus National Forest* maps.

Permits & Regulations

A permit is not required for a day hike, but a free wilderness permit is required for any overnight trip. Go to the Summit ranger station (☎ 209-965-3434) at the Pinecrest Lake turnoff on Hwy 108, 29mi east of Sonora, or the Brightman ranger station, also on Hwy 108, 2.7mi west of the Clark Fork 'Y' intersection. Nearby campgrounds along Hwy 108 are often full. Dispersed camping is allowed and even encouraged in this area; some good campsites are close to the trailhead.

GETTING TO/FROM THE HIKE

A small sign on the north side of Hwy 108 marks the St Marys Pass Trailhead, 0.9mi northwest of Sonora Pass, 73mi east of Sonora and 8.2mi east of Kennedy Meadow. It's also 16.3mi from the US 395/Hwy 108 intersection 17mi northwest of Bridgeport (see Access Towns, p148). Turn north into a small unpaved parking area (9450ft).

THE HIKE

From the trailhead sign at the north end of the parking area (9450ft), the well-worn trail heads north. Initially, it parallels a stream flowing in a slight ravine 200ft to the east, but soon heads away from the gurgling stream, rising through mixed lodgepole and whitebark pines to pass a small Carson-Iceberg Wilderness information sign five minutes from the trailhead.

Leaving the trees behind, the trail attains an open area atop a gentle low ridge, which hosts a garden of early summer wildflowers; purple lupines, red paintbrushes, yellow mule ears and golden sneezeweed sunflowers. Ascending along this low ridge, bear north-northwest, working upward toward a larger spur ridge that descends southsouthwest from **Sonora Peak.**

After 10 minutes, the trail begins to follow a tiny stream, whose source is a willow-enshrouded spring five minutes ahead. The trail crosses the trickle, lined with lovely clusters of bright yellow seep-spring monkeyflowers and, turning briefly west, crosses another trickling spring before resuming its northward ascending course.

Entering a wide, shallow ravine that descends from the pass, which is visible ahead, the trail crosses a small side stream and makes a brief, steep ascent directly to the pass. This saddle on a ridge that descends west from Sonora Peak has become known as **St Marys Pass** (10,400ft), and is marked by a small Carson-Iceberg Wilderness boundary sign and a tall orange-tipped metal pole that also carries a Carson-Iceberg Wilderness sign. The original St Marys Pass actually lies west, along the ridge on the other side of the small rock outcrop and hill adjacent to where the trail crosses the saddle. No existing trail crosses the original St Marys Pass, which for a few brief years beginning in 1862 was the principal route through the Sonora Pass area. The approximate original location of St Marys Pass is shown by the placement of the pass name on the USGS 1:24,000 *Sonora Pass* quadrangle.

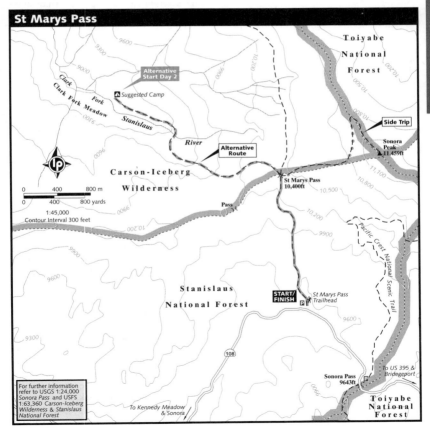

Enjoy the views to the north of Carson-Iceberg Wilderness. The distinct cone of **Stanislaus Peak** (11,233ft) rises prominently to the north-northeast. Sonora Peak is near, just east of and above the pass. To the south is a gray mass, **Leavitt Peak** (11,569ft), the highest Sierra summit north of Yosemite, with year-round snowfields on its northern flanks. Turn and retrace your steps in 30 minutes to the parking area. The descent is perhaps the most enjoyable part of the hike, as you stroll easily through wildflowers enjoying the constant views of the rugged, snowy Leavitt Peak massif and ridges.

Side Trip: Sonora Peak
1½ hours, 1.8mi (2.9km), 1059ft (318m) ascent, 1059ft (318m) descent
St Marys Pass lies on a western ridge of Sonora Peak (11,459ft). From the pass, a side trip to the summit of Sonora Peak is possible. It's 0.9mi one way. From St Marys Pass, a small trail turns east and follows the ridgeline that descends from Sonora Peak. The trail fades as you go east along the ridge until the ridge steepens and it becomes easier to traverse north-northeast to a slight saddle on the ridge that descends northwest from Sonora Peak. From the slight saddle, follow the ridgeline to the summit. Summit views stretch from the peaks south of Lake Tahoe to those along the southern boundary of Yosemite. To the north, you peer directly into the deep canyon of the **East Fork Carson River**. Return via the same route to St Marys Pass.

Alternative Route: Clark Fork Meadow
A mildly adventurous overnight trip goes from St Marys Pass via a frequented but cross-country route to beautiful Clark Fork Meadow, situated in a granite basin just 3.7mi from the St Marys Pass Trailhead.

Alternative Day 1: St Marys Pass to Clark Fork Meadow
2 hours, 2.4mi (3.9km), 950ft (285m) ascent, 1340ft (402m) descent
From the saddle where the trail crosses St Marys Pass, 1.3mi from the trailhead, do not

continue on the trail that heads north toward prominent **Stanislaus Peak**. Instead, cross the pass and turn immediately west. Contour down and across a gravelly slope, where snow often lingers until August, for five minutes to a wooden signpost in a level area north of the ridgeline of the pass and south of a yellowish granite outcrop. On the signpost are the words, one word on each side 'Are you here?' From this curious signpost, head southwest, following the descending snowmelt trickle into a concentration of yellow granite boulders and scattered whitebark pines.

Descending westward, you find small stone cairns that mark the route, and within 15 minutes from the signpost, green Clark Fork Meadow is visible below. Follow the incipient Clark Fork Stanislaus River from its headwaters down to the meadow, staying on the true left (south) bank of the ever-growing stream. You encounter a faint trail as you descend. Just before reaching the meadow the route crosses the stream to its true right bank above a small cascade. You can sleep anywhere along the northwest side of lovely granite-walled **Clark Fork Meadow** (9060ft), 2.4mi below St Marys Pass.

Alternative Day 2: Clark Fork Meadow to St Marys Pass Trailhead
2½–3 hours, 3.7mi (22km), 1340ft (402m) ascent, 950ft (285m) descent
Take the faint trail up along the creek, eventually following small stone cairns as you retrace your steps to the wooden signpost and St Marys Pass. From the pass, follow the good trail back to the trailhead parking area.

Emigrant Wilderness

The high country along the western side of the Sierra Crest south of Hwy 108 and north of Yosemite National Park forms Emigrant Wilderness, which is within Stanislaus National Forest. With rugged volcanic peaks and ridges in its northern portion and granite ridges with lakes and meadows in its southern part, it is a dramatic and varied landscape of great beauty. Its rivers flow into the Stanislaus and Tuolumne Rivers, and Leavitt Peak (11,569ft), the highest peak, rises to the south of Sonora Pass. Its many lakes and 185mi of hiking trails combine to make it a popular area that is the gateway to northwestern Yosemite National Park.

Brown Bear & Bond Passes

Duration	6 days
Distance	45.4mi (73.1km)
Standard	moderate
Start/Finish	Kennedy Meadow
Public Transport	no

Summary Following streams through big meadows, this pioneer route traverses Emigrant Wilderness across two easy passes, offering good access to northern Yosemite National Park from the western Sierra.

Along the western slopes of the central Sierra, the gentle terrain of Emigrant Wilderness, which has been shaped by glaciers and volcanoes, offers the easiest access to northern Yosemite National Park. Following a high segment of the Tahoe-Yosemite Trail (between 6400ft and 9700ft), this hike visits expansive meadows and fine fishing lakes and also crosses two gentle passes to meet the PCT just inside the national park.

HISTORY

In 1852, the Clark-Skidmore party, traveling on the West Walker route, were the first non-natives to cross Emigrant Pass. More parties crossed in 1853, but the route was soon abandoned as too difficult. The Kennedy brothers established Kennedy Meadows Resort in 1886, and the area has focused on recreation ever since. It first received protection as Emigrant Basin Primitive Area in 1931 and became a wilderness area in 1975.

PLANNING
When to Hike

The hiking season is from mid-June to September.

Maps

The USGS 1:24,000 *Sonora Pass, Emigrant Lake* and *Tower Peak* quadrangles cover the hike, as does the USFS 1:63,360 *Emigrant Wilderness* map, which includes northwestern Yosemite.

Permits & Regulations

A free wilderness permit is required for this hike. Stanislaus National Forest issues wilderness permits for Emigrant Wilderness. Go to the Summit ranger station (☎ 209-965-3434) at the Pinecrest Lake turnoff on Hwy 108, 29mi east of Sonora, or the Brightman ranger station, also on Hwy 108, 2.7mi west of the Clark Fork 'Y' intersection.

Campgrounds along Hwy 108 are often full. Dispersed camping is allowed and even encouraged near Sonora Pass. Camping is only allowed in designated campgrounds along Kennedy Meadow Rd.

GETTING TO/FROM THE HIKE

Kennedy Meadow Rd is off Hwy 108, 9.5mi west of Sonora Pass and 25.7mi east of Pinecrest.

Turn south onto Kennedy Meadow Rd and go 0.7mi, following the signs to the Kennedy Meadow Trailhead parking lot. The road continues almost a mile beyond the parking lot to the private Kennedy Meadows Resort, which has a small store and public showers, and the actual trailhead. The trail from the parking lot to the resort is signed as being 1½mi long. You may want to first drive to the end of the road, drop your gear, and then return to park your vehicle.

THE HIKE
Day 1: Kennedy Meadow to Sheep Camp

6–7 hours, 8.5mi (13.7km), 2400ft (720m) ascent

From the gated trailhead (6400ft) on the Middle Fork Stanislaus River, the route

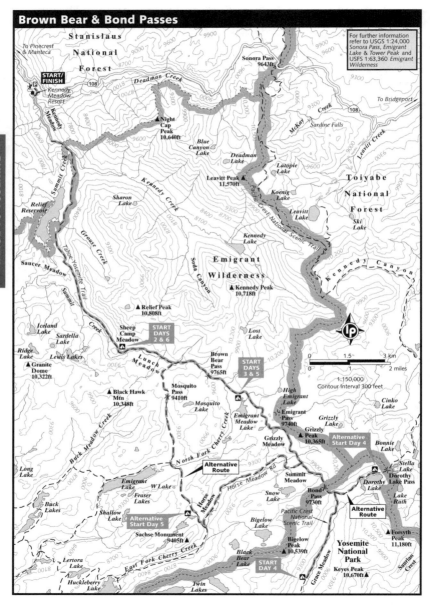

TAHOE TO YOSEMITE

Brown Bear & Bond Passes

For further information refer to USGS 1:24,000 *Sonora Pass, Emigrant Lake & Tower Peak* and USFS 1:63,360 *Emigrant Wilderness*

follows the Huckleberry Trail on a wide track south over a saddle to skirt the east side of Kennedy Meadow and enter Emigrant Wilderness. It crosses the Stanislaus and follows the river's south bank to cross Summit Creek. Ascending past the Kennedy Lake Trail junction, it traverses above the east side of Relief Reservoir and crosses Grouse Creek.

Ascending steadily, the trail rises southeast, passing an early emigrant's grave in Saucer Meadow to soon meet Summit Creek. Multicolored volcanic Relief Peak (10,808ft) looms to the north as the trail crosses a forested ridge above a bend in the creek to reach *campsites* along Summit Creek in the meadow known as Sheep Camp (8800ft).

Day 2: Sheep Camp to Emigrant Meadow Lake
4–5 hours, 7.5mi (12.1km), 1000ft (300m) ascent, 400ft (120m) descent
The trail follows Summit Creek west through Lunch Meadow, at the end of which is a junction with a trail that heads south to Emigrant Lake (see Alternative Days 4–6, below). Continuing west, the trail rises to **Brown Bear Pass** (9765ft), the watershed between the Stanislaus and Tuolumne Rivers, and descends to expansive Emigrant Meadow and Emigrant Meadow Lake (9400ft), just west of Emigrant Pass, which was a mid-19th century pioneer route. *Campsites* lie along the lake's west shore.

Day 3: Emigrant Meadow Lake to Grace Meadow
3–5 hours, 6.7mi (10.8km), 600ft (180m) ascent, 1280ft (384m) descent
The trail rises 300ft over a ridge to Grizzly Meadow and its two small lakes, then dips through the headwaters of East Fork Cherry Creek, passing the Horse Meadow road to Maxwell Lake (see Alternative Days 4–6, below) and arriving at Summit Meadow. Rising 300ft to gentle **Bond Pass** (9730ft), the boundary of Yosemite National Park, the trail descends to meet the PCT (9400ft). Hikers can turn north (left) to reach *campsites* along the west shore of beautiful Dorothy Lake (9400ft) after 0.9mi, or south (right) to continue 2.3mi to

peaceful Grace Meadow (8720ft), with *campsites* along Fall Creek.

Days 4–6: Grace Meadow to Kennedy Meadow
3 days, 22.7mi (36.6km)
Return along the same trails to Kennedy Meadow.

Alternative Days 4–6: Grace Meadow to Kennedy Meadow
3 days, 24.7mi (39.8km)
Alternatively, recross Bond Pass to Summit Meadow and turn south on the wide Horse Meadow road along the East Fork Cherry Creek 5mi to fine *campsites* on the north shore of Maxwell Lake (8700ft), beneath distinctive granite Sachse Monument (9405ft). Then return, heading north, 6mi via Emigrant Lake and **Mosquito Pass** (9410ft) to *Sheep Camp*, and back to Kennedy Meadow.

Hoover Wilderness

Accessible from Hwy 108, US 395 and Hwy 120, Hoover Wilderness lies east of the Sierra Crest along the northeastern boundary of Yosemite, within Inyo and Toiyabe National Forests. Encompassing the eastern escarpment of the Sierra Nevada, its colorful volcanic peaks abut the glacier-carved granite canyons of northeastern Yosemite. It is a wilderness of dramatic transitions, with numerous lakes and aspen-lined streams. Justifiably popular, it still receives far less visitation than adjacent areas within Yosemite. Many of its peaks rise above 12,000ft, with massive Dunderberg (12,374ft) the highest.

PLANNING
Permits & Regulations
A free wilderness permit is required for all overnight hikes in Toiyabe National Forest, which has jurisdiction over Hoover Wilderness. A permit is not required for day hikes. The Hoover Wilderness website, at W www .fs.fed.us/htnf/hoover.htm, has trail and permit information. The Bridgeport ranger station (☎ 760-932-7070), on the east side of US 395 0.6mi south of town, issues permits

for Hoover Wilderness. A quota system is in effect on most trails the last Friday in June to September 15. Reservations are accepted for 50% of the available permits and only by mail (HCR 1000, Bridgeport, CA 93517), with a $3 reservation fee per person, from March 1 to three weeks prior to the entry date. The remainder of the permits are available on a walk-in first-come, first-served basis. Permits by advance reservations are mailed. Reservations are recommended in July and August. From September 16 to the last Thursday in June, self-issuing permits are available at the Bridgeport ranger station.

ACCESS TOWNS & FACILITIES
Bridgeport

Toiyabe National Forest's Bridgeport ranger station (☎ 760-932-7070), on the east side of US 395 0.6mi south of town, issues wilderness permits, provides trail information and sells books and maps (by mail order to HCR 1000, Bridgeport, CA 93517).

Contact the Bridgeport chamber of commerce (☎ 760-932-7500) or visit W www .bridgeportcalifornia.com. On Main St (US 395) through town there are businesses. Zig's Sporting Goods (☎ 760-932-7331), 323 Main St, sells gear. Buy groceries at the General Store Market and Busters Market.

Silver Maple Inn (☎ 760-932-7383, 310 Main St) has friendly owners and a pleasant, shaded garden ($60/65 singles/doubles). *The Cain House Bed & Breakfast (☎ 760-932-7040, 800-433-2246, e cainhouse@qnet.com, W www.cainhouse.com),* run by and next to the Silver Maple Inn, has individually decorated rooms from $80 to $120. *Bridgeport Inn (☎ 760-932-7380, fax 932-1160, W www .thebridgeportinn.com),* on Main St, has older rooms with shared bath, no TV or telephone, for $59. Motel rooms in back cost $79 and suites above the restaurant cost $99.

The Barn, with patio tables, is the best bet for hungry hikers in search of burritos, tacos, burgers and milkshakes. *Rhinos Bar & Grille* is the choice for beer and pizza.

Bridgeport (6465ft), the largest town along the 125mi stretch of US 395 between Carson City and Mammoth Lakes, is 25mi north of Lee Vining and 72mi south of Carson City.

Inyo Mono Transit (☎ 800-922-1930) operates one round-trip Bridgeport-Bishop bus ($6, 3 hours), departing from Bridgeport at 8am on Monday and Wednesday.

Lee Vining

The Mono Lake Committee Information Center & Bookstore (☎ 760-647-6629, W www.leevining.com), on US 395 at Third St, has helpful staff. The Mono Basin National Forest Scenic Area visitor center (☎ 760-647-3044), on US 395, sells maps, rents bear-resistant containers ($3 per day) and issues free permits for Inyo National Forest.

The brightly red-painted Lee Vining Market sells groceries. Bell's Sporting Goods (☎ 760-647-6406), across the street, sells gear.

El Mono Motel & Latte Da Coffee Cafe (☎ 760-647-6310), on US 395 at Third St, has rooms without bathroom for $49 and ones with for $65. *Murphey's Motel (☎ 760-647-6316, 800-334-6316, e info@murpheysyosemite.com, W www.murpheysyosemite.com),* at the north end of town, costs $78/93 for singles/doubles.

Nicely's Restaurant, on US 395 at Fourth St, is a family-style restaurant. Next door is *Bodie Mike's*, a popular spot for pizza.

Lee Vining (6780ft) straddles US 395 a half-mile north of its junction with Hwy 120, which leads to Yosemite National Park. Lee Vining is 25mi south of Bridgeport and 26mi north of the US 395 Mammoth Lakes exit.

Sawtooth Ridge

Duration	6 days
Distance	51mi (82.1km)
Standard	moderate-hard
Start/Finish	Upper Twin Lake
Nearest Facilities	Annett's Mono Village
Public Transport	no

Summary This loop follows forested rivers through spectacular steep-walled granite canyons of remote northern Yosemite National Park, crossing three passes as it swings around the magnificent towers of Sawtooth Ridge.

The solid white granite pinnacles and arêtes of Sawtooth Ridge, one of the Sierra's most interesting climbing areas, range from 11,400ft to 12,281ft and form the most dramatic portion of Yosemite National Park's northeastern boundary. With four small glaciers under the northeast face, the rocky summits rise abruptly more than 5000ft only 3mi from Twin Lakes. Passing through Hoover Wilderness into the park, this rewarding hike skirts the ridge, following a segment of the PCT before returning via incomparable Matterhorn Canyon and isolated, tranquil Upper Piute Creek. Crossing three passes and two minor saddles, this demanding route explores the exquisite canyons and relatively unvisited superb high country of northern Yosemite.

PLANNING
When to Hike
The hiking season is from July to mid-September.

Maps
The USGS 1:24,000 *Twin Lakes, Dunderberg Peak, Buckeye Ridge* and *Matterhorn Peak* quadrangles cover the hike. The USFS 1:63,360 *Hoover Wilderness* map covers the trail outside the national park.

Permits & Regulations
A free wilderness permit is required (see Planning, p147). Campfires are prohibited above 9000ft in Hoover Wilderness and above 9600ft in Yosemite National Park.

NEAREST FACILITIES
Annett's Mono Village
Annett's Mono Village (☎ *760-932-7071, fax 932-7468,* W *www.monovillage.com),* a resort at the northwestern end of Upper Twin Lake, has a grocery store, gas station, ATM, shower and laundry facilities, a cafe and bar, a campground ($11 for one or two people), cabins (starting at $65) and motel rooms ($50 singles or doubles). To get to Annett's Mono Village (7000ft) from the western end of Bridgeport, turn south onto Twin Lakes Rd and follow it 14mi southwest to its end. Five desirable USFS *campgrounds* (ranging from $9 to $10) are along Twin Lakes Rd and at Lower Twin Lake.

GETTING TO/FROM THE HIKE
The only parking area is on private land at Annett's Mono Village. Drive to the signed 'gate' at the campground to register your vehicle and pay the $5 fee, which allows you to park for any length of time.

The signed 'Backpackers Parking' area is at the far end of the marina in a scenic lakeside lot. Walk back to the gate and through the campground, following an unpaved road a short distance to the signed Barney Lake Trailhead.

THE HIKE
Day 1: Upper Twin Lake to Peeler Lake
6–7 hours, 8mi (12.9km), 2400ft (720m) ascent

From the trailhead (7092ft), walk a short distance west on a dirt road, then turn right onto the actual trail. Passing amid fragrant Jeffrey pines, with cottonwoods and aspens near **Robinson Creek**, the trail ascends gently, crossing several small streams. Continuing up dry, open slopes, with good views of **Victoria** and **Hunewill Peaks,** you enter Hoover Wilderness north of Little Slide Canyon, 2.5mi from the trailhead. The trail brings you close to fir-shaded Robinson Creek, then launches into a series of well-graded switchbacks.

Turning southwest, the trail crosses a stream that descends from the slopes of Hunewill Peak and levels out as it nears warm and popular **Barney Lake**, 1.4mi from the wilderness boundary. Heading south over talus above the lake's west shore, the trail continues past its beaver-dammed inlet. Continuing south, the trail descends to cross Robinson Creek to its true right (east) bank, then ascends along the creek through red-fir forest and recrosses to its west bank.

Crossing the stream from **Peeler Lake** just above its confluence with Robinson Creek, the trail ascends up two long sets of steep switchbacks to reach a junction with the trail to **Crown Lake**. Bear right, continuing along Peeler Creek, until you make a short ascent to large **Peeler Lake** (9500ft) with *campsites* on its west and north shores.

TAHOE TO YOSEMITE

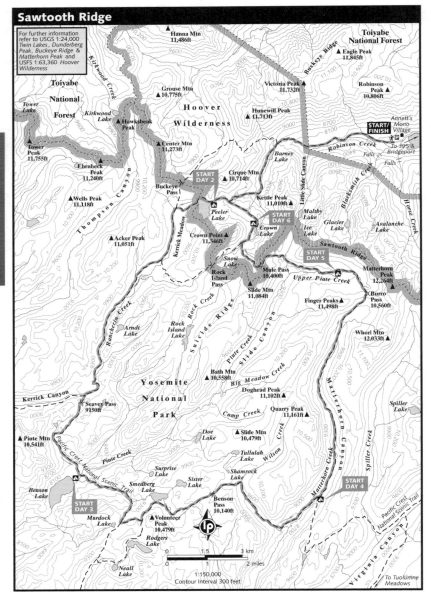

Sawtooth Ridge

For further information refer to USGS 1:24,000 *Twin Lakes, Dunderberg Peak, Buckeye Ridge & Matterhorn Peak* and USFS 1:63,360 *Hoover Wilderness*

Toiyabe National Forest

▲ Hanna Mtn 11,486ft

▲ Eagle Peak 11,845ft

▲ Robinson Peak 10,806ft

Buckeye Ridge

Kirkwood Creek

Tower Lake

Toiyabe National Forest

Kirkwood Lake

▲ Grouse Mtn 10,775ft

H o o v e r

W i l d e r n e s s

▲ Victoria Peak 11,732ft

▲ Hunewill Peak 11,713ft

START/FINISH Annett's Mono Village

To 395 & Bridgeport

Robinson Creek

Falls

Falls

Hawksbeak Peak

▲ Center Mtn 11,273ft

Barney Lake

Little Slide Canyon

Blacksmith Creek

Horse Creek

Tower Peak 11,755ft

▲ Ehrnbeck Peak 11,240ft

START DAY 2

▲ Cirque Mtn 10,714ft

Buckeye Pass

Kettle Peak 11,010ft ▲

START DAY 6

Maltby Lake

Glacier Lake

Avalanche Lake

▲ Wells Peak 11,118ft

Thompson Canyon

Peeler Lake

Crown Lake

Ice Lake

▲ Acker Peak 11,051ft

Kerrick Meadow

Crown Point ▲ 11,346ft

Snow Lake

START DAY 5

Sawtooth Ridge

Matterhorn Peak 12,264ft ▲

Rock Island Pass

Mule Pass 10,400ft

Upper Piute Creek

▲ Burro Pass 10,560ft

Rancheria Creek

Rock Creek

Slide Mtn 11,084ft

Finger Peaks ▲ 11,498ft

Whorl Mtn 12,033ft ▲

Arndt Lake

Rock Island Lake

Suicide Ridge

Piute Creek

Slide Canyon

Bath Mtn ▲ 10,558ft

Big Meadow Creek

Matterhorn Canyon

Y o s e m i t e

Doghead Peak 11,102ft ▲

Spiller Lake

Kerrick Canyon

N a t i o n a l

Camp Creek

Quarry Peak 11,161ft ▲

Seavey Pass 9150ft

P a r k

Doe Lake

▲ Slide Mtn 10,479ft

Spiller Creek

▲ Piute Mtn 10,541ft

Pacific Crest National Scenic Trail

Piute Creek

Tullulah Lake

Wilson Creek

Surprise Lake

Shamrock Lake

START DAY 4

Benson Lake

Smedberg Lake

Sister Lake

START DAY 3

Mardock Lake

▲ Volunteer Peak 10,479ft

Benson Pass 10,140ft

Pacific Crest National Scenic Trail

Rodgers Lake

LP

0   1.5   3 km

0   1   2 miles

Neall Lake

1:150,000
Contour Interval 300 feet

Virginia Canyon

To Tuolumne Meadows

Day 2: Peeler Lake to Benson Lake

6–7 hours, 10mi (16.1km), 250ft (75m) ascent, 2150ft (645m) descent

Peeler Lake sits on a ridge crest, and its waters flow both east and west. The trail goes around the lake's north end and enters Yosemite National Park. Descending along the western outlet of Peeler Lake into **Kerrick Meadow**, the trail crosses the headwaters of Rancheria Creek and meets the trail coming from Buckeye Pass. Turning left onto this trail, you descend along the west side of Kerrick Meadow past the junction with the trail to Rock Island Pass. Continue down Rancheria Creek through canyon and meadow to a junction with the PCT (8910ft), 6.5mi from Peeler Lake. Turning left onto the well-traveled PCT, the trail then rises out of Kerrick Canyon 0.6mi to granite **Seavey Pass** (9150ft). It then makes a rather rocky descent 2.5mi to the valley floor and the side trail that leads another 0.3mi to enormous blue **Benson Lake** (7590ft), with its popular sandy beach and *campsites* along its east shore.

Day 3: Benson Lake to Matterhorn Canyon

7–8 hours, 10.6mi (17.1km), 2550ft (675m) ascent, 1650ft (495m) descent

Returning 0.3mi to the PCT and turning right, the trail rises along a stream and passes two side trails as it runs beneath the west face of Volunteer Peak to reach Smedberg Lake (9220ft) in 3.9mi. It is another 2.2mi ascent to **Benson Pass** (10,140ft). Descending from the pass, the trail meets Wilson Creek and follows it down 4.2mi to the forested **Matterhorn Canyon** (8490ft), where the trail fords Matterhorn Creek to reach well-used creek-side *campsites*.

Day 4: Matterhorn Canyon to Upper Piute Creek

6–7 hours, 8.5mi (13.7km), 2070ft (621m) ascent, 1000ft (300m) descent

On the east side of Matterhorn Creek, the trail turns left, leaving the PCT, and heads up the granite-walled canyon. Crossing the creek three times, it finally runs along the west side to enter spectacular upper cirque meadows beneath Finger Peaks (11,498ft), Whorl Mountain (12,033ft) and Matterhorn Peak (12,264ft).

Traversing up, the trail makes final switchbacks to **Burro Pass** (10,560ft) 6.2mi up into the canyon, with Sawtooth Ridge rising jagged to the north. The trail descends past some fine granite climbing walls 2.3mi into the forest along **Upper Piute Creek** (9600ft), where deer often wander through *campsites*.

Day 5: Upper Piute Creek to Crown Lake

4–5 hours, 6mi (9.7km), 800ft (240m) ascent, 900ft (270m) descent

The trail traverses west through forest and crosses a side stream from the north, where you have views downvalley of the massive slide that gave Slide Canyon its name. It works up open slopes to reach **Mule Pass** (10,400ft), which marks the boundary of Yosemite National Park. The trail descends a series of benches, where snow often lingers beneath Slide Mountain (11,084ft). Crossing the stream from Snow Lake and passing the trail to Rock Island Pass, the route zigzags down to the west side of **Crown Lake** (9500ft) beneath Crown Point (11,346ft), with *campsites* along its outlet.

Day 6: Crown Lake to Upper Twin Lake

4–5 hours, 8mi (12.9km), 2400ft (720m) descent

The trail crosses the outlet and descends switchbacks along the creek, fording it above Robinson Lakes. Following along the west shore of the larger upper lake, the trail passes between the two Robinson Lakes and runs along the north shore of the smaller, shallow lower lake. The trail makes a short ascent over a saddle, and 1.5mi from Crown Lake, meets the trail to Peeler Lake. Turn right and descend, retracing your steps to Barney Lake and along Robinson Creek to the trailhead.

East Lake

Duration	4 hours
Distance	8mi (12.9km)
Standard	easy-moderate
Start/Finish	Green Creek Trailhead
Public Transport	no

Summary The pleasant wildflower- and aspen-lined trail to beautiful East Lake brings hikers to one of the most colorful settings in the eastern Sierra.

The blue depths of large and lovely East Lake, beneath the red and ochre summits of Gabbro, Page and Epidote Peaks, is one of the Sierra's most vivid settings. The verdant valley of Green Creek, which flows from the lake, offers the additional pleasure of wildflowers along a splashing stream. Together, these elements all make this a delightful day hike or an easy overnight trip into Hoover Wilderness near the northeast boundary of Yosemite National Park. The hike has 1460ft of ascent and an equal descent along a broad and well-defined trail.

PLANNING
When to Hike
The hiking season is from mid-June to October. Along Green Creek, wildflowers bloom profusely in midsummer, and in the autumn, aspens display superb fall colors.

Maps
The USGS 1:24,000 *Dunderberg Peak* quadrangle covers this hike, as does the USFS 1:63,360 *Hoover Wilderness* map.

Permits & Regulations
A permit is not required for this day hike. A free wilderness permit is required for any overnight trip (see Planning, p147). Campfires are prohibited above 9000ft.

GETTING TO/FROM THE HIKE
From Bridgeport, head 3.7mi south on US 395 to the well-signed Green Creek Rd (USFS Rd 142). Allow 20 to 30 minutes to follow this unpaved road southwest 8.4mi to the Green Creek Trailhead (8000ft).

Most hikers spend the night near the trailhead before starting a hike. The USFS *Green Creek Campground* ($10) is at the end of the road, 0.2mi beyond the trailhead. The campground only has 10 sites and is often full. When it's full, opt for any of the numerous dispersed camping options along the road. When staying in the campground, it's shorter to go to the locked gate at site 5 and walk along the private road to join the trail than to go back downvalley to the trailhead.

THE HIKE
The trail heads southwest through ponderosa pines from the trailhead (8000ft), skirting Green Creek Campground. After 12 minutes, it meets the private unpaved road that comes from the campground, and after another five minutes passes the last privately held property along the road. Soon after, the road narrows to trail width and crosses a small creek. Continuing west and paralleling **Green Creek**, the sandy trail passes numerous large western junipers and crosses a low granite rib, from where you have good views of the brownish-red rock peaks above the valley.

Never far from tumbling Green Creek, the trail makes a series of short switchbacks up a granite rib and continues rising past more junipers and through lovely aspen groves. Forty-five minutes from the trailhead, you pass the Hoover Wilderness boundary sign, near to the confluence of East Fork and West Fork Green Creeks. The trail follows along the true left bank of **West Fork Green Creek**, through aspen groves where leopard lilies,

Wend your way through aspen groves on the hike to East Lake.

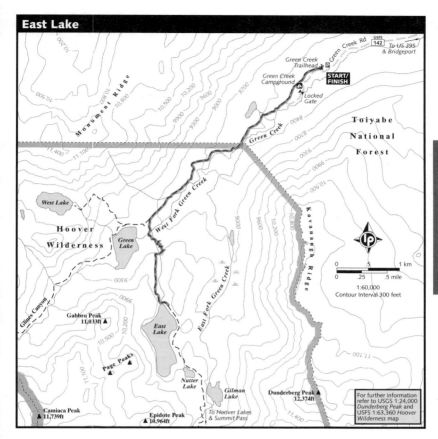

East Lake

rein orchids, shooting stars and monkeyflowers bloom in midsummer. In more open areas, paintbrushes and lupines brighten the trail.

The trail ascends an open, manzanita-dotted slope onto a spur, and the dark peaks ahead provide dramatic contrast to the green valley. About 1½ hours (2.5mi) from the trailhead, you come to a signed junction (8920ft). The right fork leads north to West Lake and the left fork leads south to East Lake. Green Lake can be reached by either trail. Turning left, head south and soon ford the large outlet of Green Lake. Later in the season, it is

possible to cross via a log. Attractive *campsites* are near the trail, along the northeast shore of large Green Lake. The area along the lakeshore is closed to camping.

Head up and away from the lake on forested switchbacks for 10 minutes and cross West Fork Green Creek to its true right bank. Walk up along the pretty stream, where tall lupines and yellow-throated bright pink monkeyflowers bloom profusely. After 10 minutes, cross the stream again to its true left bank. Heading up through mostly lodgepole pine forest with the occasional red fir, the trail levels off and continues south.

One minute after crossing its outlet, arrive at the north end of East Lake (9460ft), 1.5mi from Green Lake. The trail hugs the eastern shore of this large and lovely lake, with fabulous views out over its deep blue waters of the trio of red and ochre peaks rising above its western shore; **Epidote Peak** (10,964ft), **Page Peaks** (10,920ft) and northernmost **Gabbro Peak** (11,033ft) named for its igneous rock. *Campsites* are along the northern shore near the outlet and halfway along the eastern shore, east of a small granite-enclosed pond. Enjoy the views and return the same way to the trailhead.

Summit & Virginia Passes

Duration	2 days
Distance	18.3mi (29.4km)
Standard	moderate-hard
Start/Finish	Green Creek Trailhead
Public Transport	no

Summary Gorgeous lakes, dramatic peaks, wildflowers galore, two pass crossings and the incomparable charm of upper Virginia Canyon make this a superbly rewarding and satisfying loop hike for those seeking something slightly off the beaten path.

An excellent two-day loop through Hoover Wilderness visits upper Virginia Canyon in northeastern Yosemite National Park and offers plenty of solitude and scenic splendor, which unfolds with every mile. The trail follows a series of gorgeous lakes up along the West Fork Green Creek, a lush valley enclosed by dramatic red and brown peaks. Crossing lake-crowned Summit Pass, you enter Virginia Canyon, one of the most peaceful corners of Yosemite. You're likely to encounter no one else in this corner of the park and, although Virginia Pass is not crossed every day, it's not for lack of outstanding scenery. The mildly adventurous return over the pass and down Glines Canyon, following a mostly user-defined trail back to the trailhead, which requires some route-finding skills.

The hike has several easy stream crossings. The lack of footbridges means you may have to ford, hop rocks or walk on logs, and early in the season getting your feet wet may be unavoidable. It's possible to extend the hike by spending an extra day or more in upper Virginia Canyon to savor its remarkable beauty and tranquility, or by camping the first night at East Lake and the second night along Return Creek. Reversing the direction of this loop is discouraged; hiking up Glines Canyon is far more difficult than descending it.

PLANNING
When to Hike
The hiking season is from July to October. The trail down Glines Canyon can be snowy until mid-July. In the fall, the abundant aspens along Green Creek turn into a blaze of gold.

Maps
The USGS 1:24,000 *Dunderberg Peak* quadrangle covers this hike.

Permits & Regulations
A free wilderness permit is required for this hike (see Planning, p147). Campfires are prohibited above 9000ft in Hoover Wilderness and above 9600ft in Yosemite National Park.

GETTING TO/FROM THE HIKE
See the East Lake hike, p152, for details on how to get to the Green Creek Trailhead (8000ft).

THE HIKE
Day 1: Green Creek Trailhead to Return Creek
6½–7½ hours, 11.3mi (18.2km), 2820ft (846m) ascent, 980ft (294m) descent
See the East Lake hike, p152, for a description of the trail between the Green Creek Trailhead and East Lake. From where the trail meets East Lake, it continues following along the eastern shore, then ascends above the southeast shore and passes along the east shore of small Nutter Lake.

Continuing upvalley, the trail turns south and passes well above small Gilman Lake, which lies at the base of a dark talus slope beneath the west face of massive Dunderberg Peak (12,374ft). Secluded *campsites* are away from the trail down near **Gilman Lake**. Traversing high above Gilman Lake, the trail crosses its inlet via slippery logs, one hour from East Lake.

Turning southwest, ascend parallel to the stream's true right bank. Skirting some gray talus and passing over a low whitebark pine-speckled ridge, reach the first of two **Hoover Lakes** (9820ft), set amid rocks beneath the southeast face of Epidote Peak. Only a few trees manage to grow at this windy lake. The trail follows along its northeast shore, then crosses the stream connecting it to upper Hoover Lake and hugs that lake's rocky northwest shore.

Passing the lake's inlet, the trail rises along the meadow-lined stream where lupines, wild onions, and several types of penstemons bloom. The trail then ascends some switchbacks along the willow-lined creek, providing unfolding views back of the Hoover Lakes and imposing **Dunderberg Peak**. Cross over to the inlet's true right bank and ascend through scattered pines. A short distance ahead, 45 minutes from the

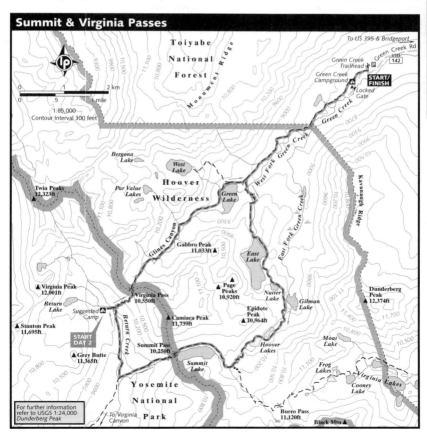

TAHOE TO YOSEMITE

Summit & Virginia Passes

Toiyabe National Forest

Monument Ridge

To US 395 & Bridgeport

Green Creek Rd

Green Creek Trailhead
USFS 142

Green Creek Campground

START/FINISH

Locked Gate

Green Creek

West Fork Green Creek

0   1   2 km
0   .5   1 mile
1:85,000
Contour Interval 300 feet

Bergona Lake

West Lake

Hoover

Par Value Lakes

Wilderness

Green Lake

East Fork Green Creek

Kavanaugh Ridge

Twin Peaks 12,323ft

Glines Canyon

Gabbro Peak 11,033ft ▲

East Lake

Virginia Peak 12,001ft

Return Lake

Suggested Camp

Virginia Pass 10,550ft

Page Peaks 10,920ft ▲

Nutter Lake

Gilman Lake

Dunderberg Peak 12,374ft ▲

▲ Stanton Peak 11,695ft

Return Creek

Camiaca Peak 11,739ft ▲

Epidote Peak 10,964ft ▲

Moat Lake

START DAY 2

▲ Grey Butte 11,365ft

Summit Pass 10,250ft

Summit Lake

Hoover Lakes

Frog Lakes

Virginia Lakes

Cooney Lake

Yosemite National Park

For further information refer to USGS 1:24,000 Dunderberg Peak

To Virginia Canyon

Burro Pass 11,120ft

Black Mtn ▲

crossing of Gilman Lake's inlet, which is 3mi from East Lake, you come to a junction (10,080ft) with the unsigned trail to the south that descends from Burro Pass (see the Virginia Lakes hike, below). A trail sign at this junction points in opposite directions; west (right) to Summit Lake and northeast (left) to Hoover Lakes.

Turn right and dip down through a stream-filled meadow and cross the stream (10,020ft), then ascend along the true right bank of a small stream flowing from Summit Lake. Cross to the stream's true left bank and ascend a gully. Continue up to the east end of **Summit Lake**, 15 minutes from the trail junction. Camping is prohibited along the east shore of the lake, which is often too windy anyway.

Wildflowers and willows line the level trail as it skirts the northern shore for 15 minutes. Whitebark pines dot the lower slopes of Camiaca Peak (11,739ft), rising dramatically above the north shore. Camping is also prohibited along the north shore. Along the west shore, clusters of whitebark pines on a grassy knoll well away from the lake offer windy, exposed *campsites*.

Just beyond the western shore is the barely noticeable **Summit Pass** (10,250ft), where you enter Yosemite National Park and leave Hoover Wilderness. The white granite peaks ahead shimmer in marked contrast to the red and brown peaks above Green Creek. The darker Grey Butte is the closest, with Stanton Peak's whitish double summit just beyond. The granite cliffs above Virginia Canyon are impressive, and to the north is the prominent reddish cone of Virginia Peak (12,001ft).

Descending the lush slopes from Summit Pass, whitebark pines quickly yield to a forest of lodgepole pines. The view down **Virginia Canyon** along forested **Return Creek** is impressive, but more impressive is the rugged glaciated granite peak of **Shepherd Crest** to the south. Reach a signed junction (9330ft) along Return Creek 35 minutes and 1.1mi below the pass. A trail, which parallels Return Creek, leads west (left) 18.6mi to Tuolumne Meadows and in the opposite direction, heads north (right)

up Virginia Canyon. Turning north, the trail is faint at first, but quickly becomes more substantial, obvious and easy to follow as you gradually ascend between Grey Butte to the west and Camiaca Peak to the east.

After 10 minutes, cross to Return Creek's true right (west) bank and ascend over a lodgepole-forested spur. Rounding the bend in the canyon, 15 minutes beyond the crossing, you get your first views of upper Virginia Canyon. **Virginia Peak** and the light gray summits of **Twin Peaks** rise above the meadow-filled valley floor where Return Creek sparkles.

Head down to meet Return Creek, cross to its true left bank and continue on the trail up this beautiful subalpine valley. Just before the trail crosses Return Creek a third time is the barely perceptible trail to Virginia Pass. Look for this junction so you know where to head up the next morning. To reach the campsite, cross to the creek's true right bank and head up two minutes into a cluster of trees along the true right bank of **Return Creek**, 1.2mi from the last trail junction. The excellent *campsite* (9840ft) here, on a bench between the confluence of two streams, makes a superb base for cross-country exploration of upper Virginia Canyon. Excursions are possible to Return Lake and the alpine plateau above it, from where you can see Spiller Lake and Matterhorn Peak at the head of Spiller Canyon.

Day 2: Return Creek to Green Creek Trailhead

3½–4½ hours, 7mi (11.3km), 810ft (243m) ascent, 2650ft (795m) descent

Retrace your steps two minutes down the trail and cross to Return Creek's true left bank. Just beyond the crossing, look for a faint track heading north up the steep slope into lodgepole pines. A couple of tiny cairns at ground level mark the start of the route to Virginia Pass. The track to the pass is essentially an eroded gully, which was once a more solid trail.

Head into the trees going up in a basically straight line, looking for occasional cairns on boulders. There are no switchbacks here. The route gets more defined 10 minutes higher, as you follow a small gravelly track up the slope. The views to the south open to include not only spectacular **Shepherd Crest** with its permanent snowfields, but also distant **Cathedral Range**, above Tuolumne Meadows. Thirty minutes up the slope, Return Lake pops into view. From this point, the trail becomes completely visible for the final 15 minutes to signed **Virginia Pass** (10,550ft), 0.4mi from Return Creek. The splendid view includes Twin Peaks, Virginia Peak, Stanton Peak, Return Lake, Shepherd Crest and the distant Cathedral Range.

The 4.1mi descent of Glines Canyon from Virginia Pass to Green Lake is steep and somewhat confusing. From the pass, follow the small but obvious trail down 200ft over the talus slope, keeping to the right (south) of the usually snow-filled gully. This section is difficult when snow covered early in the season. Below, the trail goes through overgrown vegetation and whitebark pines, keeping to the south side of a level, grassy area at the eastern end of which both pink and white heather bloom profusely. A faint trail descends from the rocky east end of this level area, following a willow-lined stream. **Green Lake** is visible well below.

Follow the stream's true right bank, continuing along the descending track. Thirty minutes from the pass, cross the stream in the middle of a short, grassy section where it flows south, perpendicular to the trail. Now on the true left bank of the main drainage, continue down over gray shale and then through stands of pine and hemlock. For 10 minutes the trail stays high above the main stream where it flows through a canyon. With Green Lake now obscured by forest, the trail nears the stream's true left bank in a level meadow.

Cascading **Glines Creek** flows over a strikingly white stone bed, whose color derives from the dissolved calcium of marble and limestone above. The trail is faint, but obvious, and in 10 minutes you encounter an old rusted automobile engine lying on a gravel patch. Walk past the broken metal pieces, away from the main stream. The route is confusing here; whatever you do, do not cross the main stream. Just beyond the engine, through the trees, is an old log **cabin** situated on a promontory overlooking Glines Canyon.

Pass close by the cabin, keeping to the left of the rock outcrop as the trail moves farther away from the main stream and drops down to cross the outlet from Par Value Lakes. Just beyond the stream, walk past old rusted mining gears, pipes and mill parts scattered on the ground.

Continue down the trail through forest, where hemlocks and firs are abundant. Reach the west shore of Green Lake (8940ft), 30 minutes from the log cabin. The trail works around the northwest shore, near the lake at first, then detouring to avoid willow thickets along the lakeshore and finally climbing on the somewhat overgrown trail to get over a rock bluff above the lake (9040ft). Your reward for making this effort is an excellent view back upvalley toward Virginia Pass. Meet the signed junction with the trail to West Lake 15 minutes farther along. In another five minutes, come to the familiar signed junction with the trail to East Lake, 4.1mi from Virginia Pass. From here, retrace your steps the final 2.5mi to the Green Creek Trailhead (8000ft).

Virginia Lakes

Duration	3 hours
Distance	6.6mi (10.6km)
Standard	easy-moderate
Start/Finish	Virginia Lakes Trailhead
Public Transport	no

Summary A day hike passes seven subalpine lakes to reach Burro Pass, offering a treat of wildflowers, mountain peaks and sweeping vistas.

Starting from one of the Sierra Nevada's most easily reached and highest trailheads, this delightful hike ascends past a chain of mountain lakes, along streams and meadows to reach the alpine heights of Burro Pass (11,120ft). Between Dunderberg Peak to the north and Black Mountain to the south, the pass has big views of the Nevada desert to the northeast and west into Yosemite National Park. The red, ochre, gray and black rocks of the high alpine basin around the pass hold snowfields late into summer. Wildflowers are exceptional along this immensely satisfying hike, which has a total elevation gain and loss of 2560ft in equal amounts of ascent and descent.

Stay on the most well-traveled trail up-valley, since many side trails lead to popular fishing spots. Along the way, you find a couple of stream crossings where there are no footbridges, so early in the season you may get your feet wet. Listen for marmot calls and try to glimpse one as they scamper around the rocky terrain.

Those who relish more can extend their hike to Green Creek (see the Summit Pass side trip, below, and the Virginia Lakes to Green Creek hike, p161) for alternative longer and highly rewarding day hikes.

PLANNING
When to Hike
The hiking season is from mid-June to October. Hikers can expect to find snow near Burro Pass until July. Ask at the Bridgeport ranger station about snow conditions.

Maps
The USGS 1:24,000 *Dunderberg Peak* quadrangle covers the hike, as does the USFS 1:63,360 *Hoover Wilderness* map.

Permits & Regulations
A permit is not required for this day hike. A free wilderness permit is required for any overnight trip (see Planning, p147). Campfires are prohibited above 9000ft.

GETTING TO/FROM THE HIKE
From Conway Summit (8138ft) on US 395, 13mi south of Bridgeport and 12mi north of Lee Vining, take the paved Virginia Lakes Rd 5.8mi west into the USFS Virginia Lakes Recreation Area. Continue 0.3mi beyond the USFS *Trumbull Lake Campground* ($10) where the pavement ends to reach the large parking lot at the Virginia Lakes Trailhead (9840ft).

THE HIKE
Skirting the shore of large upper Virginia Lake (9840ft), the trail goes through lodgepole pines and in five minutes meets the spur trail coming from the campground. After five more minutes, pass the Hoover Wilderness boundary sign and continue along the pine-forested northeast shore of Blue Lake (9880ft). The vermillion-colored rock ridge descending from massive **Dunderberg Peak** (12,374ft) forms a striking backdrop to this pretty lake. Traversing reddish scree at the base of the ridge, the trail rises above Blue Lake's north shore, the steepest ascent along the hike. Patches of pink heather decorate the slope as you ascend steeply and enter open lodgepole-pine forest above the lake's west end.

The trail becomes more gradual as it continues its steady ascent amid pines, and 30 minutes (0.8mi) from the trailhead reaches an historic log miner's cabin. Although it is in reasonably good repair, the cabin lacks

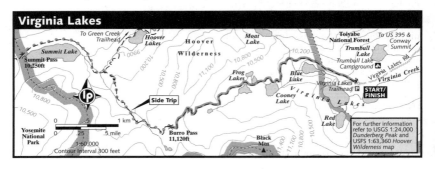

any sign to tell its no doubt interesting story. Crossing the outlet from Moat Lake, the trail winds around and comes in five minutes to the windswept western shore of **Cooney Lake** (10,260ft), 0.5mi beyond Blue Lake, where the pines are now only whitebark.

Passing north of the lake, after five minutes cross its inlet on logs and wind between the three **Frog Lakes** (10,380ft), which are popular fishing spots. Sheltered by low granite ridges, the lakes, 0.5mi and 15 minutes beyond Cooney Lake, have willows and whitebark pines along their shores. Patches of pink heather and purple and pink penstemon color the trailside, and in pockets of meadows, buttercups and cinquefoils make yellow dots amid the green grass. Continuing along the northern side of this small lake cluster, the trail passes well above and north of the highest one, affording good views east over the entire series of lakes and the distant hills near US 395.

As you rise along gentle switchbacks, trees become sparse. The good trail traverses talus and shale slopes, where patches of pink heather lie in green mats, as it follows rocky switchbacks to the pass. Strikingly beautiful clusters of pale purple timberline penstemon bloom along the trail as it passes the last stunted whitebark pines to reach **Burro Pass** (11,120ft), 45 minutes from the Frogs Lakes and 3.3mi from the trailhead.

The rocky, windswept plateau has excellent views of not only five of the seven lakes in the **Virginia Lakes Basin** to the east, but also of Virginia Peak's prominent tower and Twin Peaks, which lie inside Yosemite National Park. The high, rocky basin surrounding you holds permanent snowfields that feed Green Creek. Walk at least two minutes beyond the pass for views of **Summit Lake**, **Camiaca Peak** and other superb mountain views that are obscured from the pass itself. Return along the same trail to the trailhead in 1½ hours.

Side Trip: Summit Pass
3–3½ hours, 6mi (9.7km), 1330ft (399m) ascent, 1330ft (399m) descent
Hikers tempted by their glimpse of the upper Green Creek Basin from Burro Pass can continue through fantastic scenery to Summit Lake, on Yosemite National Park's boundary. From Burro Pass, the trail heads west, then turns northwest and in just a few minutes you glimpse large Summit Lake in the distance. As the trail descends rocky switchbacks, luscious clusters of pinkish-white and lemon-yellow columbine appear. Twenty minutes from the pass, as the trail follows a splashing stream, you reach the first grass at timberline. Whitebark pines, patches of pink heather and alpine buttercup abound in the streamside meadow (10,400ft). This makes a fine picnic spot or a solitary high wilderness *campsite*.

Continue down the trail 1mi from the pass to the signed Summit Lake/Hoover Lake trail junction (10,080ft). Turn left (west) and dip down to cross the stream (10,020ft) descending from Burro Pass. Head up the trail a scant 20 minutes to the east shore of Summit Lake (10,200ft) and continue along its north shore to Summit Pass (10,250ft). The almost white granite of the Yosemite peaks ahead are a sharp contrast to the red and brown earth tones of the peaks of Hoover Wilderness. Enjoy the view and retrace your steps to the Virginia Lakes Trailhead.

Gardisky Lake

Duration	1–1½ hours
Distance	2.6mi (4.18km)
Standard	easy-moderate
Start/Finish	Gardisky Lake Trailhead
Public Transport	no

Summary A secluded yet easily accessible timberline lake on the Tioga Crest offers outstanding views of the giant peaks along the Sierra Crest.

Gardisky Lake is an unknown gem. Nestled amid flower-filled meadows on the Tioga Crest beneath Tioga Peak (11,526ft), within a short walk from the road it has wonderful views of Mt Conness (12,590ft) and Mt Dana (13,057ft). Lying east of Yosemite National Park, the lake receives far fewer visitors that it deserves, which makes it a great place for a

TAHOE TO YOSEMITE

stroll or picnic. The hike to the lake is short but steep, with a combined elevation gain and loss of 1560ft, in equal amounts of ascent and descent. The timberline country around the lake invites you to wander cross-country for solitude or even better views.

PLANNING
When to Hike
The hiking season is from mid-June to October.

Maps
The USGS 1:24,000 *Tioga Pass* and *Mount Dana* quadrangles cover the hike.

Permits & Regulations
A wilderness permit is not required for this day hike, however, hikers are asked to sign their names in the 'Day Hiker Register' at the trailhead. Inyo National Forest issues free wilderness permits for any overnight trip.

GETTING TO/FROM THE HIKE
To reach the Gardisky Lake Trailhead, turn north onto Saddlebag Lake Rd from Tioga Rd (Hwy 120) 2.1mi east of Tioga Pass. Go up the road 1.1mi to the trailhead; the trailhead sign and parking area are on the road's west (left) side and the trailhead is on its east (right). The 9800-ft-high USFS *Sawmill Walk-in Campground* ($6) is 0.5mi beyond the trailhead.

THE HIKE
The ascent begins almost immediately from the trailhead (9720ft). Follow the trail up amid lodgepole pines five minutes and cross a creek to its true right bank. Ascend steeply along the creek, with good views of **Mt Dana** and the **Dana Plateau** off to your right (south). The trail turns north, away from the creek, then makes a switchback south toward the creek. Clusters of white-bark pine replace the lodgepole pines as you head higher and the views of **Tioga Peak** (11,526ft) get increasingly better.

After this 20-minute ascent, the trail enters a meadow along the creek and begins to level off. Continue for 10 minutes, passing a small lake that feeds the creek you fol-

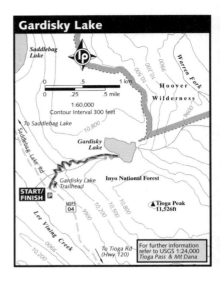

lowed and another small lake that flows east into large **Gardisky Lake** (10,500ft), whose outlet flows east into Warren Fork Lee Vining Creek. Marmots scamper in this broad grassy basin, an area with a Sierra Nevada bighorn sheep population. Enjoy the expansive views west and south along the Tioga Crest, including Mt Conness and Mt Dana. The prominent peak to the east is **Lee Vining Peak.**

For even better views, it's an easy scramble south to the ridge and then east to the top of rocky Tioga Peak. You can also wander up the meadow slope north of the lake for picnicking and solitude. Retrace your steps to the trailhead in less than 30 minutes.

Other Hikes

Grouse Lake
Grouse Lake is tucked into a quiet but easily accessible corner of Mokelumne Wilderness. The 12.4mi (20km) easy-moderate round-trip hike can be done as a day hike but is best as an overnight trip. From Hwy 88 6.3mi east of Carson Pass, go south on Blue Lakes Rd about 12mi to Middle

TAHOE TO YOSEMITE

Creek Campground. The trailhead is nearby at **Middle Creek Campground**. Head west 2.2mi to popular Granite Lake, a good swimming spot. Leaving the crowds behind at Granite Lake, continue along the trail, which contours the headwaters of Snow Creek. You rise easily over a ridge (9200ft) and gently down into Summit City Creek's large valley to Grouse Lake (8560ft) in 4mi. Grouse Lake has good fishing and plenty of solitude. Return the same way. The USGS 1:24,000 *Pacific Valley* and *Mokelumne Peak* quadrangles cover the hike, as does the USFS 1:63,360 *Mokelumne Wilderness* map.

Sardine Falls

Sardine Falls are both visible and audible from Hwy 108. It's an easy, level stroll across Sardine Meadow and through forest along McKay Creek to the base (9000ft) of the falls. The trailhead (8800ft) is on the south side of Hwy 108, 2.5mi east of Sonora Pass and 12.2mi west of the Hwy 108/ US 395 intersection. Park along the side of the highway. The falls, at their best in springtime, boom over volcanic pumice rock, throwing a shower of mist high into the air. The 2mi round-trip hike takes an hour. The USGS 1:24,000 *Sonora Pass* quadrangle covers the hike. A wilderness permit is not necessary for this easy day hike in Hoover Wilderness.

Virginia Lakes to Green Creek

If you're not opposed to vehicle shuttles, it's possible to combine outstanding features of two hikes in this chapter: the Virginia Lakes hike and the Summit & Virginia Passes hike. This popular, moderate 11.3mi (18.2km) day hike, 8mi of which are downhill, starts at the Virginia Lakes Trailhead and finishes at the Green Creek Trailhead.

See the Virginia Lakes hike, p157, for a description of the 3.3mi trail from the Virginia Lakes Trailhead to Burro Pass. See that hike's side trip for a description of the next 1mi down to the trail junction above Hoover Lakes. At this trail junction you turn right and join the trail that leads to Green Creek.

Follow the description in the reverse direction on Day 1 of the Summit & Virginia Passes hike, p154. It's 3mi downvalley to East Lake (0.7mi to Hoover Lakes, 1.3mi to Gilman Lake, and 1mi to East Lake) and 4mi from there to the Green Creek Trailhead.

To shorten the drive between trailheads, go up Virginia Lakes Rd, 4.5mi from the US 395 junction or 1.6mi from the Virginia Lakes Trailhead, where an unpaved road called Dunderberg Meadow Rd (USFS Rd 020) leads in 8mi to Green Creek. It's shorter (but dustier) than driving between trailheads on US 395.

20-Lakes Basin

Nestled between the Sierra Crest to the west and Tioga Crest to the east along Yosemite's northeastern boundary lies 20-Lakes Basin, a lake-dotted alpine landscape east of prominent Mt Conness (12,590ft) and North Peak (12,242ft). The area, which is all higher than 10,000ft, is easily visited on a 7.5mi (12.1km) day hike from Saddlebag Lake. A four- to five-hour clockwise loop passes a dozen lakes and crosses two easy passes. You can also spend several days exploring the alpine country surrounding dramatic North Peak via Class 2 routes that link Cascade Lake to Upper McCabe Lake, Upper McCabe Lake to Roosevelt Lake, and Roosevelt Lake to the Conness Lakes.

A free wilderness permit, which you can get at the Saddlebag Lake Resort, adjacent to the trailhead, is required for all overnight trips in Hoover Wilderness. Camping is not allowed in the Hall Natural Area adjacent to the national park boundary, and wood fires are prohibited everywhere in the basin. The USGS 1:24,000 *Tioga Pass* and *Dunderberg Peak* quadrangles cover the area.

To reach the Saddlebag Lake Trailhead, turn north onto Saddlebag Lake Rd from Tioga Rd (Hwy 120) 2.1mi east of Tioga Pass. Go 2.4mi to the end of the road and the Saddlebag Lake Trailhead. The resort and the USFS **Saddlebag Lake Campground** ($11) are just beyond the trailhead.

Cross Lee Vining Creek beneath the dam's spillway and follow a well-beaten trail 1.5mi over talus, paralleling the west shore of Saddlebag Lake to Greenstone Lake. Cross its outlet stream and join an old mining road that ascends northwest above Greenstone Lake's north shore. Passing north of Wasco Lake, you cross an easy, unnamed pass into the Mill Creek watershed. Continue north along the east shore of Steelhead Lake to its outlet, where the old road heads northwest to an abandoned tungsten mine. Leave the road and follow a well-established trail northeast, passing north of dramatic Shamrock Lake and descending past the north shore of Lake Helen. Turning southeast, cross Mill Creek just below Lake Helen and join the Lundy Pass Trail, which ascends south past Odell Lake, crosses **Lundy Pass** (10,300ft), and descends past the west shore of Hummingbird Lake to the north end of Saddlebag Lake, from where you retrace your steps to the trailhead.

Yosemite National Park

Yosemite National Park, with some of the most exquisite scenery in the US, is a UNESCO World Heritage Site that draws visitors from around the globe. Most visitors head for Yosemite Valley, where the incomparable granite monoliths of El Capitan and Half Dome are instantly recognizable and several of the world's highest waterfalls thunder over the rim to the valley floor.

Beyond the valley, more than 800mi of trails through the park's nearly 1200 sq miles offer hikers an uncrowded backcountry experience. Yosemite's high country is an alpine wilderness, with flower-filled meadows ringed by conifer forests and threaded by streams, where gem-like lakes shimmer beneath granite pinnacles. Tuolumne Meadows is the center for Yosemite backpacking beneath the 13,000ft Sierra Crest.

The northwestern approach to the park, along Hwy 120, provides access to the Hetch Hetchy Valley. In their hurry to reach Yosemite Valley, many people drive by this uncrowded area, unaware of the waterfalls and granite cliffs that rival its more famous counterpart. Hetch Hetchy's relatively lower elevation makes it an especially good destination in spring and fall, when the high country is in winter's grip.

Southern Yosemite along the South Fork Merced River, easily accessible from Hwy 41, is another less-visited region. The glacially formed landscape features granite domes and waterfalls without the valley's crowds.

Access to remote areas of northern Yosemite is often easier from outside the national park along Hwy 108 and US 395. For hikes in this part of the park, see the Brown Bear & Bond Passes hike, p145, Sawtooth Ridge hike, p148, and Summit & Virginia Passes hike, p154, in the Tahoe to Yosemite chapter.

HISTORY

Native American Ahwahneechee, a subtribe of the Southern or Sierra Miwok, knew of Yosemite Valley 5000 years ago and settled

Highlights

JIM WARK

Half Dome, Yosemite's most dramatic landmark, towers over the valley below.

- Standing on the summit of Half Dome after surviving the cables

- Strolling Indian Ridge to North Dome for up-close and personal views of Half Dome's sheer north face

- Climbing to Mt Dana's windswept summit for aerial views of Mono Lake and the Tuolumne high country

- Hiking from the bottom to the top of Yosemite Falls, the world's fifth-highest free-leaping waterfall

there by 1000 BC, living on black oak acorns and fish, and occasionally deer and rabbits. They lived in the valley during fall and winter, and in spring headed to the high country, where they traded with eastern Sierra Piutes.

Not until the mid-19th century did non-Native Americans visit the secluded valley.

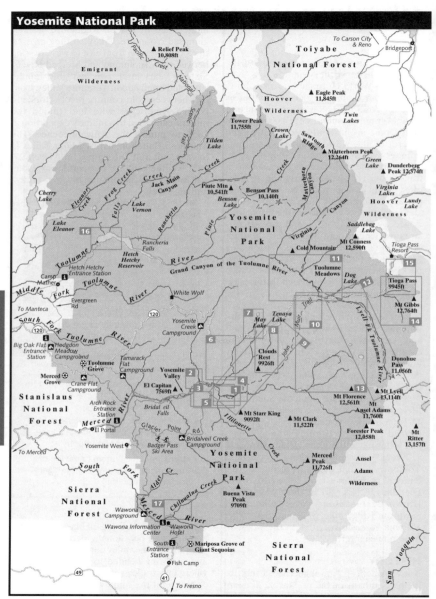

Yosemite National Park

To Carson City & Reno
Bridgeport

Toiyabe

National Forest

Relief Peak 10,808ft

Pacific

Emigrant
Wilderness

Crest

Eagle Peak 11,845ft

Hoover

Wilderness

Twin Lakes

Tower Peak 11,755ft

National

Tilden Lake

Crown Lake

Sawtooth Ridge

Matterhorn Peak 12,264ft

Green Lake

Dunderberg Peak 12,374ft

Scenic

Creek

Piute Mtn 10,541ft

Benson Pass 10,140ft

Matterhorn Canyon

Frog Creek

Creek

Jack Main Canyon

Benson Lake

Virginia Lakes

Lundy Lake

Cherry Lake

Lake Vernon

Trail

Yosemite

National

Park

Virginia Canyon

Hoover

Wilderness

Eleanor Creek

Rancheria

Falls

Creek

Piute

Saddlebag Lake

Mt Conness 12,590ft

Tioga Pass Resort

Lake Eleanor

16

Rancheria Falls

River

Cold Mountain

Virginia

11

Tuolumne Meadows

Dog Lake

15

Hetch Hetchy Reservoir

Grand Canyon of the Tuolumne River

12

Tioga Pass 9945ft

Hetch Hetchy Entrance Station

Camp Mather

Tuolumne

River

Evergreen Rd

White Wolf

Mt Gibbs 12,764ft

Middle

Fork

To Manteca

14

South Fork Tuolumne River

120

Yosemite Creek Campground

7

May Lake

Tenaya Lake

Muir Trail

10

Lyell Fk Tuolumne River

Big Oak Flat Entrance Station

Hodgdon Meadow Campground

Tuolumne Grove

Tamarack Flat Campground

6

8

9

Donohue Pass 11,056ft

120

Crane Flat Campground

Clouds Rest 9926ft

John

Merced Grove

Yosemite Valley

2

El Capitan 7569ft

4

3

1

13

Mt Lyell 13,114ft

Stanislaus

Arch Rock Entrance Station

5

Mt Florence 12,561ft

Mt Ansel Adams 11,760ft

National

Bridal eil Falls

Mt Starr King 9092ft

Mt Clark 11,522ft

Forest

River

Glacier

Point Rd

Forester Peak 12,058ft

Mt Ritter 13,157ft

Merced

El Portal

Bridalveil Creek Campground

Illilouette

To Merced

Yosemite West

Badger Pass Ski Area

Yosemite

National

Park

Merced Peak 11,726ft

Ansel

Adams

Wilderness

South

Alder Cr

Fork

Buena Vista Peak 9709ft

Sierra

National

Merced

Chilnualna Creek

17

Forest

Wawona Campground

River

Wawona Information Center

Wawona Hotel

Mariposa Grove of Giant Sequoias

Sierra

National

Forest

South Entrance Station

Fish Camp

49

41

To Fresno

San Joaquin

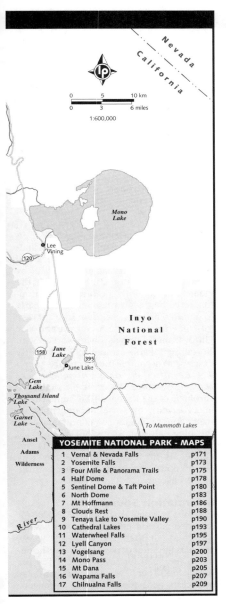

In 1833, a party of 58 fur trappers and hunters, led by Joseph Reddeford Walker, glimpsed Yosemite Valley as they crossed the Sierra Nevada from east to west, passing between the Tuolumne and Merced Rivers. Sixteen years later, two lost gold miners stumbled briefly upon Yosemite Valley. Conflict between gold country prospectors and Native Americans who had raided the miners' camps led to a military expedition in 1851 to punish the Ahwahneechee. The Mariposa Battalion, led by Major James D Savage, entered the valley on March 27, 1851, via the route of present-day Wawona Rd, forcing the capitulation of Chief Tenaya and his tribe.

In 1855, San Franciscan publisher James Mason Hutchings and artist Thomas Ayres visited the valley. Through articles byHutchings and Ayres' sketches, published nationwide, Yosemite's captivating beauty quickly attracted other tourist parties. As visitors increased, Hutchings, conservationist Galen Clark, landscape architect Frederick Law Olmsted and others recognized the importance of protecting Yosemite Valley and the Big Tree Grove (ie, Mariposa Grove) of giant sequoias south of the valley. In 1864, the US Congress passed and President Abraham Lincoln signed into law the Yosemite Grant, a bill that transferred these two areas to California as a public trust and created Yosemite State Park.

Through efforts of John Muir and editor Robert Underwood Johnson, the US Congress established Yosemite as the third national park in the US on October 1, 1890. In 1906, the US Congress approved the recession of the Yosemite Grant and incorporated Yosemite State Park into the national park.

The US Cavalry managed and administered the park from 1890 to 1914, after when administration passed to the US Department of Interior. The first civilian park rangers were employed in 1898.

The park's first General Management Plan, created in 1980, emphasized education through interpretation and environment-first (as opposed to people-first) ethics. Yosemite became a UNESCO World Heritage Site in 1984.

YOSEMITE NATIONAL PARK

The 1980 General Management Plan for Yosemite recognized a need to deal with the problems of rapidly increasing visitation. Planning started in the early 1990s and took on greater urgency following the flood of January 1997. The resulting Yosemite Valley Plan, adopted on December 29, 2000, will 'restore natural processes in Yosemite Valley, preserve cultural resource values, reduce harmful environmental impacts (including those related to traffic congestion) and continue to provide high quality visitor experiences.'

Change will not be immediate or overnight, but rather will take years to unfold. Among projects planned are creating a more natural and educational Lower Yosemite Falls area, and removing dams and some bridges and roads to restore the free-flowing wild and scenic character of the Merced River. Other projected changes include relocating horse stables and horseback riding, vehicle repair and shuttle bus maintenance facilities, some administrative activities and employee housing outside of Yosemite Valley. Also on the drawing board is consolidating visitor services and transit operations in the eastern end of Yosemite Valley, and providing a day-use parking lot sufficient (550 spaces) to accommodate all day visitors between late fall and early spring who travel by private vehicle. This latter project will also, during peak season, provide additional out-of-valley parking areas along each of the valley's three primary access roads, which will be served by an associated shuttle bus system.

NATURAL HISTORY

The park contains all the Sierra Nevada life zones from lower montane to alpine. The western part of the park is densely forested, while the eastern side of the park along the Sierra Crest is a drier, subalpine environment. Yosemite Valley, at 4000ft, is in the lower montane zone, where a mixed conifer forest of predominantly ponderosa pine, incense cedar, and Douglas fir, rises above an understory of wildflower-carpeted meadows, flowering shrubs and woodlands of black oak and California live oak.

INFORMATION
Maps

The USGS 1:125,000 *Yosemite National Park and Vicinity* map ($7), with 200ft contour intervals, covers the entire park. Tom Harrison Maps 1:125,000 *Yosemite National Park Recreation Map* ($8.95) and National Geographic/Trails Illustrated 1:100,000 *Yosemite National Park* topographic map ($9.95) give similar coverage.

Maps and books are available from the Yosemite Association Bookstore (☎ 209-379-2648, fax 379-2486, W yosemite.org), PO Box 230, El Portal, CA 95318, and at park visitor centers and stores. The Tuolumne Meadows Sport Shop, at the gas station there, also sells maps.

Books

Yosemite: Its Discovery, Its Wonders & Its People, by Margaret Sanborn, is a fascinating and thorough account of the park and its history. *Discovery of the Yosemite,* by Lafayette Houghton Bunnell MD, the medical officer with the Mariposa Battalion, is the best eyewitness account of early Yosemite history. *Indian Life of the Yosemite Region,* by SA Barrett and EW Gifford, anthropologists who worked with Yosemite Miwok around 1900, cogently describes Yosemite's Indian culture. *Camp 4 – Recollections of a Yosemite Rock-climber,* by Steve Roper, is the definitive chronicle of the heyday of Yosemite climbing. *Yosemite,* by Ansel Adams, presents the famous photographer's finest images of the place closest to his heart. *Birds of Yosemite and the East Slope,* by David Gaines, is the best reference, covering every known species in Yosemite and the Mono Lake area.

Information Sources

Yosemite National Park (☎ 209-372-0200 for recorded general information, W www.nps.gov/yose), PO Box 577, Yosemite, CA 95389, provides the latest park information. The entrance fee, valid for seven days, is $20 per vehicle or $10 per person for individual entry by cyclists, pedestrians and bus passengers. An annual pass costs $40.

The National Park Reservation Service (☎ 800-436-7275, 301-722-1257 outside the US, W reservations.nps.gov), PO Box 1600, Cumberland, MD 21502, handles bookings up to five months in advance for the campgrounds that require reservations. It is not possible to make reservations for first-come, first-served campgrounds.

Yosemite Concession Services (☎ 559-252-4848, fax 456-0542, W www.yosemitepark.com), 5410 East Home, Fresno, CA 93727, handles reservations for all lodging, including tent cabins and High Sierra Camps (see High Sierra Camp Loop, p211, for a description of these facilities). See Access Facilities under the Yosemite Valley, p168, Tuolumne, p184, and Southern Yosemite, p208, sections later in this chapter for campground and lodging details.

On the Web, W www.yosemite.com has information on the area surrounding the park, including lodging in nearby towns.

Permits & Regulations

Free wilderness use permits are required year-round for all overnight backcountry trips, but not for day hikes. A trailhead quota system is in effect. First-come, first-served permits are available from the following permit stations:

Yosemite Valley Wilderness Center
Wawona Information Station
Big Oak Flat Information Station
Hetch Hetchy Entrance
Tuolumne Meadows Wilderness Center

Go to the permit station nearest your trailhead. See Information under Access Facilities in the Yosemite Valley, p168, and Tuolumne, p184, sections for more details about these wilderness centers. Call the park (☎ 209-372-0200) or ask at any visitor center to verify when each permit station is open.

Permits are also available by reservation, with a $5 non-refundable processing fee per person (payable to the Yosemite Association; credit cards accepted), from six months to two days in advance of an entry date.

Reservations are recommended for popular trailheads from May to September.

You can either mail a completed reservation form to Wilderness Permits (☎ 209-372-0740, 9am to 4pm weekdays), PO Box 545, Yosemite, CA 95389, or make reservations online by visiting W www.nps.gov/yose/wilderness.

The use of bear-resistant food containers is required by law at all backcountry campsites above 9600ft and at the High Sierra Camps. Containers are readily available for rent for $3 per trip from any of 10 park locations, including where you get your wilderness permits.

No campfires are allowed above 9600ft. Camping is only allowed 4mi beyond Yosemite Valley, Tuolumne Meadows, Glacier Point Rd, Hetch Hetchy and Wawona, or at least 1mi from any other road.

Help! Trailhead Quota Is Full!

You need a wilderness permit for your backpacking trip, but the park ranger tells you that the trailhead quota is full for the day you want to start. Dejected, you wish you had paid the fee to reserve a permit in advance, and you ponder whether your vacation is ruined. This is an all-too-frequent reality for summer hikers, especially those wanting to start a hike from Yosemite Valley. Fortunately, if you're flexible, several strategies exist for getting to where you want to go.

The easiest solution is to do a day hike, which doesn't require a permit, instead of an overnight trip. If you can wait a day, the following day's quota may have space available. For those set on backpacking, consider starting your hike from a different trailhead – try the Four Mile Trail Trailhead in Yosemite Valley or Glacier Point outside the valley. If Half Dome is your goal, consider approaching it from the Sunrise Lakes Trailhead at Tenaya Lake. Picking any hike that avoids camping in Little Yosemite Valley helps too. Finally, consider a less 'popular' and often-overlooked hike near Tuolumne, such as North Dome, Mt Hoffmann or Mt Dana, each with great views and intriguing overnight options.

Other Information

The nearest HI/AYH hostels are in Midpines and Merced. *The Yosemite Bug Hostel* (☎ 209-966-6666, fax 966-6667, e] bughost@yosemite bug.com, w] www.yosemitebug.com), PO Box 81, Midpines, CA 95345, at 6979 Hwy 140 just 9.5mi northeast of Mariposa, ranges from $14 to $16 for a dormitory bed. YARTS has 10 daily buses that stop at the Yosemite Bug;

Warning

Many hikes in Yosemite National Park go to the top of powerful waterfalls. The smooth granite along the edge of these rivers and streams is very slippery, even when not wet. Slipping into the swift-moving water and tumbling over a fall is almost certain to be fatal. Despite warning signs in different languages and protective railings in many places, every year people die needlessly. Approach any waterfall with caution and use common sense. Above all, don't get into the water!

round-trip tickets to Yosemite Valley cost $10, including the park entrance fee. Hop on Bus (☎ 866-467-6628, 415-777-1995, e] hoponbus@ aol.com, w] www.hoponbus.com) is an inexpensive hostel-to-hostel van service in California that stops at The Yosemite Bug three times a week.

Merced Home Hostel (☎ 209-725-0407, e] merced-hostel@juno.com), PO Box 3755, Merced, CA 95344, charges from $14 to $16 for a dormitory bed; advance reservations are required. They offers free pickup from the Greyhound and Amtrak stations in Merced and also rent tents ($5 per night) and sleeping bags ($3 per night).

Yosemite Valley

Sheer, glacially sculpted granite cliffs tower more than half a mile above the incomparable Yosemite Valley, through which courses the Merced River. World-renowned granite monoliths and waterfalls line both sides of this 7mi-long and half-mile wide meadow-carpeted valley. The dramatic scale dazzles hikers who take any of the trails from the valley floor to its rim. The western park (including Yosemite Valley), undoubtedly the Sierra Nevada's single most sensational and busy destination, experiences a mild climate. The best months to visit are May, June, September and October, although the valley is enjoyable year-round. Summer crowds, especially on key holiday weekends, can fill the valley almost to bursting. At such times hikers will find not only less-crowded trails but also much cooler and more pleasant temperatures in the high country, above the valley floor.

ACCESS FACILITIES
Yosemite Valley

Information A visitor center and wilderness center are in Yosemite Village. The Yosemite Valley visitor center, west of the post office at shuttle bus stops 5 and 9, provides general information. The nearby wilderness center, adjacent to the Ansel Adams Gallery, is the place to go for wilderness permits and trail information, not the visitor center. It is open daily 7am to 6pm. Backpackers starting from Yosemite Valley park their vehicles in the Wilderness Permit Holders Parking Lot south of Curry Village near Upper Pines campground.

Supplies & Equipment The Village Store in Yosemite Village is stocked with every imaginable item, including groceries and souvenirs. The Yosemite Valley Sport Shop sells gear and bear-resistant food containers.

The Mountain Shop in Curry Village, which is also home to the mountaineering school, has a wide variety of gear including everything from tents to bear-resistant food containers. An adjacent store sells groceries.

Places to Stay & Eat Wilderness permit holders are allowed to camp in the *Backpackers' Walk-in Camp* from April to October on the night before their permit entry date and the night of the permit exit date. Sites ($5 per person, cash or check only) are available on a first-come, first-served basis. Intentionally not marked on park maps, the camp is along the north bank of Tenaya Creek behind North Pines campground.

At the west end of the valley is the usually crowded first-come, first-served *Camp 4 Walk-in campground* ($5 per person), which is open year-round. Reservations are necessary at *North Pines campground* ($18, open April to September), the year-round *Upper Pines campground* ($18) and *Lower Pines campground* ($18, open March to October) at the valley's eastern end.

Valley lodging ranges from *Housekeeping Camp* ($54.75 for one to four people), *Curry Village* ($48 canvas tent cabin, $57.25 cabin without bathroom, $74.75 cabin with bathroom, $102.75 standard room, all based on double occupancy) and *Yosemite Lodge* ($102.75 standard room, $141.97 lodge room, both based on double occupancy) to the elegant *The Ahwahnee* (starting from $318.75). Public showers are available ($2) at Housekeeping Camp and Curry Village.

See Information Sources, p166, for details on how to make campground and lodging reservations.

Yosemite Village has three restaurants, including a deli. *Pavilion Buffet*, in Curry Village, serves breakfast and dinner, and several snack stands serve food throughout the day. Yosemite Lodge has a *food court* and two restaurants. *Mountain Room* is only open for dinner, but the bar and lounge there serve a la carte continental breakfast and lunch, as well as offering snack service throughout the day and evening. A trip to the *dining room* in The Ahwahnee (☎ 209-372-1489, dinner reservations recommended) is unforgettable, but formal and expensive, with dinner entrees starting at $20.

Getting There & Away The nearest international airports are in the Los Angeles area (a six hour drive), San Francisco area (a 3½ hour drive) and in Reno. Regional airports are in Fresno (90mi from the South Entrance) and Merced (73mi from the Arch Rock Entrance). Visitors usually rent a vehicle and drive to the park.

Three park entrances on the western side of the Sierra Nevada lead to the valley: South Entrance on Hwy 41 (Wawona Rd) north of Fresno, convenient from southern California; Arch Rock Entrance on Hwy 140 (El Portal

Rd) east of Merced, convenient from northern California; and Big Oak Flat Entrance on Hwy 120 (Big Oak Flat Rd) east of Manteca, also convenient from northern California. Gasoline is not available in Yosemite Valley.

Amtrak has several daily round-trip trains serving the Central Valley city of Merced, where you can transfer to public transportation to Yosemite Valley. From major airports, the first leg of Amtrak service is by bus to the nearest train station. From San Francisco ($30/54 one way/round trip, including the bus service), the bus goes to Emeryville, where you board the train to Merced. From Los Angeles ($29/55), the bus goes to Bakersfield, and from Reno ($29/55), the bus goes to Sacramento. Greyhound also runs to Merced from San Francisco ($26 one way, five hours) and Los Angeles ($29, seven hours).

The Yosemite Area Regional Transportation System (YARTS, ☎ 877-989-2787, W www.yarts.com) operates two bus routes to Yosemite Valley: daily year-round service from Merced along Hwy 140, and summer-only weekend service from Coulterville along Hwy 132 and Hwy 120. YARTS buses ($20/40 one way/round trip) depart Merced's Greyhound bus terminal at 16th St between N and O Sts (called Transpo), daily at 7, 8:45, 10:50am and 5:25pm, stopping a few minutes later at the Merced Amtrak train station at K and 23rd Sts. From there the bus goes to Yosemite Valley.

Return buses depart Yosemite Valley for Merced at 9:38am and 3:20, 3:55, 4:20, 5:20 and 7:50pm. A YARTS bus ($10/20 one way/round trip) departs Coulterville at 9am for Yosemite Valley, and departs Yosemite Valley for Coulterville at 7:25pm. Obtain your ticket before boarding the bus; contact any of the numerous local ticket sellers. Verify schedules and the location of ticket sellers directly with YARTS. VIA Adventures, Inc (☎ 800-842-5463), a private tour and charter bus company, operates the VIA Yosemite Connection (☎ 888-727-5287). These buses also operate between Merced and Yosemite Valley in conjunction with YARTS, following the same schedule.

The Tuolumne Meadows Tour & Hikers Bus ($14.50/23 one way/round trip, 2½ hours,

YOSEMITE NATIONAL PARK

56mi) plies between Yosemite Valley and Tuolumne Meadows mid-June to mid-September. The bus departs daily (Curry Village at 8am, Yosemite Village at 8:05am and Yosemite Lodge at 8:20am,) stops at Crane Flat ($5/9.50), White Wolf ($8.50/15.50), Yosemite Creek ($9.50/17.50), May Lake junction ($11.50/22), Olmsted Point and Tenaya Lake ($12.50/22), and arrives at Tuolumne Meadow Store at 10:20am and Tuolumne Meadows Lodge at 10:30am. Reservations are recommended; call ☎ 209-372-1240 up to one week in advance. You can be dropped off or picked up anywhere along the route by flagging down the bus.

Mammoth YARTS operates a round-trip bus ($15/20 one way/round trip) between Yosemite Valley and Mammoth Lakes once a day on weekends in June and September and once daily in June and July. The bus departs Yosemite Valley at 5pm. The fare just to ride the bus between Yosemite Valley and Tuolumne Meadows is $15 one way. For information on schedules or to make a reservation call Mammoth California Vacations (☎ 800-626-6684), which handles Mammoth YARTS bookings.

Getting Around The free Yosemite Valley Visitor Shuttle stops at 21 numbered locations around eastern Yosemite Valley year-round, operating daily at 15- to 20-minute intervals. A parking lot (shuttle bus stop 1) is centrally located near Yosemite Village.

Vernal Fall

Duration	2–3 hours
Distance	2.6mi (4.2km)
Standard	easy-moderate
Start/Finish	Happy Isles
Public Transport	yes

Summary Hiking on the Mist Trail along the Merced River as it ascends 1000ft to the top of Vernal Fall is one of Yosemite's most scenic day hikes.

Vernal Fall, which the Miwok people called Pai-wai'-ak, tumbles 317ft over a vertical cliff. The top of Vernal Fall is the easiest of Yosemite's waterfalls to reach, making it one of the valley's most popular day hikes. The wide, once-paved trail, however, has 1000ft elevation gain and another 1000ft elevation loss.

PLANNING
When to Hike
The hiking season is from May to November.

Maps
Tom Harrison Maps 1:24,000 *Map of Yosemite Valley* covers the hike, as does the USGS 1:24,000 *Half Dome* quadrangle.

Permits & Regulations
A permit is not required for this day hike. Camping is not allowed along this trail.

GETTING TO/FROM THE HIKE
The trailhead is Happy Isles (shuttle bus stop 16), which is near the south end of Upper Pines campground.

THE HIKE
(See the Vernal & Nevada Falls map.)
From Happy Isles (4035ft), cross the road bridge over the **Merced River** and head up its true right (east) bank. Opposite the footbridge that was destroyed by a 1999 flood, join the once-paved trail, which gently ascends 400ft in 0.7 miles to the **Vernal Fall footbridge**. Along the way you have views of 370ft Illilouette Fall. The very popular footbridge, with a restroom and drinking fountain on its southern side, has photogenic views of Vernal Fall.

Continue beyond the footbridge 0.3mi to a trail junction where the John Muir Trail turns right. Continue straight on the Mist Trail. Expect to get wet on this aptly named trail, as sheets of water from the falls spray your path. On sunny days, the spray dances with rainbows. From the junction, it is 0.3mi to the top of Vernal Fall. A final short but steep rock staircase, protected by a railing, brings you to the top of the fall, where you can dry off and enjoy the views and a picnic. Return to Happy Isles via the same trail, taking care on the often-slippery wet rock.

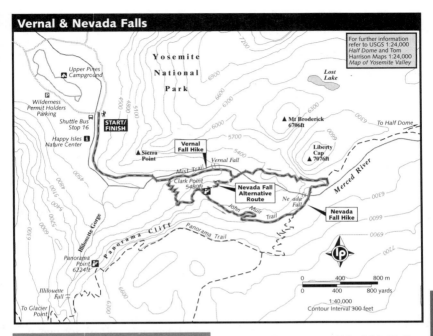

Nevada Fall

Duration	4–5 hours
Distance	6.5mi (10.5km)
Standard	moderate
Start/Finish	Happy Isles
Public Transport	yes

Summary Offering more scenic diversity than any other hike in Yosemite Valley, the day hike to the top of Nevada Fall ascends 1850ft to reach the valley's rim.

At Nevada Fall, the Merced River cascades 594ft over a polished cliff beneath the striking dome of Liberty Cap (7076ft). Originally called Yo-wai'-yik by the Miwok people, it is the tallest fall on the Merced River.

The hike to the valley's rim at the top of the fall has more than 3700ft of total elevation change – half up and half down. The hike description follows the gentler switchbacks of the renowned John Muir Trail up to the fall and the far more spectacular, yet steeper, Mist Trail down. To turn this into an overnight trip, continue 1mi beyond Nevada Fall and camp in Little Yosemite Valley along the Merced River.

PLANNING
When to Hike

The hiking season is from May to November. In early spring and late autumn, portions of the John Muir Trail below Nevada Fall and the Mist Trail near Vernal Fall may be closed due to snow, ice or avalanche danger.

The top of Nevada Fall, however, is usually still accessible to hikers. Take the John Muir Trail to Clark Point, detour down to cross the Merced River on the footbridge above Vernal Fall and follow the Mist Trail to Nevada Fall in both directions. Seasonal trail status is posted along the way.

Maps

Tom Harrison Maps 1:24,000 *Map of Yosemite Valley* covers the hike, as does the USGS 1:24,000 *Half Dome* quadrangle.

Permits & Regulations

A permit is not required for this day hike. A free wilderness permit is required to camp in Little Yosemite Valley (see Permits & Regulations, p167).

GETTING TO/FROM THE HIKE

The trailhead is Happy Isles (shuttle bus stop 16), which is near the south end of Upper Pines campground.

THE HIKE

(See the Vernal & Nevada Falls map.)
From Happy Isles (4035ft), cross the road bridge over the Merced River, turn right, and follow its east bank upstream to join the gentle pathway that ascends 400ft in 0.7mi to the popular Vernal Fall footbridge. A couple of minutes beyond the scenic footbridge is the junction of the John Muir Trail and Mist Trail, 1mi from the trailhead. Turn right, staying on the John Muir Trail; the Mist Trail continues straight to the top of Vernal Fall.

Follow the gentle switchbacks up the canyon 1.3mi, opposite the south wall of Sierra Point, through forest of Douglas fir and gold-cup oak to **Clark Point** (5480ft). Continue on a more level trail 1.0mi to the junction with the Panorama Trail. Stay on the John Muir Trail 0.2mi, crossing the footbridge over the Merced River at the top of **Nevada Fall** (5907ft), 3.5mi from Happy Isles. Picnic or relax on the granite rocks along the northeast brink of the fall. A spectacular but often overlooked scenic viewpoint lies a short distance down a spur trail on the river's north side. The terrace, protected by an iron railing, is at the very edge of the waterfall.

To avoid retracing your steps back to Yosemite Valley, the shorter but steeper Mist Trail leads back to Happy Isles in 2.8mi. From the top of Nevada Fall, walk 0.2mi farther northeast beyond the footbridge and look for the trail junction near a solar toilet. Turn left onto the Mist Trail beneath Liberty Cap and descend steeply on the 500-step rock staircase

alongside Nevada Fall. Cross another footbridge over the Merced River (5120ft) at the **Silver Apron** and continue along the Emerald Pool 0.1mi to Vernal Fall on a more gentle trail. Below Vernal Fall, descend another short rock staircase and follow the paved pathway from the Vernal Fall footbridge, reaching Happy Isles, 1.3mi from the top of Vernal Fall.

Another alternative, yet longer, return route leaves the Mist Trail at the footbridge (5120ft) at the Silver Apron and ascends 360ft in 0.5mi to Clark Point with great views overlooking Vernal Fall. From Clark Point, follow the John Muir Trail back to Happy Isles, 4.2mi from the top of Nevada Fall.

Yosemite Falls

Duration	5–6 hours
Distance	6.8mi (10.9km)
Standard	moderate-hard
Start/Finish	Camp 4
Public Transport	yes

Summary The classic hike to the top of Yosemite's most extraordinary waterfall, which has more than 4800ft total elevation change, offers a close-up experience of Yosemite's sheer vertical wonder.

Cho'lok, or Yosemite Falls, plunges 2425ft in three cascades – the upper fall is 1430ft, the middle 675ft, and the lower 320ft – creating the world's fifth-highest free-leaping waterfall. An excellent trail leads from the valley floor to the top of the falls along the valley's north rim, but the stiff ascent of 2410ft and equivalent descent makes this a strenuous day hike. When doing the side trip to spectacular Yosemite Point, it's an even stiffer ascent, of almost 3000ft.

PLANNING
When to Hike

The hiking season is from mid-May to mid-November. This south-facing trail is free from snow earlier than other trails to the valley rim, making it a desirable hike in May and June, when the falls are most powerful. By August they can be just a trickle in comparison.

Maps

Tom Harrison Maps 1:24,000 *Map of Yosemite Valley* covers the hike. The USGS 1:24,000 *Half Dome* and *Yosemite Falls* quadrangles also cover the hike.

Permits & Regulations

A permit is not required for this day hike. A free wilderness permit is required to camp at the top of the falls (see Permits & Regulations, p167).

GETTING TO/FROM THE HIKE

The trailhead is behind Camp 4, which is shuttle bus stop 7. The next nearest shuttle bus stops are 6 (Lower Yosemite Falls), 0.6mi from the trailhead along the Valley Floor Trail, and 8 (Yosemite Lodge), from where a very short walk across Northside Drive leads to the trailhead.

THE HIKE

From the east side of Camp 4 Walk-in campground (3990ft), go up slope for a minute to the northside Valley Floor Trail. Head west for a minute to the start of the Yosemite Falls Trail.

The trail ascends four dozen short switchbacks immediately, ascending steeply up a talus slope through gold-cup oaks. After 0.8mi, the trail becomes more gradual and follows switchbacks east to reach **Columbia Rock**, a viewpoint a mile from the trailhead and 1000ft above the valley floor with impressive views of Half Dome and Quarter Dome to the east.

In another 0.4mi, the trail approaches **Lower Yosemite Falls**, where breezes may shower you with a fine, cooling mist. After a few more switchbacks, the trail traverses northeast, bending north for views of the upper fall.

The trail then makes numerous switchbacks steadily up a rocky cleft in the cliffs to the valley rim. This cleft was once the route of Yosemite Falls, but when the last major glacier receded some 130,000 years ago, it left glacial moraine that blocked the river and shifted its course eastward to the cliff face, forming today's spectacular free-leaping waterfall.

The trail tops out 3.2mi from the trailhead and bends east. At the junction, the trail going straight leads to Eagle Peak. Turn right at this junction and follow the trail 0.2mi to the brink of upper Yosemite Fall at the **Yosemite Falls Overlook** (6400ft). The view of the falls is impressive, but views of El Capitan and Half Dome are obscured. For better views, go to Yosemite Point (see the Side Trip below). It's also possible to do this hike as an overnight trip. *Campsites* are in a forested area above Yosemite Creek's true right bank. Return along the same trail, back to Camp 4.

Side Trip: Yosemite Point

1½ hours, 1.6mi (2.6km), 536ft (161m) ascent, 536ft (161m) descent
From either the Eagle Peak Trail junction or the Yosemite Falls Overlook, head downhill to Yosemite Creek and cross the footbridge to its true left bank. The 0.8mi-long trail climbs gently, first heading north and then turning back east up switchbacks and south to the valley rim and Yosemite Point (6936ft). From this viewpoint are superb views of Half Dome, North Dome, Clouds Rest, Glacier Point, Cathedral Rocks and the best close-up view of Lost Arrow Spire.

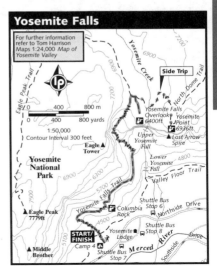

Yosemite Falls

For further information refer to Tom Harrison Maps 1:24,000 *Map of Yosemite Valley*

Camp 4: Fifty Years of Hard Rock in Yosemite

Along the base of the Middle Brother, not far from Leidig Meadow in Yosemite Valley, is a dusty, boulder-punctuated campground. In the 1950s and early 1960s, when the pioneers of Yosemite climbing first tackled the valley's big walls, the place was known as Camp 4. To climbers, Camp 4 was the center of the universe – a home away from home, a place to hang out, share stories and learn about the latest climbing gear and techniques. In the early 1970s, the National Park Service (NPS) changed the campground's name to Sunnyside. The name never really caught on, and valley regulars always referred to it as Camp 4.

Shock rippled through the climbing community in 1997 when word got out that the NPS planned to build employee housing at Camp 4. Legendary climber Tom Frost launched a vigorous grassroots effort, joined by the nonprofit Friends of Yosemite Valley, to save Camp 4. Climbers from every country with a mountaineering tradition joined in a successful worldwide letter-writing campaign to have Camp 4 declared eligible for the National Register of Historic Places. By 1998, Camp 4's eligibility established its permanent place in rock-climbing history.

On September 25, 1999, as the light of the full moon shimmered on Yosemite's granite walls and towers, the climbing community gathered to celebrate Camp 4's reprieve and 50 years of Yosemite climbing. The American Alpine Club sponsored the event, and many luminaries of the Yosemite climbing scene attended, including David Brower, Warren 'the Bat' Harding, Royal Robbins, Yvon Chouinard, Tom Frost, TM Herbert, Allen Steck, Galen Rowell, John Bachar, Don Reid, Peter Croft and Hans Florine. The NPS announced that the official name of the site would once again be Camp 4, and a replica of the original Camp 4 sign, which had been extracted from the El Portal dump by a climber some 25 years ago, was presented to the park.

Tom Frost described the event as 'a once in a lifetime moment in climbing history – a reunion for all who love climbing and Camp 4, a celebration of the historic significance of Camp 4 in the world of climbing and, as such, its determination of eligibility for the National Register.'

Four Mile & Panorama Trails

Duration	6½–8 hours
Distance	12.6mi (20.3km)
Standard	moderate-hard
Start	Leidig Meadow
Finish	Happy Isles
Public Transport	yes

Summary A classic near-loop hike with 3900ft of ascent taking in Glacier Point, Panorama Cliff and the Merced Canyon serves up a visual feast of waterfalls, granite domes and big walls at every turn.

A brilliantly fulfilling day hike from Yosemite Valley ascends to Glacier Point, traverses the valley's south rim, and follows the cascading Merced River back to the valley floor. Most of the hike provides a continually changing perspective on the rounded, glacially polished west and south sides of world-famous Half Dome. Passing alongside three of the valley's major waterfalls, the hike has 7800ft of elevation gain and descent, roughly in equal amounts, making it a demanding yet highly rewarding experience. Much of the trail is forested, providing welcome shade on the big climbs without obscuring the many breathtaking views.

Hikers not inclined to make the steep 3200ft ascent on the Four Mile Trail can instead start the hike from Glacier Point, which is served by the Glacier Point Hikers' Bus from Yosemite Valley ($10.50 one way; 1 hour, 30mi).

The bus departs from Yosemite Lodge at 8:30 and 10am and 1:30pm June to September, and at 8:30am and 1:30pm in

October. Reservations are recommended; call ☎ 209-372-1240 one day to one week in advance to reserve a seat.

The only way to turn this hike into an overnight trip is to detour 1mi beyond the top of Nevada Fall and camp in Little Yosemite Valley, saving the descent to Yosemite Valley for a short hike the next morning.

PLANNING
When to Hike
The hiking season is from July to October. The shady, north-facing Four Mile Trail remains closed longer than other trails early in the season due to possible patches of snow and ice.

Maps
Tom Harrison Maps 1:24,000 *Map of Yosemite Valley* and 1:31,680 *Half Dome Trail Map* covers the hike, as does the USGS 1:24,000 *Half Dome* quadrangle.

Permits & Regulations
A permit is not required for this day hike. A free wilderness permit is required to camp in Little Yosemite Valley (see Permits & Regulations, p167).

GETTING TO/FROM THE HIKE
To the Start
Start from Leidig Meadow (4000ft) along Southside Drive at Yosemite Valley's western end. The nearest shuttle stop is 7 (Camp 4), where a short walk west along a paved footpath leads over Swinging Bridge, which is just above sandy Sentinel Beach, to Southside Drive. Parallel the road west one to two minutes a very short distance to the signed Four Mile Trail Trailhead, just before the Yellow Pine/Sentinel Beach picnic area.

From the Finish
The trailhead is Happy Isles (shuttle bus stop 16), which is near the south end of Upper Pines campground.

THE HIKE
Follow the Four Mile Trail, which is more like 4.6mi, steadily up 2½ to four hours to **Glacier Point** (7214ft), a 3200ft cliff overlooking Yosemite Valley. The trail passes by 2000ft Sentinel Fall and beneath Sentinel Rock (7038ft) as it traverses Yosemite Valley's shady, north-facing wall. It reaches **Union Point** 3mi from the trailhead near a large tree, where the first Half Dome views

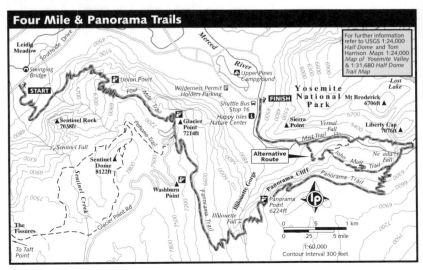

Four Mile & Panorama Trails

The First Ascent of El Capitan

The Yosemite Miwok tell that two bear cubs fell asleep on a rock along the Merced River. As they slept, the rock began to grow, reaching higher and higher, till the little bears' faces scraped against the moon. The animal people of Ah-wah'-nee Valley (Yosemite) gathered to try to bring the young cubs back. Each animal tried to leap up the great rock, but none could succeed, not even mountain lion, who was the best leaper. Finally Tul-tak-a-na, the green measuring worm, began to creep up the rock wall. Slowly he climbed, inch by inch, until finally he reached the top and brought the two bear cubs back down. Ever since, the boulder that grew into a great rock (El Capitan), has been called Tu-tok-a-nu'-la in honor of its first climber, the measuring worm.

appear. The construction of Four Mile Trail in 1871–72 was planned and financed by James McCauley as a toll trail to Glacier Point, then the site of a hotel that burned in 1969. With impressive views of El Capitan, Cathedral Spires, Three Brothers and Yosemite Falls, and unique perspectives of Royal Arches, Washington Column, North Dome and Half Dome, Glacier Point is a heavily visited spot. Its snack bar also makes it a good rest spot after the long ascent.

From Glacier Point, look for the signed start of the Panorama Trail. Descend the gentle, open, fire-scarred hillside south 2mi to cross a solid footbridge over **Illilouette Creek**, whose shaded banks offer delightful picnic spots. The distant roar from Vernal Fall is audible. As the trail leaves the creek, you have good views of the 370ft Illilouette Fall.

Ascending east to **Panorama Point** and farther to the top of **Panorama Cliff** high above Merced River brings amazing views of the Glacier Point apron, Half Dome, Mt Broderick (6706ft), Liberty Cap and Mt Starr King (9092ft). The trail descends to a junction, where the John Muir Trail heads to the left. Follow the trail to the right 0.2mi to

the top of **Nevada Fall**, 3.2mi from Illilouette Creek. From Nevada Fall, descend on the Mist Trail via Vernal Fall, or else on the 0.6mi longer and more gentle John Muir Trail, to Happy Isles at the eastern end of the valley. See the Nevada Fall hike, p171, earlier in this section for a description.

Yosemite's Classic Domes

Rising 4800ft above the eastern end of Yosemite Valley is Half Dome, the most glorious and monumental granite dome on earth. Its sheer vertical north face towers above Tenaya Canyon, directly opposite the smooth rounded summit of North Dome, which offers a stunning perspective on its colossal neighbor. Across Yosemite Valley to the southwest rises Sentinel Dome, the most accessible of these three domes. No trip to Yosemite is complete without standing on top of at least one of these magnificent examples of Yosemite's unique geology and savoring the panoramic 360-degree view over the incomparable valley.

Half Dome

Duration	2 days
Distance	17mi (24.4km)
Standard	hard
Start/Finish	Happy Isles
Public Transport	yes

Summary It is an awesome hike to the summit of this world-famous granite dome, towering above Yosemite Valley.

Rising more than 4800ft above the eastern end of Yosemite Valley, the granite monolith of Half Dome (8842ft) has awed visitors since the park's inception. Its 2000ft vertical north face has attracted climbers from around the globe since the first ascent (of the northeast face) in 1875 by George Anderson, a Scottish sailor and gold prospector who worked as a valley blacksmith. Hikers,

YOSEMITE NATIONAL PARK

too, covet this imposing landmark. The trail from Yosemite Valley, which passes two dramatic waterfalls, culminates in 360-degree panoramic views.

The rigorous hike is most enjoyable as a two-day trip, although fit hikers can attempt it as a demanding 10- to 12-hour day hike. If you consider this alternative, keep in mind there is a total of 9684ft total elevation change. Day hikers need to start by 6am in order to return before dark; carrying a flashlight is recommended. For those hikers intent on reaching the summit of a Yosemite dome for whom the Half Dome hike sounds like a bit too much of a trek, see the Sentinel Dome & Taft Point hike, p179, and North Dome hike, p182.

PLANNING
When to Hike

Hiking to the top of Half Dome is only allowed when the cable route to the top is open. Depending upon snow conditions, the NPS puts the cables up as early as late May and takes them down in mid-October. If you're planning an early season or late season trip, it's essential to confirm that the cables are in place (see Permits & Regulations, p167).

Maps

Tom Harrison Maps 1:24,000 *Map of Yosemite Valley* and 1:31,680 *Half Dome Trail Map* cover the hike, as do the USGS 1:24,000 *Half Dome* and *Yosemite Falls* quadrangles.

Permits & Regulations

A free wilderness permit is required, whether you camp on the northeast shoulder or in Little Yosemite Valley (see Permits & Regulations, p167). When trailhead quotas starting from Yosemite Valley are full, consider approaching Half Dome from Tenaya Lake (see the Tenaya Lake to Yosemite Valley hike, p189, or starting from Glacier Point along the Panorama Trail (see the Four Mile & Panorama Trails hike, p174).

GETTING TO/FROM THE HIKE

The trailhead is Happy Isles (shuttle bus stop 16), which is near the south end of Upper Pines campground.

THE HIKE
Day 1: Happy Isles
to Northeast Shoulder
4–5 hours, 8mi (12.9km), 3600ft (1080m) ascent

From Happy Isles (4035ft), ascend the paved pathway 400ft to the Vernal Fall bridge. Just beyond the bridge, turn right, staying on the John Muir Trail; the Mist Trail continues straight to Vernal Fall. Follow gentle switchbacks 2mi up to Nevada Fall (5907ft), 3.4mi from Happy Isles, and cross the footbridge over the Merced River. Continue over a low rise and reach level **Little Yosemite Valley** with views of the massive, rounded, golden southern side of Half Dome. Solar composting toilets testify to the popularity of its many *campsites*. Many people camp here to avoid carrying their backpacks higher. At the east end of Little Yosemite Valley, the Merced Lake Trail heads east (right) along Merced River. Stay on the John Muir Trail, which turns north (left) and climbs steeply through forest 1.3mi to the Half Dome Trail junction.

Turn west (left) onto the Half Dome Trail, where a signpost reads 2mi to Half Dome. Ten minutes above the junction on the left side of the trail is a somewhat hard-to-spot seasonal spring. This trickle is the last source of water, so fill up your water bottles. Continue for 30 minutes, first up through forest and then up switchbacks to the **northeast shoulder** (7600ft). Protect your food at all times from varmints scampering around this busy spot. The views from the pleasant *campsites* are spectacular, yet few people

Warning

No reliable drinking water source exists above the Merced River at Little Yosemite Valley. To avoid dehydration, drink up before going above Little Yosemite Valley. Carry at least 1L for a day hike and 3L when camping on the northeast shoulder. Heed this warning; people have fainted while on the cables.

Lightning strikes on Half Dome have been recorded every month of the year, so do not proceed above the northeast shoulder when storm clouds are visible on the horizon.

Half Dome

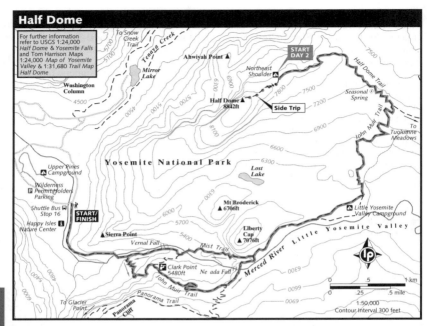

For further information
refer to USGS 1:24,000
Half Dome & Yosemite Falls
and Tom Harrison Maps
1:24,000 *Map of Yosemite
Valley* & 1:31,680 *Trail Map
Half Dome*

ever spend the night here. Since this is a dry campsite, bringing prepared food that requires no cooking is recommended.

Side Trip: Half Dome's Summit
1¾–3 hours, 1mi (1.6km), 1242ft (373m) ascent, 1242ft (373m) descent

The exposed route above the northeast shoulder campsite keeps some hikers from ever going beyond it. However, backpackers who camp there can visit the top of Half Dome in the late afternoon for sunset and again the next morning for exquisite solitude when the top is all but deserted.

A rocky trail snakes 650ft up two dozen switchbacks in 20 to 30 minutes to a notch at the top of the dome's shoulder and to the base of the **cables**. From here, steel cables bolted to the granite provide handholds, and intermittent wooden cross-boards provide footholds for the final 600ft ascent up an exposed 45-degree rock face. To protect the skin on your hands from the steel cables, you

can grab a pair of gloves from the pile at the base. A trip up uncrowded cables takes only 15 minutes, but on crowded cables (or if you are intimidated), it may take 30 minutes or longer. From the relatively flat five-acre expanse on top, enjoy the amazing views of Yosemite Valley – especially from the over-

JOHN MOCK

hanging northwest point – **Mt Starr King**, Clouds Rest (9926ft), the Cathedral peaks, Unicorn Peak and the Sierra Crest. Most people spend from 30 minutes to an hour on top. Watch the time carefully to avoid having to descend in the dark.

Camping on top of Half Dome is prohibited for three reasons: to protect the threatened Mt Lyell salamander's habitat, which was being disturbed by people moving rocks to build wind shelters; to reduce human waste left on top; and to protect the **last remaining tree**, as six of the seven trees previously growing there were illegally cut for campfires. Respect the camping ban and protect this fragile ecosystem.

Day 2: Northeast Shoulder to Happy Isles
4 hours, 8mi (12.9km), 3600ft (1080m) descent

Retrace steps to Little Yosemite Valley. At the northeast brink of Nevada Fall, turn right onto the Mist Trail just before the footbridge, and descend the 500-step rock staircase alongside Nevada Fall. Cross the footbridge above Vernal Fall, and continue to the fall on a more gentle trail. Descend another short rock staircase and follow the paved pathway from the Vernal Fall footbridge to Happy Isles.

Sentinel Dome & Taft Point

Duration	2½–3 hours
Distance	5.1mi (8.2km)
Standard	easy
Start/Finish	Sentinel Dome & Taft Point Trailhead
Public Transport	yes

Summary Get on top of a Yosemite dome with 360-degree views and hike past remarkable geological formations to a spectacular south rim viewpoint above Yosemite Valley.

Sentinel Dome (8122ft) and Taft Point (7503ft) are two easily reached viewpoints along the south rim of Yosemite Valley. The hike to Sentinel Dome is the shortest and easiest way anywhere in Yosemite to stand on top of a granite dome. For those who can't go to the top of Half Dome, Sentinel Dome offers an equally outstanding perspective on Yosemite's wonders. **Taft Point** is a fantastic, hair-raising viewpoint at the edge of a sheer 3000ft vertical cliff, with an impressive perspective on El Capitan and Yosemite Valley.

Because both viewpoints share the same trailhead along Glacier Point Rd, a vista-packed loop hike is possible by doing a counterclockwise circumambulation of Sentinel Dome. This 5.1mi loop has a total elevation change of 1958ft, which is an ascent of 979ft and an equal descent. Many hikers just visit one of the viewpoints on a 2.2mi round-trip hike, or backtrack on the same trails to each viewpoint, hiking a total of 4.4mi with almost 1500ft of total elevation change. The loop, which is only 0.7mi longer and avoids nearly all backtracking, offers more big views with comparatively little additional effort.

PLANNING
When to Hike
The trails are open whenever the Glacier Point Rd is open, usually mid-May to November. The hike is also nice in July, when wildflowers are at their peak bloom. Try timing your visit to the top of Sentinel Dome for sunrise or sunset, or better yet, a full moon.

Maps
Tom Harrison Maps 1:24,000 *Map of Yosemite Valley* covers the hike, as does the USGS 1:24,000 *Half Dome* quadrangle.

Permits & Regulations
A permit is not required for this day hike. Camping is not allowed anywhere along this trail, but the ***Bridalveil Creek Campground*** ($12; 7200ft) is nearby along Glacier Point Rd.

GETTING TO/FROM THE HIKE
From Hwy 41 (Wawona Rd) at Chinquapin (6000ft), turn east onto Glacier Point Rd and drive 13mi to the signed Sentinel Dome & Taft Point parking lot (7740ft) on the north (left) side of the road.

From Yosemite Valley, hikers can ride the Glacier Point Hikers' Bus ($10.50 one way; 1 hour, 30mi) to the trailhead 3mi before Glacier Point. The bus departs from Yosemite Lodge at 8:30 and 10am and 1:30pm June to September, and at 8:30am and 1:30pm in October. Reservations are recommended; call ☎ 209-372-1240 one day to one week in advance to reserve a seat.

THE HIKE

Just beyond the roadside parking lot, the trail divides. Take the right fork, heading north. The trail rises gently, contouring through an open area and then through mixed forest of white firs, Jeffrey pines and lodgepole pines. As you approach the base of Sentinel Dome after 20 minutes, several signs indicate the trail as it heads northwest across open granite slabs dotted with manzanitas. Turn north again, skirting the dome's base to join an old service road. Several signs here point back to the trailhead.

Continue up along the broad old road, passing a signed junction where the trail to the right leads to Glacier Point. Stay on the road, veering to the northwest (left) to emerge onto the **northeast shoulder** of Sentinel Dome. Another sign points in one direction to Glacier Point and in the opposite direction back to the parking lot. From these signs, turn abruptly to the southwest (left) 90 degrees, and head five minutes up the obvious gentle granite slope to the top of Sentinel Dome (8122ft), 1.1mi (35 minutes) from the trailhead.

The gnarled, bleached bones of a **Jeffrey pine** crown the dome's summit. The tree, famously photogenic when alive, died in a drought in the late 1970s. Allow at least 30 minutes on top to soak up the 360-degree views. To the west, Cathedral Rocks and El Capitan frame the Merced River and Yosemite Valley. To the north, Yosemite Falls leap from the valley's north rim to its floor, with Mt Hoffmann prominent in the distance. North Dome, Basket Dome and Mt

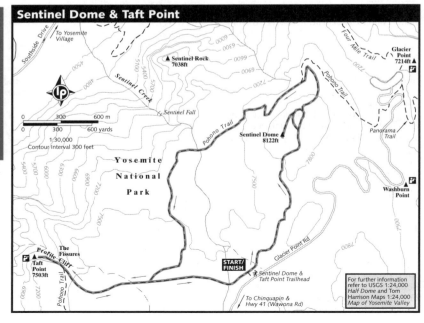

Watkins line the valley's northeast side. A distant **Mt Conness** locates the Sierra Crest, and much closer, Clouds Rest and Half Dome rise dramatically above Tenaya Canyon. In the distance, above Nevada Fall, are notable peaks of the Cathedral and Ritter Ranges – Mt Lyell, Banner Peak and Mt Ritter. Nearby to the east is the unmistakable smooth granite of Mt Starr King in the foreground of the **peaks of the Clark Range** – Mt Clark, Gray Peak, Red Peak and Merced Peak. To the south are the gentler, forested Buena Vista Crest and Horse Ridge.

From the summit, return down the open slope for two minutes to a trail sign that reads 'Glacier Point 1.3mi.' Follow this trail north, descending 300ft toward a small building that houses a radio facility. (Ignore the longer switchbacks of another service road.) The trail passes west (left) of the building, then turns sharply to the southwest to the junction with the Pohono Trail, 0.5mi and less than 15 minutes from Sentinel Dome.

Head southwest 15 minutes on the well-made Pohono Trail. The near-level traverse through a dense, **white-fir forest** as you pass beneath Sentinel Dome has breathtaking views of the purposeful bends in the Merced River and the lush meadows guarding it. Here you also see the full length of Yosemite Falls, a perspective gained from no other vantage point. T

wo gently graded switchbacks descend the soft, conifer-needle-covered trail to emerge at the forest's edge, where a large, fallen tree points toward the valley rim. The spectacular views of El Capitan and distant Mt Hoffmann along with the thunder of Yosemite Falls invite you to step away from the trail and enjoy the splendor.

The trail continues southwest for 15 minutes, leaving the valley rim, and descends through a deep, peaceful forest to arrive at **Sentinel Creek** (7340ft). A short distance downstream on either side of the creek are open rocky areas at the valley's rim that offer excellent picnic spots with superb views above Sentinel Rock and Sentinel Fall. Cross the creek via a fallen log when the water is high, or hop rocks when it's low.

Seeing a golden eagle on a high-elevation hike can be a thrill.

The trail ascends gently for 30 minutes through mixed forest to a signed junction with the Taft Point Trail. (This junction is 1.8mi from the building and the junction of the Pohono Trail and the trail from Sentinel Dome.) Turn right and continue southwest easily through forest. After 10 minutes, emerge from the forest heading northwest and descend in five minutes on an open, rocky slope following the unnamed creek that flows by the fissures. Pass the **fissures** on your right, four narrow chimney-like slots that drop hundreds of feet to Yosemite Valley along the edge of Profile Cliff. Across the valley are views to the **Three Brothers**, which have similar yet longer cracks in the rock. At the fourth fissure, the Pohono Trail splits off from the Taft Point Trail.

Ahead 0.1mi, the sheer drop at **Taft Point** (7503ft) is guarded by a metal railing. Looking west through binoculars, you can spot climbers on the southeast face and on the famous nose of El Capitan. You can also get a remarkable view of El Capitan's southwest face in profile. After soaking up the views, which include a close-up look at Cathedral Spires, return 1.1mi on the Taft Point Trail through forest, crossing and recrossing an upper portion of Sentinel Creek, to the parking lot.

North Dome

Duration	4½–5 hours
Distance	8.4mi (13.5km)
Standard	easy-moderate
Start/Finish	Porcupine Creek Trailhead
Public Transport	yes

Summary Hike along a vividly scenic ridge to spectacularly situated North Dome for consummate full-frontal exposure to Half Dome.

North Dome is arguably the best vantage point anywhere along Yosemite Valley's entire rim. Yet this spectacular spot above the north rim sees comparatively few hikers. Its perspective on Half Dome, Quarter Domes and Clouds Rest all rising above granite Tenaya Canyon is unrivaled.

The trail has 1000ft of descent but only 422ft of ascent on the way to North Dome, making the round-trip hike a total of 2844ft of elevation change. The side trip to the natural arch on Indian Ridge adds another 480ft of total elevation change. Keep in mind that it's mostly downhill on the way out to North Dome and uphill on the way back, although the gradient is almost never steep.

Longer variations of this hike are possible by descending to Yosemite Valley following either the Snow Creek Trail down to Tenaya Canyon and Mirror Lake at Yosemite Valley's east end, or by following the trail west to Yosemite Point and Yosemite Falls Overlook, from where you can take the Yosemite Falls Trail down to Camp 4 at Yosemite Valley's west end.

Or, you can start from Yosemite Valley and visit North Dome on a very demanding round-trip day hike of eight to 10 hours. It's also possible for fit hikers to traverse the valley's north rim via North Dome on an equally challenging day hike, by ascending the Snow Creek Trail's 100-plus switchbacks to the valley's north rim and returning via Yosemite Point on the Yosemite Falls Trail.

PLANNING
When to Hike
The hiking season is from mid-June to mid-October.

Maps
The USGS 1:24,000 *Yosemite Falls* quadrangle covers the hike, as does Tom Harrison Maps 1:31,680 *Half Dome Trail Map*.

Permits & Regulations
A permit is not required for this day hike. A free wilderness permit is required for any overnight trip (see Permits & Regulations, p167).

GETTING TO/FROM THE HIKE
The well-signed Porcupine Creek Trailhead (8120ft) is on Tioga Rd (Hwy 120) at road marker T19, 1.3mi east of Porcupine Flat campground. When camping at Porcupine Flat, walk across Hwy 120 from the campground entrance and follow the footpath that parallels the south side of Hwy 120 east to reach the trailhead.

The Tuolumne Meadows Tour & Hikers Bus from Yosemite Valley to Tuolumne Meadows passes the trailhead at about 9:30am ($10.50/20 one way/round trip). The shuttle bus from Tuolumne Meadows to Yosemite Valley passes the trailhead at about 2:45pm ($5/9).

THE HIKE
Follow an abandoned road, which once led to a now-closed campground, downhill

The Legend of Tisse'yak

Tisse'yak and her husband arrived in Yosemite Valley after a long journey across the mountains. Tisse'yak had carried a heavy conical basket, but her husband had only a light load. Tisse'yak arrived first and thirstily drank from Lake Awai'a (Mirror Lake), draining it dry. Her husband, angry that no water was left for him to drink, beat his wife. She became enraged and flung her basket at him. As they stood in anger, facing each other, they were transformed into stone for their wickedness. He is North Dome, the basket is Basket Dome, and she is Half Dome, whose face is stained black from tears.

0.7mi (20 minutes) through red-fir forest. The pavement ends and the trail turns right to cross a creek and then the larger lodgepole pine-lined Porcupine Creek (7840ft) via a log. Ascend gently and re-enter open red-fir forest, where you get the first glimpses of Clouds Rest and the Clark Range, and continue 30 minutes to a signed trail junction (7853ft), 1.5mi from trailhead. The Snow Creek Trail to Yosemite Valley via Mirror Lake turns left (east) here. Continue straight at this junction and go 50ft (0.1mi) farther to a second trail junction. At the second junction, take the left fork, which is signed to North Dome.

The trail traverses gently up the forested western slopes of Indian Ridge 10 minutes to an inviting viewpoint (7880ft). Granite boulders, open manzanita scrub and a few Jeffrey pines form the foreground to expansive views across Yosemite Valley to Sentinel Dome and Taft Point. Continue along the ridge's side through open red-fir forest, where white-flowering manzanitas lie low along the trail, 15 minutes to a seasonal creek. A short distance ahead, the trail turns back sharply east (left) and ascends steadily for 10 minutes to gain the ridgeline at the signed Indian Rock trail junction (8120ft), 1.1mi from the previous junction.

A worthwhile, but optional, side trip leads to the only **natural arch** visible in Yosemite National Park. (There is another arch, but it's submerged in the Tuolumne River.) Follow the short but steep spur trail 10 minutes and 0.3mi up the sandy slope one way to the arch (8360ft), which has good views of Clouds Rest, the Clark Range, Mt Starr King and Sentinel Dome. Clambering onto the rock presents a view of Half Dome framed through the arch. The arch is also referred to as Indian Rock, although the USGS topographic quadrangle and other maps name Indian Rock as the highest point (8522ft) on Indian Ridge several minutes' walk north of the natural arch. Allow 30 minutes for the 0.6mi natural arch round trip.

From the Indian Rock trail junction, the hike's highest point, the main trail continues south, descending gently along the

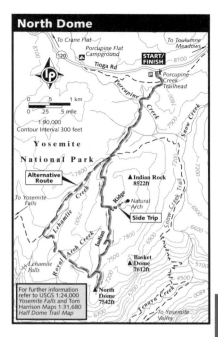

open ridge 10 minutes to a spectacular **viewpoint** at the end of the ridge that makes a fantastic ***campsite*** (8000ft). If you decide to spend the night here (or on North Dome), you need to bring water, since none is available nearby. From this viewpoint, directly in front of Half Dome, you also get a view across Yosemite Valley of the hard-to-see **Illilouette Fall**. North Dome is directly below to the south, and Basket Dome's round granite top (7612ft) is below to the southeast.

At a large, lightning-cropped Jeffrey pine, the trail drops southeast (left) off the ridgeline in the direction of Half Dome and descends on switchbacks through open Jeffrey pines and manzanitas 10 minutes onto open granite. Cairns mark the route, a few minutes across the rock to the signed North Dome Trail junction (7560ft), 1mi from the Indian Rock trail junction.

Turn east (left) onto the North Dome Trail for the final 0.5mi. The rough trail descends along a steep granite rib, then through white-fir forest to a saddle (7400ft) before making the short, easy five-minute ascent over granite to the summit of **North Dome** (7542ft). To the west are the Sentinels, Cathedrals, El Capitan, the Three Brothers and Yosemite Point; Yosemite Falls are hidden. To the northeast are Basket Dome, Mt Watkins and the distant peaks of the Cathedral Range. Horse Ridge fills the horizon to the south. But looming in front of everything is the sheer north face of **Half Dome**, surely one of the most impressive sights in all Yosemite.

Retrace your steps along Indian Ridge back to the trailhead in two to 2½ hours.

Alternative Route

To avoid retracing your steps along Indian Ridge, an alternative return route from North Dome via Lehamite Creek offers more solitude, on a peaceful, shady trail through forest. It foregoes the big ridge-top views and is 0.7mi longer than the trail along Indian Ridge; a stiff ascent adds more than 886ft total elevation change. It's a good option, however, if the weather turns stormy and you want to stay off the ridge. From North Dome, return to the main trail, turn southwest (left) and descend to cross Royal Arch Creek (7100ft). Climb to a high spot (7250ft) and descend through forest to cross Lehamite Creek above Lehamite Falls. A short distance beyond is a trail junction (7000ft), 1.3mi (30 minutes) from the North Dome Trail junction. Turn northeast (right) and ascend steadily 1.5mi along Lehamite Creek to rejoin the main trail from Indian Ridge in 45 minutes. Follow it 1.6mi back to the trailhead, making a 9.1mi clockwise loop.

Tuolumne

Smooth, dome-like peaks once covered by glaciers today stand opposite jagged peaks that rose above the ancient ice. Flowing from the Sierra Crest, the Lyell Fork and Dana Fork of the Tuolumne River converge in the 2½mi long Tuolumne Meadows, the Sierra Nevada's largest subalpine meadow.

This high elevation granite-crowned region enjoys a brief and glorious summer. The meadows' blossoms peak in July, after the June snowmelt and before the first August frosts. Hikers can escape Yosemite Valley's summer heat in Tuolumne Meadows and its surrounding high country, which are between 15°F and 20°F cooler. Snow can fall here in any month of the year, typically as late as June and as early as September.

ACCESS FACILITIES
Tuolumne Meadows

Information An information station is at Big Oak Flat Entrance on Hwy 120, and a visitor center is in Tuolumne Meadows at road marker T30, which is also shuttle bus stop 6. Facilities and trails along Tioga Rd are only open during the months when the road is open. At the start of the season, the road typically opens one to two weeks before facilities do.

The Tuolumne Meadows Wilderness Center, shuttle bus stop 3, is the place to go for wilderness permits and trail information, not the visitor center. It is open daily 7am to 6pm. The wilderness center is the building adjacent to the backpackers' parking lot 0.6mi east of the bridge over the Tuolumne River on the south side of Tioga Rd (Hwy 120).

Supplies & Equipment A well-stocked grocery store geared toward backpackers is in Tuolumne Meadows, adjacent to the Tuolumne Meadows Grill. The Tuolumne Meadows Sport Shop and Yosemite Mountaineering School and Guide Service, at the gas station, sell a variety of backpacking gear, including maps, dehydrated food and bear-resistant food containers. A small grocery store is at Crane Flat, but it sells mostly snacks, and it would be hard to outfit an extended backpacking trip here.

Places to Stay & Eat Some *walk-in sites* ($5 per person; cash or check only) are available for backpackers on first-come, first-served basis June to September behind Tuolumne Meadows *campground*. Other first-come, first-served campgrounds along the 39mi of Tioga Rd between Crane Flat and Tuolumne Meadows are *Tamarack Flat Campground* ($8, 6315ft), at road marker T2; *White Wolf Campground* ($12; 8000ft), at road marker T9; *Yosemite Creek Campground* ($8, 7659ft); and *Porcupine Flat Campground* ($8, 8100ft), at road marker T17. Reservations are required May to September at *Hodgdon Meadow Campground* ($18, 4872ft) and *Crane Flat Campground* ($18, 6192ft), and year-round for half of the sites at *Tuolumne Meadows Campground* ($18, 8600ft), at road marker T31. Hodgdon Meadow campground is open year-round, Crane Flat and Tamarack Flat campgrounds are open June to early September, and the others are open July to early September. When campgrounds along Hwy 120 are full, try any of the eight USFS campgrounds outside of the national park along the 12mi stretch of Hwy 120 between Tioga Pass and US 395, and along Saddlebag Lake Rd.

Tuolumne Meadows Lodge ($56 canvas tent cabin), shuttle bus stop 1, and *White Wolf Lodge* ($52 canvas tent cabin, $71 cabin with bathroom), which are only open mid-May to mid-September, provide everything except sleeping sheets or bags.

Both lodges serve a la carte breakfast and family-style dinners (☎ 209-372-8413 dinner reservations recommended), and have public showers ($2).

See Information Sources, p166, for details on how to make campground and lodging reservations.

Tuolumne Meadows Grill, adjacent to the store at shuttle bus stop 5, is open 8am to 6pm daily. It serves breakfast, hamburgers and frosties. Seating is only outdoors at picnic tables.

Getting There & Away The 56mi east-west section of Hwy 120 between Crane Flat and US 395 at Lee Vining, called Tioga Rd, is the only road to bisect the park and access Tuolumne Meadows. Visitors enter the park via the Big Oak Flat Entrance, east of Manteca off US 99, from the western Sierra or via Tioga Pass Entrance (9945ft), 7mi east of Tuolumne Meadows and 10mi west of Lee Vining, from the eastern Sierra. Typically the road is closed due to snow from mid-November to mid-May, although in years with heavy snowfall it may not open until late June.

The Tuolumne Meadows Tour & Hikers Bus ($14.50/23 one way/round trip; two hours, 56mi) plies between Tuolumne Meadows and Yosemite Valley from mid-June to mid-September. The bus departs once daily (Tuolumne Meadow Lodge at 2:05pm and Tuolumne Meadows Store at 2:15pm), stops at Tenaya Lake ($3/5), Olmsted Point, May Lake junction ($4/7), Yosemite Creek ($6/11), White Wolf ($7/13) and Crane Flat ($10/19), and arrives at Curry Village at 4pm, Yosemite Village at 4:05pm and Yosemite Lodge at 4:15pm. Reservations are recommended; call ☎ 209-372-1240 one day to one week in advance. You can be dropped off or picked up anywhere along the route by flagging down the bus.

Mammoth YARTS operates a round-trip bus between Mammoth Lakes and Yosemite Valley, which stops in Tuolumne Meadows, once a day on weekends in June and September and once a day in June and July. The eastbound bus ($15) to Mammoth Lakes passes through Tuolumne Meadows just before 7pm.

The westbound bus ($15) to Yosemite Valley passes through Tuolumne Meadows at 8:50am. For information on schedules or to make a reservation call Mammoth California Vacations (☎ 800-626-6684), which handles Mammoth YARTS bookings.

Getting Around The free Tuolumne Meadows Shuttle Bus plies Tioga Rd between Olmsted Point and Tioga Pass daily from 7am to 7pm mid-June to mid-September. The shuttle travels between Tuolumne Meadows Lodge and Olmsted Point, starting from Tuolumne Lodge at 7am and operating at roughly 30-minute intervals from 8:30am to 5:30pm. The last eastbound shuttle departs Olmsted Point at 6:30pm. Another shuttle goes between Tuolumne Meadows Lodge and Tioga Pass, departing at 9am, noon and 3 and 5pm.

YOSEMITE NATIONAL PARK

Mt Hoffmann

Duration	4–5 hours
Distance	6mi (7.7km)
Standard	moderate
Start/Finish	May Lake Trailhead
Public Transport	yes

Summary Mt Hoffmann, the park's geographical center, commands outstanding views of Yosemite's high country, with more than 50 peaks visible.

Hiking up Mt Hoffmann (10,850ft) takes just a few hours following a good trail that presents no difficulties. The broad summit plateau offers a superb perspective, from which almost the entire park is visible, a feature that drew the first California Geological Survey party in 1863. They named the peak after Charles F Hoffmann, the party's topographer and artist. It was the first peak climbed in Yosemite and remains one of the park's most frequently visited summits.

The hike has a total elevation gain and loss of 4008ft, with equal amounts of ascent and descent. A small solar-powered weather station sits atop the rocky western summit. Hiking only as far as May Lake gives good views of Half Dome and the peaks above Tuolumne.

To turn this into an overnight trip, it's easiest to stay at the campsites at May Lake, although camping on the summit plateau is nothing less than sublime.

PLANNING
When to Hike
The hiking season for this trail is from July to October.

Maps
The USGS 1:24,000 *Tenaya Lake* and *Yosemite Falls* quadrangles cover the hike.

Permits & Regulations
A permit is not required for this day hike. A free wilderness permit is required for any overnight trip (see Permits & Regulations, p167).

GETTING TO/FROM THE HIKE
Start from the May Lake Trailhead (8846ft), 1.7mi up paved Old Tioga Rd, which turns north off Hwy 120 (Tioga Rd) at road marker T21, 2.2mi west of Olmsted Point and 3.2mi east of Porcupine Flat campground.

The Tuolumne Meadows Tour & Hikers Bus from Yosemite Valley to Tuolumne Meadows stops at the May Lake junction at 9:45am ($11.50/22 one way/round trip). The bus from Tuolumne Meadows to Yosemite Valley passes the trailhead at 2:35pm ($4/7).

THE HIKE
The good 1.2mi trail to May Lake (9350ft) is very easy, with fine views of Cathedral Peak to the east, Mt Clark to the southeast, and Clouds Rest and Half Dome to the south. The lake, ringed by pines and hemlocks, is nestled beneath the rocky summits of Mt Hoffmann. At May Lake the trail forks; the right fork leads a short distance to *May Lake High Sierra Camp*, and the left fork to

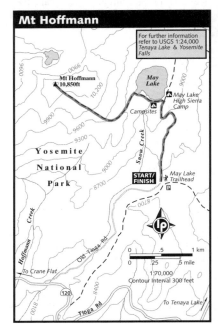

Mt Hoffmann. Heading west (left) through attractive **campsites** along the lake's southern shore, the trail crosses its outlet.

From the lake's southwest corner, the trail turns south and ascends, passing through a talus field where it becomes indistinct, although the route is obvious. Following along the left side of a small stream, the trail reaches a small meadow. Beyond the meadow it heads southwest and angles upward for 150yd and turns sharply back northwest directly toward Mt Hoffmann's eastern summit. Several paths marked with cairns leading up this rocky slope can cause hesitation, but they all converge above and go northwest though a broad meadow toward the western, highest summit, which is reached by a short, easy Class 2 scramble.

Camping is possible on the vast **plateau** near the eastern summit, although water must be carried from May Lake or melted from snow lying in the north-facing couloirs that lingers through July. The 360-degree views from the summit plateau are outstanding. Retrace your steps back to the May Lake Trailhead.

Clouds Rest

Duration	6–7 hours
Distance	14.4mi (23.2km)
Standard	moderate-hard
Start/Finish	Sunrise Lakes Trailhead
Public Transport	yes

Summary Ascending to the top of Yosemite's biggest chunk of granite is a classic day hike with awesome views.

Clouds Rest (9926ft), the largest granite expanse in Yosemite, rises 4500ft above Tenaya Creek, with spectacular views from the summit and along the trail. More than 1000ft higher than nearby Half Dome, Clouds Rest may well be Yosemite's best panoramic viewpoint. The hike has 5270ft of total elevation change – 2205ft ascent plus 430ft descent on the way to the summit and equal amounts on the way back – but getting there is worth the effort.

As a longer alternative to retracing your steps to Tenaya Lake, you can descend to Yosemite Valley from the summit of Clouds Rest (see the Tenaya Lake to Yosemite Valley hike, p189, later in this section).

PLANNING
When to Hike
As its name implies, clouds often settle on Clouds Rest. For the best views, hikers should look for an optimal day to visit the summit. The summit is accessible from mid-June to October, and even later if snow has not begun to accumulate.

Maps
The USGS 1:24,000 *Tenaya Lake* quadrangle covers the hike, as does Tom Harrison Maps 1:31,680 *Half Dome Trail Map*.

Permits & Regulations
A permit is not required for this day hike. A free wilderness permit is required for any overnight trip (see Permits & Regulations, p167).

GETTING TO/FROM THE HIKE
The well-signed Sunrise Trailhead at Tenaya Lake's western end is along Hwy 120 (Tioga Rd) west of Tuolumne Meadows. Trailhead parking is limited, and the parking lot frequently fills early. The free Tuolumne to Olmsted Point shuttle stops at the Sunrise Lakes Trailhead, shuttle bus stop 10.

The Tuolumne Meadows Tour & Hikers Bus from Yosemite Valley to Tuolumne Meadows stops at Tenaya Lake at 10:05am ($12.50/22 one way/round trip). The bus from Tuolumne Meadows to Yosemite Valley stops at 2:30pm ($3/5).

THE HIKE
A paved footpath heads east a short distance from the parking lot (8151ft) into lodgepole pines near the southwest shore of Tenaya Lake. It soon reverts to a trail and crosses the lake's shallow outlet stream, the start of Tenaya Creek. Entering the Yosemite Wilderness, the trail passes a left fork that leads to Tuolumne Meadows and continues straight (southeast) along the true

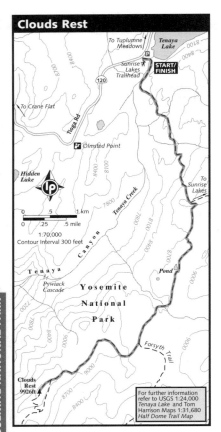

Tuolumne Peak (10,845ft) to the north. After 30 minutes of steady ascent, the granite steps end and the trail eases off over soft earth amid large red firs. A signed junction (9220ft) with the trail to Sunrise Lakes is 10 minutes ahead, 2.5mi from the trailhead. Tall western white pines whisper in the frequent breeze atop this open plateau.

As you descend southwest over a granite outcrop, distant Yosemite Valley and Sentinel Dome come into view and the trail soon reaches the level, forested floor west of the granite slopes of **Sunrise Mountain** (9974ft). Paintbrushes, lupines and wandering daisies bloom here, along with mats of pink heather and bushes of poisonous white-flowered labrador tea. The trail crosses a small creek and, 30 minutes beyond the junction, passes a shallow pond with a granite rock in the middle. Fifteen minutes beyond the pond, cross a larger creek (8870ft). This is the last water en route to Clouds Rest, so fill up your water bottles! The trail rises along a small branch of the creek for a few minutes, and 20 minutes from the crossing reaches a signed junction (9100ft). The trail to the southeast (left) is called the Forsyth Trail, although it is not labeled as such on this trail sign.

The trail to Clouds Rest bears southwest (right) from this junction, ascending through an open forest of western white pines and red firs along the ridgeline that culminates in Clouds Rest. To the southeast are fabulous views of wedge-shaped Mt Clark (11,522ft), the granite **Cascade Cliffs** and **Bunnell Point** of the Merced Canyon, and the granite hummock of Mt Starr King (9092ft) rising to the southwest. The trail passes over a low rise and through a slight, but obvious **saddle** (9360ft) on the ridge 25 minutes beyond the Forsyth Trail junction.

Beyond the saddle, the trail turns west and soon south as it ascends, emerging from the trees onto the ridge crest. At a large white pine, 20 minutes from the saddle, a small unsigned trail forks left. It's sometimes called the 'horse trail' and is recommended for those not willing or able to take the more exposed summit path.

Just above the white pine, a sign reading 'Clouds Rest Foot Trail' leads you along the

left bank of Tenaya Creek to the right and a granite rib to the left. Continuing about five minutes along the creek, ascend slightly and cross the granite rib, from where you catch your first glimpse of Clouds Rest and the shining granite of Tenaya Canyon, 20 minutes from the trailhead.

Leaving the moist lodgepole forest after another 15 minutes, the trail begins a steady ascent into a mixed fir forest, heading up well-constructed switchbacks. As you climb higher, the **view over the granite canyon** expands to include prominent Mt Hoffmann (10,850ft) to the northwest and granite ridge crest. The crest narrows rather thrillingly in one place, although it is never less than 5ft wide. The narrowest section might look intimidating to some hikers – more so than it actually is, since it only takes five to 10 second to cross it. After a few footsteps, the ridge quickly broadens and reaches the summit of **Clouds Rest** (9926ft), where the views are truly breathtaking. Half Dome immediately to the southwest is spectacular as you look down on its summit, with Yosemite Valley beyond. The view stretches from the Sawtooth Ridge and Matterhorn Peak along Yosemite's north border to Mt Ritter and Banner Peak, tall, dark and prominent to the southeast. Mt Conness and Mt Dana on the Sierra Crest and the nearer granite Cathedral Range are all outstanding. This is undoubtedly one of the Sierra Nevada's most amazing spots. Savor the view before retracing your steps back to the trailhead.

Tenaya Lake to Yosemite Valley

Duration	2 days
Distance	17.2mi (27.7km)
Standard	moderate-hard
Start	Sunrise Lakes Trailhead
Finish	Happy Isles
Public Transport	yes

Summary Traverse Clouds Rest and pass close to two waterfalls on this scenic approach to Yosemite Valley.

Instead of driving to Yosemite Valley, why not consider hiking there? It's not only ecologically sound, but is also mostly downhill when you start from trailheads along Tioga Rd. The most spectacular approach traverses the summit of Clouds Rest (9926ft), which is arguably Yosemite's finest panoramic viewpoint. An easier variation bypasses Clouds Rest completely and follows Sunrise Creek. Both hikes bring you down the giant staircase of the Merced River past world-renowned Nevada and Vernal Falls. Either can include a side trip to

the top of Half Dome (see the Half Dome hike, p176) for an outstanding tour of Yosemite granite.

The other classic approach is the John Muir Trail from Tuolumne Meadows via Cathedral Pass (see the Cathedral Lakes hike, p192, and the John Muir Trail, p289).

Tenaya Lake may be named for the Ahwahneechee chief, but it was he who resisted this dubious distinction by pointing out that the lake already had a name – Pywiack – meaning 'lake of shining rocks.' Set amid glacier-polished granite slopes that mirror sunlight just like a calm lake, Tenaya is a heart-achingly beautiful prelude to the symphony of granite on this remarkable hike.

PLANNING
When to Hike
The hiking season is mid-June to October. On stormy days, do not attempt to visit Clouds Rest.

Maps
The USGS 1:24,000 *Tenaya Lake, Yosemite Falls* and *Half Dome* quadrangles cover the hike, as does Tom Harrison Maps 1:31,680 *Half Dome Trail Map.*

Permits & Regulations
A free wilderness permit is required for this hike (see Permits & Regulations, p167).

GETTING TO/FROM THE HIKE
The trailheads are almost 50mi apart by road. Unless you shuttle two vehicles, use YARTS or the Tuolumne Meadows Tour & Hikers Bus to get between the trailheads.

To the Start
The well-signed Sunrise Trailhead at the western end of Tenaya Lake is along Hwy 120 (Tioga Rd) west of Tuolumne Meadows. Trailhead parking is limited, and the parking lot frequently fills early. The free Tuolumne to Olmsted Point shuttle stops at the Sunrise Lakes Trailhead, shuttle bus stop 10.

The Tuolumne Meadows Tour & Hikers Bus from Yosemite Valley to Tuolumne Meadows stops at Tenaya Lake at 10:05am ($12.50/22 one way/round trip). The bus

YOSEMITE NATIONAL PARK

from Tuolumne Meadows to Yosemite Valley stops at 2:30pm ($3/5).

From the Finish

Happy Isles, shuttle bus stop 16, is at the south end of Yosemite Valley's Upper Pines campground.

THE HIKE
Day 1: Sunrise Lakes Trailhead to Little Yosemite Valley

5½–6½ hours, 12.8mi (20.6km), 2205ft (662m) ascent, 4256ft (1277m) descent

See the Clouds Rest hike, p187, for a description of the 7.2mi-long trail to the summit of Clouds Rest. Having attained the summit perspective, head down granite steps off the southern end of the often-windy crest to the forested ridge below in five minutes, where white pines stand amid manzanitas and chinquapins on the sandy soil. Reach a signed junction with the bypass trail for horses after 0.6mi. Continue straight, down switchbacks on the hot, sunny, open slope amid scattered ponderosa pines, chinquapins and manzanitas. The southwest aspect enables ponderosa pines to grow here, well above their usual elevation band. Twenty minutes below the horse trail junction, pass beneath granite domes southwest of Clouds Rest where the trail turns sharply northwest. Continue the long, hot and dry descent on

Warning

Park rangers reportedly call Tenaya Canyon the 'Bermuda Triangle of Yosemite' – hikers who ignore the posted warnings to stay out of the canyon have a way of disappearing mysteriously. There are no trails and the canyon is dangerous. Navigating its hundreds of technical obstacles requires a rope, climbing skills and a couple of days. If you end up here, you're blowing it badly. Nobody wants to launch a costly search-and-rescue mission, so resist any temptation to think that a route down along a creek through a canyon is your quickest way to Yosemite Valley. It's not.

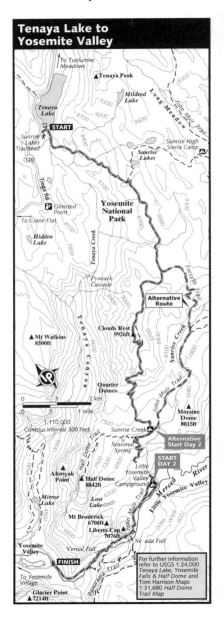

switchbacks heading southwest for another hour. Near the bottom of the knee-pounding 2726ft descent, the trail enters forest with refreshing shade.

Two hours (3.8mi) from the summit of Clouds Rest, reach the signed junction with the John Muir Trail (7200ft). Nearby Sunrise Creek provides the first water since well before Clouds Rest and offers several *campsites* in the forest. Turn west (right) onto the John Muir Trail and descend 15 minutes on a gentle grade 0.5mi to the signed junction with the heavily traveled Half Dome Trail. Go south (left) and head down the trail 1.3mi to established and busy *campsites* in **Little Yosemite Valley** (6100ft) along the Merced River. Both Sunrise Creek and Little Yosemite Valley experience chronic problems with bears.

Alternative Campsite: Sunrise Creek

Some hikers camp near the junction of John Muir Trail and Clouds Rest Trail along Sunrise Creek (7200ft). *Campsites* on the far side of the creek are more desirable than those right near the trail junction. This stop breaks up the 3826ft descent between Clouds Rest and Little Yosemite Valley by limiting it to 2726ft over 3.8mi on Day 1. Then on Day 2, descend another 1100ft over 1.8mi to Little Yosemite Valley.

Camping along Sunrise Creek, just 0.5mi before the Half Dome Trail junction, also puts you in the most desirable position if you decide you want to do the side trip to Half Dome (see the Half Dome hike, p176) before descending to Little Yosemite Valley. It's also possible to push on beyond Sunrise Creek to the northeast shoulder of Half Dome to camp.

Alternative Day 1: Tenaya Lake to Little Yosemite Valley

5–6 hours, 11.6mi (18.7km), 1299ft (390m) ascent, 3350ft (1005m) descent
Those not inclined to take in the top of Clouds Rest can follow an easier, forested trail along Sunrise Creek. Follow the Day 1 description for 2½ hours (4.7mi) to the signed junction (9100ft), where the trail to

Clouds Rest turns southwest (right) to follow the ridge crest to the summit, and the Forsyth Trail turns southeast (left).

From this junction in open, white-pine forest, bear left and follow the Forsyth Trail, which crosses a moist, lodgepole pine-lined meadow and then re-enters an open landscape of large white pines and granite boulders. The trail begins to descend along the true left bank of a creek amid red firs 15 minutes from the junction. The angle soon steepens as the trail descends south. Turning southeast, the trail makes a long, gradual traverse down the open red-fir-forested slope, with good views of the Clark Range, Merced Canyon and Mt Starr King, then turns and traverses west. High above to the right through the trees is the granite outline of Clouds Rest. Resuming its course south, the trail descends rather steeply through an area burned by a wildfire caused by a lightning strike. Beyond the charred area, the trail descends to cross a lupine-lined branch of **Sunrise Creek**. The angle eases, and the trail follows along the true right (north) bank of pretty Sunrise Creek 10 minutes, then crosses it above the confluence with another

You may spot a spotted owl nesting in a stand of Douglas firs.

branch. A slight ascent takes you away from the creek to the signed junction (8000ft) with the John Muir Trail, here known also as the Sunrise Trail. This junction marks the end of the 3.1mi Forsyth Trail.

Go southwest (right) on the John Muir Trail just 0.1mi to another junction, where a trail to Merced Lake goes east (left). Stay on the John Muir Trail, heading west (right) down along Sunrise Creek where the red firs yield to ponderosa pines. Lined with fragrant and delicate mountain azalea, Sunrise Creek splashes along as you walk along its true left bank, then soon cross to its true right bank and descend switchbacks. Reach the signed junction (7200ft) with the trail descending from Clouds Rest, 2mi from the Sunrise Trail junction.

Continue walking for 0.5mi to meet the busy Half Dome Trail. Go south (left) at this junction, following the descending John Muir Trail 1.3mi to established **campsites** in **Little Yosemite Valley** (6100ft) along the Merced River.

Day 2: Little Yosemite Valley to Happy Isles

2–2½ hours, 4.4mi (7.1km), 2065ft (620m) descent

See Day 2 of the Half Dome hike, p176, and the Nevada Fall hike, p171, for descriptions of the trails between Little Yosemite Valley and Happy Isles.

Cathedral Lakes

Duration	4–5 hours
Distance	7.6mi (12.2km)
Standard	easy-moderate
Start/Finish	Cathedral Lakes Trailhead
Public Transport	yes

Summary The gem-like Cathedral Lakes, lying beneath the unique white granite spires and fins of the Cathedral Range, invite day hikers to picnic, swim or contemplate the peaks' reflections on the water.

The Cathedral Range runs northwest from the Sierra Crest, separating the Tuolumne and Merced Rivers. The striking granite pinnacles and cockscombs of the range give it a unique beauty, and the many lakes, streams and meadows among the high forests endow the range with a truly park-like atmosphere. The hike has a total elevation gain and loss of 2276ft, with equal amounts of ascent and descent.

Cathedral Lakes offer fine swimming. Camping is possible at both lakes, but chronic problems with bears make a visit to the lakes more enjoyable as a day hike rather than an overnight trip.

PLANNING
When to Hike
The hiking season extends from mid-June to September.

Maps
The USGS 1:24,000 *Tenaya Lake* quadrangle covers the hike.

Permits & Regulations
A permit is not required for this day hike. A free wilderness permit is required to camp at the lakes (see Permits & Regulations, p167).

GETTING TO/FROM THE HIKE
The hike starts from a parking area on the south side of Hwy 120 (Tioga Rd), 1.7mi west of Tuolumne Meadows Visitors Center. The free Tuolumne to Olmsted Point shuttle stops at the Cathedral Lakes Trailhead (8562ft), shuttle bus stop 7.

THE HIKE
Joining the John Muir Trail about 500ft from the trailhead (8562ft), the trail rises steadily southwest, moving away from Budd Creek. It descends slightly, with views of **Unicorn Peak**, and crosses Cathedral Creek, then ascends past a spring and skirts the west side of Cathedral Peak, reaching a junction in about 2.8mi. The right fork leads in half a mile to Lower Cathedral Lake (9288ft), while the main John Muir Trail goes south slightly more than a mile, passing Upper Cathedral Lake (9585ft) – which beautifully reflects **Cathedral Peak** (10,911ft) – to

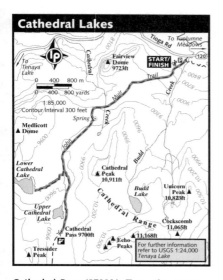

Cathedral Pass (9700ft). From the pass are fine views of the peaks of the Cathedral Range, including Tresidder Peak, Echo Peaks and the Matthes Crest. From the high point, return along the same trail.

Waterwheel Falls

Duration	2 days
Distance	18mi (29km)
Standard	moderate
Start/Finish	Glen Aulin Trailhead
Public Transport	yes

Summary Hike here along the Tuolumne River, passing a series of six waterfalls, to reach the Grand Canyon of the Tuolumne.

The Grand Canyon of the Tuolumne River stretches 15mi between Tuolumne Meadows and Hetch Hetchy Reservoir. Waterwheel Falls is the last and most impressive in a series of six cascades before the Tuolumne River plunges even farther into the canyon. Within the canyon lies forested Glen Aulin, a peaceful interlude between the otherwise continuous cascades.

The canyon itself was scoured smooth during the Tioga glacial period, just 20,000 years ago, when the massive Tuolumne Glacier, a 2000ft-thick river of ice, coursed from the Sierra Crest through Tuolumne Meadows and completely filled Hetch Hetchy Valley. The contrasting shapes of the peaks around Tuolumne depict this glaciation – the smooth dome-like peaks were under the glacier, whereas the sharp, jagged summits of the Cathedral Range and Sierra Crest remained above the ice that quarried their slopes. These features are eminently and delightfully visible as you walk along the river through the meadow and into the resplendent colorful granite canyon.

You could, if fit, do this hike in a single monumental day, but you would scarcely savor the remarkable falls, canyon and forested glen. Or you could go on a day hike only as far as White Cascade near Glen Aulin High Sierra Camp. You would not be disappointed, but you would miss the forested glen, the Tuolumne River's most impressive series of cascades and its largest waterfall – Waterwheel Falls. Walk down, spend the night and walk back the next morning, relishing the Grand Canyon of the Tuolumne and its exquisite falls.

PLANNING
When to Hike
The hiking season is from mid-June to October, but the falls are at their best before August.

Maps
The USGS 1:24,000 *Tioga Pass* and *Falls Ridge* quadrangles cover the hike.

Permits & Regulations
A free wilderness permit is required for this hike (see Permits & Regulations, p167).

GETTING TO/FROM THE HIKE
To reach the trailhead from Tuolumne Meadows, head east on Tioga Rd (Hwy 120) 0.1mi beyond the bridge over the Tuolumne River to the Lembert Dome parking area on north side of Tioga Rd. Turn left (north) onto the unpaved road and go 0.3mi to its

end at the signed Glen Aulin Trailhead (8580ft). The trailhead is a 0.3mi walk from shuttle bus stop 4.

THE HIKE
Day 1: Tuolumne Meadows to Waterwheel Falls

4 hours, 9mi (14.5km), 120ft (36m) ascent, 2260ft (678m) descent

Beyond the locked gate at the trailhead (8580ft), the trail follows a gravel road parallel to the Tuolumne River through John Muir's 'meadow in the sky.' Across Tuolumne Meadows to the south soar the Cathedral Range's granite summits. After 10 minutes, the road divides. Take the right fork ascending slightly and curving around Soda Spring to the Yosemite Wilderness boundary sign, 0.5mi from the trailhead.

Turn right onto the Glen Aulin Trail and hike through open lodgepole pine forest 20 minutes to a crossing of shallow Delaney Creek. Continue 10 minutes more to a signed junction with the Young Lakes Trail, 1.3mi from Soda Spring. Take the left fork, heading northwest through lodgepole pines 15 minutes to emerge into meadows along the river to inspiring views of **Fairview Dome**, **Cathedral Peak** and **Unicorn Peak**.

Another 30 minutes farther, the level, cairn-dotted trail crosses an open, vast, glacially polished granite slab, dotted by a few erratics, where the Tuolumne River flows. Soon the roar of the river signals the end of Tuolumne Meadows and the start of the cascades.

The trail climbs briefly over a granite rib, affording distant views of Matterhorn Peak (12,264ft) and Virginia Peak (12,001ft) on Yosemite's northern boundary, and a first view of the huge, orange-tinged granite cliff above Glen Aulin. Descend from the granite rib through forest to a two-part wooden footbridge (8320ft) spanning the Tuolumne River, 2.3mi from the Young Lakes Trail junction.

The granite-constructed and gently stepped trail, now on the river's true left bank, descends steadily, alternating between forest and the riverside as it winds down to the first large cataract, **Tuolumne Falls** in 15

minutes. Mt Conness (12,590ft) comes into view to the northeast. Continue along the plunging river another 15 minutes to a signed junction with the May Lake Trail, 1.1mi from the footbridge. From this junction, descend 0.2mi along the Tuolumne River as it flows over **White Cascade**. In five minutes come to a steel girder footbridge (7880ft) spanning the river just below the pool beneath White Cascade, a good picnic area.

Cross the footbridge to the river's true right bank and come immediately to two trail junctions in close succession. To the right, a footbridge crosses Conness Creek to the Glen Aulin High Sierra Camp. Do not cross this, but go straight to the second trail junction a few steps beyond. Here the PCT continues north (straight) to nearby *campsites* adjacent to Glen Aulin High Sierra Camp, and on to Cold Canyon and Virginia Canyon. Turn west (left) onto the trail to Waterwheel Falls, 3.3mi downstream.

From the junction, the trail crosses a low granite rib and descends an orange-stained granite slope into **Glen Aulin**, a long, level forested valley where the river flows green and tranquil beneath a massive water-stained granite wall. Pass through a ghost forest of standing dead lodgepole pines, their down-curving white branches intact and delicately brittle.

Aspens cling to the Tuolumne River's bank, and a few hemlock deepen the forest green. Abundant lupines add a splash of purple to open patches, where both fire and avalanches have taken their toll on the trees. The trail wanders between the forest and the river's edge, inviting a dip in the placid waters, and crosses an area made marshy by a stream descending cliffs from Cold Mountain (10,301ft) to the north.

After 40 minutes of strolling, reach the far end of the peaceful glen, where the river flows deceptively smoothly to the brink of the first of a series of near continual cascades. The trail, too, plunges along the river, dropping over gorgeous orange-tinted granite, and as you walk the view over the Grand Canyon of the Tuolumne stretches ahead as far as the eye can see. Big, red-barked

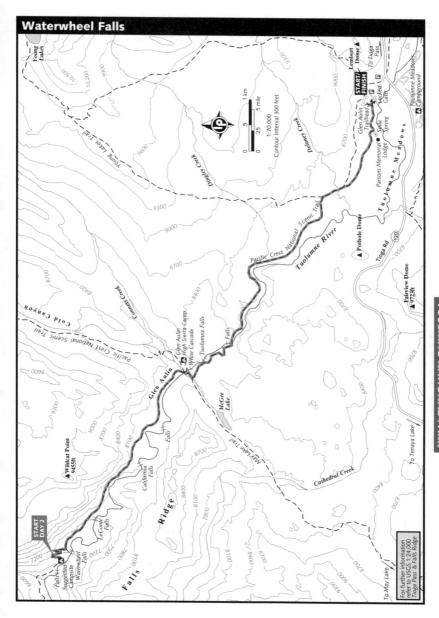

Waterwheel Falls

Young Lakes

10,500
10,200
9900
9600

Young Lakes Trail

Delaney Creek

9300

9000

8700

Pacific Crest National Scenic Trail

Tuolumne River

9600

Lembert Dome
To Tioga Pass

START/FINISH

Glen Aulin Trailhead
Soda Spring
Parsons Memorial Lodge

Lecked Gate

Tuolumne Meadows Campground

T u o l u m n e   M e a d o w s

▲ Pothole Dome

Tioga Rd
120

8700

Fairview Dome
▲ 9723ft

YOSEMITE NATIONAL PARK

N

1 km
.5 mile
.25 .5
0

1:70,000
Contour Interval 300 feet

Conness Creek

8400

Cold Canyon

Pacific Crest National Scenic Trail

Glen Aulin
High Sierra Camp
White Cascade

Tuolumne Falls

Falls

9600

9300

McGee Lake

May Lake Trail

8700

8400

Cathedral Creek

8700

8400

To Tenaya Lake

▲ Wildcat Point
9455ft

Falls

California Falls

LeConte Falls

Glen Aulin

R i d g e

8400

8100

7800

9000

8700

8600

8500

START DAY 2

Falls
Suggested Campsite
Waterwheel Falls

7200

7500

F a l l s

6600

For further information refer to USGS 1:24,000 Tioga Pass & Falls Ridge

YOSEMITE NATIONAL PARK

junipers cling to the granite as you descend, leaving the lodgepole behind and entering into mixed forest of firs and pines. Walk along the aquamarine river beneath the huge, sheer, polished northern granite walls of Wildcat Point (9455ft), with the 8000ft granite wall of Falls Ridge rising above the opposite, southwestern bank. **California Falls** and **LeConte Falls** are the most prominent cascades in this section, yet most are unnamed. If you ask yourself, 'Are these the Waterwheel Falls?' keep going; they're not. Waterwheel Falls are obvious.

An hour after leaving the glen, as the trail descends through pine and manzanita, you come to a small unsigned junction (6820ft), where a hard-to-see spur trail branches southwest (left) to a viewpoint of Waterwheel Falls. Their obvious roar tells you this is the spot, although you will find the falls are somewhat hidden from view by trees. From the main trail, walk two minutes to the edge of massive **Waterwheel Falls**, named for distinctive 15ft- to 20ft-high plumes of water that curl into the air like a wheel midway down the more than 600ft-long falls.

After viewing the thundering falls, return to the main trail, turn west (left) and continue 10 minutes downvalley. As you approach some scattered junipers next to an obvious dark granite rib that is perpendicular to the trail, turn south (left) and head down a sandy slope through manzanitas, following a use trail that runs parallel to the rock rib. It leads to a large, level forested *campsite* (6440ft), which is partly visible from the main trail above. Camp beneath big ponderosa pines and incense cedars, about 0.3mi below Waterwheel Falls, with the green and tranquil Tuolumne River about 200ft away.

Day 2: Waterwheel Falls to Tuolumne Meadows

4 hours, 9mi (14.5km), 2260ft (678m) ascent, 120ft (36m) descent

Retrace your steps to the trailhead. The initial and steepest ascent takes you back to Glen Aulin. Once across the steel bridge over the Tuolumne River, watch the trail

carefully where it crosses open granite areas, being careful not to wander off the trail. Small stones mark the way. The final stretch through forest along Tuolumne Meadows to Soda Spring seems long, but is relieved by frequent and spectacular vistas over the Cathedral Range.

Stop for a thirst-quenching sip at **Soda Spring** before the last few easy minutes to the trailhead. No trip to Tuolumne is complete without a sip of the naturally carbonated mineral water issuing forth from this spring in the heart of the Sierra Nevada's largest subalpine meadows. First described in 1863 by California Geological Survey botanist William H Brewer as 'pungent and delightful to the taste,' these bubbly founts continue to delight and amaze travelers. Bring your own cup to dip from the several pools inside a split rail enclosure near McCauley Cabin, an early residence now used by the National Park Service, and Parsons Memorial Lodge, built by the Sierra Club in 1914, which now hosts interesting exhibits.

Lyell Canyon

Duration	2 days
Distance	17.6mi (28.3km)
Standard	easy-moderate
Start/Finish	Lyell Canyon Trailhead
Public Transport	yes

Summary Following the Lyell Fork Tuolumne River, this level segment of the John Muir Trail meanders through quintessential subalpine meadows and forest to the base of Mt Lyell, Yosemite's highest peak, from where an ascent is possible.

The John Muir Trail along the Lyell Fork Tuolumne River is surely the most level stretch of trail anywhere in the Sierra Nevada, gaining only 200ft over 8mi. Strolling the lovely forested meadows along the winding Lyell Fork beneath the Sierra Crest is an unforgettably scenic hike that offers experienced hikers an opportunity to climb Mt Lyell.

PLANNING
When to Hike
The hiking season is from July to September.

Maps
The USGS 1:24,000 *Vogelsang Peak* quadrangle covers the hike, and the *Mt Lyell* quadrangle covers the side trip to Mt Lyell.

Permits & Regulations
A free wilderness permit is required for this hike (see Permits & Regulations, p167).

GETTING TO/FROM THE HIKE
The Lyell Canyon Trailhead (8700ft) is unusual because it is not along a road. Any of four footpaths lead a short distance to the signed trailhead, which is along the true left bank of the Dana Fork Tuolumne River on the south side of the only footbridge that crosses this river.

From Tuolumne Meadows Lodge (shuttle bus stop 1), walk southwest 0.2mi and cross the footbridge to the trailhead. From the Dog Lake parking lot (shuttle bus stop 2), which is along the road to the lodge, cross the road to the John Muir Trail sign and walk south one minute across the meadow and follow the true right bank of the Dana Fork upstream to the east-southeast 0.3mi (about six to eight minutes) to the trailhead across the footbridge.

From the parking lot at the Tuolumne Meadows Wilderness Center (shuttle bus stop 3), look for a hidden trail sign saying 'Tuolumne Lodge, John Muir Trail,' and walk southeast along the trail paralleling the road to the lodge and the Dana Fork upstream 20 minutes to the trailhead across the footbridge.

From the Tuolumne Meadows campground, walk to an alternative trailhead that starts in 'A Loop,' opposite site A88, and follow it along the true left bank of the Lyell Fork. The trailhead sign here reads, 'To Pacific Crest, John Muir.' It joins the John Muir Trail, and in 30 minutes (about a mile), meets the trail from the Lyell Canyon Trailhead, 0.4mi beyond that trailhead and 0.8mi before the junction with the trail heading up Rafferty Creek.

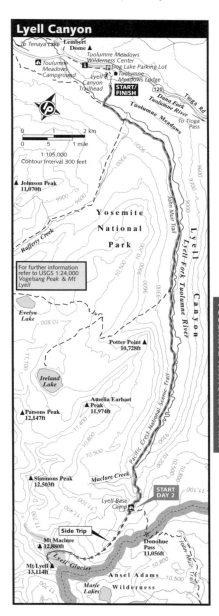

YOSEMITE NATIONAL PARK

THE HIKE
Day 1: Lyell Canyon Trailhead to Lyell Base Camp
5–6 hours, 8.8mi (14.2km), 340ft (102m) ascent

The trail parallels the road to Tuolumne Meadows Lodge a short distance, then turns south and follows the Dana Fork Tuolumne River before crossing it and heading south half a mile to a set of bridges over the Lyell Fork Tuolumne River. Across the river, the trail meets the John Muir Trail and turns left onto it. Soon the trail crosses Rafferty Creek and turns southeast into Lyell Canyon, along the river's meadow-lined south bank. Passing the trail to Ireland and Evelyn Lakes, the trail crosses Ireland Creek and, passing beneath Potter Point, continues to *Lyell Base Camp* (9040ft) on a forested bench at the base of the John Muir Trail's ascent to Donohue Pass.

Side Trip: Mt Lyell
5–7 hours, 4074ft (1222.2m) ascent, 4074ft (1222.2m) descent

Mt Lyell (13,114ft), named for British geologist Sir Charles Lyell, is Yosemite's highest peak, first climbed in 1871. The easiest and most popular route is Class 2 to 3 over the north glacier and the north face, but requires prudence. Difficulty varies with snow conditions, and a rope should be carried for safety. If you're uncertain about attempting the peak alone, hire a guide (see Guides, p39).

From Lyell Base Camp, head southeast across the upper basin, crossing talus and the west end of the Lyell Glacier to the saddle between Mt Lyell and Mt Maclure (12,880ft). From here, sloping Class 2 ledges above the glacier lead toward the summit. A short, steep Class 3 crack with some exposure is the crux. Allow three to four hours for the ascent and two to three hours for the descent.

Day 2: Lyell Base Camp to Lyell Canyon Trailhead
5 hours, 8.8mi (14.2km), 340ft (102m) descent

Follow the John Muir Trail along the Lyell Fork back to the trailhead.

Vogelsang

Duration	3 days
Distance	27mi (43.4km)
Standard	moderate
Start/Finish	Lyell Canyon Trailhead
Public Transport	yes

Summary A loop hike crossing two passes through the Cathedral Range takes hikers on a visual feast of lakes and meadows, cascades and domes, with exhilarating panoramic views.

Crossing Tuolumne and Vogelsang Passes through Yosemite's **Cathedral Range** offers a remarkable circuit through John Muir's 'Range of Light.' The smooth curve of polished pale granite walls, domes and ridges crowned by upthrust summit blocks tells the story of once-vast glaciers, where beautiful lakes now fill the cirques and bowls. The vast and sloping subalpine meadows and streams on either side of the gentle Tuolumne Pass (9992ft) provide some of the Sierra Nevada's most delightful hiking. With multiple cascades and sweeping views of distant peaks in several mountain ranges, including the hard-to-see Clark Range, the hike is a visual feast. Camping at **Vogelsang Lake** and crossing the alpine **Vogelsang Pass** (10,660ft) may be the highlights, but the hike never lets down, continually rewarding you with some of the best the Yosemite high country has to offer as it circumambulates Vogelsang Peak.

PLANNING
When to Hike
The hiking season is from July to September.

Maps
The USGS 1:24,000 *Tioga Pass, Vogelsang Peak, Mt Lyell, Merced Peak* and *Tenaya Lake* quadrangles cover the hike, as does the Tom Harrison Maps 1:63,360 *Yosemite High Country* map ($8.95).

Permits & Regulations
A free wilderness permit is required for this hike (see Permits & Regulations, p167).

GETTING TO/FROM THE HIKE

See the Lyell Canyon hike, p196, for details on how to get to the Lyell Canyon Trailhead (8700ft).

THE HIKE
Day 1: Lyell Canyon Trailhead to Vogelsang Lake

4 hours, 7.4mi (11.9km), 1641ft (492m) ascent

From the trailhead sign across the footbridge along the true left bank of the Dana Fork Tuolumne River, walk 15 minutes southeast through a lodgepole-pine forest over a low rise and then turn southwest to cross two wooden footbridges that span Lyell Fork Tuolumne River. The river flows clear over granite bedrock with an idyllic meadow expanse on the far side. Two minutes beyond the footbridges is a junction where the trail from the Tuolumne Meadow campground from the northwest joins the John Muir Trail.

Turn southeast (left), staying on the John Muir Trail as it enters lodgepole forest beyond the riverside meadow. Twenty minutes (0.8mi) ahead turn south (right), leaving the John Muir Trail. The 2½ hour long 4.9mi ascent along Rafferty Creek begins with a rutted ascent up the hillside. The trail, gouged out by the steel-shod hooves of pack horses and mules that keep the Vogelsang High Sierra Camp supplied during summer, clambers over granite steps and cobblestones through forest for some 20 to 30 minutes before it eases off and nears Rafferty Creek's true left bank. To the north, you see Mt Conness and White Mountain, and nearby to the east, the Lyell Fork Meadows some 500ft below. As you ascend, continual expansive views of **Kuna Crest** and **Sierra Crest** with Mt Conness and Mt Dana unfold.

With the steepest part of the trail now behind, you begin a continual gradual ascent heading gently up the attractive little valley. The trail crosses a small branch stream and soon draws near chuckling Rafferty Creek, following along its left (west) bank, with a splendid granite spur ridge of the Cathedral Range to your right. The forested trail continues up gently another 30 to 40 minutes, then enters a small open meadow, a harbinger of things to come. Passing again amid lodgepole pines and crossing several more small branch streams, the well-worn trail finally emerges into a lovely, open meadow along Rafferty Creek.

Lupines and penstemons splash color along the creek, while Fletcher Peak's bulky mass and Vogelsang Peak's pointed granite summit rise above the open horizon ahead. The blocky granite ridge that includes Johnson Peak (11,070ft) and Rafferty Peak is dramatically close, to the right. Follow the nascent creek ever upward, crossing its small willow-lined feeders. You pass several small ponds and, 6.1mi from the trailhead, arrive at gentle **Tuolumne Pass** (9992ft). A clump of whitebark pines offers shade and a place to sit and have a bite to eat. Belding's ground squirrels approach close in hope of a handout, but don't feed them!

At the signed Tuolumne Pass junction, take the left fork and head southeast. The trail has enticing views of Boothe Lake and the granite ridge above it as it traverses up 0.8mi to **Vogelsang High Sierra Camp** (10,130ft). The camp's white tent cabins along the ridgeline beneath Fletcher Peak (11,408ft) are picturesque. Three trails diverge here at a signed junction. To the left (east) 0.1mi is Fletcher Lake and a backpackers' **campground** equipped with bear boxes and toilets. To the right (west) is a trail down Fletcher Creek, which eventually leads to Merced Lake High Sierra Camp. Take the trail that continues straight ahead (south) and leads to Vogelsang Pass.

Cross Fletcher Creek immediately beyond the High Sierra Camp and skirt the base of Fletcher Peak as the trail ascends past clusters of whitebark pine. In the western distance you can see Clouds Rest, the top of Half Dome, and the white spot of Sentinel Dome. Just 0.5mi (20 minutes) beyond the High Sierra Camp, arrive at large **Vogelsang Lake** (10,341ft), set in a picture-perfect cirque beneath Fletcher and Vogelsang Peaks. Named for the Vogelsang brothers, who headed the California Fish and Game Board from 1896 to 1910, the name itself translates aptly from German as

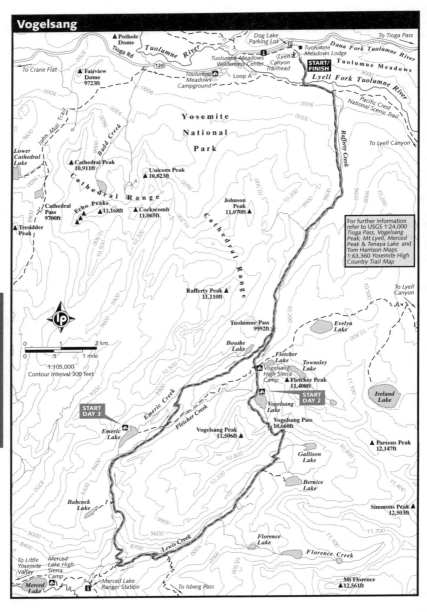

'a meadow where birds sing.' Above the northeast shore near the base of Fletcher Peak are *campsites* among whitebark pines.

Day 2: Vogelsang Lake to Emeric Lake

5½–6 hours, 10.2mi (16.4km), 1557ft (467m) ascent, 2560ft (768m) descent

Cross the lake's outlet stream on logs and contour up around the west side through subalpine meadows. The trail ascends above the lake's southwest end and, 45 minutes from the outlet, you cross a large, cold stream just below its spring-fed source. The view of the granite-framed lake below and the Cathedral Range beyond is sublime. Five minutes beyond the spring is the obvious pass in the serrated granite ridge descending from Vogelsang Peak (11,506ft). The level alpine **Vogelsang Pass** (10,660ft) holds a small meadow and a pond.

From the actual pass, the trail traverses east briefly, rising a bit higher and providing a sweeping view of the upper Lewis Creek Basin. Lovely Gallison Lake, surrounded by meadow, sends forth a cascading stream. Large Bernice Lake lies at the base of a massive granite ridge beneath Mt Florence (12,561ft). Half a dozen more lakes lie hidden in a chain above Gallison Lake, fed by the permanent snow on the slopes of Simmons Peak (12,503ft) at the valley's head. To the southwest is the more distant Clark Range, sweeping from the west to the southeast: Mt Clark (11,522ft), Gray Peak (11,574ft), Red Peak (11,699ft), Merced Peak (11,726ft) and Triple Divide Peak (11,607ft).

Head down switchbacks, following the course of a small stream that you cross twice. The south-facing slope is warm and dry, with sagebrush, lupines, paintbrushes and penny-royals along the trail. At the base of this 30-minute descent, enter a lodgepole-pine forest along the level valley floor and in five minutes cross to the true left bank of the outlet stream that descends from Gallison Lake. Braided streams course across the lush meadow where you recross Gallison Lake's outlet stream and, two minutes later, cross the larger outlet stream from Bernice Lake. The two streams join to form **Lewis Creek**.

Follow its true left bank several minutes downstream through forest to a signed junction with the trail to Bernice Lake, 1.5mi (45 minutes) below Vogelsang Pass.

Continue straight at the junction, heading downstream along Lewis Creek through a deepening hemlock forest as the angle of descent steepens. In 20 minutes, cross **Florence Creek**, which cascades down granite slabs dramatically. Passing through deep hemlock and fir forest, the trail runs next to a 15ft-high, almost overhanging granite wall. Descending across an open granite slab, the trail comes close to tumbling Lewis Creek.

Traversing up and away from the creek, the trail passes the junction with the trail to Isberg Pass, 3mi from the junction with the trail to Bernice Lake and 45 minutes after crossing Florence Creek. Continuing 1mi down the trail through **a dramatic canyon**, you have a view of distant Half Dome, just before descending past large junipers to the signed junction (8160ft) with the trail to Merced Lake. It's only 1.8mi (45 minutes) from this junction to Merced Lake, but camping is not allowed at the lake itself. Backpackers must camp away from the lake in a dense forest behind the Merced Lake High Sierra Camp. Walking a short distance down this trail offers a nice view of Merced Lake, more than 1000ft below. The view is sufficient, for the lake hardly justifies the dusty descent and subsequent ascent the next morning.

Instead, turn north (right) at the signed junction and follow the trail up Fletcher Creek. The trail makes a short descent to cross a wooden footbridge (8100ft) over Lewis Creek five minutes from the junction. A short distance beyond the footbridge is a possible *campsite*, if you are not inclined to go farther, although stopping here leaves you with a long day back to Tuolumne Meadow. It makes a much better lunch spot.

The trail ascends along Fletcher Creek as it cascades down around the base of an **enormous granite dome** that sits right in the middle of the valley. Crossing several side streams, the trail stays mostly in the shade as it climbs high above the true left bank of this beautiful stretch of Fletcher Creek. The views back of the Clark Range improve continuously as you ascend along granite slabs until, about one hour from the footbridge, the trail levels out and attains a **fabulous viewpoint** over Merced Canyon and the interesting peaks of the Clark Range.

Leaving these views behind, head into lodgepole-pine forest and quickly reach the signed junction with the 0.3mi-long trail to Babcock Lake, 1.6mi from the junction of the trail to Merced Lake. Small and warmish Babcock Lake offers few enticements to visit other than solitude.

Continuing on amid pines, the trail ascends gently along placid Fletcher Creek, then begins to ascend more steeply along the creek, which tumbles over granite. After 25 minutes of easy ascent, the trail emerges into a lovely meadow, with another smaller granite dome rising northwest of Fletcher Creek. Stroll 20 minutes through the charming granite-lined meadow, with the familiar Vogelsang and Fletcher Peaks rising ahead, to a four-way trail junction, which is 2mi above the Babcock Lake trail junction. Here the trail to Emeric Lake leaves the main trails upvalley. Turn northwest (left) and head 0.4mi to the large **Emeric Lake** (9338ft). Cross its inlet to reach good *campsites* above the northwest shore.

Day 3: Emeric Lake to Lyell Canyon Trailhead

4–4½ hours, 9.4mi (15.1km), 654ft (196m) ascent, 1292ft (387m) descent

Retrace your steps 0.4mi in 15 minutes to the four-way junction, which looks very much like the letter 'X', along Fletcher Creek. Looking upvalley, the trail to the northeast (right) leads in 2.2mi back to the Vogelsang High Sierra Camp, and is dustier from more use. Take the north (left) trail, a less-traveled trail to Boothe Lake. Both trails eventually lead to Tuolumne Pass, but the trail via Boothe Lake has 150ft less ascent, is 0.1mi shorter and altogether more pleasant.

Rising up onto a ridge through open lodgepole-pine forest, the trail passes a shallow lake and then another small but pretty lake that reflects Fletcher and Vogelsang Peaks above its southeast shore. Paralleling a granite rib for a few minutes, the trail passes a third small and narrow lake and, topping a small rise, comes to **Boothe Lake**, 2.5mi (one hour) from the junction. Large and lovely Boothe Lake, the original site of the High Sierra Camp before it was moved to it present location and renamed Vogelsang, has granite slopes on its northwest side that rise to a rocky summit. Lodgepole pines line its southeast shore. The trail stays well above the lake, where camping is prohibited. Arrive once again at **Tuolumne Pass**, 0.4mi and 15 minutes beyond Boothe Lake. Retrace your steps easily in two hours, 4.9mi down along Rafferty Creek to the John Muir Trail and then 30 minutes and 1.2mi to the Lyell Canyon Trailhead. Either fork of the Tuolumne River beckons you for a refreshing dip to wash off the trail dust.

Mono Pass

Duration	3½–4½ hours
Distance	7.4mi (11.9km)
Standard	easy-moderate
Start/Finish	Mono Pass Trailhead
Public Transport	yes

Summary A delightful day hike ascending 915ft to an historic pass on the Sierra Crest visits subalpine meadows and lakes with great views of the Tuolumne high country.

Mono Pass (10,604ft), a saddle on the Sierra Crest between the rounded summits of Mt Gibbs (12,764ft) and Mt Lewis (12,296ft), was the highest point on an ancient Native American trade route that linked the Mono Lake area with Tuolumne and continued to Yosemite Valley via Cathedral Pass. Native Americans crossed the pass in both directions, trading pine nuts, obsidian and edible brine-fly pupae from Mono Lake for acorns and forest products from Yosemite Valley. Along the trail and on the historic pass itself are remnants of late-19th-century log buildings.

The day hike from Dana Meadows along the Dana Fork Tuolumne River follows the well-marked historic trail past meadows through open forest to the expanse of the lake-crowned pass, and returns via the same gentle, scenic path. The hike has a total elevation change of 1830ft, in equal amounts of ascent and descent.

Or, it's possible to cross Mono Pass and descend Bloody Canyon, following the ancient route to the Bloody Canyon Trailhead (7935ft) at Walker Lake along the June Lake Loop west of US 395 and south of the Hwy 120/US 395 junction. Unless you have two vehicles or arrange for someone to drop you off or pick you up, you have to take the YARTS bus serving the June Lake Loop to get back to Dana Meadows.

PLANNING
When to Hike
The hiking season is from mid-June to September.

Maps
The USGS 1:24,000 *Tioga Pass, Mount Dana* and *Koip Peak* quadrangles cover the hike.

Permits & Regulations
A permit is not required for this day hike. Camping is prohibited in the Dana Fork Tuolumne River watershed. If you wanted to make this into an overnight trip, you could legally camp at Upper Sardine Lake east of Mono Pass, which is beyond the Dana Fork watershed and outside the national park in Inyo National Forest.

GETTING TO/FROM THE HIKE
The well-signed Mono Pass Trailhead (9689ft) is on Hwy 120 (Tioga Rd) at road marker T37, 1.4mi south of Tioga Pass and 5.6mi east of the bridge over the Tuolumne River in Tuolumne Meadows.

The free eastbound Tuolumne to Tioga Pass shuttle departs from Tuolumne Lodge at 9am and noon and then 3 and 5pm, reaching the Mono Pass Trailhead in 10 minutes. The westbound shuttle to Tuolumne Meadows departs less than 15 minutes later.

THE HIKE
The trail heads southeast through open lodgepole-pine forest, with the reddish bulk

of Mt Dana (13,053ft) prominent to the northeast. After 0.5mi of easy hiking along the edge of Dana Meadows, the well-worn trail crosses two shallow branches of the Dana Fork Tuolumne River in quick succession. Rising east over two small, timber-covered ridges that descend from the shoulder of **Mt Gibbs** (12,764ft), the trail passes amid stately lodgepole pines along the edge of several small, buttercup-filled meadows. Emerging from the pines, the trail ascends gently along meadow-lined Parker Pass Creek, with the reddish rock of Mt Gibbs close above to the east.

The pines grow shorter as the trail rises to a signed junction (10,000ft) with the trail to Spillway Lake, 2mi (one hour) from the trailhead. Follow the left fork, which has a sign reading Mono Pass and Parker Pass, although the right fork also leads to Parker Pass.

From the junction, the trail to Mono Pass makes its only steep ascent for five minutes, heading southeast away from the creek. Small whitebark pines begin to appear amid the lodgepole pines, and lodgepole chipmunks scamper about. The trail passes the remains of a log cabin and opens into a large

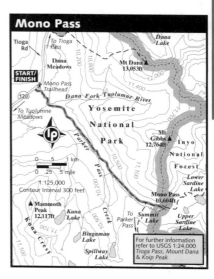

Mono Pass

meadow along a small creek descending from the pass. Views downvalley of the rocky Kuna Crest and Mammoth Peak (12,117ft) are impressive. Thirty minutes (1.4mi) from the signed junction with the trail to Spillway Lake, a small, unsigned use trail marked only by a rock arrow branches south (right), heading across the creek and meadow toward Parker Pass. One minute and 150ft farther, a metal sign (10,600ft) informs you that Mono Pass is just 0.3mi ahead.

Passing clusters of wind-twisted whitebark pine, the gentle trail turns east and passes above two small lakes to the south and arrives quickly at broad, grassy **Mono Pass** (10,604ft). Tiny Summit Lake lies just west of the pass, and larger Upper Sardine Lake lies east of and just below the pass. The even larger Lower Sardine Lake is farther down Bloody Canyon, beneath the first of multiple cascades down the canyon. Tree frogs call from the banks of Summit Lake in early summer, and along its north side are meadows where scrub willows, Sierra onions and yellow potentillas flourish. Whitebark pines cling to its south shore. At the southern end of the pass sit three historic log cabins, one of which has a partially intact roof.

Retrace your steps back to the trailhead, enjoying the expansive views of the Kuna Crest and over Dana Meadows as you descend.

Mt Dana

Duration	6–7 hours
Distance	5.8mi (9.3km)
Standard	hard
Start/Finish	Tioga Pass
Public Transport	yes

Summary Reaching the rocky summit of Yosemite's second highest peak involves a short but steep 3108ft ascent, with unrivaled views of Mono Lake and the Yosemite high country.

Mt Dana (13,057ft) is Yosemite's second highest peak, named for American geologist James Dwight Dana. Only 5.8mi round trip, but with a vertical rise of more than 3100ft above Tioga Pass (9945ft), this strenuous day hike offers unrivaled views of Mono Lake, the Grand Canyon of the Tuolumne River and the rest of the Yosemite high country. Prior acclimatization helps make the hike more enjoyable.

PLANNING
When to Hike
The hiking season is from July to mid-September. Snow may block the trail early in summer. Do not start out on the hike if a storm threatens. In July, beautiful deep-blue-violet flower clusters of sky pilot, with its sweet and musky fragrance, bloom near the summit.

What to Bring
The summit is always windy, and often draws afternoon clouds, so start in the morning and carry a jacket. No water is available, so carry at least 2L, along with lunch.

Maps
The USGS 1:24,000 *Tioga Pass* and *Mount Dana* quadrangles cover the hike, but other larger scale maps (see Maps, p166) help to identify the peaks visible from the summit.

Permits & Regulations
A permit is not required for this day hike. Camping is prohibited along the Dana Fork Tuolumne River, but is allowed on top of Mt Dana. A free wilderness permit is required for any overnight trip (see Permits & Regulations, p167).

GETTING TO/FROM THE HIKE
The trail begins at Tioga Pass Entrance on Hwy 120, 8mi northeast of Tuolumne Meadows and 12mi west of Lee Vining. Parking areas can be found on either side of the entrance.

The free eastbound Tuolumne to Tioga Pass shuttle departs from Tuolumne Lodge at 9am and noon, and 3 and 5pm, reaching the trailhead at Tioga Pass in 15 minutes. The westbound shuttle to Tuolumne Meadows departs within a few minutes after the eastbound shuttle arrives.

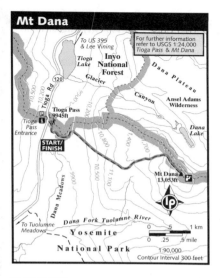

Mt Dana

For further information refer to USGS 1:24,000 Tioga Pass & Mt Dana

To US 395 & Lee Vining

Tioga Lake

Inyo National Forest

Glacier

Tioga Pass 9945ft

Tioga Pass Entrance

START/ FINISH

Dana Plateau

Canyon

Ansel Adams Wilderness

Dana Lake

Mt Dana 13,053ft

Dana Meadows

To Tuolumne Meadows

Dana Fork Tuolumne River

Yosemite National Park

0   5   1 km
0   .25   .5 mile
1:90,000
Contour Interval 300 feet

THE HIKE

The unsigned trailhead is on the east side of Tioga Pass. The trail heads east, passing between two broad shallow pools, then begins ascending. The angle soon steepens, and the trail passes through flower-filled meadows about halfway up the 1700ft climb to a west-descending ridge, marked by a large, loose cairn, 1.8mi from Tioga Pass.

From this cairn, several indistinct paths head up the rocky, Class 1 western slope to the summit, still 1.1mi (a 1400ft ascent) away. Avoid the left-most path through difficult talus blocks along the northwest ridge in favor of paths to the right that offer easier footing. The views from Mt Dana's summit are so outstanding that some hikers spend the night on top, where there are two small rock windbreaks. From the summit, retrace your steps downhill to the trailhead.

Hetch Hetchy

The Hetch Hetchy Valley, gateway to the Grand Canyon of the Tuolumne River, lies today submerged by O'Shaughnessy Dam. Beneath the placid waters is one of Yosemite's most beautiful valleys. Native American Ahwahneechee and Piute once came each summer to gather acorns in Hetch Hetchy Valley, whose name comes from the native word *hatchatchie* for an edible grass that grew in this beautiful, glacier-carved valley.

In 1900, the USGS recommended Hetch Hetchy as a potential reservoir to provide water for San Francisco. Despite vigorous protests from John Muir, who decried the project as tantamount to submerging a cathedral, the US Congress passed the Raker Act in 1913, authorizing construction of a dam on the Tuolumne River. O'Shaughnessy Dam, named for San Francisco's city engineer, was

---

Restore Hetch Hetchy

Probably no other issue exists that symbolizes the hopes and dreams of environmentalists more than the quest to restore Hetch Hetchy, and with it, to protect the integrity of America's national parks.

In 1970, the Sierra Club board of directors recommended the removal of O'Shaughnessy Dam and the restoration of Hetch Hetchy. In 1987, President Reagan's Secretary of the Interior, Donald Hodel, proposed the restoration of Hetch Hetchy Valley, and in 1988 the US Department of the Interior completed a preliminary study outlining scenarios for restoring Hetch Hetchy while still allowing use of the Tuolumne River for water and electric power. Current detailed proposals to restore Hetch Hetchy without reducing water and electricity for San Francisco exist, but the political will is lacking.

The Sierra Club continues its long-standing call for the removal of the dam and restoration of Hetch Hetchy Valley, which once rivaled Yosemite Valley in beauty and grandeur. The non-profit organization Restore Hetch Hetchy (☎ 209-379-9334, ⓔ info@ hetchhetchy.org, ⓦ www.hetchhetchy.org), PO Box 289, Yosemite, CA 95389, works to address the future of Hetch Hetchy and the Tuolumne River.

YOSEMITE NATIONAL PARK

the largest structure on the West Coast when it was dedicated in 1923. Originally 312ft high, it went to 430ft in 1938, with a projected life span of 100 years. When you take a drink of water in San Francisco, you are drinking Tuolumne River water from the Hetch Hetchy Reservoir. *Hetch Hetchy: Requiem for a Valley,* by Brooks Anderson, tells the story of this valley drowned for a drink.

Wapama Falls

Duration	2½–3 hours
Distance	5.4mi (8.7km)
Standard	easy
Start/Finish	O'Shaughnessy Dam
Public Transport	no

Summary Stroll to the base of two of Yosemite's most exhilarating yet least known waterfalls, in the quiet western corner of the park.

Nowhere else in the park does a trail bring you so close to the shower and roar of a big waterfall. The name of these falls is less well known than the reservoir into which they tumble. Along the northern shore of beautiful Hetch Hetchy Reservoir, two side-by-side waterfalls tumble more than 1000ft over fractured granite walls into the reservoir: the seasonal, free-leaping Tueeulala Fall and the triple cascades of the enormous, year-round Wapama Falls. The two falls can be photographed together, along with Hetch Hetchy Dome (6197ft) to their immediate east. The gentle trail rolls along the reservoir's shore with less than 800ft of total elevation gain and loss, in equal amounts.

Warning

Poison oak grows along the trail, particularly between the footbridge beneath Tueeulala Fall and Wapama Falls. The trail is broad, however, so it's easy to avoid. Rattlesnakes and some other snakes, although rare, live in this area. Leave your swimsuits and fishing poles behind, as both swimming and fishing in the reservoir are prohibited.

PLANNING
When to Hike
The hiking season is from May to November, but the hike is most enjoyable early in the season when it's cooler, butterflies are abundant and spring wildflowers are in bloom.

Maps
The USGS 1:24,000 *Lake Eleanor* quadrangle covers the hike.

Permits & Regulations
A permit is not required for this day hike. Camping is not allowed along this trail.

GETTING TO/FROM THE HIKE
From the Big Oak Flat Entrance (4872ft), exit the park and go north 1mi on Hwy 120 to Evergreen Rd. Turn right (east) onto Evergreen Rd and go 7.3mi to the junction with the Hetch Hetchy Rd at Camp Mather. Turn right, and in 1mi re-enter the park at the Hetch Hetchy Entrance. Continue 8.9mi to the end of the road. Since it's far to Hetch Hetchy, you may want to camp at the *Hetch Hetchy Backpackers Campground* adjacent to the trailhead parking lot at O'Shaughnessy Dam. From Yosemite Valley, it's a 40mi drive.

When traveling east from Manteca on Hwy 120, turn left (east) onto the Hetch Hetchy Rd beyond Buck Meadows and before reaching the Big Oak Flat Entrance.

THE HIKE
From the parking lot (3813ft), walk across O'Shaughnessy Dam and take the opportunity to sip from the continually flowing drinking fountain on the dam. Continue through the large tunnel on its far side, where a sign announces your entry into the Yosemite Wilderness. The broad, oak-shaded trail heads northeast, well above and parallel to the shore of the reservoir. Rising gradually past several small seasonal streams, you come to a signed trail junction (4050ft), 1.1mi (30 minutes) from the start. The trail to Lake Vernon, the source of Falls Creek, heads left.

Take the right (east) fork, following the sign reading 1.6mi to Wapama Falls. The trail descends gently, winding through small flower-filled meadows, then turns left onto

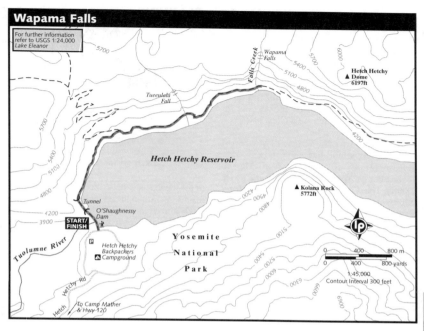

Wapama Falls

For further information refer to USGS 1:24,000 Lake Eleanor

Falls Creek

Wapama Falls

Hetch Hetchy ▲ Dome 6197ft

Tueeulala Fall

Hetch Hetchy Reservoir

▲ Kolana Rock 5772ft

Tunnel

O'Shaughnessy Dam

START/ FINISH

Tuolumne River

Hetch Hetchy Backpackers Campground

Y o s e m i t e

N a t i o n a l

P a r k

Hetchy Rd

Hetch

To Camp Mather & Hwy 120

0   400   800 m
0   400   800 yards
1:45,000
Contour Interval 300 feet

broad, polished granite slabs. Hopping a seasonal rivulet, you cross the delightful open granite expanse, where pink and yellow harlequin lupines grow along the trail in springtime. **Tueeulala Fall** (pronounced **twee**-lala) springs spectacularly from the cliffs more than 1000ft above the trail, 20 minutes from the junction. Most of its water flows under a wooden footbridge, but in the spring, a small section of the trail fills with runoff. By June, the falls are usually dry.

The trail continues 10 minutes gently down a staircase that switchbacks to the base of thundering Wapama Falls (3900ft), where wooden footbridges span **Falls Creek**. In spring, water cascades over the trail beyond the first footbridge and almost covers the second footbridge. When the water is high, crossing is dangerous, but at other times, the flow is ankle deep. The frothy, gushing torrents create billowing clouds of mist that drench the entire area and are refreshingly cool on a warm after-

noon. Southeast across the deep waters of the reservoir, the dark towering bulk of the vertical north face of Kolana Rock (5772ft) provides nesting sites for peregrine falcons. Enjoy the sights and sounds of beautiful Wapama Falls and Hetch Hetchy, then return to the trailhead via the same route.

Southern Yosemite

Yosemite's southern boundary follows the South Fork Merced River. Forests and rushing streams characterize this area, whose granite domes and cascading falls display its glacial origin. Hwy 41 today follows the original Yosemite Road, passing through Wawona, where Galen Clark built the park's first hotel in 1857. The Wawona Hotel, built in 1875, still operates today. The Wawona area is the center of Yosemite's human history and offers year-round hiking and camping in an uncrowded and peaceful setting.

YOSEMITE NATIONAL PARK

ACCESS FACILITIES
Wawona

Go to Hill's Studio (☎ 209-375-9501), the small building adjacent to the Wawona Hotel (4000ft), for visitor information and wilderness permits. It's only open seasonally. You can self-register for wilderness permits for trailheads at Wawona and those along Glacier Point Rd. To get permits for hikes starting in Yosemite Valley, however, you must go to the valley.

A store, post office and ATM are off Forest Drive behind the gas station.

Reservations are required from May to September at **Wawona Campground** ($18, 4000ft). The Victorian-style **Wawona Hotel** exudes a turn-of-the-20th century ambiance, with its handsome broad porches and expansive lawns. Singles or doubles without bathroom cost $99, and those with a bathroom cost $157.50. The hotel restaurant serves daily meals, and has a popular Sunday brunch. See Information Sources, p167, for details on how to make campground and lodging reservations.

Wawona is on Hwy 41 (Wawona Rd), 4mi north of the South Entrance (63mi from Fresno) and 35mi south of Yosemite Valley. No public transport serves Wawona. Between April and October, a free shuttle bus plies the road between the Wawona store, the park's South Entrance and the Mariposa Grove gift shop.

Watch out for rattlesnakes!

Chilnualna Falls

Duration	4–5 hours
Distance	8.6mi (13.8km)
Standard	moderate
Start/Finish	Chilnualna Falls Trailhead
Public Transport	no

Summary The 2240ft ascent to the top of southern Yosemite's most impressive waterfalls is in a seldom-visited area of park.

Chilnualna Creek tumbles over the northern shoulder of the forested Wawona Dome (6897ft) in an almost continuous series of cascades. The largest and most impressive of all these cascades, called Chilnualna Fall, thunders into a deep and narrow chasm. Both above and below this main waterfall are other impressive cascades. Although they are not free-leaping like their Yosemite Valley counterparts, their continual, energetic white-water rush makes this an attractive day hike. The trail ascends 2240ft over 4.3mi beneath Turner Ridge to a nice spot for picnicking at the top of the falls. Carry all the water you need, since the route can be hot.

Warning

Rattlesnakes, though not aggressive, often bask in the sun along the trail. Keep a watchful eye on the trail a few feet ahead of where you're walking.

PLANNING
When to Hike

The hiking season is from March to November. Chilnualna Falls, like all Yosemite waterfalls, are best in spring when streams are at their height. The trail is open as early as March, and the falls are at their peak between April and June. July and August are often too hot to hike in the afternoon, and by September, the falls are reduced by low water.

Maps

The USGS 1:24,000 *Wawona* and *Mariposa Grove* quadrangles cover the hike.

Permits & Regulations

A permit is not required for this day hike. A free wilderness permit is required for any Yosemite overnight trip (see Permits & Regulations, p167).

GETTING TO/FROM THE HIKE

Follow Hwy 41 (Wawona Rd) 0.25mi north of the Wawona Hotel and store. Across the bridge over the South Fork Merced River, turn (east) right, onto Chilnualna Falls Rd. Follow it 1.7mi to its end, passing through a private enclave to the signed parking area on the right.

THE HIKE

The pavement extends a few hundred feet beyond the parking area (4200ft). Follow the signs to the Chilnualna Falls footpath. The trail along the northwest bank of Chilnualna Creek goes 0.1mi to the first series of tumbling cascades, which in springtime shower the trail with cool mist. Ascend

several brief sets of granite steps along the cascades. Above, the stock trail joins the footpath at the Yosemite Wilderness boundary, a short but steep 0.2mi and 600ft above the trailhead. Here a sign reads 4.1mi to Chilnualna Falls.

The trail rises gently, yet continually, through open, mixed-conifer forest, and levels out as it passes near the rushing creek. It then moves away from the creek, taking you on long, sweeping gradual switchbacks beneath the shade of incense cedar and ponderosa pine. Mountain misery *(Chamaebatia foliolosa),* a low shrub with fern-like, feathery foliage and small white flowers that Miwok's called kit-kit-dizze, is a profuse ground cover along most of the trail. The sheer granite curve of Wawona Dome fills the view to the east as you rise above the forested Wawona Valley. One to 1½ hours from the trailhead is an unobstructed view from a granite overlook (5400ft) that includes the first good views of the falls. To the

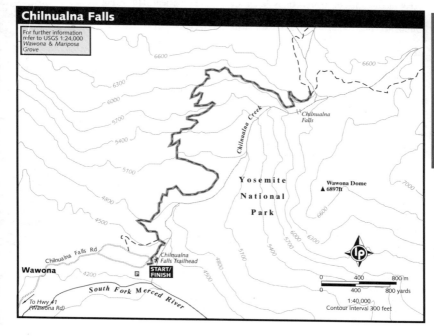

Chilnualna Falls

For further information refer to USGS 1:24,000 Wawona & Mariposa Grove

Chilnualna Creek

Chilnualna Falls

Yosemite National Park

Wawona Dome ▲ 6897ft

Chilnualna Falls Rd

Chilnualna Falls Trailhead

Wawona

START/FINISH

South Fork Merced River

To Hwy 41 (Wawona Rd)

0   400   800 m
0   400   800 yards

1:40,000
Contour Interval 300 feet

southwest are expansive views of the forested Chowchilla Mountains.

The trail continues steadily up on well-graded switchbacks, after 15 minutes passing a small, seasonal stream flowing over a granite outcrop. The trail makes a final dynamite-constructed switchback across a granite cliff to bring you to the top of Chilnualna Falls (6200ft) in another 15 minutes. Mist swirls above the black, water-stained chasm into which the falls disappear.

This spot offers the best views of the falls, but it's worthwhile to continue 15 minutes farther to a better **picnicking spot**. As the trail turns to parallel Chilnualna Creek, another series of cataracts tumbles above the main falls. The trail continues toward them, staying above the bank of the creek. It then sharply veers away, climbing through manzanita scrub before it turns back again toward the creek to bring you to the top of the second cataract. A short distance ahead is a signed trail junction (6440ft). Yet another series of cascades on Chilnualna Creek are visible, but stop here and walk over to the confluence of a small seasonal stream with Chilnualna Creek and picnic anywhere along the water's edge. If you want to make this an overnight trip, campsites are farther up both Chilnualna Creek and Deer Creek.

Retrace your steps 4.3mi to the trailhead in two to 2½ hours, ignoring an inaccurate sign that reads '5.6mi to Wawona.' At the trail junction just 0.2mi from the trailhead, avoid the tempting broader stock and horse trail (which comes out at a different trailhead) in favor of the footpath that turns to the left and heads back down along the creek.

Other Hikes

Pohono Trail

Romantically named Bridalveil Fall was called Po-ho-no by the Ahwahneechee, who regarded it as bewitched. An evil spirit whose breath is a fatal wind lived at the base of the fall, and to sleep near it meant certain death. The voices of people who drowned in the fall could be heard warning others to stay away from Po-ho-no.

Today, the name Pohono is given to a trail that follows Yosemite Valley's south rim 13.8mi (22.2km) between Glacier Point and the Wawona Tunnel parking area. The highlights of the Pohono Trail are its **seven stunning viewpoints** overlooking Yosemite Valley: Glacier Point (7214ft), Taft Point, Dewey Point (7385ft), Crocker Point (7090ft), Stanford Point, Old Inspiration Point and Inspiration Point. The trail traverses high above three waterfalls – Sentinel, Bridalveil and Silver Strand.

The seven- to nine-hour day hike is best done from east to west, starting at Glacier Point. The well-signed trailhead is near the snack bar. The trail descends more than 2800ft, so hiking from west to east makes for a less pleasant hike, with an initial relentlessly steep 3.8mi ascent between the Wawona Tunnel parking area and Stanford Point. You need to have two vehicles or to arrange for someone to drop you off, since the trailheads are many miles apart. The Glacier Point Hikers' Bus can get you to the Glacier Point Trailhead from Yosemite Valley, but it doesn't stop at the Wawona Tunnel parking area trailhead. The USGS 1:24,000 *El Capitan* and *Half Dome* quadrangles cover the hike.

See the Sentinel Dome & Taft Point hike, p179, earlier in this chapter for a description of the most scenic segment of the Pohono Trail.

TUOLUMNE
Lembert Dome

Named for Jean Baptiste Lembert, a 19th century shepherd who homesteaded in Tuolumne Meadows, prominent Lembert Dome (9450ft) provides the most easily attained perspective on the unique beauty of Tuolumne Meadows and the surrounding peaks.

The easy 2.4mi (3.9km) round-trip hike takes one to 1½ hours and has a total elevation gain and loss of 1500ft, with equal amounts of ascent and descent. The USGS 1:24,000 *Tioga Pass* quadrangle covers the hike.

Two similarly named trailheads access Lembert Dome: the Lembert Dome/Dog Lake Trailhead (8580ft) and the Dog Lake Trailhead (8700ft) via the Young Lakes Trail. The former is amid lodgepole pines at the signed Lembert Dome parking area's north end, on the north side of Tioga Rd 0.1mi beyond the bridge over the Tuolumne River.

This is a steeper trail, which has been damaged by storms and is not recommended. To reach the preferred Dog Lake Trailhead, you need to head east from Tuolumne Meadows on Tioga Rd (Hwy 120) and go 0.6mi beyond the bridge. Then turn south onto the road leading to Tuolumne Meadow Lodge and go 0.4mi to the signed Dog Lake parking lot, which is shuttle bus stop 2.

From the Dog Lake Trailhead (8700ft), follow the Young Lakes Trail three minutes as it ascends and crosses to the north side of Tioga Rd. Continue up the lodgepole-pine-forested slope heading north. A series of well-graded switchbacks takes you steadily but easily up the slope. The switchbacks come to an end 20 minutes from the trailhead, as you continue more easily through the pines. In another five minutes, you reach a signed junction, where the trail to Lembert Dome forks northwest (left). Continue six to eight minutes along the easy, sandy trail to a forested saddle, 0.9mi from the trailhead, between Lembert Dome and the smaller Dog Dome, where a sign points west to 'Lembert Dome Parking' and east to 'Dog Lake Parking.'

The 0.3mi one-way route to the top of Lembert Dome leaves the trail at this saddle. Turn southwest and walk up the easy, sloping granite 10 minutes to the summit. The Sierra Crest from Mt Conness to the Kuna Crest stretches to the east, with the Cathedral Range to the south and Tuolumne Meadows immediately below to the west. Relax and enjoy the view, perhaps best accompanied by a picnic lunch, before retracing your steps in 30 minutes back to the Dog Lake parking lot.

Alternatively, it's possible to avoid retracing your steps and complete a 3.7mi counterclock-wise circumambulation of Lembert Dome by turning west at the forested saddle and following the heavily eroded trail steeply down through forest 1.7mi to the Lembert Dome parking lot, shuttle bus stop 4. From this parking lot, a level trail crosses to the south side of Tioga Rd, where it joins the John Muir Trail. Follow the trail 0.5mi east, paralleling the road to the lodge as it passes the Tuolumne Meadows Wilderness Center, to the Dog Lake parking lot. Allow two hours for this hike.

High Sierra Camp Loop

In the Yosemite backcountry are five enormously popular High Sierra Camps: dormitory-style canvas tent cabins with beds, shower facilities and a central dining tent where meals are provided. Guests hike in and provide their own sleeping sheet or bag.

The camps, all within a leisurely day's hike – ranging from 5.7mi (9.2km) to 10mi (16.1km) – of one another, are at Glen Aulin, May Lake, Sunrise, Merced Lake and Vogelsang. The Tuolumne Meadows Lodge completes the circuit, although the lodge is also open to the public. The camps are on the north and south sides of Hwy 120 (Tioga Rd) west of Tuolumne Meadows.

Hiking to all the High Sierra Camps creates a week-long loop hike on established trails. The camps are only for guests, but adjacent backpackers' campsites and the trails between the camps are open to everyone.

Guests have the option to arrange for a park ranger to lead the daily hikes between camps. Backpackers can take advantage of camping the High Sierra Camps and utilizing the bear boxes, toilets and potable water taps. The use of bear-resistant food containers is required by law at the High Sierra Camps.

The convenience of not having to carry a tent and food is appealing, and, of course, it makes it possible for people to enjoy the wilderness who otherwise couldn't carry a full backpack. The camps, however, are supplied by cowboy-led pack strings that have a high impact on the environment.

The High Sierra Camps are part of the park's western heritage, but have also become romantic relics of a bygone era that have been grandfathered into park management.

Reservations are mandatory, and applications for a reservation lottery, which is held in mid-December, are accepted only between October 15 and November 30 for the following year. Contact Yosemite Concession Services (☎ 559-253-5674 for the High Sierra desk, W www.yosemitepark.com), 5410 East Home, Fresno, CA 93727. You can also

Look for nesting peregrine falcons on the north face of Kolana Rock.

call at the last minute to check if any cancellations have created available space at any of the camps.

It's also possible to call a day or two in advance to reserve meals only at a camp, which can ease the burden of carrying your own food for any back-packing trip that passes by a High Sierra Camp. The trails between the camps are busier than other park trails, but by getting a reasonably early start to a hiking day you can avoid most of the foot traffic, which tends to come in a big wave midmorning.

Sequoia & Kings Canyon National Parks

Isolated groves of sequoia and deep granite gorges characterize the adjacent, yet unique, Sequoia and Kings Canyon National Parks. These parks cover almost 1350 sq miles, ranging in elevation from 1300ft to almost 14,500ft, and showcase the splendor of the southern Sierra, offering limitless day hiking and backpacking opportunities.

The towering granite peaks of the Great Western Divide, a southern branch of the Sierra, bisect Sequoia National Park. To its west are the canyons created by four forks of the Kaweah River – the Marble, Middle, East and South. To its east is the north-south flowing Kern River, which descends from Forester Pass and the lofty peaks on the Kings-Kern Divide. The vast canyon created by the Kern River separates the Great Western Divide from the Sierra Crest, which forms the park's eastern boundary and is crowned by Mt Whitney.

Kings Canyon National Park consists of two noncontiguous segments: a small, finger-like protrusion that's centered around Grant Grove and the vast Kings Canyon high country adjacent to the northern boundary of Sequoia National Park. Kings Canyon is the most wild and rugged part of the Sierra Nevada, where the Middle and South Forks Kings Rivers, separated by the Monarch Divide, descend from the High Sierra to form the Kings River. The canyon through which the river flows, first cut by streams and enlarged by glaciers, is among the deepest in the US, reaching a depth of 7891ft from the summit of Spanish Mountain (10,051ft) to the river.

Roads penetrate a tiny fraction of both parks only from the western side of the Sierra Nevada. No trans-Sierra roads cross either park, and access to the parks from the eastern Sierra is by foot only (see the Eastern Sierra chapter, p240). Five passes access Kings Canyon National Park from the eastern Sierra. From north to south. They are Bishop Pass (11,972ft; see the Humphreys &

Highlights

The Four Guardsmen of the Giant Forest tower above trucks and beasts alike.

- Standing in awe beneath a monumental giant sequoia tree
- Looking back at an idyllic Rae Lakes campsite from the heights of Glen Pass
- Waking up along Lake Reflection's shore to see Mt Jordan mirrored in the placid waters
- Sitting for a while on Sawtooth Pass, meditating on the Great Western Divide

Evolution Basins hike, p263); Taboose Pass (11,400ft); Sawmill Pass (11,347ft); Baxter Pass (12,270ft); and Kearsarge Pass (11,823ft; see the Sixty Lake Basin hike, p270). Four passes access Sequoia National Park from the eastern Sierra. They are, from north to south, Shepherd Pass (12,050ft); Trail Crest (13,777ft; see the Mt Whitney hike, p274); New Army Pass (12,300ft) and Cottonwood

SEQUOIA & KINGS CANYON

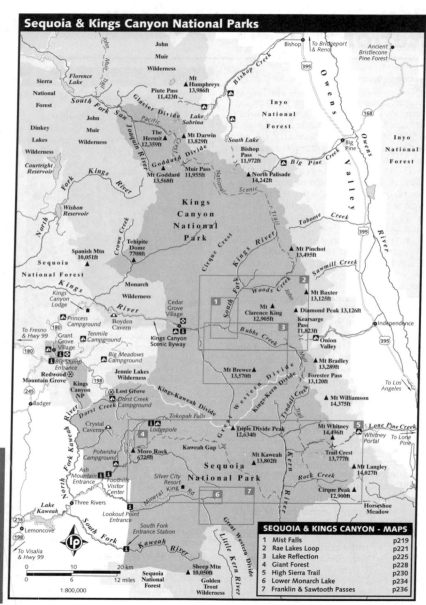

Sequoia & Kings Canyon National Parks

1:800,000

Pass (11,140ft; see the New Army & Cottonwood Passes hike, p277). Trail Crest is the most frequently crossed pass, followed by New Army, Kearsarge and Bishop Passes.

HISTORY

Native American Yokuts were the original inhabitants of the lowest elevation western foothills. The Monache, or Western Mono, migrated from the eastern Sierra's Owens Valley to the middle western foothills and high country about 500 years or 600 years ago. By the mid-19th century, the Monache were dominant, living in three groups at about 250 sites. The Potwisha group lived near Hospital Rock, the Wuksachi near the North Fork Kaweah River, and the Wobonuch near Grant Grove. The Monache traded with the Owens Valley Piutes, following the route from Kings Canyon up Bubbs Creek and crossing the Sierra Crest at Kearsarge Pass.

In 1805, Spanish missionaries, led by Gabriel Moraga, discovered the Kings River, calling it *Rio de los Santos Reyes* or 'River of the Holy Kings,' an indication they camped there on January 6, the day of the Epiphany. Jedediah Smith passed through in 1827 on a failed attempt to be the first white man to cross the Sierra. With the onset of the California gold rush, ranchers, miners and loggers flocked to the region, settling it in the mid-19th century and displacing the Monache by 1865. The growing population soon devastated the environment, and by the 1870s a conservation effort led by Visalia journalist George Stewart began.

Sequoia became the second national park in the US on September 25, 1890. Six days later, at the same time as Yosemite, Grant Grove became the 4-sq-mile General Grant National Park. In 1926, Kern Canyon and Mt Whitney became part of Sequoia National Park.

Protection for Kings Canyon, however, waited for half a century. Although the US Congress had considered creating John Muir–Kings Canyon National Park in the 1930s, it was not until 1940 that Harold Ickes, secretary of the interior under President Franklin Roosevelt, succeeded in persuading the US Congress to establish the park. Grant Grove National Park was absorbed into the new park, but Muir's name was omitted – as were the actual Kings Canyon itself and Tehipite Valley on the Middle Fork Kings River, which were viewed as potential reservoir sites. These two areas were incorporated in 1965.

The two parks have been jointly managed since 1943, initially for reasons of economy during WWII, an effective policy that endures. In 1976 the parks were internationally recognized as a UNESCO biosphere reserve. In 2000, to further convey protection for sequoia groves, more than 327,000 acres of land in Sequoia National Forest adjacent to the national parks were officially declared Giant Sequoia National Monument.

NATURAL HISTORY

The parks contain all four of the Sierra's vegetation zones, from lower montane to alpine. In a 60mi stretch south of the Kings River are 68 of the world's 75 giant sequoia groves. Kings Canyon contains the world's largest grove, Redwood Mountain, which contains more than 15,000 trees. The parks' lower-elevation western foothills also have extensive, open woodlands, where oak and digger pine rise above profusely flowering buckeye, coffeeberry and poison oak.

Also prevalent as high as 5000ft is chaparral, composed of aromatic evergreen shrubs adapted to hot, dry summers and cool, rainy, yet snow-free winters. This vegetation, unique to California and adjacent southern Oregon and northern Baja California, is adapted to fire, and most of its seeds germinate only with intense heat. Common plants here are white-flowered chamise, blue-flowering ceanothus, scrub oak and smooth, red-barked manzanita. Early summer visitors to Sequoia via Ash Mountain Entrance spot the dramatic, tall flowering stalk of Our Lord's Candle *(Yucca whipplei)* along the roadside.

INFORMATION
Maps

The USGS 1:125,000 *Sequoia and Kings Canyon National Parks and Vicinity,* with 200ft contour intervals, is a superb planning and backpacking map for all routes in both parks. The excellent, yet massive, USFS 1:63,360 *John Muir Wilderness (Inyo and Sierra National Forests) and National Parks Backcountry (Sequoia and Kings Canyon National Parks)* series ($10) includes three sheets: *North Section,* areas north from Evolution Basin in northern Kings Canyon National Park; *Central Section,* all of Kings Canyon National Park except areas south of the South Fork Kings River; and *South Section,* areas of Kings Canyon National Park south of the South Fork Kings River and all of Sequoia National Park.

Tom Harrison Maps 1:125,000 *Sequoia & Kings Canyon National Parks Recreation Map* ($8.95), with 200ft contour intervals, covers the parks and their eastern Sierra approaches. Two Tom Harrison Maps provide more detail and are recommended for backpacking.

The 1:63,360 *Kings Canyon High Country Trail Map* ($8.95) provides greater detail of the area from Bubbs Creek to Wanda Lake, and 1:63,360 *Mt Whitney High Country Trail Map* ($8.95) provides greater detail of the area between Kings Canyon's Roads End and Sequoia's Mineral King.

National Geographic/Trails Illustrated 1:111,850 *Sequoia/Kings Canyon National Park* topographic map ($9.95) shows both national parks.

The Sequoia Natural History Association (SNHA) publishes large-scale topographic *Cedar Grove, Lodgepole, Giant Forest* and *Mineral King* maps ($2) that show most day hikes from these areas. These maps are readily available at visitor centers in the park.

Books

From Pioneers to Preservationists: A Brief History of Sequoia and Kings Canyon National Parks, by Douglas H Strong, follows the efforts to save the giant sequoias and pristine wilderness areas. *Exploring the Highest Sierra,* by James G Moore, explains the exploration and natural history of the parks with etchings, maps, photographs, charts and diagrams. *Sequoia & Kings Canyon: The Story Behind the Scenery* by William C Tweed is a fine reference for nature lovers.

Maps and books are available by mail from SNHA (☎ 559-565-3759, fax 565-3728, @ a-seqnha@inreach.com, W www.sequoia history.org), HCR-89 Box 10, Three Rivers, CA 93271, as well as at park visitor centers and ranger stations.

Information Sources

Sequoia and Kings Canyon National Parks (☎ 559-565-3341, 335-2856, W www.nps.gov/ seki), 47050 Generals Hwy, Three Rivers, CA 93271-9651, are jointly administered. The entrance fee, valid for seven days for both parks, is $10 per vehicle or $5 per person for cyclists, bus passengers and walk-ins. An annual pass for both parks costs $20.

To make your lodging reservations at Grant Grove and Cedar Grove, you can contact Kings Canyon Park Services (☎ 866-522-6966, 559-335-5500, fax 559-335-2498, W www.sequoia-kingscanyon.com), 5755 East Kings Canyon Rd, Suite 101, Fresno, CA 93727. To make lodging reservations in Sequoia National Park, contact Delaware North Parks Services (W www.visitse-quoia.com). Dorst Creek and Lodgepole campgrounds in Sequoia National Park accept reservations. Contact the National Park Reservation Service (☎ 800-436-7275, 301-722-1257 outside the US, W reservations.nps.gov), PO Box 1600, Cumberland, MD 21502, up to five months in advance for campground reservations. All other campgrounds in both parks are on a first-come, first-served basis, and it is not possible to make reservations. The websites of both concessionaires offer general park information as well as online lodging reservations.

Permits & Regulations

A free wilderness permit is required for all overnight hikes. A permit is not required for day hikes. First-come, first-served permits are available year-round at Sequoia's Foothill and Lodgepole visitor centers (7am to 4pm) and at Kings Canyon's Grant Grove visitor center. First-come, first-served permits are available seasonally at Sequoia's South Fork and Mineral King ranger stations and Kings Canyon's Roads End (7:15am to 2:45pm) and Cedar Grove visitor center (after 2:45pm). Some trailheads have self-issuing permits. First-come, first-served permits are available the day of your trip or after 1pm for the next day.

Reservations are available for trips starting between May 21 and September 21, and are recommended for weekend entry dates. To make a reservation, mail or fax your request (along with a $10 per-permit reservation fee) after March 1 and no later than three weeks before a desired entry date or by August 31, to Wilderness Permit Reservations, Sequoia & Kings Canyon National Parks (☎ 559-565-3708, fax 559-565-4239), HCR 89 Box 60, Three Rivers, CA 93271.

Pick up a copy of the park brochure *Backcountry Basics,* a trip-planning guide packed with useful information as well as regulations. A copy of the 'permit reservation application' is inside the brochure.

Bear-resistant food containers are available for rent and sale at any ranger station or visitor center that issues wilderness permits. Campfires are prohibited higher than 10,000ft.

The parks' wilderness office (☎ 559-565-3708) can help you arrange food resupplies for long backpacking trips. You can also mail food to yourself at the Cedar Grove and Mineral King ranger stations.

Kings Canyon

The canyon that lends its name to Kings Canyon National Park rivals Yosemite Valley in its depth and sheer granite walls, but lacks the dramatic free-leaping waterfalls. Through this deep, glacially carved canyon flows the powerful South Fork Kings River. At the canyon's head, called Roads End, are several trails leading into the Kings Canyon high country.

ACCESS FACILITIES
Grant Grove

The Grant Grove visitor center provides general information as well as trail information and issues wilderness permits.

The Grant Grove Market is well-stocked with essentials and has an adjacent restau-rant.Near Grant Grove Village (6589ft) are **Sunset Campground** ($14), **Azalea Campground** ($14) and **Crystal Springs Campground** ($14). The year-round **John Muir Lodge** has $128 rooms, cabins with ($88) and without (ranging from $45 to $55) bathrooms and summer-only tent cabins ($38). Public showers ($3) are available at Grant Grove Village (from 11am to 4pm); go to Lodging Information-Registration.

Getting There & Away The nearest international airports are in the Los Angeles (a four-hour drive) and San Francisco (a five-hour drive) areas. The nearest regional airport is in Fresno.

Amtrak has several daily round-trip train routes serving the Central Valley city of Fresno, from where you must rent a vehicle, since there is no public transportation to either national park. From major international airports, the first leg of Amtrak service is by bus to the nearest train station. From San Francisco ($34/65 one way/round trip including the bus service), the bus goes to Emeryville, from where you board the train to Fresno. From Los Angeles ($23/44 one way/round trip), the bus goes to Bakersfield. Greyhound also has bus service to Fresno; the six-hour trip from San Francisco costs $31 one way, and the six-hour trip from Los Angeles costs $22.

From Fresno, Hwy 180 leads 53mi east to Kings Canyon's Big Stump Entrance, a 1½-hour drive. Just beyond the entrance, Generals Hwy branches southeast to Sequoia NP (see Giant Forest, p226, and Mineral King, p233). Yosemite's South Entrance is a three-hour drive from Big Stump Entrance.

Cedar Grove

A ranger station is adjacent to Sentinel campground, 0.25mi south of Cedar Grove Village, and another one is at Roads End, 6mi beyond Cedar Grove.

Cedar Grove Village (4635ft) is basically one building with a motel, market and snack bar, but no restaurant. **Cedar Grove Lodge**, open May to October, has basic rooms ($90) above the market and a few kitchenettes on the ground floor below it.

SEQUOIA & KINGS CANYON

Public showers ($3), open 8am to 7pm, and laundry facilities are in a nearby building. Four first-come, first-served campgrounds are in Cedar Grove along the river: *Sheep Creek Campground* ($14); *Sentinel Campground* ($14), the closest to Cedar Grove Village; *Canyon View Campground* ($14), a tent-only campground; and *Moraine Campground* ($14).

Hwy 180 drops 3200ft along South Fork Kings River into an impressive canyon 2mi beyond the entrance to Grant Grove Village. Beyond Grant Grove Village, Hwy 180 is known as the Kings Canyon Scenic Byway and is open from mid-April to mid-November. It leads 30mi to Cedar Grove Village and 6mi farther to its terminus at Roads End. Allow one hour to drive between Grant Grove and Cedar Grove.

Other Campgrounds

Six campgrounds in the Hume Lake and Stony Creek areas of Sequoia National Forest offer alternatives when national park campgrounds at Grant Grove and Cedar Grove are full. Of these, the best choices that accept reservations are: *Stony Creek Campground* ($16) on Generals Hwy near Sequoia's Lost Grove; and *Princess Campground* ($12) along Hwy 180 north of Kings Canyon's Grant Grove. The first-come, first-served *Tenmile Campground*, 5.5mi north of the Kings Canyon's Redwood Mountain Overlook off Generals Hwy, is also nice.

Mist Falls

Duration	4–5 hours
Distance	9.2mi (14.8km)
Standard	easy
Start/Finish	Roads End
Public Transport	no

Summary Enjoy a fine day hike, ascending just more than 600ft gently along the South Fork Kings River, and a picnic at one of Kings Canyon's most magnificent waterfalls.

Mist Falls, one of Kings Canyon's largest and most impressive waterfalls, makes a great picnic destination. The falls are named for the remarkable plume of mist that rises like a specter from their base.

PLANNING
When to Hike

The hiking season is from May to October. The falls are at their peak in late spring and early summer.

Maps

The SNHA 1:30,000 *Cedar Grove* map ($2) covers the hike, as does the USGS 1:24,000 *The Sphinx* quadrangle.

Permits & Regulations

A permit is not required for this day hike. Camping is not allowed downstream of Paradise Valley. If you want to visit the falls on an overnight hike, you must continue upvalley at least 1.9mi beyond the falls to the first of three campsites in Paradise Valley (see the Rae Lakes Loop hike, below).

GETTING TO/FROM THE HIKE

The trail begins at Roads End (5036ft), 6mi east of the Cedar Grove Village turnoff.

THE HIKE

From Roads End (5036ft), the nearly level trail to Mist Falls heads east and quickly crosses Copper Creek over a footbridge and goes over level, sandy ground through stands of open pine and cedar forest for 30 minutes. It then enters a shaded fern-filled area and, in 20 minutes, reaches the junction of the Paradise Valley Trail with the Bubbs Creek Trail, 1.9mi from the trailhead. The Bubbs Creek Trail turns right (northeast) and immediately crosses the South Fork Kings River over a steel **Bailey bridge**. You stay on the trail to Mist Falls, which turns left (north) at this junction and begins a steady, gradual ascent along the river on the Paradise Valley Trail.

Ascending through forest, the trail meets the river's edge in 20 minutes. The ascent upvalley continues and, in another 20 minutes, you approach a series of dramatic cataracts, then surmount a granite hillside with striking views back downvalley of **Avalanche Peak** and **The Sphinx** (9143ft),

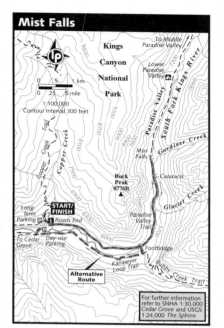

Mist Falls

Kings Canyon National Park

To Middle Paradise Valley

Lower Paradise Valley

South Fork Kings River

Paradise Valley

Gardiner Creek

Mist Falls

Cataract

Buck Peak 8776ft

Copper Creek Trail

Copper Creek

Long-term Parking

START/FINISH Roads End

Glacier Creek

Paradise Valley Trail

To Cedar Grove

Day-use Parking

Footbridge

Kanawyer Loop Trail

Bubbs Creek Trail

Alternative Route

0   .5   1 km
0   .25   .5 mile
1:100,000
Contour Interval 300 feet

For further information refer to SNHA 1:30,000 *Cedar Grove* and USGS 1:24,000 *The Sphinx*

Rae Lakes Loop

Duration	5 days
Distance	41.5mi (66.8km)
Standard	moderate
Start/Finish	Roads End
Public Transport	no

Summary The best loop hike in Kings Canyon National Park tours gorgeous forests and meadows, crosses one pass, and passes a chain of jewel-like lakes beneath the Sierra Crest in the heart of the Kings Canyon high country.

Deservedly Kings Canyon's most popular hike, this clockwise circumambulation of King Spur, a cluster of high peaks, offers access to many less frequently visited parts of the park. It traverses the Rae Lakes and Glen Pass segments of the combined PCT (Pacific Crest National Scenic Trail) and John Muir Trail. The Rae Lakes are some of the most beautiful and picturesque lakes in the Sierra Nevada. They are named after Rachel 'Rae' Colby, wife of William E Colby, who joined the Sierra Club in 1898 and, as both its secretary and president, was instrumental in the founding of Kings Canyon National Park. Taking a layover day allows time to explore this beautiful region.

PLANNING
When to Hike
The hiking season is from mid-June to September. Early in the season, streams and rivers may be too high to cross. Especially tricky is the South Fork Kings River crossing in Upper Paradise Valley. Snow also makes the north side of Glen Pass difficult early in the season. Mid-July to mid-August is the peak season, when permit quotas often fill.

Maps
The SNHA 1:62,500 *Rae Lakes Loop Trail Map* ($4) covers the hike, as do the USGS 1:24,000 *The Sphinx* and *Mt Clarence King* quadrangles. Tom Harrison Maps 1:63,360 *Kings Canyon High Country Trail Map* ($8.95) and *Mt Whitney High Country Trail Map* also cover the hike.

---

high above Bubbs Creek. This lower series of cataracts, although formidable, should not be mistaken for Mist Falls.

The trail continues 15 minutes through forest to reach **Mist Falls** (5663ft), which are readily identified by a signpost. Mist Falls are 2.7mi from the Bubbs Creek Trail junction. Return leisurely to Roads End via the same trail.

Alternative Route
On your return, from the Bubbs Creek Trail junction, try a pleasant alternative route between the Bailey bridge and Roads End. Turn left (northeast) onto the Bubbs Creek Trail and cross the Bailey bridge. Turn right shortly after the bridge onto the Kanawyer Loop Trail.

This less-frequently used, level 2.6mi trail hugs the true left bank of the South Fork Kings River, recrossing the river downstream on a sturdy footbridge near the day-use parking lot at Roads End.

Permits & Regulations

A free wilderness permit is required for overnight trips (see p216). Permits are issued at Roads End from 7:15am to 2:45pm. Permits for the next day are issued at 1pm. After 2:45pm, go to the Cedar Grove ranger station.

A one-night camping limit applies to Paradise Valley, and a two-night camping limit to each of the Rae Lakes. Camping is allowed only in designated, numbered campsites at one of three campgrounds in Paradise Valley. Camping is prohibited downstream (west) of Sphinx Creek on the Bubbs Creek Trail.

Bears are active all along the hike. Hikers are required to use bear-resistant food containers and are encouraged to also use bear boxes at designated campsites.

GETTING TO/FROM THE HIKE

The trail begins at Roads End (5036ft), 6mi east of the Cedar Grove Village turnoff.

THE HIKE
Day 1: Roads End to Middle Paradise Valley

4–4½ hours, 7.6mi (12.2km), 1583ft (474.9m) ascent

See the Mist Falls hike, p218, for a description of the 4.6mi trail from Roads End to the falls. A series of short switchbacks takes you to the top of the falls. Beyond Mist Falls, a larger and longer set of rocky switchbacks leads you up and into forest above the river. The trail levels out amid aspens and cottonwoods and enters Paradise Valley, one hour from the falls. The South Fork Kings River flows placidly through forest and meadows inviting you five minutes farther to the first *campsites* at **Lower Paradise Valley** (6586ft), 1.1mi beyond Mist Falls. The most attractive campsites, which are often full, are in the forest to the right of the trail near the river. Continue up the beautiful valley, at times along the river and at times through fir forest, 1.1mi (30 minutes) farther to the ponderosa- and sugar-pine-shaded *campsites* at **Middle Paradise Valley** (6619ft). Middle Paradise Valley, which has a nice beach, is typically less crowded than Lower Paradise Valley and offers more open views of granite cliffs.

Day 2: Middle Paradise Valley to Woods Creek

4–4½ hours, 7.8mi (12.6km), 1873ft (561.9m) ascent

A short distance beyond the campsite, the trail passes through an open area cleared of trees by avalanches from the polished granite cliffs above. Ascend through some rocky areas near the cascading river, passing amid ponderosa pines, white firs and incense cedars. The trail ascends gradually for 50 minutes before dropping back down along the river in a dense forest to **Upper Paradise Valley** (6876ft), at the confluence of the South Fork Kings River and Woods Creek, 2.2mi from Middle Paradise Valley.

Continue past the pleasant *campsites* and cross a massive log spanning the South Fork Kings River. Head south a couple of minutes along the river's true left (east) bank and cross a tiny log footbridge. The trail turns southeast, passing some large sugar pines, and begins a steady ascent up dusty switchbacks on an open slope. Crossing the shoulder of a granite ridge, you enter the forested canyon above Woods Creek.

The trail traverses east, ascending gently, high above rushing Woods Creek. The trail gradually draws near the creek and continues up the forested valley. Ascending an open, manzanita-covered slope amid small granite boulders, the dusty trail rises to a gated fence (8113ft), two hours from the river crossing.

Pass through the gate and descend to the open avalanche-formed **Castle Dome Meadow** beneath the spectacular, polished white granite of the Castle Domes. Cross the aspen-dotted meadow in 10 minutes and re-enter a pine forest. The views of the multiple summits of the Castle Domes gets better and better as you continue 30 minutes and ascend some stone steps to another gated fence. Pass through the gate, over a granite rib and down amid some cottonwoods and aspens along Woods Creek 15 minutes to a signed junction with the John Muir Trail.

Turn right (east) onto the southbound John Muir Trail and cross Woods Creek on a large wooden-planked steel suspension bridge, whose over-engineered structure is justified by the extremely high springtime

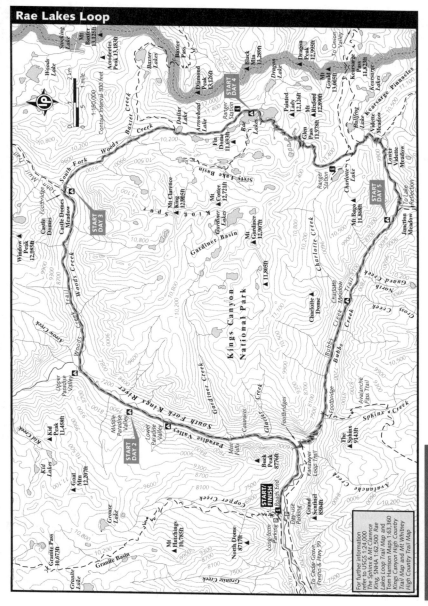

Rae Lakes Loop

SEQUOIA & KINGS CANYON

For further information refer to USGS 1:24,000 The Sphinx & Mt Clarence King, SNHA 1:62,500 Rae Lakes Map Trail Maps, Tom Harrison Maps 1:63,360 Kings Canyon High Country Trail Map and Mt Whitney High Country Trail Map

water level of Woods Creek. Summer hikers, however, may wonder why the NPS spent its scarce resources so lavishly. Two *campsites* (8492ft) are on the south side of **Woods Creek**; one near the trail and the other downstream a short distance.

Day 3: Woods Creek to Middle Rae Lake

3½–4 hours, 5.8mi (9.3km), 2058ft (617.4m) ascent

Heading south, the trail rolls easily on open slopes along the west side of South Fork Woods Creek, with good views back of **Castle Domes** and the granite high country above the confluence. Forty-five minutes from the campsite, cross a side stream that descends from a lake northeast of Mt Clarence King. Continue upvalley 30 minutes, as lodgepole pines become more frequent. South Fork Woods Creek cascades through granite bedrock, and the trail rises over granite to descend into a small, lodgepole-lined meadow, where you cross a small wooden footbridge over a stream that is often dry by late summer.

Ten minutes farther, cross the stream (via logs) that cascades over a cleft in the rock as it drains Sixty Lake Basin. This is a good place to stop for water. Beyond the stream, pass through a gated 'drift' fence, which prevents stock animals from drifting outside of permitted grazing areas. Foxtail pines dot the dry, granitic slope above the trail as you continue up to small, lovely **Dollar Lake** (10,240ft), which is 2½ hours (3.7mi) from the Woods Creek crossing.

Near the north end of Dollar Lake, a faint trail branches east, leading to Baxter Pass (12,270ft). The striking view of **Fin Dome** (11,693ft) above Dollar Lake sets the theme of mountain splendor that typifies Rae Lakes. Skirting Dollar Lake's west shore, continue up and arrive in 20 minutes at the larger **Arrowhead Lake** (10,300ft), which has attractive *campsites* near the northeast shore, west of the trail.

Crossing the outlet, follow along Arrowhead Lake's east side, with fine views of Fin Dome. Moving away from the lake, the trail ascends gradually in 20 minutes to large and beautiful **Lower Rae Lake**, with *campsites* along the lake's east shore. The high walls enclosing the upper valley, which you cross via Glen Pass on Day 4, are impressive ahead. The trail rolls gently through the attractive lake setting, crossing several small side streams and passing the signed spur trail to the usually unoccupied Rae Lakes ranger station; the backcountry ranger generally stays at Charlotte Lake, south of Glen Pass. Continue 15 minutes to the signed turnoff for the *campsites* above the eastern shore of **Middle Rae Lake** (10,550ft) and descend past some foxtail and lodgepole pines toward the clear azure lake.

Day 4: Middle Rae Lake to Junction Meadow

5–5½ hours, 9.9mi (15.9km), 1428ft (428.4m) ascent, 3898ft (1169.4m) descent

Return to the John Muir Trail and turn right (south). The trail soon turns southwest across the isthmus separating Middle and Upper Rae Lakes. Walk along the northern shore of Upper Rae Lake, where two tree-decorated granitic islands delight your eye, and the view of Fin Dome remains marvelous. In 20 minutes you cross the connector stream between the lakes and come to a signboard for the Rae Lakes area, where the faint trail to Sixty Lake Basin heads northwest (right), leaving the John Muir Trail.

At this junction, stay on the John Muir Trail, which continues south (left). Ascend well-graded switchbacks above the west side of Upper Rae Lake. The ascent eases off as the trail follows a small willow-lined creek in a meadowy swale. Above, more switchbacks take you up a talus slope to a tarn-filled basin, from where Glen Pass is visible ahead on the dark, rocky ridgeline. A few stunted whitebark pines cling to the rock here at timberline. The trail passes nine aqua tarns, which glisten in the barren cirque to the west. Turning southwest, you ascend above another aquamarine tarn east of the trail, then make a series of switchbacks up talus, with dramatic views back to the north, to narrow **Glen Pass** (11,978ft), 2mi (1½ hours) from the Sixty Lake Basin junction. In the distance to the southwest are massive Mt Brewer (13,570ft), with its snowy northeast face, and other peaks along the Great Western Divide and Kings-Kern Divide. Mt Bago (11,868ft) is the distinctive reddish peak in the foreground.

Glen Pass is a narrow ridge topped with black rock and ranging in width from 10ft to 20ft. Traverse southwest one to two minutes along the length of this saddle to start your descent. Gravelly but well-graded switchbacks take you down on a steep scree slope toward the pothole tarn at tree line 15 minutes below. A few whitebark pines grow along its southern shore. Get water here, for the next reliable water is not until the outlet of Bullfrog Lake several miles ahead.

Head steeply down the narrow canyon, passing well above a snow-fed, talus-lined pool. As you exit the canyon, trees reappear and the trail swings south. Twenty minutes from the pothole tarn, you have a view of charming **Charlotte Lake** and remarkable **Charlotte Dome**. The trail then contours high above forested Charlotte Lake, amid foxtail and lodgepole pines. Passing an eastbound trail to Kearsarge Pass 2.1mi from Glen Pass, the trail arrives after 0.2mi at a sandy four-way junction. The west (right) fork leads to Charlotte Lake and the northeast (left) fork is another trail to Kearsarge Pass.

Continuing south (straight), you catch a glimpse of distant Forester Pass, the highest pass on the John Muir Trail, at the head of Bubbs Creek as you cross a low rise and begin the descent to Bubbs Creek. Fifteen minutes (0.7mi) from the four-way junction, reach the junction with the trail heading northeast (left) to Bullfrog Lake and Kearsarge Lakes. The scenic descent south twice crosses the outlet from Bullfrog Lake to reach **Lower Vidette Meadow** (9480ft) in 30 minutes (1.5mi).

Leaving the John Muir Trail, which continues southeast (left), turn right (southwest) and follow the trail down Bubbs Creek past two *campsites* along the forested edge of pretty Lower Vidette Meadow. Descending west along tumbling Bubbs Creek, the trail crosses several side streams and a large rock slide, then finds shade beneath some large, red firs.

Beneath soaring granite walls on either side of the canyon, the trail drops steadily down a hot manzanita slope, then along narrow, rushing Bubbs Creek and into a cooler red fir forest. Passing a large waterfall where Bubbs Creek tumbles over a substantial granite bench, your descent continues a short distance to aspen-filled **Junction Meadow** (8080ft), 2.9mi from Lower Vidette Meadow.

Pass the signed junction with the trail to East Lake and Lake Reflection (see the Lake Reflection hike, p224) in a beautiful aspen-dotted meadow. Continue five minutes, to grassy *campsites* beneath tall lodgepole pines. Additional *campsites* are 10 minutes farther, beyond a gated drift fence beneath red firs along the north side of Bubbs Creek.

Day 5: Junction Meadow to Roads End
5–5½ hours, 10.4mi (16.7km), 3044ft (913.2m) descent

From the west end of Junction Meadow, the trail continues downvalley through alternating cool red fir and fern forest and hot open shrub-filled slopes. Granite walls tower on both sides of the valley, and you see a particularly enormous monolith on the north side above the confluence with Charlotte Creek. As you descend toward Charlotte Creek, the forest is predominantly ponderosa pines and white firs, signaling your descent into a lower-elevation vegetation zone. To the north, Charlotte Dome, with some superb rock climbs on its granite face, comes into view.

Pass the *campsite* at **Charlotte Meadow**, beneath white firs just east of Charlotte Creek, 3.8mi from Junction Meadow. Crossing Charlotte Creek, the trail continues west, through mixed ponderosa pine and white fir forest 3mi down Bubbs Creek to *campsites* at **Sphinx Creek** (6240ft), where the trail to Avalanche Pass crosses Bubbs Creek on a wooden footbridge.

The Bubbs Creek Trail descends steeply on hot, open switchbacks, with sweeping views into Kings Canyon and of the granite pinnacle of The Sphinx towering above Bubbs Creek. At the valley floor, the trail crosses braided Bubbs Creek over four separate wooden footbridges in close succession and continues across the steel Bailey bridge over the South Fork Kings River. Beyond the bridge is the junction of the Bubbs Creek Trail with the Paradise Valley Trail, 1.7mi from Sphinx Creek. From here, retrace your steps from Day 1 over level ground, 1.9mi back to Roads End (5036ft).

Lake Reflection

Duration	4 days
Distance	30mi (48.3km)
Standard	moderate
Start/Finish	Roads End
Public Transport	no

Summary A quintessential Sierra lake nestles beneath the 13,000ft-high peaks of the Kings-Kern Divide, with outstanding mountain views and idyllic campsites.

Lake Reflection (10,005ft) lives up to its name. The peaks of the Kings-Kern Divide – Mt Jordan (13,344ft), Mt Genevra (13,055ft) and South Guard (13,224ft), among others close at hand – reflect beautifully in the lake's transparent, aqua waters. The spectacularly situated campsites along the lakeshore are ideal for early morning photography, and the lake's deep waters are perfect for swimming.

PLANNING
When to Hike
The hiking season is from mid-June to September. Early in the season, the Bubbs Creek crossing may be difficult due to high water.

Maps
The SNHA 1:62,500 *Rae Lakes Loop Trail Map* ($4) covers the hike, as do the USGS 1:24,000 *The Sphinx, Mt Clarence King* and *Mt Brewer* quadrangles.

Permits & Regulations
A free wilderness permit is required for this hike (see Permits & Regulations, p216). Camping is prohibited below Sphinx Creek on the Bubbs Creek Trail. Campfires are prohibited above East Lake.

GETTING TO/FROM THE HIKE
The trail begins at Roads End (5036ft), 6mi east of the Cedar Grove Village turnoff.

THE HIKE
Day 1: Roads End to Junction Meadow
5–6 hours, 10.4mi (16.7km), 3044ft (913.2m) ascent

From Roads End, the nearly level trail heads east 1.9mi to a signed junction just before the steel Bailey bridge over South Fork Kings River. Take the right (northeast) fork and cross the bridge, then cross a series of four wooden footbridges in close succession over Bubbs Creek. Once on the true right bank of Bubbs Creek, the trail climbs out of the forest on a long series of switchbacks. The view steadily improves as you ascend the hot, open, west-facing slope, where pinyon pines, unusual for the western side of the Sierra Nevada, grow, along with oaks and incense cedars.

Reaching the top of the switchbacks, the trail enters a canyon along Bubbs Creek and soon comes to the *campsites* at Sphinx Creek, where a trail to Avalanche Pass heads south across a wooden footbridge over Bubbs Creek, 1.7mi from the Bailey bridge. Continue along the north side of Bubbs Creek, amid white firs and ponderosa pines, 3mi to **Charlotte Meadow**, where *campsites* are beneath white firs east of Charlotte Creek.

Ascending steadily along Bubbs Creek, beneath soaring granite walls, the trail continues 3.8mi to **Junction Meadow** (8080ft). The first *campsites* are beneath red firs. Two minutes beyond, you pass through a gated

Bailey bridges help you cross those snow-swollen streams.

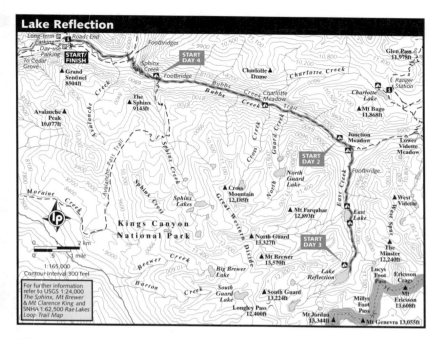

Lake Reflection

drift fence and, after another 10 minutes, you come to more grassy *campsites* beneath tall lodgepole pines standing at the meadow's western end.

Day 2: Junction Meadow to Lake Reflection

2½–3 hours, 4.6mi (7.4km), 1925ft (577.5m) ascent

From Junction Meadow's western end, continue five minutes upvalley to the signed junction amid aspens, where the trail to East Lake turns right (south). Bubbs Creek soon presents itself as an obstacle to cross. Walk two minutes downstream and cross the large log spanning the creek. Across the log, you find *campsites* in a dense and dark red fir forest on the south side of Bubbs Creek and the west side of East Creek.

The trail ascends amid red firs and emerges on an open manzanita slope. Several short switchbacks take you up across granite slabs, and on both sides of East Creek

dramatic granite walls give a small preview of the beautiful granite peaks ahead. The trail levels off and comes to a wooden footbridge crossing to the true right bank of East Creek, 30 minutes from Junction Meadow.

Continuing through red fir forest, you ascend steadily up a rutted trail worn by pack animals. Switchbacks take you up the steepest sections. Now well above East Creek, you traverse east and cross a fern-lined stream that descends from a small lake beneath **West Vidette peak**, 45 minutes from the footbridge. Below, East Creek tumbles through chutes and falls over granite. After a few short, final switchbacks, the trail levels out and continues 15 minutes through lodgepole pines to **East Lake** (9445ft), which has *campsites* at both its north and south end. A sandy beach and better mountain views make the north shore a more desirable spot to camp.

The trail hugs East Lake's eastern shore, offering inspiring views of the granite peaks and ridges above the lake and of distant **Mt Brewer** (13,570ft) and **North Guard** (13,327ft) at the head of Ouzel Creek. Beyond the campsite near the inlet, the trail ascends along a lodgepole pine-lined meadow and passes through a gated drift fence 10 minutes above the lake.

The trail ascends steadily, crossing a small talus slope after 20 minutes and another larger talus slope five minutes later. The route across the talus slopes, and in a few other sections is marked by easy-to-follow cairns. Nearby, East Creek flows over granite. Continuing, the trail crosses a willow-choked side stream that descends from small lakes beneath **Deerhorn Mountain**, beyond which you step onto large glacier-polished slabs overlooking East Creek.

Following the granite slabs upward, the trail enters a moist area of lodgepole pines. It then ascends more granite benches to reach **Lake Reflection** (10,005ft), 45 minutes from the gate. The best *campsites* are reached by crossing the outlet as soon as possible, before it widens, and following it a short way to an incredibly scenic spot on the northwest lakeshore. Mt Jordan fills your view to the south across the lake, but the best views and photography spots are from a granite outcrop 10 minutes along the east shore. Mt Genevra is in the background to the south, with South Guard rising above the lake's western shore.

Day 3: Lake Reflection to Sphinx Creek

4–4½ hours, 11.4mi (18.3km), 3765ft (1129.5m) descent

Retrace your steps easily from Lake Reflection to East Lake in 45 minutes and down to Bubbs Creek in another hour. Once across Bubbs Creek, follow the Bubbs Creek Trail downvalley to Sphinx Creek. *Campsites* (6240ft) are along the north side of the trail before the footbridge over Bubbs Creek.

Day 4: Sphinx Creek to Roads End

1½–2 hours, 3.6mi (5.8km), 1204ft (361.2m) descent

Retrace your steps into Kings Canyon to the trailhead at Roads End.

Sequoia National Park – Giant Forest

The aptly named Giant Forest, Sequoia National Park's most popular destination, is a 5-sq-mile area of redwood groves where four of the earth's five largest trees and hundreds of others tower above tranquil and picturesque meadows. More than 40mi of hiking trails wind through the spectacular trees, streams and meadows of Giant Forest.

ACCESS FACILITIES

Information Foothills visitor center is beyond Ash Mountain Entrance and Lodgepole visitor center is at Lodgepole Village. At Lodgepole Village, the wilderness permits office is in the same building as the visitor center. Its entrance is to the left of the main doors. At the time of writing, a new visitor center was to be opened in Giant Forest in 2002.

Places to Stay & Eat The low-elevation and often too-hot *Potwisha Campground* ($14; 2080ft) and *Buckeye Flat Campground* ($14; 2820ft) are along Generals Hwy, northeast of Ash Mountain Entrance. *Lodgepole Campground* ($16; 6720ft) is 4mi north of Giant Forest and 0.4mi off Generals Hwy in Tokopah Canyon, along the Marble Fork Kaweah River. *Dorst Creek Campground* ($16; 6720ft), also along Generals Hwy west of Lodgepole, is near the Lost Grove. Dorst Creek and Lodgepole are the only campgrounds that accept reservations; contact National Park Reservation Service (☎ 800-365-2267, 301-722-1257 from outside the US, fax 301-722-1174, ⓦ reserva tions.nps.gov). Reservations are recommended on summer weekends and especially during August. Lodgepole Market Center, near the Lodgepole campground, has a grocery store, snack bar and public showers ($3) and laundromat.

Wuksachi Village & Lodge (☎ 888-252-5757, 559-253-2199 from o erseas), at 7200ft, sits 2mi west of Lodgepole above Generals Hwy and has spectacular views of Tokopah Valley. Open year-round, rooms range from $110 (economy) and $125 (standard) to $155 (deluxe). The dining room serves daily meals; reservations are required for dinner (☎ 559-565-4070).

Getting There & Away The 45.8mi-long Generals Hwy (Hwy 198) meanders through the western portion of the park between Sequoia's Ash Mountain Entrance, 36mi from Visalia, to Hwy 180 between Kings Canyon's Big Stump Entrance and Grant Grove Village. The Giant Forest is a one-hour drive from either Grant Grove or the Ash Mountain Entrance.

Late June through Labor Day, a free shuttle bus operates every 30 minutes from 9am to 6pm between Wuksachi Village and the Crescent Meadow trailhead, stopping at Lodgepole, Wolverton, Giant Forest and Moro Rock.

Congress Trail

Duration	1–1½ hours
Distance	2.1mi (3.4km)
Standard	easy
Start/Finish	General Sherman Tree
Public Transport	no

Summary The paved Congress Trail takes visitors on a self-guided hike amid the most outstanding examples of unique giant sequoia trees on the planet.

The Congress Trail, a paved loop in the heart of Giant Forest, is the star attraction of Sequoia National Park. Understandably popular, it offers the best introduction to what John Muir called 'the most beautiful and majestic woods on earth.' A pamphlet for this impressive self-guiding nature trail is available at the trailhead.

PLANNING
When to Hike
The hiking season is from May to November.

Maps
The SNHA 1:9500 *Giant Forest* map ($2) covers the hike.

Moro Rock

The easily accessible exfoliating granite formation called Moro Rock rises 4000 vertical feet above the Middle Fork Kaweah River. A mere quarter-mile-long trail climbs 400 steps, rising 300ft to the summit of the dome (6725ft), which has commanding views of much of Sequoia National Park. Moro Rock was first climbed in 1861, and a wooden stairway was built in 1917, followed by construction of the present stone staircase in 1931. In 1978, Moro Rock became listed on the National Register of Historic Places. A quick trip to the top and a glimpse of the peaks of the Great Western Divide, such as Sawtooth Peak, may immediately inspire hikers to head to Mineral King for a backpack (see the Mineral King section, p233). From Generals Hwy in the Giant Forest, drive 1.5mi southeast on Crescent Meadow Rd to the trailhead.

Permits & Regulations
A permit is not required for this day hike. Camping is not allowed anywhere in the Giant Forest.

GETTING TO/FROM THE HIKE
Take the Generals Hwy, 2mi southwest of Lodgepole, to the General Sherman Tree parking lot and the well-signed trailhead.

THE HIKE
(See the Giant Forest map.)
First, walk to the 2300- to 2700-year-old **General Sherman Tree**, the largest of the giant sequoias and the largest living organism on earth. Begin this clockwise loop by walking south on the easy trail, and in 0.9mi reach the Chief Sequoyah Tree and giant President Tree. Just 0.2 farther is the imposing **Senate Group**, followed by the equally impressive **House Group** and the **General Lee Tree**. Turn north at the McKinley Tree and continue 0.7mi to the parking lot.

To spend more time hiking in the Giant Forest, combine this hike with the Trail of

Giant Forest

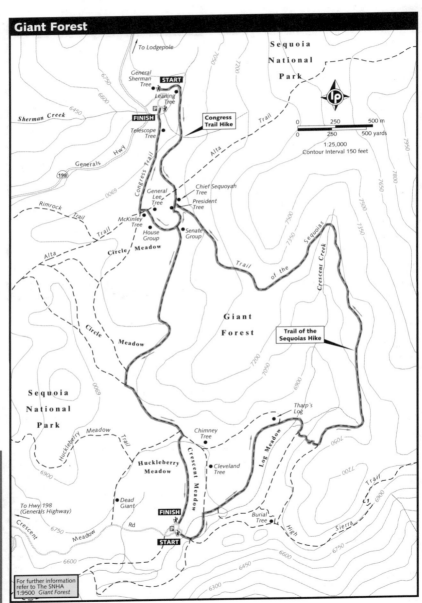

the Sequoias for a combined 7.2mi loop. Leave the paved path just past the Chief Sequoyah Tree and do the Trail of the Sequoias in a clockwise direction, rejoining the Congress Trail at the Senate Group after 5.1mi.

Trail of the Sequoias

Duration	2½–3 hours
Distance	5.1mi (8.2km)
Standard	easy
Start/Finish	Crescent Meadow
Public Transport	no

Summary The peaceful Trail of the Sequoias immerses hikers in the quiet serenity of the Giant Forest, as it loops past meadows and along streams through exquisite stands of sequoia trees.

A counterclockwise loop through the eastern part of the Giant Forest on the Trail of the Sequoias takes you to the finest groves in the Giant Forest and touches many of the renowned trees of the Congress Trail. The mostly shaded trail skirts three named meadows, where only lush grasses grow, because the soil is too wet to support tree growth. The gentle trail rolls along with a total elevation gain and loss of only 1240ft in equal amounts of ascent and descent.

PLANNING
When to Hike
The hiking season is from May to November.

Maps
The SNHA 1:9500 *Giant Forest* map ($2) covers the hike.

Permits & Regulations
A permit is not required for this day hike. Camping is not allowed anywhere in the Giant Forest.

GETTING TO/FROM THE HIKE
From Generals Hwy in the Giant Forest, 4mi southwest of Lodgepole, drive 3.5mi southeast to the parking lot and trailhead at the end of Crescent Meadow Rd (6700ft).

THE HIKE
(See the Giant Forest map.)
Follow the Crescent Meadow-Log Meadow trail east around the south end of Crescent Meadow (6700ft) and along the west side of Log Meadow 0.8mi to historic **Tharp's Log**, a huge hollow log that served as the summer home of Hale Tharp, Giant Forest's first settler, from 1861 to 1890. Join the Trail of the Sequoias here and follow it east, around the north end of **Log Meadow**. After crossing Crescent Creek, ascend 160ft in 0.2mi, then turn north and parallel Crescent Creek. The trail recrosses the creek, ascends gently over a small ridge (7320ft) and descends through beautiful forest to join the Congress Trail near massive **Chief Sequoyah Tree**.

Turn south and follow the combined trails a few minutes to the Senate Group. Here, the Trail of the Sequoias leaves the paved path and continues south 1mi, past the small, intimate Circle Meadow. Continue another 0.5mi to the north end of Crescent Meadow. Turn south on the Crescent Meadow trail and walk 0.5mi along the west side of this tranquil meadow to the trailhead.

High Sierra Trail

Duration	8 days
Distance	72.2mi (116.2km)
Standard	hard
Start	Crescent Meadow
Finish	Whitney Portal
Public Transport	no

Summary This classic trans-Sierra route from west to east across Sequoia National Park crosses two passes and traverses the Kern River canyon, linking the sequoias of the Giant Forest to Mt Whitney.

The High Sierra Trail traverses the very heart of the High Sierra across Sequoia National Park. Starting from giant sequoia groves, this varied hike crosses the Great Western Divide at its lowest pass, skirts the multicolored Kaweah peaks, ascends the Kern River canyon, crosses a high plateau and reaches Mt Whitney's summit before descending to the eastern Sierra. Backpackers should be in top shape to enjoy the splendors of this long and strenuous route.

The trailheads are almost 400mi apart by road, which takes six to seven hours of driving time. To overcome this logistical obstacle, you need to have two vehicles, along with patience and time to drive shuttles, or to arrange for someone to drop you off or pick you up. If you prefer support for a hike this long, contact the companies listed under Organized Hikes, p38, in the Facts for the Hiker chapter.

PLANNING
When to Hike

The hiking season for this trail is from July to mid-September.

Maps

The USGS 1:24,000 *Lodgepole, Triple Divide Peak, Mt Kaweah, Chagoopa Falls* and *Mt Whitney* quadrangles cover the hike,

as does Tom Harrison Maps 1:63,360 *Mt Whitney High Country Trail Map* ($8.95).

Permits & Regulations

A free permit is needed (see p216).

GETTING TO/FROM THE HIKE
To the Start

From Generals Hwy in Giant Forest, drive 3.5mi east on Crescent Meadow Rd to its end at the trailhead.

From the Finish

From Whitney Portal, a road leads 13mi east to Lone Pine (see Lone Pine, p262).

THE HIKE
Day 1: Crescent Meadow to Bearpaw Meadow

6–7 hours, 11mi (17.7km), 1100ft (330m) ascent

Skirting Crescent Meadow and Log Meadows (6700ft), passing some giant sequoias and

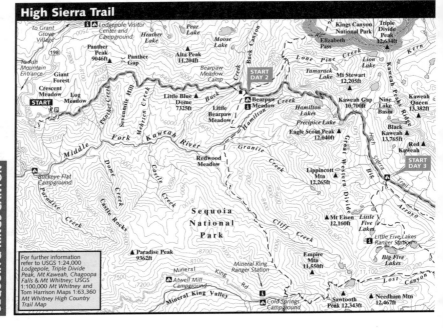

swinging by Eagle View Overlook, the High Sierra Trail begins an undulating traverse high along the forested north side of the canyon of the Middle Fork Kaweah River. Crossing numerous streams, many with small *campsites*, the trail presents a continuous panorama of the Kaweah Basin and the peaks of the Great Western Divide. Shortly after crossing Mehrten Creek, it passes a spur trail leading north to the Alta Trail, and continues to the bridge over Buck Creek, from where it ascends to **Bearpaw Meadow** (7800ft) and intersects a trail leading north to Elizabeth Pass and descending south to Little Bearpaw and Redwood meadows. Heavily used *campsites* lie a few yards ahead and south of the trail in the forest. A ranger station and Bearpaw Meadow Camp are on either side of the trail a short distance ahead. ***Bearpaw Meadow Camp (☎ 888-252-5757, 559-253-2199 from outside the US)***, open mid-June to mid-September, is a tent 'hotel' ($150 per person including two daily meals)

that offers complete bedding and showers; reservations are required.

Day 2: Bearpaw Meadow to Big Arroyo Creek Junction
6–7 hours, 11mi (17.7km), 2900ft (870m) ascent, 1100ft (330m) descent

Continue east and go northeast 2mi to cross Lone Pine Creek and pass the Tamarack Lake trail junction. The trail ascends toward fantastic, granite-walled Hamilton Lakes and Kaweah Gap. It contours the cliff face and zigzags up, across Hamilton Creek below smaller, lower Hamilton Lake, recrossing it below upper **Hamilton Lake** (8200ft), which has overused *campsites* to its northwest.

Rising steeply out of the cirque, the trail, engineered by blasting, passes tunnel-like across the cliff face. Climbing past Precipice Lake, which lies beneath towering Eagle Scout Peak, the trail emerges at **Kaweah Gap** (10,700ft) on the Great Western Divide, to face Nine Lake Basin and the jagged

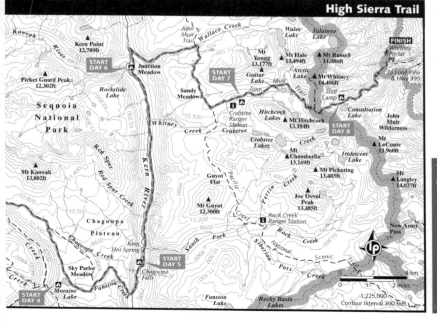

High Sierra Trail

spires of the Kaweah peaks. Descending along the west side of Big Arroyo Creek, then crossing to its east side, the trail enters forest and crosses streams coming from Black Kaweah and Red Kaweah. It comes to *campsites* (9600ft) shortly before the junction with the Big Arroyo Creek and Little Five Lakes trails, 2mi from Kaweah Gap.

Day 3: Big Arroyo Creek Junction to Moraine Lake

5–6 hours, 8mi (12.9km), 1040ft (312m) ascent, 1340ft (402m) descent

Pass the trail junction and ascend eastward along the northern slopes of Big Arroyo Creek to broad **Chagoopa Plateau**, south of the Kaweah peaks. Descending gradually along this sloping tableland, the trail crosses a branch of Chagoopa Creek and comes to a junction. The left fork continues 3.3mi to Sky Parlor Meadow beyond Moraine Lake, where it rejoins the right fork. Follow the right fork and head down to *campsites* along the southern shore of Moraine Lake (9300ft).

Day 4: Moraine Lake to Kern Hot Spring

4–5 hours, 7mi (11.3km), 2500ft (750m) descent, 80ft (24m) ascent

Heading east through Sky Parlor Meadow and fording Funston Creek, the trail rejoins the High Sierra Trail after a mile. Continuing east, it begins an ever-steepening descent into **Kern Canyon**, paralleling Funston Creek to meet the Kern River Trail 3.7mi from the junction. Turning left, it heads north up the deep canyon, through meadows and forest. The trail crosses a bridge to the east side of the Kern River and passes opposite **Chagoopa Falls**, tumbling down the canyon's west wall. Just beyond the crossing of South Fork Rock Creek lies Kern Hot Spring (6880ft) where a *campsite* is just north and east of the hot spring, near the Kern River.

Day 5: Kern Hot Spring to Junction Meadow

4–6 hours, 8mi (12.9km), 1156ft (346m) ascent

Ascending steadily north along the east side of the Kern River, beneath impressive high granite cliffs, the trail crosses the Guyot Flat stream, Whitney Creek and Wallace Creek to arrive at Junction Meadow (8036ft), which has heavily used *campsites* along the river.

Day 6: Junction Meadow to Crabtree Ranger Station

5–6 hours, 9mi (14.5km), 2664ft (799.2m) ascent

Ascending steadily north along the Kern River for a mile, the trail comes to a junction where it turns sharply right, leaving the Kern River Trail. Working southeast, the High Sierra Trail rises into the **Wallace Creek** canyon and parallels the creek 3.5mi to a junction (10,390ft) with the combined PCT and John Muir Trail.

Turning right onto this well-traveled route, the High Sierra Trail crosses Wallace Creek, rolls up and over the saddle west of Mt Young, skirts **Sandy Meadow** and, 3.5mi from the junction, the High Sierra and John Muir Trails turn east (left), leaving the PCT. The trail continues for just less than a mile to the Crabtree ranger station, with *campsites* (10,700ft) just south of Whitney Creek.

Day 7: Crabtree Ranger Station to Trail Camp

7–8 hours, 12.2mi (19.6km), 3077ft (923.1m) ascent, 1777ft (533.1m) descent

Staying north of Whitney Creek, the trail climbs above tree line, passing **Timberline** and **Guitar Lake**s. It crosses the outlet from Arctic Lake, traverses a meadow and begins a long series of switchbacks up the western slopes of Mt Whitney to reach the junction with the trail to the summit of Mt Whitney. The junction is 5.5mi from Crabtree ranger station.

Many hikers leave their backpacks here and turn north along the spectacular ridge crest, continuing 2mi to the summit. As you return to **Trail Crest** (13,777ft) from the summit, with its breathtaking view, the trail turns east, leaving Sequoia National Park, and descends many short, steep switchbacks to the heavily used **Trail Camp** (12,000ft), among the boulders above Consultation Lake.

Day 8: Trail Camp to Whitney Portal

3–4 hours, 6mi (9.65km), 3635ft (1090.5m) descent

Follow the busy trail down to Whitney Portal (see the Day 1 description of the Mt Whitney hike, p276).

Sequoia National Park – Mineral King

Mineral King is a scenic subalpine valley, surrounded by half a dozen smaller valleys (each with lakes in alpine basins) and passes leading to more distant backcountry. Hiking anywhere from Mineral King involves a steep climb out of the valley along strenuous trails.

HISTORY

Mineral King, as the name implies, was a mining center that rose to prominence in the late 1870s. Prospectors built the first road into the valley and established a small town, but hopes of endless silver ore faded after just a few years. In 1893 Mineral King became part of the Sierra Forest Preserve, and soon after, the USFS leased land to summer vacationers. By 1926, Sequoia National Park expanded, encircling Mineral King. In the ensuing years, developers fought to turn it into a large-scale ski resort. Fortunately, Mineral King was saved when the US Congress made it part of Sequoia National Park in 1978.

ACCESS FACILITIES
Mineral King

Mineral King has no services, but private Silver City Resort, about 3mi west of the ranger station on Mineral King Rd, has a small restaurant and store. Drinking water and a food storage hut are opposite the ranger station.

Along Mineral King Rd are the first-come, first-served *Atwell Mill Campground* ($8; 6540ft) and *Cold Springs Campground* ($8; 7580ft).

The 25mi-long Mineral King Rd begins at Hwy 198, 4mi north of Three Rivers and

Warning: Munching Marmots

An abundant yellow-bellied marmot population in Mineral King is creating havoc for some unsuspecting motorists. From early spring through mid-July, these largest members of the ground squirrel family (*Marmota flaviventris*) chew on the hoses, belts and wiring of vehicles to get the salt (sodium) they crave before their winter hibernation. The only known system for protecting vehicles parked at all Mineral King trailheads is to physically enclose the vehicle in chicken wire weighted down with rocks. (One-inch or 2in hex netting that is 36in or 48in high and 50ft long costs $15 to $20.) Marmots have been known to stow away in engines regardless of the precautions you take, so look under the hood before driving off.

2mi south of Sequoia's Ash Mountain Entrance. The first 17mi of this steep and narrow winding road are open year-round, but the last 8mi are closed during winter and reopen Memorial Day weekend. The drive to the trailheads at its end takes 1½ hours one way.

Lower Monarch Lake

Duration	2 days
Distance	10mi (16.1km)
Standard	moderate
Start/Finish	Mineral King
Public Transport	no

Summary Hike to a scenic lake nestled beneath the western flanks of the Great Western Divide with commanding views of Sequoia National Park's Mineral King Valley.

Lower Monarch Lake lies in a rocky bowl above tree line beneath jagged Sawtooth Peak (12,343ft), which dominates Mineral King Valley, and between colorful Empire and Rainbow Mountains. It's possible to visit Lower Monarch Lake on a steep and strenuous day hike, but overnight backpackers are well rewarded with photogenic views from on high at sunset.

PLANNING
When to Hike
The hiking season is from mid-June to September.

Maps
The USGS 1:24,000 *Mineral King* quadrangle covers the hike.

Permits & Regulations
A free wilderness permit is required for this hike (see Permits & Regulations, p216).

GETTING TO/FROM THE HIKE
See Mineral King, p233, under Access Facilities earlier in this chapter. Park your vehicle at the Sawtooth-Monarch Parking Area.

THE HIKE
Day 1: Mineral King to Lower Monarch Lake
3½–4 hours, 5mi (8.1km), 2540ft (762m) ascent

From the Sawtooth-Monarch Parking Area (7840ft), follow the dusty Sawtooth Pass

Trail as it makes a long traverse through sagebrush to the junction with the Timber Gap Trail after about a mile. Bear right at the junction and go up the hot, open slope, past some trees, into the Monarch Creek canyon, reaching Groundhog Meadow in another mile. Cross the creek into cool forest and zigzag relentlessly up the ridge, reaching the Crystal Lake Trail junction in 2.2mi. Continue along the Sawtooth Pass Trail, traversing easily north across the shoulder of the ridge to regain the Monarch Creek drainage, with glimpses of Sawtooth Peak and nearby Glacier Pass. Passing through a rocky area, the trail traverses to meet Monarch Creek, crosses it twice, and arrives at the west end of **Lower Monarch Lake** (10,380ft), which has *campsites* above the north shore.

Side Trip: Sawtooth Pass
3 hours, 2.4mi (3.9km), 1220ft (366m) ascent, 1220ft (366m) descent

A side trip to **Sawtooth Pass** (11,600ft), on the Great Western Divide, follows a steep, difficult and faint trail over pulverized granite, and rewards with views of the Kaweah Peaks and the Whitney Crest.

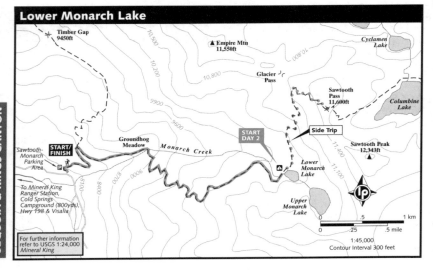

Day 2: Lower Monarch Lake to Mineral King
3–3½ hours, 5mi (8.1km), 2540ft (762m) descent
Retrace your steps to the trailhead.

Franklin & Sawtooth Passes

Duration	4 days
Distance	30mi (48.3km)
Standard	moderate-hard
Start/Finish	Mineral King
Public Transport	no

Summary Two scenic passes over the Great Western Divide, forested canyons and beautiful lakes with excellent fishing make this Sequoia National Park's most popular loop from Mineral King.

The highly popular loop from Mineral King crosses two passes, Franklin and Sawtooth, as well as the Great Western Divide. For some backpackers, the beginning of this route offers an alternative western approach to Mt Whitney via direct access to the Kern River Basin. Hiking to Lower Franklin Lake and visiting Franklin Pass makes an excellent, shorter overnight option.

PLANNING
When to Hike
The hiking season is from mid-June to September.

Maps
The USGS 1:24,000 *Mineral King* and *Chagoopa Falls* quadrangles cover the hike.

Permits & Regulations
A free wilderness permit is required for this hike. (see Permits & Regulations, p216).

GETTING TO/FROM THE HIKE
See Mineral King, p233, under Access Facilities earlier in this chapter. The hike starts near the Eagle-Mosquito Parking Area and finishes at the Sawtooth-Monarch Parking Area. You can park at either of these two areas, which are only a few minutes' walk apart.

THE HIKE
Day 1: Mineral King to Lower Franklin Lake
4–5 hours, 6mi (9.7km), 2480ft (744m) ascent
From Eagle-Mosquito Parking Area (7840ft), walk back over the bridge and follow the road a few minutes south past the pack station, where the pavement ends. The trail soon narrows and fords **Crystal Creek** after a mile.

Rising gently above the green valley, the trail fords **Franklin Creek**, then rises in a series of switchbacks and long traverses through meadows to the junction with the Farewell Gap Trail in 2.5mi. Follow the left fork, which continues north and then east, climbing to a second ford of Franklin Creek. Passing through contrasting, dark, multicolored, metamorphic rock and pale granite, the trail switchbacks above the north bank of Franklin Creek to cross a granite shoulder above dammed **Lower Franklin Lake** (10,320ft). Attractive **campsites** are above the northeast shore.

Day 2: Lower Franklin Lake to Little Claire Lake
4–6 hours, 7mi (11.3km), 1480ft (444m) ascent, 1350ft (405m) descent
The trail rises through the last bit of forest, then makes a series of well-graded switchbacks up the pulverized granite slope as it ascends out of the cirque. It crosses two tiny, year-round, flower-lined streams, and works steadily upward to a long traverse to panoramic **Franklin Pass** (11,800ft), 2.5mi from the lake.

Descending switchbacks from the pass into forested upper Rattlesnake Canyon, the trail soon comes to the junction with the Shotgun Pass Trail. A quarter mile below (beyond) this junction, the trail forks. The right fork crosses Rattlesnake Creek and descends along the creek to the Kern River, which serves as the alternative route to Mt Whitney. Follow the left fork, which goes a mile to Forester Lake. Beyond Forester

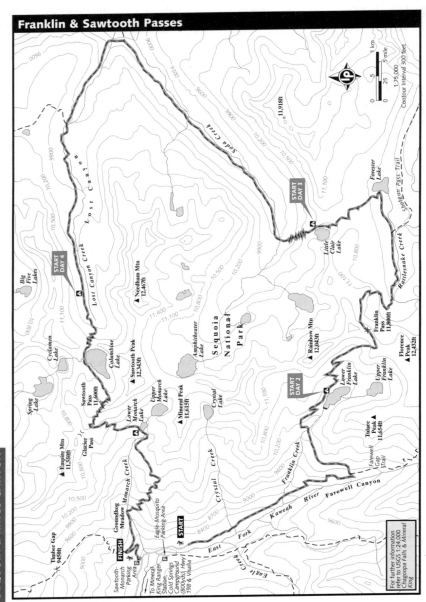

Franklin & Sawtooth Passes

START DAY 4

START DAY 3

START DAY 2

START

FINISH

Big Five Lakes

Cyclamen Lake

Spring Lake

Empire Mtn 11,550ft

Sawtooth Pass 11,600ft

Glacier Pass

Columbine Lake

Sawtooth Peak 12,343ft

Upper Monarch Lake

Lower Monarch Lake

Mineral Peak 11,615ft

Needham Mtn 12,467ft

Amphitheater Lake

Crystal Lake

Rainbow Mtn 12,043ft

Franklin Pass 11,800ft

Florence Peak 12,432ft

Lower Franklin Lake

Upper Franklin Lake

Tulare Peak 11,654ft

Little Claire Lake

Forester Lake

11,918ft

Sequoia National Park

Lost Canyon

Lost Canyon Creek

Soda Creek

Rattlesnake Creek

Shotgun Pass Trail

Crystal Creek

Monarch Creek

Groundhog Meadow

Eagle-Mosquito Parking Area

Franklin Creek

Farewell Gap Trail

Kaweah River

Farewell Canyon

East Fork

Eagle Creek

Timber Gap 9450ft

Sawtooth-Monarch Parking Area

To Mineral King Ranger Station; Cold Springs Campground; (800yds), Hwy 198 & Visalia

For further information refer to USGS 1:24,000 Chagoopa Falls & Mineral King

1 km

5 mile

1:75,000

Contour Interval 300 feet

Lake, ascend through forest, over a ridge, and down into the Soda Creek drainage and to Little Claire Lake (10,450ft) with good *campsites* at its outlet.

Day 3: Little Claire Lake to Upper Lost Canyon

5–6 hours, 9mi (14.5km), 1400ft (420m) descent, 1200ft (360m) ascent

The trail descends in switchbacks west of the outlet from Little Claire Lake, down a steep, forested slope to a ford of Soda Creek. Keeping north of Soda Creek, the trail descends through forest to a trail junction about 5mi from Little Claire Lake. The right fork descends to Big Arroyo Canyon. Take the left fork, which climbs through open brush and enters **Lost Canyon**, crossing that creek to its north side. The trail then rises steadily for more than a mile to a junction with the Big Five Lakes Trail. Just beyond the junction, the Lost Canyon Trail fords the creek, which it recrosses within another mile. The trail then ascends steeply through meadows and mixed forest to grassy *campsites* amid scattered pines (10,200ft), with Needham Mountain rising to the south.

Day 4: Upper Lost Canyon to Mineral King

5–6 hours, 8mi (12.9km), 1400ft (420m) ascent, 3760ft (1128m) descent

The trail rises above timberline and ascends a rocky slope. Crossing this low saddle, the trail drops down to dramatic **Columbine Lake**, beneath Sawtooth Peak, and crosses its outlet. Circling the northern lakeshore, the trail climbs steeply to **Sawtooth Pass** (11,600ft). From the pass, marked by a small cairn, the trail descends northwest toward Glacier Pass. Many paths head steeply down over loose pulverized granite, but the best route stays high, aiming northwest toward a saddle with a few trees several hundred yards south of Glacier Pass. From above the saddle, the route works down a grassy gully between granite outcrops, then makes a level traverse to popular **Lower Monarch Lake** (10,380ft), from where you see sweeping views west over Mineral King and spectacular sunsets. A good trail descends to Sawtooth-Monarch Parking Area, visible more than 3700ft below (see the Lower Monarch Lake hike, p233).

Other Hikes

Redwood Canyon

Redwood Mountain Grove is the world's largest grove of sequoias, with more than 15,000 trees. Three decades of a sustainable management program, including prescribed burns, has led to a successful rejuvenation of these majestic trees. A choice of three half-day loop hikes will have you winding your way past impressive groves and noteworthy individual trees and through an impressive canyon.

This is a little-visited area, despite its close proximity to the Big Stump Entrance of Kings Canyon National Park and busy Grant Grove Village. Two things contribute to this – the lack of a sign telling visitors where **Redwood Mountain Grove** is, and the rough, single-lane, unpaved road to it. But don't let a little inconvenience stand in the way of your going to this magnificent, pristine corner of Kings Canyon.

Look for the 'Hume Lake/Quail Flat' sign on Generals Hwy 3.6mi east of the 'Y' intersection, which is 1.7mi east of the Big Stump Entrance. Just opposite it is an unsigned, unpaved, single-lane road along which is a sign indicating you are 'Entering Kings Canyon National Park.' Turn right (south) onto the road and drive 1.8mi down to a fork called Redwood Saddle; turn left at the fork and go 0.1mi to the parking area. The Redwood Saddle Trailhead (6200ft) is at the parking area's northeast corner.

Bring water with you since none is available here. Two trails start at this trailhead. The one to the left is called the Hart Tree/Redwood Canyon Trail, and the one to the right is the Sugar Bowl Trail.

The first hike is a 6mi (9.7km) loop to Hart Tree, Barton's Post Camp and Fallen Goliath. Turn left from the trailhead and walk half a mile to a junction with the trail down Redwood Canyon. Turn left and reach Barton's Post Camp, an old sequoia logging site with a cabin made from one huge log, in half a mile. It's 2.5mi farther to Hart Tree, 1mi beyond which is Fallen Goliath. Continue half a mile to a junction with the Redwood Canyon trail. Turn right and go uphill 1.5mi back to the trailhead.

The second hike visits two groves, **Burnt Grove** and **Sugar Bowl Grove**, making another 6mi loop. Head right at the trailhead and hike 1mi to the Burnt Grove. The Sugar Bowl Grove is 1.5mi farther.

Two miles downhill beyond that, reach Redwood Canyon and the trail from Fallen Goliath. Continue 1.5mi up the canyon back to the trailhead. Seeing thousands of flourishing sequoia seedlings that demonstrate the effectiveness of the burn policy makes this hike unique.

The third hike combines the two shorter loops for a spectacular 10mi (16.1km) trip.

The USGS 1:24,000 *General Grant Grove* quadrangle covers the hike. A wilderness permit is not necessary for day hikes, but is required for any overnight trip. Go to the Grant Grove visitor center to get one. Camping is prohibited within 2mi of the trailhead.

Silliman & Elizabeth Passes

A 52mi (83.7km) five-day, clockwise near-loop hike crosses two passes, starting from the Twin Lakes trailhead (6740ft) and finishing at Crescent Meadow (6700ft). The highlight of this moderate-hard hike is ascending Deadman Canyon and crossing Elizabeth Pass (11,360ft).

The USGS 1:24,000 *Lodgepole, Mt Silliman, Sphinx Lakes* and *Triple Divide Peak* quadrangles cover the hike, as does Tom Harrison Maps 1:63,360 *Mt Whitney High Country Trail Map*. A wilderness permit is required for this hike.

The Twin Lakes trailhead is at Lodgepole campground in Sequoia National Park. Drive 0.3mi past the campground kiosk into the Lodgepole campground and park at the huge long-term parking lot.

Walk 0.1mi beyond the parking lot and cross the bridge over the Marble Fork Kaweah River. Two trailheads are immediately visible to the right after the bridge. Pass by the first trailhead, which goes to Tokopah Falls, and start from the second trailhead nearby, which is the Twin Lakes Trailhead.

The Twin Lakes Trail ascends out of the Marble Fork Kaweah River valley and turns north to cross forested **Cahoon Gap** (8650ft) and descends to the East Fork Clover Creek.

Turning right (east) you ascend along the creek past Twin Lakes (9445ft) and continue up to **Silliman Pass** (10,165ft), entering Kings Canyon National Park. A steep descent brings you to Ranger Lake (9180ft), with campsites on its southwest shore.

From the lake, the trail heads north to Sugarloaf Creek and turns east into Sugarloaf Valley, beneath polished granite Sugarloaf Dome

(7995ft). Crossing the creek, the trail climbs a ridge and descends into Roaring River Valley to campsites near Roaring River ranger station (7430ft), at the junction with the trail to Avalanche Pass. Follow the trail to Elizabeth Pass, south along the west bank of Deadman Creek into Deadman Canyon, crossing it several times as you ascend.

The polished granite canyon walls rise above narrow Ranger Meadow as you continue to campsites in Upper Ranger Meadow (9200ft). The cirque wall at the head of the canyon looks impossibly steep as you make the ascent amid talus along the cascading creek. A final steep ascent on the faint and rugged trail brings you to **Elizabeth Pass** (11,360ft), where you re-enter Sequoia National Park. Switchbacks then take you steeply down to campsites located at Bearpaw Meadow (7800ft) on the High Sierra Trail. From here, follow the High Sierra Trail west to Crescent Meadow (6700ft).

Little Five Lakes Loop

Another popular loop hike, this one from Mineral King in Sequoia National Park, is the 31mi (49.9km), four-day loop to Little Five Lakes. This strenuous route crosses three passes, one of which is on the **Great Western Divide**, and visits five fishing lakes.

From the Sawtooth-Monarch Parking Area (7840ft), the trail ascends north 2mi to Timber Gap (9450ft). It then drops steeply through forest, along flower gardens at the head of Timber Creek, and down through forest to a crossing of Cliff Creek (7040ft). North of the creek are campsites and a trail junction.

The trail turns east (right), ascends along the north side of Cliff Creek, passing the falls on **Cliff Creek**, and ascends to cross the outlet from Pinto Lake.

A short right spur leads to Pinto Lake (8650ft), 8.5mi from the trailhead. Returning from this campsite and then turning east (right), the main trail switchbacks steadily upward to Black Rock Pass (11,650ft) with immense views of Little Five Lakes, Big Five Lakes, the towering Kaweah peaks, and the distant Sierra Crest. The trail descends southeast, then takes a turn northeast to pass near the Little Five Lakes (10,500ft), 7mi from Pinto Lake.

The trail then crosses the outlet of the main Little Five Lake and descends through forest about a mile, then rises to a ridge above the Big Five Lakes.

At the start of the descent to these lakes, a side trail forks right to upper Big Five Lakes. The main trail continues down switchbacks and passes east of the lowest Big Five Lake, with campsites near the outlet (9840ft). A rocky ascent then leads to the ridge south of the Big Five Lakes and to the north side of a small, unnamed lake (10,000ft), 5mi from Little Five Lakes.

The trail then switchbacks down to join the Lost Canyon Trail before ascending west several miles into upper **Lost Canyon**. Continuing west, it crosses Sawtooth Pass and returns via Lower Monarch Lake to Mineral King.

Eastern Sierra

The eastern Sierra is for many backpackers the Sierra Nevada's most appealing area, spanning more than 250mi of five contiguous wilderness areas – Ansel Adams, John Muir, Golden Trout, South Sierra and Dome Land – from north to south. Here the jagged crest of the Sierra Nevada rises abruptly almost 2mi above the high desert, with 14 peaks higher than 14,000ft and Mt Whitney as the crown jewel. Most trails access one of these wilderness areas, and more than a dozen major passes cross over the Sierra Crest into Yosemite, Kings Canyon and Sequoia National Parks.

The connecting highway between Los Angeles and Reno, US 395, follows the length of the eastern Sierra through the Owens Valley between Deadman Summit and Hwy 178. Paved roads lead west from US 395 and go several thousand feet up steep canyons to popular high elevation trailheads, offering quick access to the high country. In most of these inviting canyons, where creeks and rivers tumble from formidably steep granite pinnacles, are USFS recreation areas with convenient campgrounds, and an occasional small, private resort or store.

INFORMATION
Maps

The USGS 1:125,000 *Sequoia and Kings Canyon National Parks and Vicinity* with 200ft contour intervals is a superb planning and backpacking map for all eastern approach routes in both parks. The excellent, yet massive, USFS 1:63,360 *John Muir Wilderness (Inyo and Sierra National Forests) and National Parks Backcountry (Sequoia and Kings Canyon National Parks)* series ($10) includes three sheets: *North Section,* areas north from Evolution Basin in northern Kings Canyon National Park; *Central Section,* all of Kings Canyon National Park except areas south of the South Fork Kings River; and *South Section,* areas of Kings Canyon National Park south

of the South Fork Kings River and all of Sequoia National Park.

Tom Harrison Maps 1:125,000 *Sequoia & Kings Canyon National Parks Recreation Map* ($9) with 200ft contour intervals covers the parks and their eastern Sierra approaches. The USFS 1:126,720 *Inyo National Forest* map is also useful for secondary roads, campgrounds and some trails.

Books
Sierra East: Edge of the Great Basin, by Genny Smith, is a lavishly illustrated, comprehensive and accessible account of the natural and unnatural history of the eastern Sierra.

Information Sources
For general wilderness information, call Inyo National Forest at ☎ 760-873-2485 or visit the website at Ⓦ www.r5.fs.fed.us/inyo.

Permits & Regulations
A free wilderness permit is required year-round for all overnight hikes in this chapter. A permit is not required for any day hikes except Mt Whitney (see the Mt Whitney hike, p274, for permit information specific to that hike only). Inyo National Forest (☎ 760-873-2408 general information, ☎ 760-873-2485 wilderness information, ☎ 760-873-2483 wilderness permit reservations), which extends along 175mi of the eastern Sierra from Lundy Canyon north of Mono Lake to the southern end of the Owens Valley, issues permits for these wilderness areas: Hoover, Ansel Adams, John Muir, Golden Trout and South Sierra, which include all the hikes in this chapter.

A quota system is in effect on most trails from the last Friday in June to September 15. Advance reservations, which are recommended for weekend entry dates, are available (for a $5 per-person reservation fee) during the quota period for 60% of the permits. The other 40% are available on a walk-in first-come, first-served basis.

Walk-in permits are available starting at 11am the day prior to the entry date at ranger stations and visitor centers. From September 16 to the last Thursday in June, permits are available on a self-issuing basis.

You can submit applications for advance reservations by fax (fax 760-873-2484) or mail (Wilderness Reservation Office, Inyo

National Forest, 873 N Main St, Bishop, CA 93514) starting March 1, or by telephone (☎ 760-873-2483 from 1 to 5pm weekdays) from May 1 up to two days prior to your planned entry date. Wilderness permit applications can be downloaded from the national forest website at Ⓦ www.r5.fs.fed.us/inyo/vvc/permits.htm.

To pick up your wilderness permit, go to any of the following ranger stations or visitor centers, preferably the one nearest your trailhead:

Mono Basin National Forest Scenic Area visitor center (☎ 760-647-3044), on US 395 half a mile north of Lee Vining

Mammoth ranger station (☎ 760-924-5500), 2500 Main St (Hwy 203), inside the Mammoth visitor center, 3mi west of US 395 in Mammoth Lakes

White Mountain ranger station (☎ 760-873-2500), 798 N Main St (US 395) at Yaney St, at the north end of Bishop

Mt Whitney ranger station (☎ 760-876-6200), on US 395 at Inyo St, at the south end of Lone Pine

Inyo National Forest ranger stations are typically open 8am to 5pm daily during summer.

Bear-resistant food containers are required in many areas and are available for rent and purchase at the above locations. Some Inyo National Forest trailheads have bear boxes, typically in areas with the greatest bear problems.

Implementation of a new management plan for Inyo National Forest begins in 2002. Changes are scheduled to occur in the wilderness permit system, quotas and advance reservations resulting in differences in how, where and when you can get a permit or make reservations. Visit their website at Ⓦ www.r5.fs.fed.us/inyo before your trip for the most recent updates. Inyo National Forest has the most daunting rules, regulations and procedures of any federal agency in the Sierra Nevada, but don't let the somewhat harsh tone of their literature discourage you. When you get through the bureaucracy of permits and regulations, life on the trail is pleasantly uncomplicated.

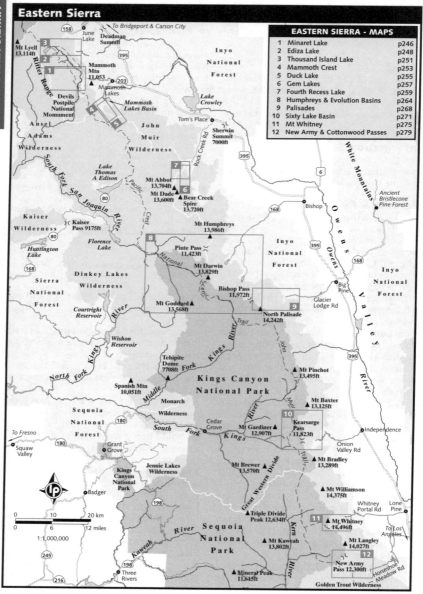

Eastern Sierra

To Bridgeport & Carson City

Mt Lyell
13,114ft

June Lake

Deadman Summit

Ritter Range

Inyo

National

Forest

Mammoth Mtn
11,053ft

Mammoth Lakes

Devils Postpile National Monument

Mammoth Lakes Basin

Lake Crowley

Tom's Place

Sherwin Summit 7000ft

Ansel

Adams

Wilderness

John

Muir

Wilderness

Rock Creek Rd

South Fork San Joaquin River

Pacific Crest

Lake Thomas A Edison

Mt Abbot
13,704ft

Mt Dade
13,600ft

Bear Creek Spire
13,720ft

White Mountains

Bishop

Ancient Bristlecone Pine Forest

Kaiser Wilderness

Kaiser Pass 9175ft

Florence Lake

Mt Humphreys
13,986ft

Piute Pass
11,423ft

Inyo

National

Forest

Owens

Owens Valley

Inyo

National

Forest

Huntington Lake

Sierra

National

Forest

Dinkey Lakes Wilderness

Courtright Reservoir

National

Scenic

Kings River

Mt Darwin
13,829ft

Mt Goddard
13,568ft

Bishop Pass
11,972ft

North Palisade
14,242ft

Big Pine

Glacier Lodge Rd

Wishon Reservoir

North Fork

Tehipite Dome
7708ft

Middle Fork

Kings River Trail

John

Muir

Trail

Spanish Mtn
10,051ft

Monarch

Wilderness

Kings Canyon

National Park

Mt Pinchot
13,495ft

To Fresno

Squaw Valley

Sequoia

National

Forest

Grant Grove

Jennie Lakes Wilderness

Cedar Grove

South Fork

Kings

Mt Gardiner
12,907ft

Mt Brewer
13,570ft

Mt Baxter
13,125ft

Kearsarge Pass
11,823ft

Independence

Onion Valley Rd

Mt Bradley
13,289ft

Badger

Kings Canyon National Park

Great Western Divide

Mt Williamson
14,375ft

Whitney Portal Rd

Lone Pine

Triple Divide Peak 12,634ft

Kern River

Mt Whitney
14,496ft

Mt Langley
14,027ft

To Los Angeles

Sequoia

National

Park

Mt Kaweah
13,802ft

New Army Pass 12,300ft

Horseshoe Meadow Rd

Three Rivers

Mineral Peak
11,615ft

Golden Trout Wilderness

Kaweah River

0   10   20 km
0   6   12 miles
1:1,000,000

Defenders of Freedom

The R-2508 Complex is an airspace designated for military use by the US Department of Defense that includes the skies above the eastern Sierra and Kings Canyon and Sequoia National Parks. Wilderness boundaries are clearly delineated on the ground, but the skies above are entirely another matter. This special, military-use airspace is used daily for aircraft research and development of weapons system technology. Pilots may be students engaging in proficiency testing or those training for 'Top-Gun' air combat maneuvering. Military aircraft, usually flying low and fast or maybe doing spins or testing their craft's supersonic cruising capabilities, roar overhead disrupting the otherwise tranquil wilderness. Pilots are not supposed to fly lower than 3000ft above ground level, but occasionally they do. When this happens, note the time, location, and direction of flight, describe the aircraft, and report it to authorities and park officials.

Other Information

Privately owned shuttle services transport hikers between Owens Valley towns and all Inyo National Forest trailheads. To make a reservation, contact Inyo Trailhead Transportation (call Walt Pettis at work, ☎ 760-876 5518; or home, ☎ 760-876-0035; for Lone Pine shuttles – anywhere from Taboose Creek south, and ☎ 760-872-1901 for Bishop shuttles), which is affiliated with Inyo-Mono Dial-A-Ride (☎ 800-922-1930), or Kountry Korners Trailhead Shuttle Service (☎ 877-656-0756, 760-872-3951), 771 N Main St, Suite 59, Bishop. Rates vary widely depending on itineraries and number of passengers.

Mammoth

The year-round resort town of Mammoth Lakes, home of California's largest ski resort, Mammoth Mountain, is also the gateway to two heavily used hiking areas, the Mammoth Lakes Basin and the Ritter Range, which includes the Minarets. Mammoth Lakes Basin and the Mammoth Crest are south of the town, while the Ritter Range and the Minarets lie west, across the deep, broad valley of the Middle Fork San Joaquin River. Both the PCT and John Muir Trail pass through these areas, and with the added attraction of Devils Postpile National Monument, Mammoth is extremely popular. Hiking trails in the Minarets lie at comparatively low elevation – mostly below 10,000ft – which means the area is quite hot during summer. Trailheads in the Minarets offer easy one-day access to the base of big peaks.

The many pinnacles of the knife-edged Minarets are part of the Ritter Range; hard, dark metamorphosed mountains more than 100 million years older than the granite peaks in adjacent Yosemite National Park. The Ritter Range was part of the national park until 1905. The twin summits of Mt Ritter (13,157ft) and Banner Peak (12,945ft) are the highest of the central Sierra and this range. The lakes nestled at the base of the magnificent Minarets are some of the most beautiful in the Sierra Nevada, as well as some of the most accessible, making them a photographer's delight.

Volcanic activity is evident, especially around Mammoth Mountain (11,053ft) itself, a dormant volcano on the rim of a huge, 760,000 year old caldera. Volcanic activity last occurred as recently as 500 years ago, and the Mammoth region today is California's most active seismic zone.

PLANNING

A free wilderness permit is required for all overnight hikes in the Ansel Adams and John Muir Wilderness Areas. A permit is not required for day hikes. The USFS ranger station (☎ 760-924-5500), which is inside the Mammoth visitor center on Hwy 203 (Main St), 3mi west of US 395, provides trail information, reserves campgrounds, issues wilderness permits and rents bear-resistant containers ($5 per week).

ACCESS TOWN & FACILITIES
Mammoth Lakes

The Mammoth visitor center, on Hwy 203 (Main St), houses the Mammoth Lakes visitors bureau and USFS ranger station. The visitors bureau (☎ 888-466-2666, 800-367-6572, 760-934-2712, fax 760-934-7066, e mmthvisit@qnet.com, w www.visitmammoth.com) provides general information in addition to 24-hour lodging information. The ranger station (☎ 760-924-5500) provides trail information, reserves campgrounds, issues free wilderness permits for the Ansel Adams and John Muir Wilderness Areas, and sells books and maps. The free *Mammoth Lakes Area Visitor Guide* for Inyo National Forest, published by the Eastern Sierra Interpretive Association, is very useful for general orientation. The station is open 8am to 5pm daily.

For local weather information, contact the National Weather Service (☎ 760-873-3213), USFS (☎ 760-934-6611), and in Mammoth Lakes call ☎ 760-934-7669.

Mammoth Mountaineering Supply (☎ 760-934-4191), 437 Old Mammoth Rd at Meridian Blvd, in the Minaret Village shopping center next to Vons Food and Drug, sells gear.Lodging is expensive, so it helps to utilize the visitors bureau. Try *Alpenhof Lodge* (☎ 800-828-0371, 760-934-6330, 6080 Minaret Rd), with its European ambiance, starting at $62, or *Econo Lodge* (☎ 800-845-8764, 760-934-6855, 3626 Main St), starting at $54.

Base Camp Cafe (☎ 760-934-3900), on Main St across from the post office, beyond the junction of Old Mammoth Rd, is a good choice for grabbing a bite to eat. *Roberto's Cafe* (☎ 760-934-3667, 271 Old Mammoth Rd), serves authentic Mexican cuisine, good margaritas and vegetarian fajitas.

Getting There & Away The town of Mammoth Lakes is on Hwy 203, 3mi west of US 395 south of Deadman Summit (8041ft), north of Los Angeles (5½ hours, 325mi), south of Reno (3 hours, 164mi) and east of San Francisco (5½ hours, 300mi). The turnoff is 25mi south of the Hwy 120 junction and 39mi north of Bishop.

Inyo Mono Transit (☎ 800-922-1930) stops at the McDonalds restaurant in Mammoth Lakes on its twice-weekly Bridgeport-Bishop route. The northbound bus ($2.50, 1½ hours) to Bridgeport departs Mammoth Lakes at 4:15pm, and the southbound bus ($3.50, 1¼ hours, 39mi) to Bishop departs at 9:30am, both on Monday and Wednesday. Inyo Mono Transit has a Dial-a-Ride service, which functions much like a taxi; call their dispatcher to make a reservation. This is an inexpensive way to get to trailheads in the Mammoth Lakes Basin.

Mammoth YARTS operates a round-trip bus between Mammoth Lakes and Yosemite National Park once a day on weekends in June and September and once daily in June and July. The bus stops in Mammoth Lakes are at Shilo Inn and Shady Rest campground on Hwy 203 west of the ranger station, Sierra Nevada Rodeway Inn on Old Mammoth Rd, Juniper Springs at the end of Meridian Blvd, and Mammoth Mountain Inn. The bus ($15/20 one way/round-trip) departs Mammoth Lakes right at 7am, then stops in Tuolumne Meadows at 8:50am, and arrives in Yosemite Valley at 10:45am. The return bus departs Yosemite Valley at 5pm. The fare to ride the bus only between Mammoth Lake and Tuolumne Meadows or between Tuolumne Meadows and Yosemite Valley is $15 one way. For information on schedules or to make a reservation call Mammoth California Vacations (☎ 800-626-6684), which handles Mammoth YARTS bookings.

The Mammoth Shuttle (☎ 760-934-3030 information, 760-934-6588 reservations) operates a shuttle service between the Reno/Tahoe International Airport, the nearest airport, and Mammoth Lakes. It costs $125 for one person, $100 each for two people and $75 each for three or more people.

Reds Meadow Area & Devils Postpile

Places to Stay & Eat Six busy campgrounds off Minaret Rd typically fill every day, even midweek. The five USFS campgrounds (from north to south) are: *Agnew Meadows Campground* ($15; 8400ft), the prettiest and quietest of the campgrounds, with spread-out sites, which is 2.6mi from the Minaret Summit entrance station and 0.6mi north of Minaret Rd; *Upper Soda Springs Campground* ($15; 7700ft); *Pumice Flat Campground* ($15; 7700ft); *Minaret Fall Campground* ($15; 7600ft) along the river; and *Reds Meadow Campground* ($15; 7600ft), 0.9mi beyond the Devils Postpile turnoff, with desirable walk-in sites ($5). Reds Meadow campground has a bath house fed by natural hot springs where showers are free for everyone. The undesirable NPS *Devils Postpile Campground* ($12; 7500ft), 4.5mi beyond the Agnews Meadows turnoff, is little more than a dusty, unpaved parking area adjacent to the national monument's day-use parking lot.

Red's Meadow Mule Tradin' General Store, at the private Reds Meadow Resort, 0.6mi beyond Reds Meadow campground, sells groceries and basic supplies.

Getting There & Away The Reds Meadow area and Devils Postpile are on Minaret Rd west of Mammoth Lakes and Mammoth Mountain. Follow Hwy 203 (Main St) west through Mammoth Lakes to the intersection of Minaret Rd. Turn right (north) onto Minaret Rd, which Hwy 203 now follows, and ascend 4mi to Mammoth Mountain Inn and the helpful USFS Information Station.

The vast parking lot here is the staging area for a mandatory shuttle bus system, which has been in operation since 1979. Beyond here, the road is closed to private vehicles from 7:30am to 5:30pm daily, late June to mid-September. During these hours everyone must use the Reds Meadow/Devils Postpile Shuttle Service, except those with confirmed campground reservations. (A wilderness permit does not entitle backpackers to drive their own vehicles to trailheads during these hours.) The shuttle operates every 20 minutes and makes 10 stops, including the turnoffs to the area's six campgrounds and Reds Meadow Resort. The first daily shuttle departs from Mammoth Mountain Inn (☎ 760-934-0686) at 8am; the last departs at 5:30pm. The last bus departs Reds Meadow Resort at 6:15pm. The one-way/round-trip fares are

as follows: cyclists (of any age) and adults, $5/9; ages 13–18, $4/7; ages 5–12, $3/5; and children four or younger, free.

Anyone without a campground reservation and wanting to drive their own vehicle must do so before 7:30am or after 5:30pm. Motorists can proceed 1.3mi beyond Mammoth Mountain Inn to the Minaret Summit entrance station (9175ft) and wait with the typically long line of other vehicles until the road opens at 5:30pm. Beyond the entrance station, the road is a steep, single-lane paved road with turnouts for 2.4mi, after which it returns to being a two-lane road. It's easier to find a campsite when driving in before 7:30am than when driving in after 5:30pm, when a furious rush is on for the few available campsites. Motorists are free to drive out of the area any time of day.

Several policy changes for the Reds Meadow Area and Devils Postpile are proposed to start in 2002. These changes include making it a fee-based area, instituting a user fee for everyone, reducing the cost of the mandatory shuttle bus to more affordable levels and extending the daily shuttle bus hours and season of operation. Check with the USFS before visiting this area to find out what, if any, changes are in effect.

Minaret Lake

Duration	2 days
Distance	15.6mi (25.1km)
Standard	moderate
Start/Finish	Devils Postpile ranger station
Public Transport	yes

Summary A forested trail along a creek passes a waterfall and goes to a gorgeous lake at the base of the Minarets, whose spires are reflected in the lake's placid water.

Minaret Lake offers the most intimate and best up-close views of the Minarets. More than half a dozen towers of the southern Minarets rise dramatically above the lake, with the highest summit almost 2500ft

EASTERN SIERRA

above the water. Although the beginning of the hike is rather unpromising, it keeps getting better and better until it culminates in the spectacularly situated, deep blue lake. Minaret Lake is often used as a base camp for climbs on these towers. Adventurous hikers can spend an extra day exploring the ridges around the lake.

PLANNING
When to Hike
The hiking season is from mid-June to October.

Maps
The USGS 1:24,000 *Mammoth Mountain* and *Mt Ritter* quadrangles cover the hike, as do Tom Harrison Maps 1:63,360 *Mammoth High Country Trail Map* and USFS 1:63,360 *Ansel Adams Wilderness* map.

Permits & Regulations
A free wilderness permit is required for this hike (see Mammoth Lakes, p244, for the nearest ranger station). Bear-resistant food containers are required. Campfires are prohibited anywhere upstream from the outlet of Minaret Lake.

GETTING TO/FROM THE HIKE
From the Minaret Summit entrance station, go 0.5mi on Minaret Rd to the intersection with the paved Devils Postpile Rd. Turn onto this road and pass the overnight parking area on the right in 0.1mi. Park here if you're doing this hike in two days, otherwise continue 0.4mi down the Devils Postpile Rd to the large day-use parking area. The shuttle bus stops in front of the ranger station, and the trailhead (7560ft) is on its south side.

THE HIKE
Day 1: Devils Postpile to Minaret Lake
3½–4 hours, 7.8mi (12.6km), 2233ft (670m) ascent
Walk south from the ranger station (7560ft), following the John Muir Trail signs. This is also the way to Devils Postpile National Monument. After five minutes come to a signed junction, where the trail to Devils Postpile goes straight.

Turn right (west), following the sign to the John Muir Trail North. Cross a sturdy footbridge over the Middle Fork San Joaquin River. Across the footbridge, follow the sign for Minaret Lake and soon

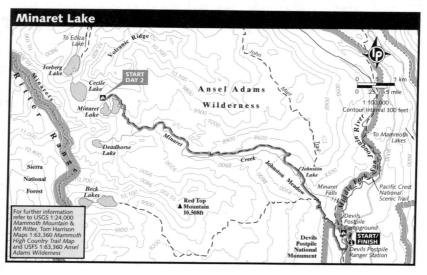

come to a signed junction of the John Muir Trail and Pacific Crest National Scenic Trail (PCT), which are one and the same south of this point, but go on to separate paths heading north.

Go northwest (straight) on the John Muir Trail North, which is also signed to Minaret Lake, leaving the national monument's boundaries and entering into Inyo National Forest. The trail ascends a granite-boulder-strewn, red-fir slope, traversing steadily up, above the river far below. Making a long gradual switchback as it ascends, the trail then nears Minaret Creek, flowing along in a granite cleft toward Minaret Falls well below.

The trail turns away from the main north-south river valley and heads west, ascending briefly along the creek to a signed junction where the trail to Beck Lakes heads southwest (left). Staying on the John Muir Trail, you pass through a gate in a barbed-wire fence and soon cross placid **Minaret Creek** via a large log.

Continuing on the level trail past shallow **Johnston Lake**, you reach a trail junction one hour (1.9mi) from the ranger station. A small sign on a big lodgepole pine indicates that the John Muir Trail bears right (north), and the trail to Minaret Lake bears left (northwest). This area is quite marshy, and the lake and meadow do not offer any possible campsites.

Take the left fork and ascend steadily through lodgepole-pine forest. After 30 minutes, the trail again nears Minaret Creek, which flows through a small granite gorge. Mammoth Mountain and Mammoth Crest are visible to the east and southeast. Continue up through pine forest, and, one hour from the junction, you should come to the base of some **large waterfalls** on Minaret Creek. The lower section is free-falling, but the much larger upper section cascades down a rock face. To the left above the cascade you'll see aptly named **Red Top Mountain** (10,508ft), a prominent landmark.

The trail zigzags up the open sagebrush slope and, reaching the top of the falls, you are rewarded with the first views of the Minarets ahead. The forest cover thins, and the open grassy slopes with granite outcrops are a welcome change from the dense lodgepole forest below. A series of long, gradual switchbacks takes you up, passing the now-closed and hard-to-find spur trail leading to Minaret Mine.

The trail levels as you near Minaret Creek, passing through a meadow where Labrador tea and heather bloom. The trail crosses a branch of Minaret Creek via a log and follows the true left (north) bank of the main creek.

Continuing up through stands of deep forest cover of red fir and hemlock, the trail draws along the splashing creek, where lilies, daisies and paintbrushes bloom profusely. Across the creek you see another stream, the outlet from Deadhorse Lake, cascading over a cliff amid tall red firs. *Campsites* are tucked in the forest between the two streams in this attractive bowl.

Leaving the creekside, follow switchbacks 10 minutes up a sagebrush-covered slope. At the top, cross a slight rocky ridge and drop down to the outlet of deep blue **Minaret Lake** (9793ft). The lake is completely surrounded by rock towers, with Riegelhuth (10,560ft), Pridham (10,960ft), Kehrlein (11,440ft), Ken (11,760ft) and Clyde (12,281ft) Minarets rising clockwise above. The trail continues to the right around the north shore and ends. *Campsites* are beneath trees on both the north and south shores. The serpentine boulders that line the lakeshore are an ideal spot for sunrise photography.

Day 2: Minaret Lake to Devils Postpile

2½–3 hours, 7.8mi (12.6km), 2233ft (670m) descent

Retrace your steps downhill all the way from the lake. Cross the bridge over the Middle Fork San Joaquin River. At the trail junction, turn right and walk a couple of minutes to the base of Devils Postpile (see the Devils Postpile boxed text, p249). After taking a few minutes to marvel at the sight, return to the ranger station and parking lot.

EASTERN SIERRA

Ediza Lake

Duration	2 days
Distance	14.8mi (23.8km)
Standard	easy-moderate
Start/Finish	Shadow Lake/River Trail Trailhead
Public Transport	yes

Summary A classic hike along a gorgeous cascading creek brings you to two scintillating lakes and campsites beneath the imposing crags and summits of the Ritter Range.

Ediza Lake, beneath Mt Ritter, Banner Peak and the glacier-draped Minarets, enjoys one of the loveliest settings of any lake in the Sierra Nevada. Coupled with the delightful trail past Shadow Lake along Shadow Creek, this is a truly enjoyable hike, suitable for almost anyone. Of course, these attractions also make it one of the Sierra's more popular destinations. Hiking as far as Shadow Lake makes a good day hike for those wishing to picnic, swim and bask in the warm summer sun. The hike offers full views of Mt Ritter and partial views of Mt Banner and the Minarets, although the views are more distant than those from Minaret Lake.

PLANNING
When to Hike
The hiking season is from mid-June to October. The relatively lower elevations on this hike make it particularly suitable for early and late season, although it's enjoyable throughout the summer.

Maps
The USGS 1:24,000 *Mammoth Mountain* and *Mt Ritter* quadrangles cover the hike, as do Tom Harrison Maps 1:63,360 *Mammoth High Country Trail Map* ($8.95) and USFS 1:63,360 *Ansel Adams Wilderness* map.

Permits & Regulations
A free wilderness permit is required for this hike (see Mammoth Lakes, p244, for the nearest ranger station). Bear-resistant food containers are required. Camping is prohibited on the south side of Ediza Lake and in the meadows on the west. Campfires are prohibited upstream from Ediza Lake's outlet. Other camping restrictions apply; pick up the list of regulations when you get your wilderness permit or refer to posted bulletins along the trail.

GETTING TO/FROM THE HIKE
On Minaret Rd 2.6mi northwest of the Minaret Summit entrance station, an unpaved road heads to Agnew Meadows campground. This intersection is a bus stop, so you can ride to here and walk the rest of the way to the trailhead. Turn onto this road and go 0.4mi to the second of two parking areas, which is the Shadow Lake/River Trail trailhead (8300ft). Agnew Meadows campground is 0.2mi farther.

THE HIKE
Day 1: Shadow Lake/River Trail Trailhead to Ediza Lake
3–3½ hours, 7.4mi (11.9km), 1225ft (367.5m) ascent, 260ft (78m) descent

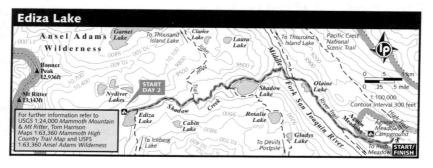

From the southeast corner of the parking area (8300ft), head southwest, skirting the south side of **Agnew Meadows**, which is enclosed by a barbed-wire fence, and cross a log over a small stream flowing into the lush meadows. The broad, level trail continues amid lodgepole pines, which provide cool morning shade, and after 15 minutes passes a small Ansel Adams Wilderness sign on a pine tree. One minute farther, you come to a signed junction where a trail to Reds Meadow turns left. Continue on the Shadow Lake Trail, which forks right and traverses northwest, heading down toward the Middle Fork San Joaquin River. You pass another, larger Ansel Adams Wilderness sign two minutes beyond the junction (in case you missed the first one).

Traversing down the open hillside past rocky outcrops, the west-facing trail offers morning shade and views across the river valley, where you can pick out the cleft of Shadow Creek ahead. The end of this pleasant 15-minute descent over 0.6mi brings you to the valley floor and another junction with a trail to Reds Meadow, 1.5mi from the trailhead. The combined Shadow Lake Trail and River Trail head upvalley beneath the shade of dense lodgepole pines, ascending steadily but moderately. In 10 minutes, reach the shallow, reed-lined **Olaine Lake**, which is separated from the river by a long, narrow, granite outcrop. Passing along the lake's east shore, the trail continues, and in another 10 minutes reaches the signed junction, 2.3mi from the trailhead, where the Shadow Lake Trail turns left and the River Trail to Thousand Island Lake heads right (northwest).

Turning left (west), you pass some large aspens, then cross an open area with some large junipers, pass a stand of cottonwoods, and in five minutes come to the sturdy wooden footbridge (8040ft) over the **Middle Fork San Joaquin River**. Across the footbridge, well-graded switchbacks take you up the open, east-facing slope, where manzanitas flourish. The slope is warm and sunny in the morning, and a few large, red-barked junipers offer occasional shade

Devils Postpile

The 40ft- to 60ft-high, four- to seven-sided columns of blue-gray basalt at Devils Postpile National Monument are the most conspicuous and interesting product of the area's volcanic activity. The columns formed less than 100,000 years ago when lava erupted near Pumice Flat and filled the entire 3mi-wide valley to a depth of 400ft. As the lava cooled, it fractured vertically, forming postpile-like columns. Then, about 10,000 years ago, glaciation quarried away the upper part of the lava, exposing the columns you see today and giving them a cracked, yet polished and shiny surface. Scrape marks from the glacier are visible on the tops of the columns.

Although originally included in 1890 as part of Yosemite National Park, mining interests almost immediately began lobbying to exclude the region from the park, and in 1905, Congress acted to remove Devils Postpile and 500 surrounding acres from the national park. In 1910, the USFS received an application to dynamite Devils Postpile to create a rock-fill dam on the Middle Fork San Joaquin River to provide electricity for mining operations. Alarmed, the Sierra Club and Professor Joseph LeConte of the University of California wrote to the US president and members of his cabinet, urging that Devils Postpile be preserved. In 1911, President Taft declared the area a national monument, restoring its federally protected status.

The 0.4mi trail to the columns takes 10 minutes one way, starting from the ranger station. Allow 30 minutes round trip for a visit. A spur trail, which branches off before reaching the exhibit, leads to the top of the columns.

along the trail. Views downvalley of Mammoth Mountain and of **Two Teats**, a prominent rock horn on the ridge to the east, keep this ascent interesting.

Near the top of the slope, the trail turns west toward cascading Shadow Creek and traverses a rock face. As you head into the gorge above Shadow Creek, thick vegetation lines the trail before it emerges at Shadow Lake's eastern shore, 30 minutes to 45 minutes from the footbridge. With rock walls at its east end, tall green lodgepole pines around its shore and views of Mt Ritter and Banner Peak to the west, beautiful **Shadow Lake** (8737ft) is a favorite of all who visit. Granite outcrops along the north shore offer places to sun and swim.

Stroll 15 minutes along the north shore to the lake's inlet, where you meet the John Muir Trail on the north side of the wooden footbridge spanning Shadow Creek, 1.9mi from the junction with the River Trail. The combined Shadow Lake and John Muir Trails continue northwest (to the right) 0.9mi along the true left bank of lovely, cascading Shadow Creek. All too quickly, you reach the junction where the John Muir Trail heads north (right) toward Thousand Island Lake and the trail to Ediza Lake continues west (left) toward the now prominent Mt Ritter and Banner Peak.

The trail follows the quintessential meadow-lined stream, which shimmers over its pebbly bed. Rising over several rock ribs through which the creek tumbles and falls, the trail finally crosses to Shadow Creek's true right bank over sturdy logs, 30 minutes after leaving the John Muir Trail.

Looking upstream from the logs, Mt Ritter is perfectly framed by the creek's banks. Another brief 10-minute ascent brings you to deep blue waters of **Ediza Lake** (9265ft), beneath Mt Ritter with the tip of Banner Peak peering overhead. The Minarets, with permanent snowfields and glaciers at their base, are lovely, and the whole setting is exquisite. Ford the outlet and follow the trail along the lake's northern shoreline to reach good *campsites* beneath trees along the northwest shore, 2.3mi from the John Muir Trail junction.

Day 2: Ediza Lake to Shadow Lake/River Trail Trailhead

3 hours, 7.4mi (9.7km), 260ft (78m) ascent, 1225ft (37.5m) descent
Retrace your steps to the trailhead.

Thousand Island Lake

Duration	2 days
Distance	20.4mi (32.9km)
Standard	easy-moderate
Start	Shadow Lake/River Trail Trailhead
Finish	High Trail Trailhead
Public Transport	yes

Summary This very popular loop hike takes in some of the Sierra Nevada's most photogenic lakes – Shadow Lake, Garnet Lake and incomparable Thousand Island Lake – with fabulous views of the Minarets thrown in as a bonus.

Scenic, enormous, granite-sprinkled **Thousand Island Lake**, at the base of **Banner Peak**, has become a Sierra icon, due largely to the memorable B&W photographs taken by Ansel Adams. The high peaks of the **Ritter Range** reflected in the island-dotted lake surface are indeed spectacular, and it is fitting that this wilderness area now bears the name of the man who made it famous. The classic approach to the lake is via the equally famous John Muir Trail. Although not the shortest or even the easiest approach, it is the finest.

The best return from the lake is via a segment of the PCT called the High Trail. With nearly continual views of the Ritter Range and the Minarets from the Sierra Crest above the Middle Fork San Joaquin River, it makes a perfect finish to this rewarding hike.

PLANNING
When to Hike

The hiking season for this trail is from mid-June to October.

Maps

The USGS 1:24,000 *Mammoth Mtn* and *Mt Ritter* quadrangles cover the hike, as does the USFS 1:63,360 *Ansel Adams Wilderness* map.

Permits & Regulations

A free wilderness permit is required for this hike (see Mammoth Lakes, p244, for the nearest ranger station). Bear-resistant food containers are required. Camping and campfires are prohibited anywhere within a quarter of a mile of Thousand Island Lake's outlet.

GETTING TO/FROM THE HIKE

On Minaret Rd, 2.6mi west of the Minaret Summit entrance station, an unpaved road heads to Agnew Meadows campground. This intersection is a shuttle bus stop, so hikers can ride to here and walk the rest of the way to the trailheads.

Turn onto this unpaved road and go 0.3mi to the first of two trailhead parking areas. This is signed as the High Trail trailhead (8400ft), from where the PCT heads north, and is the finishing point for this hike. Continue 0.1mi beyond this trailhead to the Shadow Lake/River Trail trailhead (8300ft), the hike's starting trailhead. Agnew Meadows campground is 0.2mi farther.

THE HIKE
Day 1: Agnew Meadows to Thousand Island Lake

5–6 hours, 10.7mi (17.2km), 2572ft (771.6m) ascent, 1038ft (311.4m) descent

From the trailhead (8300ft), follow the combined Shadow Lake Trail and River Trail to the signed junction where the Shadow Lake Trail turns west (left). Those in a hurry to get to Thousand Island Lake can continue north 5.5mi on the mostly forested River Trail. Turning left and ascending to Shadow Lake and then following the John Muir Trail past Garnet Lake to Thousand Island Lake is, however, infinitely more scenic.

Follow the Shadow Lake Trail past Shadow Lake, where it meets the John Muir Trail and continue to the junction (9030ft) where the trail to Ediza Lake goes west and the John Muir Trail turns right (also see Day 1 of the Ediza Lake hike, p248, for a detailed description to this point).

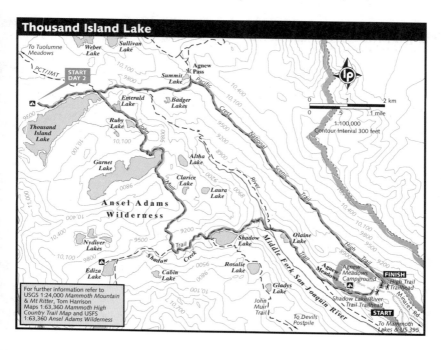

Turn north on the John Muir Trail, which ascends steadily through forest cover and emerges on a granite ridge top (10,130ft) overlooking Garnet Lake, with sweeping views of Mt Ritter, Banner Peak and Mt Davis. Descend to lovely **Garnet Lake** (9678ft), passing briefly along its south shore, and cross a rickety wooden footbridge over its outlet, 2.5mi from the junction with the trail to Ediza Lake. Camping is prohibited around the outlet.

The trail turns west and briefly follows the lake's north shore, then turns north and zigzags up the very rocky slope to the ridge top above (10,160ft). The trail drops down and passes along Ruby Lake's east shore and then along Emerald Lake's west shore to arrive at **Thousand Island Lake** (9834ft). Just across the footbridge over the outlet is the junction of the John Muir Trail and the PCT, 2.6mi from Garnet Lake. Turn west and follow a good use trail along the north shore to *campsites*. Camping near the outlet is prohibited.

Day 2: Thousand Island Lake to Agnew Meadows

4–5 hours, 9.7mi (15.6km), 280ft (84m) ascent, 1714ft (514.2m) descent

From the junction (9834ft) of the John Muir Trail and PCT, follow the PCT east along the outlet (the headwaters of the Middle Fork San Joaquin River), then ascend briefly around a granite outcrop to return to the river after 1mi and reach a junction (9560ft) where the River Trail heads south. Continue east on the High Trail, passing the junction (9640ft) of a trail leading to Clark Lakes after 0.4mi. The combined PCT and High Trail passes the shallow, grassy **Badger Lakes** and continues half a mile to a junction (9520ft) with the first of two trails leading to Agnew Pass.

Stay on the High Trail, which ascends southeast over 0.7mi to a ridge-top junction (9720ft) with a second trail leading to Agnew Pass. From this junction, the highest point of the trail, the trail traverses steadily along the mostly sage-brush covered west side of the ridge, crossing many small, flower-lined streams feeding the river below. Beyond these streams and springs, you come to a

point directly opposite the cleft formed by Shadow Creek that beautifully frames Shadow Lake. From this remarkable viewpoint, the trail continues its traversing descent along the open slope, then drops into forest above Agnew Meadows and follows a series of steep, dusty switchbacks down to the High Trail trailhead (8400ft), 6.6mi from the last trail junction to Agnew Pass.

Mammoth Crest

Duration	2 days
Distance	11mi (17.7km)
Standard	moderate
Start/Finish	Crystal Crag Trailhead
Public Transport	no

Summary Walk for hours along a stunning ridge crest that rewards you with commanding views of four mountain ranges and finishes at an inviting lakeside campsite.

Fabulous views that sweep from Yosemite's Clark Range over the Ritter Range and the Minarets to the Silver and Mono Divides make this one of the most outstanding hikes anywhere in the Sierra. A steady initial ascent brings you to the magnificent Mammoth Crest. The rest of the trail follows along the crest to the gorgeous Deer Lakes, nestled under snow-covered crags that beckon you to camp along their shores. Wildflowers all along the crest add colorful delight to the trail.

No other hike in the Sierra Nevada offers such rewards or such perspective, guaranteed to keep a smile on your face all day long. The hike is part of the Sierra High Route (see Other Hikes, p281, for more information) and, because of the high elevation, prior acclimatization is necessary. Fit hikers with prior acclimatization can enjoy it as a day hike, but most hikers will be happiest spending a night at Deer Lakes and returning to the trailhead easily the next morning.

PLANNING
When to Hike

The hiking season for the Mammoth Crest is from July to September.

Maps

The USGS 1:24,000 *Crystal Crag* and *Bloody Mtn* quadrangles cover the hike, as does Tom Harrison Maps 1:63,360 *Mammoth High Country Trail Map* ($8.95).

Permits & Regulations

A free wilderness permit is required for this hike (see Mammoth Lakes, p244, for the nearest ranger station). Bear-resistant food containers are required.

GETTING TO/FROM THE HIKE

From Mammoth Lakes, continue west on Hwy 203 (Main St) to the intersection with Minaret Rd, where Hwy 203 turns right. Go straight on what is now Lake Mary Rd and continue 4mi south toward its end. Following the well-marked signs for the Lake George campground, turn left and drive 0.4mi through the USFS **Lake Mary Campground** ($14). At the stop sign, turn right, following the signs to 'Lake George,' and drive 0.2mi into the USFS Lake George Recreation Site. At the large parking lot you find the Crystal Crag trailhead (9185ft) on the right and the USFS **Lake George Campground** ($14) to the left.

THE HIKE
Day 1: Crystal Crag Trailhead to Deer Lakes

3–3½ hours, 5.5mi (8.9km), 2101ft (630.3m) ascent, 606ft (181.8m) descent
The Crystal Lake Trail, which gets wonderful early morning sunshine, starts from the Crystal Crag trailhead (9185ft). Switchbacks take you southwest for 10 minutes up through red-fir forest dotted with granite boulders and scattered manzanita, until you are above private cabins along **Lake George**. The trail then traverses to the ridgeline, well above the lovely blue lake. Alternating between the ridge's shady west side and its sunny east side overlooking Lake George, you ascend the ridgeline, with Crystal Crag above the lake commanding your view. The views over Lake George, Lake Mary and distant Mammoth Mountain are an excellent promise of even better views to come.

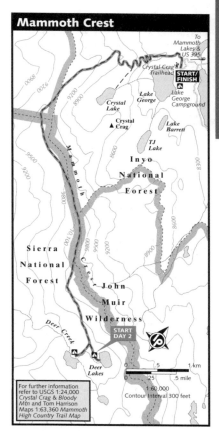

Reach a signed junction (9645ft), 1mi and 30 minutes from the trailhead. The left (southeast) fork goes to Crystal Lake. Take the right (southwest) fork which heads toward Mammoth Crest. Switchbacks bring you in 15 minutes to a viewpoint south of and high above **Horseshoe Lake**. The view over the Mammoth Lakes Basin, Mammoth Mountain and the town of Mammoth Lakes is another taste of better things ahead. A minute farther, the distant Ritter Range comes into view, with the Minarets, Mt Ritter and Banner Peak clearly identifiable.

Continue up 15 minutes and then enter John Muir Wilderness near the base of a red volcanic rock outcrop. Soon after, you come to the top of the initial 850ft ascent and the trail dips down to a faint junction marked only by a pile of rocks. Take the left (southwest) fork that contours through a subalpine meadow in a sheltered basin past scattered whitebark pines on a pumice trail. Fifteen minutes farther, reach the actual Mammoth Crest.

Here the trail continues south a short distance, then turns southeast. It takes almost 20 minutes to walk across an almost level, barren and windswept plateau of fine granite gravel, with outstanding views of Mt Ritter and Banner Peak. As the trail gradually ascends, the distant Silver Divide to the south comes into view.

Staying along the west side of the crest, the trail rises amid stunted whitebark pines, and the view is continually spectacular. Even the Clark Range in Yosemite National Park and the peaks of the distant Kaiser Wilderness far to the west are visible as you look out over a major portion of the San Joaquin River Basin. A steady, 45-minute ascent brings you to the trail's highest point (11,286ft), from where a three minute detour to the actual ridge top gives a truly remarkable view east over the entire Mammoth Lakes Basin. Here you are well above Mammoth Mountain, which appears dwarfed from this perspective.

The trail descends to a large notch in the ridge, which is snow-filled year-round, and continues on its southeast course. **Bear Creek Spire** (13,720ft) and **Mt Abbot** (13,704ft) above the Mono Divide come into sight, and your view stretches for more than 100mi along the Sierra Crest. Descending through flower-filled meadows 20 minutes from the highest point, you get the first glimpse of the dreamy Deer Lakes ahead. The upper lake is almost hidden and the middle lake is partially visible. The lower lake is an ethereal azure and turquoise color. The trail curves southeast and descends 30 minutes farther to reach the three **Deer Lakes** (10,680ft), where good

campsites are in the streamside meadow between the upper and lower lakes.

Day 2: Deer Lakes to Crystal Crag Trailhead
2½–3 hours, 5.5mi (8.9km), 606ft (181.8m) ascent, 2101ft (630.3) descent
Retrace your steps to the trailhead, savoring the remarkable views all the way.

Duck Lake

Duration	2 days
Distance	11mi (17.7km)
Standard	easy-moderate
Start/Finish	Duck Pass Trailhead
Public Transport	no

Summary A chain of lakes leads you across a rocky alpine pass on the Mammoth Crest to a massive lake with good views of the peaks of the Silver Divide.

A chain of lakes – Heart, Arrowhead, Skelton and Barney – along Mammoth Creek flow northward from Duck Pass (10,797ft) into Lake Mary, in the Mammoth Lakes Basin. A popular trail follows these lakes to the pass, from where the deep blue waters of Duck Lake invite you down to its shores for camping.

PLANNING
When to Hike
The hiking season for this trail is from mid-June to September.

Maps
The USGS 1:24,000 *Bloody Mtn* quadrangle covers the hike, as does Tom Harrison Maps 1:63,360 *Mammoth High Country Trail Map* ($8.95).

Permits & Regulations
A free wilderness permit is required for this hike (see Mammoth Lakes, p244, for the nearest ranger station). Camping and campfires are prohibited within 300ft of Duck Lake, and all camping is prohibited at the

southwest end of Duck Lake. Bear-resistant food containers are required.

GETTING TO/FROM THE HIKE

From Mammoth Lakes, continue west on Hwy 203 (Main St) to the intersection where Hwy 203 (now called Minaret Rd) goes right. Go straight on what is now the Lake Mary Rd and continue 3.5mi south toward its end. Following the well-marked signs for Lake Mary and Coldwater campground, turn left and drive 0.6mi through the USFS *Pine City Campground* along Lake Mary's shore (8910ft). Turn left again into the USFS *Coldwater Campground* ($14), driving 0.8mi through the campground to the Duck Pass trailhead (9120ft) at its far end. Lake Mary General Store, 0.1mi west of the entrance to Coldwater campground, has public showers ($3) and laundry facilities.

THE HIKE
Day 1: Lake Mary to Duck Lake
3 hours, 5.5mi (8.9km), 1677ft (503.1m) ascent, 315ft (94.5m) descent

Head east on the Duck Pass Trail from the trailhead (9120ft) and soon turn southwest (right) where the trail from the pack station joins the one from the trailhead. Note that on your way back, look for a sign that reads 'Coldwater parking' to get back to the trailhead. Soon you reach the John Muir Wilderness boundary sign. Pass a spur trail to the left (southeast) at a signed junction to **Arrowhead Lake**, which is partially visible through the trees below the main trail. Continue straight (south) on the main trail. Almost an hour from the trailhead, the views finally start to open up. The trail is now along Mammoth Creek's true left bank and soon follows the shoreline of **Skelton Lake**.

Cross to the true right bank of the outlet from Barney Lake, which is to the right at the head of the valley. Five minutes beyond Barney Lake reach the base of the ascent to Duck Pass. Switchbacks take you in 30 to 45 minutes to **Duck Pass** (10,797ft), 4.7mi from the trailhead. The views stretch northwest along the length of the Mammoth Crest and as far as Mt Ritter and Banner Peak in the

Ritter Range, and north and south to the many lakes below.

From the pass, the bulk of Duck Lake fills the bowl, below, with Pika Lake against the rocky cliffs to the east. The views southwest to the Silver Divide include Devils Top (9938ft), Double Peak (10,663ft and 10,649ft), Sharktooth Peak (11,640ft), Silver Peak (11,878ft) and Graveyard Peak (11,520ft). Descend toward Duck Lake (10,482ft), veering left to follow cairns marking the route toward Pika Lake, where attractive *campsites* are between the two lakes.

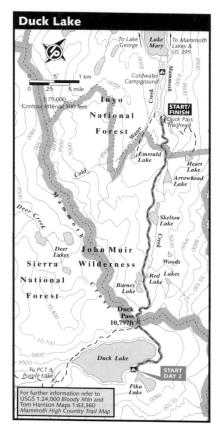

Day 2: Duck Lake to Lake Mary

2½ hours, 5.5mi (8.9km), 315ft (95m) ascent, 1677ft (503m) descent

Retrace your steps back to the trailhead. More adventurous hikers may consider a Class 1 cross-country route leading from Duck Pass to Deer Lakes (see the Mammoth Crest hike, p252) and returning to Mammoth Lakes Basin along the Mammoth Crest.

Little Lakes Valley

Picture-perfect Little Lakes Valley is one of the eastern Sierra's most popular hiking areas, and with good reason. It's the highest elevation trailhead in the Sierra, easily accessible by a good paved road, and hikers find themselves in an idyllic setting right from the start. Broad Rock Creek splashes through green, lodgepole pine-lined meadows, and snow-draped summits fill the skyline. Bear Creek Spire (13,720ft), Mt Dade (13,600ft), Mt Abbot (13,704ft), Mt Mills (13,451ft) and other lesser peaks, passes and ridges ring the valley in alpine splendor, offering desirable goals for mountaineers. Blue lakes sparkle in pine-dotted granite bowls, which offer seclusion and tranquility for day hikers and backpackers alike. Perhaps no other eastern Sierra valley offers such a combination of attractions and such delights to every hiker.

PLANNING

A free wilderness permit is required for all overnight trips. A quota system is in effect from the last Friday in June to September 15. Get the permit from either the ranger station in Mammoth Lakes (see Mammoth Lakes, p244) or in Bishop (see Bishop, p261). The USFS Information Center, on Rock Creek Rd at Tom's Place, beyond the junction of Crowley Lake Rd, issued permits in prior years but was not staffed in 2001. This may change in the future. Bear-resistant food containers are required, and campfires are prohibited in Little Lakes Valley.

GETTING THERE & AWAY

From US 395, 14.6mi southeast of Mammoth Lakes and 24mi northwest of Bishop, turn south onto Rock Creek Rd at Tom's Place, which is marked on most maps. Hikes start from the Little Lakes Valley trailhead (10,230ft), which is at the end of Rock Creek Rd, 10.2mi from US 395. (Some maps still call the trailhead Mosquito Flat.) Rock Creek Rd is a two-lane, paved road for 9mi to the Rock Creek Pack Station, but beyond that it becomes one-lane, with turnouts. The trailhead parking lot is usually full. An overflow area is 0.6mi before the trailhead, on the left side of the road. A picnic-only area, just 0.3mi before the trailhead, has a few parking spaces that are also used as overflow, although it's less obvious that overnight parking is permitted here.

ACCESS FACILITIES

The USFS Rock Creek Recreation Area runs from Tom's Place to the Little Lakes Valley Trailhead. More than six campgrounds ($13-$14, between 7000ft and 9600ft) are on the 8.5mi section of Rock Creek Rd between US 395 and Rock Creek Lake.

Two minutes above the Little Lakes Valley Trailhead is the **Mosquito Flat Walk-in Campground** (10,230ft). Not only is it free and convenient, but its setting in a forest across the footbridge along Rock Creek's true right bank is peaceful. This campground is only open to holders of a wilderness permit valid for the next day. (An old Mosquito Flat campground is marked on many maps, but no longer exists. The day-use picnic area is now in its place.)

Gem Lakes

Duration	2 days
Distance	6.6mi (10.6km)
Standard	easy
Start/Finish	Little Lakes Valley Trailhead
Public Transport	no

Summary This short and gentle hike to the lovely lakes at the foot of Bear Creek Spire offers outstanding rewards with relatively little effort.

Gem Lakes are only a few of several picturesque lakes in Little Lakes Valley. The trail

Top: Miles of azure waters are visible from the Sand Harbor Overlook on the Tahoe Rim Trail.
Bottom: Sunrise at Garnet Lake, on the John Muir Trail, illuminates the sky over Banner Peak in the Ansel Adams Wilderness.

Left: A giant sequoia soars skyward in Grant Grove, Sequoia National Park.
Top Right: A hiker ascends Clouds Rest Trail in Yosemite National Park.
Bottom Right: The still waters of Garnet Lake at sunrise reflect the trees and rocky water's edge.

JOHN MOCK

JOHN MOCK

JOHN ELK III

upvalley is always busy, filled with everyone from families with toddlers and octogenarians to mountaineers coveting any of several objectives. Gem Lakes are easy to reach, but it's worthwhile spending the night. It also lends itself to setting up a base for cross-country exploration of the upper valley.

Alternatively, you can enjoy a day hike to Gem Lakes, camp at the walk-in campground at the trailhead, and then head to Fourth Recess Lake (see the hike, p258) the next day to see more of the area.

PLANNING
When to Hike
The hiking season is from July to September, because of the high starting elevation.

Maps
The USGS 1:24,000 *Mt Morgan* and *Mt Abbot* quadrangles cover the hike, as does Tom Harrison Maps 1:63,360 *Mono Divide High Country Trail Map* ($8.95).

Permits & Regulations
A free wilderness permit is required for this hike (see Permits & Regulations, p241).

GETTING TO/FROM THE HIKE
See Getting There & Away, p256, earlier in this section, for information.

THE HIKE
Day 1: Little Lakes Valley Trailhead to Gem Lakes
1½–2 hours, 3.3mi (5.3km), 690ft (207m) ascent

The broad trail parallels the west bank of Rock Creek, into whose cool water anglers often wade in pursuit of trout. Ahead, Bear Creek Spire and Mt Abbot dominate the horizon.

Passing the John Muir Wilderness boundary sign a scant five minutes from the trailhead (10,230ft), walk up a series of gradual, widely spaced steps to reach the signed junction with the trail to Mono Pass after another five to 10 minutes. The trail up Little Lakes Valley, which leads to Gem Lakes and Morgan Pass, continues straight (south), descending slightly into the green

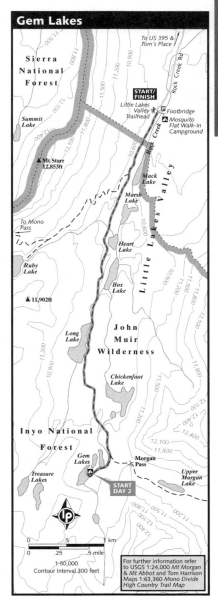

Gem Lakes

and well-watered valley, passing close to meadow-fringed Mack Lake and grass-filled Marsh Lake.

Stepping across an inlet to Heart Lake, 20 minutes from the junction, the trail crosses a small wooden footbridge over a second inlet two minutes later and passes along the open western lakeshore. Heading into stands of mixed lodgepole and white-bark pines, ascend easily out of the bowl to emerge well above the west shore of beautiful **Box Lake**. A few large lodgepole pines persist along the trail, but the trees are now mostly whitebark pines, whose red pollen-bearing clusters decorate its branch tips in midsummer.

The trail crosses an almost imperceptible rise and crosses to the true right bank of the outlet from **Long Lake** (10,543ft), the largest of the little lakes along the trail. As you hike 10 minutes along Long Lake's east shore, with a rocky cliff alongside the trail, Bear Creek Spire and Mt Abbot seem to fill the entire view upvalley.

Beyond Long Lake the trail ascends through whitebark pines and in 10 minutes passes a signed spur trail to the left leading to Chickenfoot Lake. Fifteen minutes farther, reach the outlet (10,840ft) from the Gem Lakes.

Hop rocks to the outlet's true right bank and immediately look for an unsigned use trail that follows this bank upstream. Leaving the broad trail to Morgan Pass, which bears southeast, head southwest up the well-defined but smaller trail. The trail soon turns south, and three minutes ahead is the first Gem Lake. Pass through a pretty little meadow along the stream and in another five minutes reach upper **Gem Lake** (10,920ft), 0.3mi from the main trail. The largest of the Gem Lakes, it lies beneath dramatic Bear Creek Spire and has a talus slope on its south end and whitebark pines along its northern edge. Cross its outlet stream and find a ***campsite*** away from the lake. Avoid the restoration sites near the lakeshore, which are signed with knee-high blue posts. In order to read the tiny writing on these signposts, which tells you not to walk in this area or camp here, you have to

walk in the area. Similar signposts appear elsewhere in Little Lakes Valley too.

From Gem Lakes, you can explore the upper valley for an afternoon or even a few days, perhaps visiting the even more austere and beautiful alpine Treasure Lakes or remote Dade Lake, which is farther south.

Day 2: Gem Lakes to Little Lakes Valley Trailhead

1¼–1½ hours, 3.3mi (5.3km), 690ft (207m) descent

Return easily via the same route to the Little Lakes Valley Trailhead.

Fourth Recess Lake

Duration	2 days
Distance	14.6mi (23.5km)
Standard	moderate-hard
Start/Finish	Little Lakes Valley Trailhead
Public Transport	no

Summary An alpine pass with sweeping views of rugged peaks along the Mono Divide and the Silver Divide leads to a subalpine lake in a granite cirque with a 1000ft waterfall tumbling into it.

Mono Pass (12,040ft) is the eastern back-door into the Mono Recesses, a series of four steep-walled side valleys along the south side of the valley formed by Mono Creek. Although the trail over Mono Pass requires crossing the Sierra Crest from east to west, it provides the easiest and quickest access to this remote and spectacular region of John Muir Wilderness.

Fourth Recess, the easternmost of the sequentially numbered (from west to east) Mono Recesses, is a deep, glacially carved cirque that holds large and beautiful Fourth Recess Lake. Surrounded by trees on its east and west sides, with a lovely meadow at its north end, the lake is fed by a 1000ft cascade tumbling over a sheer granite wall at its south end. The subalpine lake makes a perfect destination for an overnight trip, or a good base from which to explore the Mono Recesses. The lake's remarkable beauty makes it a popular destination and almost guarantees you won't be alone.

Alternative access to the Mono Recesses is from the western Sierra via Hwy 168 from Fresno to Huntington Lake, followed by 15mi of paved but steep road over Kaiser Pass and an additional 7mi to Lake Thomas A Edison and the Vermilion Valley trailhead. From this trailhead it is 5.5mi to Quail Meadows and the junction with the John Muir Trail, and from the junction, 10mi up Mono Creek to Fourth Recess Lake.

PLANNING
When to Hike
The hiking season for the trail is from July to September.

Maps
The USGS 1:24,000 *Mt Morgan* and *Mt Abbot* quadrangles cover the hike, as does Tom Harrison Maps 1:63,360 *Mono Divide High Country Trail Map* ($8.95).

Permits & Regulations
A free wilderness permit is required for this hike (see Permits & Regulations, p241).

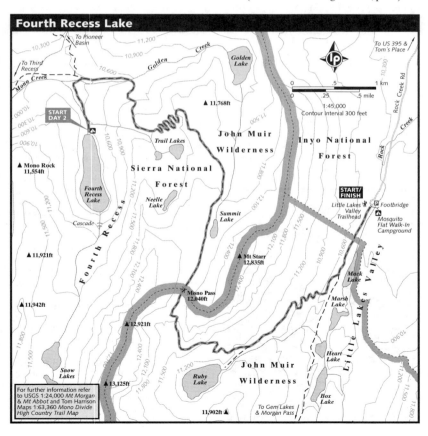

GETTING TO/FROM THE HIKE
See Getting There & Away, p256

THE HIKE
Day 1: Little Lakes Valley
Trailhead to Fourth Recess Lake
4–4½ hours, 7.3mi (11.8km), 1810ft (543m) ascent, 1908ft (572.4m) descent

Hike 0.5mi south up Little Lakes Valley, 15 minutes to the signed junction of the trails to Morgan Pass and Mono Pass. Turn right (southwest), following the sign to Mono Pass. A few minutes from this junction, pass a barely noticeable spur trail that comes from the pack station. Ascend steadily through the pine-scattered granite landscape, making occasional switchbacks that give great views over Little Lakes Valley.

The trail traverses southwest along a granite bench beneath the dramatic rocky ribs of Mt Starr (12,835ft), with constant superb views of Bear Creek Spire and Mt Abbot and other peaks at the head of Little Lakes Valley. Pass a small pond and cross its willow-lined inlet shortly beyond. A short ascent brings you to a signed junction 1.3mi from the Morgan Pass trail junction, where a spur trail leads left (southwest) 0.3mi to Ruby Lake (11,121ft), one hour from the trailhead.

Go right at this junction. The trail begins a series of long, well-graded switchbacks, working steadily west 45 minutes until it is high above the sparkling indigo waters of Ruby Lake. The trail turns a corner, leaving the views of Little Lakes Valley behind as it heads north, dipping slightly before the final, gradual 15-minute ascent to **Mono Pass** (12,040ft), 1.7mi from the Ruby Lake junction. The sandy north-south saddle is marked by a plain wooden post. To the east of and about 10 minutes above the pass, the ridge descending from Mt Starr offers superb views of Little Lakes Valley and the peaks above it. Mono Pass is also the boundary between Inyo National Forest to its east and Sierra National Forest to its west, both of which are in John Muir Wilderness.

The descent from the barren and windy pass heads north, passing along Summit Lake's west shore. From the lake's outlet, the trail dips through a sandy bowl, then heads northwest up and over a granite knoll where whitebark pines are mere shrubs, 30 minutes from the pass. The knoll offers the first sweeping views of the lake-dotted **Pioneer Basin**, and distant Red and White Mountain (12,816ft) and Mt Izaak Walton (12,077ft) on the **Silver Divide**.

Dropping off the knoll, the trail crosses another sandy area, turns southeast and descends back below tree line, where whitebark pines line the switchbacks down to pretty Trail Lakes. A small and solidly built stone hut with a wooden shake shingle roof (a Snow Survey shelter) sits along the northwest shore of the largest lake.

The trail follows the lake's outlet down through a small meadow, then turns north and descends deeply rutted switchbacks 25 minutes to a crossing of **Golden Creek**, 2.8mi from Mono Pass. The fragile soil in this section is easily eroded, and the regular horse and mule traffic has taken a heavy toll on the trail.

Turning west along the true right (north) bank of Golden Creek, the trail eventually zigzags down a southwest-facing, forested slope to a signed junction with the trail to the Fourth Recess, 20 minutes (0.5mi) after crossing the creek. The sign is small and has fallen down at times, so look carefully for the junction. The trail to Pioneer Basin is a quarter of a mile beyond this junction.

Turn left (south) on the smaller trail and recross Golden Creek after two minutes. A cairn is along Golden Creek to mark the spot, and a few more cairns get you headed in the right direction beyond the creek. Continue on the almost level trail another 15 minutes (0.5mi) to **Fourth Recess Lake** (10,132ft). Beautiful lakeside *campsites* are beneath a few stands of large lodgepole pines mixed among mostly whitebark pines above the northeast shore. Early morning light invites lakeside photography of the peaks and the waterfall reflected on the lake surface.

The lake is surrounded by forest on three sides, with Mono Rock (11,554ft) rising dramatically above the western lakeshore. The granite walls of Mt Mills are prominent to the south at the head of Fourth Recess. To the north are square-topped Mt Hopkins (12,302ft) and pointed Mt Crocker (12,457ft) flanking the western side of Pioneer Basin.

Day 2: Fourth Recess Lake to Little Lakes Valley Trailhead
4 hours, 7.3mi, 1908ft (572.4m) ascent, 1810ft (543m) descent
Retrace your steps back to the trailhead. From the granite knoll above Trail Lakes, follow an old footpath along the ridge crest west of the trail, which gives constant outstanding views of Mono Creek, Pioneer Basin and the peaks of the Silver Divide, avoids walking in the horse trough, and brings you directly to Mono Pass. This easy-to-follow ridge route is actually quicker and more aesthetically pleasing. It takes you slightly higher than Mono Pass, but the incredible views are worth the few minutes of effort they take.

High Sierra

The Owens Valley lies between the eastern base of the Sierra Nevada and the ancient White Mountains. Native American Piute

and Shoshone thrived in the Owens Valley, calling it *inyo,* a Piute word for 'dwelling place of the great spirit.' John C Frémont named it Owens Valley, after his cartographer Richard Owens. Towns began as mining settlements in the 1860s, and later became ranching centers. Basque emigrants from the Pyrenees won fame as sheepherders. The Owens Valley was once a productive agricultural region watered by Sierra streams, but since the early 20th century, water from the Owens River has been drained away by the Los Angeles Aqueduct, reducing the valley to a desert-like wasteland. Owens Dry Lake, once 30ft deep, is a notable casualty of these 'water wars.' Hollywood discovered the area in the 1920s, and current visitors to Whitney Portal pass the Alabama Hills, location of such famous TV westerns as *The Lone Ranger, Rawhide* and *Maverick*. Recreation is now the main focus of this high desert region.

ACCESS TOWNS & FACILITIES
Bishop
Main St, which is US 395, is the primary north-south road, and Hwy 168 follows W Line St, the main east-west road. The Bishop Area chamber of commerce and visitor bureau (☎ 760-873-8405, e info@bishopvis itor.com, w www.bishopvisitor.com), 690 N Main St, is nearby, next to the city park. Pick up the annual *Bishop's Visitors Guide*, which is packed with useful information.

The White Mountain ranger station (☎ 760-873-2500), 798 N Main St at Yaney St at the north end of town, sells books and maps. It issues wilderness permits and rents bear-resistant containers ($5 per week).

Wilson's Eastside Sports (☎ 760-873-7520), 224 N Main St, and Sierra Sherpas, 115 W Line St, sell maps and gear, and rent bear-resistant food containers. Joseph's Bi-Rite Market, 211 N Main St, is a convenient grocery store.

Places to Stay & Eat A mile south of town at US 395 and Schober Lane, *Brown's Town* (☎ *760-873-8522)* is a nicely shaded campground ($14) with guest-only shower facilities

($1), a grocery store and deli. *The Trees Motel* (☎ 760-873-6391, e 395trees@gte.net, 796 W Line St), owned by very accommodating and friendly folks, has quiet, clean and all non-smoking rooms ($42 for one or two people). *Mountain View Motel* (☎ 760-873-4242, fax 873-3409, 730 W Line St), starting at $57, is a busy and popular spot, with friendly owners and a pool. *Village Motel* (☎ 760-872-8155, 286 W Elm St at N Warren St), at the north end of town, starts at $45 and also has a pool.

Kava Coffeehouse (☎ 760-872-1010, 206 N Main St) has the best coffee and smoothies in town. Its friendly staff, trendy ambiance and Internet services ($0.10 per minute) keep hungry hikers content. The breakfast and lunch menu features quiche, bagel sandwiches, daily baked goods and vegetarian options. *Las Palmas Mexican Restaurant* (☎ 760-873-4337, 136 E Line St), with its festive decor, serves inexpensive and hearty authentic dishes. *Erick Schat's Bakkery* (☎ 760-873-7156, 763 N Main St), is a local favorite for breads and pastries.

For public showers ($3), head to the Wash Tub (☎ 760-873-6627), 236 N Warren St, west of and parallel to Main St between Academy and Church Sts.

Getting There & Away Bishop (4140ft) is on US 395, 39mi southeast of Mammoth Lakes and 15mi north of Big Pine.

Inyo Mono Transit (☎ 800-922-1930) operates two bus routes, Bishop-Bridgeport and Bishop-Lone Pine. The northbound Bishop-Bridgeport bus ($6, 3 hours) departs Bishop at 3pm on Monday and Wednesday. The southbound Bishop-Lone Pine bus ($4, 1 hour, 59mi) departs at noon and 5:15pm weekdays. Buses depart from the KMart, 910 N Main St, at the intersection of US 395 and Hwy 6.

Lone Pine

The Inter Agency visitor center (☎ 760-876-6222), 1.5mi south of town at the US 395/Hwy 136 intersection, offers a plethora of information, and sells books and maps. You'll find the Lone Pine chamber of commerce (☎ 760-876-4444, fax 876-9205,

e info@lone-pine.com, w www.lone pine.com), 126 S Main St, PO Box 749, Lone Pine, CA 93545, is also helpful.

The Mt Whitney ranger station (☎ 760-876-6200), PO Box 8, Lone Pine, CA 93545, is on US 395 at Inyo St at the south end of town. They issue wilderness permits and rent bear-resistant containers ($5 per week).

Lone Pine Sporting Goods (☎ 760-876-5365), 220 S Main St, and Whitney Portal Store Too (☎ 760-876-0030), 238 S Main St, rent bear-resistant food containers ($2 per day). Joseph's Bi-Rite Market, 119 S Main St, is a convenient place to buy groceries.

Places to Stay & Eat The *Historic Dow Hotel*, at the southeast corner of US 395 and Post St, has $38 rooms without bathroom and telephone, and $52 rooms with a bathroom and without telephone. Adjacent to it is *Motel Dow Villa* (☎ 800-824-9317, 760-876-5521, fax 760-876-5643, e dow illa@qnet.com, w www.dow illamotel.com, 310 S Main St) ($80/80 singles/doubles). *Alabama Hills Inn* (☎ 800-800-6468, 760-876-8700, fax 760-876-8704, e ahi@schat.com, w www .alabamahillsinn.com, 1920 S Main St) is a clean, friendly place on the southern outskirts of town ($68 for one or two people). Kirk's Barbershop (☎ 760-876-5700, 114 S Main St) has public showers ($4).

The Mt Whitney Restaurant (☎ 760-876-5751, 227 S Main) is proud of its Hollywood memorabilia display and boasts the best burgers in town, including buffalo and venison versions.

Getting There & Away Lone Pine is on US 395, 16mi south of Independence, 59mi south of Bishop and about 200mi north of Los Angeles.

Inyo Mono Transit (☎ 800-922-1930) operates two daily round-trip Lone Pine-Bishop buses ($4, 1 hour, 59mi) weekdays, departing from Lone Pine at 6:30am and 12:30pm and stopping at Independence and Big Pine. Buses depart from Statham Hall at the corner of Bush and Jackson Sts, one block east of US 395, opposite the Lone Pine post office.

Humphreys & Evolution Basin

Duration	7 days
Distance	53.8mi (86.6km)
Standard	hard
Start	North Lake
Finish	South Lake
Public Transport	no

Summary This superb circuit through the High Sierra of northern Kings Canyon National Park features the famous Muir Pass and Evolution Valley and crosses three passes, entering and exiting steeply from the eastern Sierra over the range's crest.

This classic one week near-loop circumambulates Glacier Divide and is one of the most impressive longer hikes in the High Sierra. The trail crosses three high passes, traverses alpine basins and passes through northern Kings Canyon National Park. It is a demanding and beautiful route, ranging between 8000ft and 12,000ft in elevation. Hikers should be in top shape to enjoy it.

PLANNING
When to Hike
The hiking season is from July to September.

Maps
The USGS 1:24,000 *Mt Thompson, Mt Darwin, Mt Tom, Mt Hilgard, Mt Henry, Mt Goddard* and *North Palisade* quadrangles cover the hike, as do Tom Harrison Maps 1:47,520 *Bishop Pass Trail Map* and 1:63,360 *Mono Divide High Country* ($8.95).

Permits & Regulations
A free wilderness permit is required for this hike (see Bishop, p261, for the nearest ranger station). Campfires are prohibited along the drainages for the Piute Pass and Bishop Pass Trails.

GETTING TO/FROM THE HIKE
The North Lake and South Lake trailheads are 12mi apart, which necessitates using a vehicle shuttle or planning to hitchhike or walk on the road between the trailheads. Shuttle services can drop your vehicle at the finishing trailhead and drive you to the starting trailhead for about $60. See Other Information, p243, at the beginning of this chapter for shuttle services. You can also inquire about arranging shuttles from the pack stations near the trailheads; try Bishop Pack Outfitters (☎ 760-873-4785) at North Lake, and Parcher's Resort (☎ 760-873-4177) at South Lake.

From downtown Bishop, drive west 14mi on Hwy 168 (W Line St) to the South Lake Rd junction. To reach North Lake, continue straight 3mi farther, beyond Aspendell toward Lake Sabrina, and turn onto the single-lane 2mi-long partly paved road to the North Lake trailhead parking lot. Walk 0.6mi along the road to North Lake campground, from where the Piute Pass Trail begins and this hike starts. To reach South Lake, turn left onto South Lake Rd and go 7mi to its end at the Bishop Pass trailhead.

Almost a dozen campgrounds (ranging from $13 to $14) between 7500ft and 9500ft, most with very few sites, are in the USFS Bishop Creek Recreation Area west of Bishop. Beyond the South Lake Rd turnoff, on the way to Lake Sabrina, are three campgrounds, and beyond North Lake is *North Lake Campground*, at the Piute Pass trailhead (9360ft). Four campgrounds are along South Lake Rd. The largest and easiest in which to find a site is *Four Jeffrey Campground*, although *Willow Campground* is closest to the Bishop Pass trailhead. Two small stores and two signed public shower facilities are also along South Lake Rd.

THE HIKE
Day 1: North Lake to Upper Golden Trout Lake
5–6 hours, 8mi (12.9km), 2063ft (618.9m) ascent, 570ft (171m) descent
The Piute Pass Trail, heavily used by pack strings, is dusty and rutted as it ascends through aspens along North Fork Bishop Creek. It soon enters John Muir Wilderness and crosses the creek twice in quick succession. After zigzagging up a small granite bench, the trail levels off through forest,

Humphreys & Evolution Basins

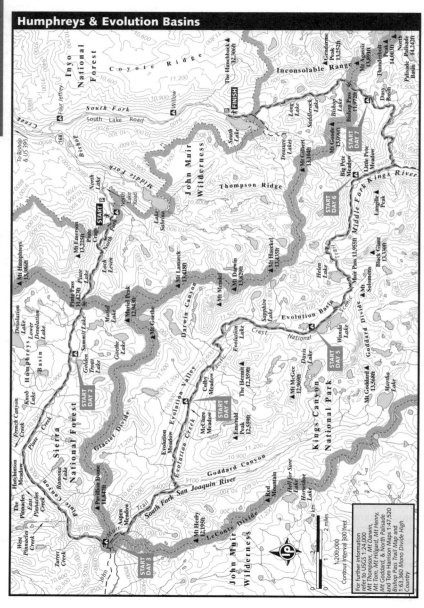

then works its way up the north slope, across red rock beneath Piute Crags. Turning back toward the cascading creek, the well-engineered trail surmounts an enormous granite bench to emerge at **Loch Leven** (10,700ft), lying in a broad, glacially formed granite valley, with **Piute Pass** visible ahead.

The walking is easy up this meadow-dotted bowl with impressive granite peaks on either side. Passing a few *campsites* at the east end of Loch Leven, the trail rolls upward north of the splashing stream to **Piute Lake** (10,985ft), 3.5mi from the trailhead. The trail rises over grassy benches, and switchbacks up a final granite rib to **Piute Pass** (11,423ft), 1.5mi from the lake. The broad vista sweeps from the Glacier Divide to the distant Pinnacles, and across the Humphreys Basin to Mt Humphreys (13,986ft), rising north of the pass.

The trail swings north of grass-lined Summit Lake, as it descends over alpine terrain, crossing several streams and passing a trail leading north to Desolation Lake. Where the trail crosses the outlet from Desolation Lake, head south half a mile to *campsites* around **Upper Golden Trout Lake** (10,850ft), 3.5mi from the pass.

Day 2: Upper Golden Trout Lake to Piute Creek
5–6 hours, 9mi (14.5km), 2800ft (840m) descent

The trail descends into forest and passes through many meadows as it follows Piute Creek to **Hutchinson Meadow** (9438ft), just west of the confluence with French Canyon Creek and 4.5mi from the lake. From this lovely meadow, the trail stays on the north side of Piute Creek and crosses East Pinnacle Creek, the last reliable water until it reaches the South Fork San Joaquin River. Soon it leaves the forest and descends rocky slopes into the narrowing Piute Canyon, staying high above the creek. A series of dry switchbacks brings the trail to seasonal Turret Creek, and it then descends to meet the combined PCT and John Muir Trail and turns southeast (left) to cross **Piute Creek** over a steel bridge (8080ft) that marks the boundary of Kings Canyon National Park.

Campsites are located along the creek beyond the bridge.

Day 3: Piute Creek to McClure Meadow
4–5 hours, 7.3mi (11.8km), 1200ft (360m) ascent

The trail ascends along the north side of the South Fork San Joaquin River, passing level Aspen Meadow. Continuing up the canyon, the trail ascends over rock and crosses the river on a bridge to its south side. As the canyon opens, the trail crosses meadows and passes a trail that leads south up Goddard Canyon. Turning east, the trail crosses the South Fork San Joaquin River and begins a series of switchbacks that brings it to a crossing of Evolution Creek and into **Evolution Meadow** (9280ft). The forested trail along the north side of the Evolution Valley soon arrives at large **McClure Meadow** (9600ft), which has abundant *campsites*.

Day 4: McClure Meadow to Wanda Lake
5–6 hours, 8mi (12.9km), 1800ft (540m) ascent

The trail continues 1.5mi to **Colby Meadow** (9840ft). It rises to cross Darwin Creek, then zigzags up out of forest and turns southeast to the northern shore of exquisite **Evolution Lake** (10,850ft). Continuing along the eastern lakeshore, the trail fords its inlet, then rises to pass west of beautiful Sapphire Lake and follows switchbacks up to cross the outlet of dramatically barren **Wanda Lake** (11,426ft) in the midst of Evolution Basin. Stark *campsites* near the lake's outlet afford spectacular views.

Day 5: Wanda Lake to Big Pete Meadow
5–6 hours, 8.5mi (13.7km), 530ft (159m) ascent, 2755ft (826.5m) descent

Tracing the eastern lakeshore, the trail rises to pass southeast of Lake McDermand and then continues up to **Muir Pass** (11,955ft), 2.2mi from Wanda Lake. It crosses the Goddard Divide, where you find a stone hut erected as a memorial to John Muir. Stony switchbacks bring the trail to the southern end of barren Helen Lake to cross its inflow stream, the source of the Middle Fork Kings River. After skirting Helen Lake's southeast shore, the trail descends along its outflow stream to an unnamed lake, fords its inlet and outlet, and continues down to a meadow at the inlet of a second unnamed rocky lake east of Helen Lake. The trail skirts its south shore and fords its outlet, then turns south and descends steep talus into forested **LeConte Canyon** to reach Big Pete Meadow (9200ft), with plentiful *campsites* amid the trees.

Day 6: Big Pete Meadow to Dusy Basin

4–5 hours, 6mi (9.7km), 480ft (144m) descent, 2600ft (780m) ascent

The trail heads south to **Little Pete Meadow** (8880ft), then descends to a junction with the Bishop Pass Trail (8710ft). Here, the trail to Bishop Pass leaves the combined PCT and John Muir Trail and turns east (left). Two steep series of switchbacks take you up through forest along the Dusy Branch of the Middle Fork Kings River, which you cross twice, to the sparsely forested **Dusy Basin**. Passing north of the lowest lake, turn north and ascend to *campsites* at the west end of the northernmost large lake (11,350ft) in the stark alpine basin.

Day 7: Dusy Basin to South Lake

5–6 hours, 7mi (11.3km), 625ft (187.5m) ascent, 2200ft (660m) descent

The trail continues up, over granite and sand, and swings east to broad **Bishop Pass** (11,972ft), from where it descends between Thompson Ridge and the Inconsolable Range past the headwaters of South Fork Bishop Creek and its chain of lakes. From the pass, the good trail follows switchbacks down a granite buttress, then across talus blocks to pass northeast of Bishop Lake and then along the east shore of **Saddlerock Lake** (11,128ft). It crosses the lake's outlet, and descends along the tumbling stream past pretty Timberline Tarns. Crossing their outlet, the trail traverses down a rocky slope high above Spearhead Lake to *campsites* at the southern end of **Long Lake** (10,753ft). Following along

the east shore of this aptly named lake beneath Chocolate Peak (11,682ft), it passes the junction with the trail to Ruwau Lake, and continues down, passing a side trail to Bull and Chocolate Lakes. The trail drops past two granite ribs and makes several switchbacks down to more level forest and passes the side trail to Treasure Lakes. A final descent above the east side of South Lake (9768ft) brings you to the trailhead.

Palisades

Duration	2 days
Distance	15mi (24.1km)
Standard	moderate
Start/Finish	Big Pine Creek Trailhead
Nearest Town	Big Pine
Public Transport	no

Summary Milky North Fork Big Pine Creek flows from the Big Pine Lakes, a chain of seven numbered lakes; the first three, fed by the Palisade Glacier, are turquoise gems beneath soaring crags.

Rising almost 2mi above the Owens Valley town of Big Pine, the granite Palisades in John Muir Wilderness are the Sierra Nevada's second highest group of peaks and the most ruggedly alpine in character, with six summits higher than 14,000ft. Glaciers, the southernmost in the contiguous US, lie at their eastern base, and the Palisade Glacier is the Sierra's largest (2.5mi long by 1mi wide). The loop hike follows the North Fork Big Pine Creek, passing two waterfalls to reach the Big Pine Lakes.

It is possible to see the many prominent **peaks of the Palisades** – Mt Gayley (13,510ft), Mt Sill (14,153ft), Thunderbolt Peak (14,003ft), Mt Winchell (13,775ft), Mt Agassiz (13,893ft), Aperture Peak (13,265ft) and Mt Robinson (12,967ft) – all rising in a semicircle above the **Palisade Glacier** – up close on either an overnight trip or a more strenuous seven- to eight-hour day hike. Countless variations of this hike are possible by spending more time and camping at different lakes. Camping is possible at most every lake, but the most desirable campsites are at First, Third and Fifth Lakes. The trail gets little shade, so get an early start to avoid the hot midday sun.

PLANNING
When to Hike
The hiking season for this trail is from mid-June to mid-October.

Maps
The USGS 1:24,000 *Coyote Flat, Split Mtn* and *Mt Thompson* quadrangles cover the hike and the *North Palisade* quadrangle covers the side trip. Tom Harrison Maps 1:63,360 *Kings Canyon High Country Trail Map* ($8.95) covers the entire hike.

Permits & Regulations
A free wilderness permit is required for this hike (see Bishop, p261, for the nearest ranger station). Campfires are prohibited.

NEAREST TOWN
Big Pine
The Big Pine chamber of commerce (☎ 760-938 2114), 126 S Main St (US 395), PO Box 23, Big Pine, CA 93513, offers general information.

Glacier View Campground ($14, 3900ft), just north of town on Hwy 168 at the intersection with US 395, is a large and pleasant county-run site shaded by aspens. *Big Pine Motel* (☎ 760-938-2282, 370 S Main St) is tidy and has all queen-sized beds ($36/40 singles/doubles) and a nice garden. Rooms at *Bristlecone Manor Motel* (☎ 760-938-2067, fax 938-3107, 101 N Main St at Crocker St) cost $36/40. *Carroll's Market (136 S Main St)* is the place to stock up on supplies.

Big Pine is on US 395, just 15mi south of Bishop and 26mi north of Independence.

GETTING TO/FROM THE HIKE
From US 395 in Big Pine (4000ft), drive west on Crocker St, which becomes Glacier Lodge Rd. It enters the USFS Big Pine Creek Area and in 8mi passes the *Sage Flat Campground* ($13, 7400ft), amid a pleasant aspen and pine forest, the first of three USFS campgrounds. Continue 1.6mi farther, or a total of 9.6mi from Big Pine, to the turnoff on your right to the Big Pine Creek trailhead (7700ft). The turnoff is 0.2mi beyond the *Upper Sage Flat Campground* ($13, 7600ft) and just 0.1mi beyond the Clyde Glacier Group Camp, both of which have more easily visible signs. Turn right and drive 0.2mi uphill to the large trailhead parking lot.

Glacier Lodge Rd continues 0.7mi beyond the turnoff to the trailhead parking lot and ends at a small day-use parking lot near the forested *Big Pine Creek Campground* ($13, 7800ft). You may want to drive to the North & South Forks trailhead (7800ft) at the day-use parking lot and drop your gear, which saves almost a mile of walking uphill with a full backpack. This alternative trail starts at the locked gate and is described below.

THE HIKE
Day 1: Big Pine Creek Trailhead to Fifth Lake
3½–4 hours, 7.9mi (12.7km), 3087ft (926.1m) ascent
South Fork Big Pine Creek and the peaks rising above it are visible from the trailhead. The peaks above North Fork Big Pine Creek are hidden from view until you get above First Falls. From the northwest end of the trailhead parking lot, the North Fork Trail heads west, traversing up an open sagebrush slope. Passing above Glacier Pack Train, the local pack station, the dusty trail ascends steadily, with good views, up South Fork Big Pine Creek of Middle Palisade Glacier and Norman Clyde Peak (13,920ft). After 1mi, you turn northwest toward North Fork Big Pine Creek. Just below the trail is small, but free *First Falls Walk-in Campground*, along the creek's true left (northeast) bank. The road once came this far, but was destroyed by a 1982 flood. Beyond, you can look down and see the short lateral trail that descends in one minute to a wide trail near a wooden footbridge, 1.5mi from the trailhead.

Alternatively, when starting from the day-use parking lot, a small wooden sign at the locked metal gate says 'North & South Fork Trails.' Head southwest along the river's true left bank, past private cabins, as the old road

Palisades

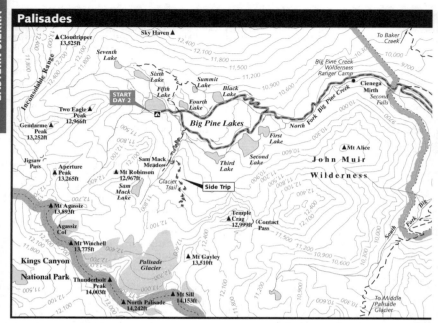

narrows to a footpath in five minutes. Cross a footbridge below **First Falls**, the cascades along North Fork Big Pine Creek, five minutes farther. Beyond the footbridge is a trail junction where the South Fork Trail goes left. Turn right (northwest) onto the North Fork Trail and ascend steep switchbacks 15 minutes on a sage-covered hillside. At the top of the switchbacks, cross the wooden footbridge back to the true left bank of the North Fork Big Pine Creek. A confusing sign here reads 'Upper Trail,' which is a shortcut ascending to the main trail coming from the Big Pine Creek trailhead. Turn left (northwest) to head upvalley on the broadest trail.

If starting from the Big Pine Creek trailhead, you can continue on the narrow, dustier path staying high above the broad lower path 20 to 25 minutes to a junction where both trails meet. Or, you can descend the short lateral trail toward the footbridge and turn right (northwest) to ascend the broad gently graded trail upvalley to the

junction. The almost level, broad, sandy trail follows the well-shaded true left bank of the North Fork Big Pine Creek. A few scattered ponderosa pines stand on the slope above. As the broad trail heads up the floor of the wide canyon, you catch a glimpse of Second Falls ahead. The trail leaves the valley floor and turns east, ascending gently to a signed junction. Here it meets the other trail, which comes from the right (east) and is signed as 'Trailhead Parking.' Another trail goes northeast up the steep slope. At this junction, turn sharply left, back to the northwest.

The trail traverses amid manzanita and mountain mahogany toward Second Falls, and a few short switchbacks up the granite wall bring you in 15 minutes to the top of the falls and into John Muir Wilderness.

Continuing west along the creek, you enter **Cienega Mirth**, an aspen- and lodgepole-pine-shaded glade. Numerous lilies here are glorious in bloom. In 20 minutes, you come to the **Big Pine Creek**

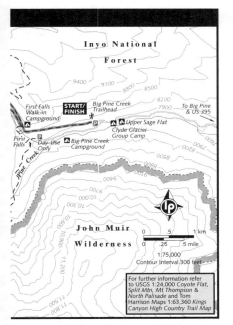

through the trees, where a use trail marked by cairns leads left (southeast) to ***campsites*** on a granite bench above the lake and right (northwest) to a spring above the trail. This is a good place to get water. A short ascent brings you to a viewpoint overlooking the **First Lake** (9961ft). The remarkable turquoise color of the lake is due to dissolved glacial silt.

Continue easily up for five minutes, over a granite outcrop overlooking the lake, to **Second Lake** (10,059ft). The view of Temple Crag above the lighter turquoise lake is truly memorable. The seemingly unreal color of the water against the imposing dark granite crag, rising almost 3000ft above the lake and framed by the clear blue sky, makes an indelible impression. Boulders and cliffs encircling the lake prevent any camping here. It takes 15 minutes to walk around the lake to its cascading inlet surrounded by forest.

Continuing up five minutes, you come to milky blue-green **Third Lake**, with the best view of Temple Crag's north face. Climbers come from around the world for routes on this face and its arêtes. ***Campsites*** are to the left of the trail on shaded granite benches high above the lake.

From here, a series of switchbacks takes you up 15 minutes to a small meadow. Cross a small wooden footbridge over a stream, another good place to fill water bottles. Two minutes beyond the stream, reach the signed junction (10,600ft) with the Glacier Trail (see Side Trip: Palisade Glacier, p270), 2.4mi from the junction with the trail from Black Lake. The Glacier Trail turns left (west).

Continue right (northwest) 0.3mi farther to a signed four-way junction (10,760ft) and turn left (west) to Fifth Lake. From this junction, a longer option is to go straight (northwest), passing along the west side of Fourth Lake (10,750ft), which is visible through the trees. Nearby Fourth Lake also has possible ***campsites*** along its east shore, but it's shallow, and the mountain views are better from Fifth Lake. This trail passes the trail to Summit Lake and ascends the trail to Sixth and Seventh Lakes, which offer more seclusion at the base of the Inconsolable Range.

The trail to Fifth Lake turns left (west) from the junction, and 10 easy minutes

Wilderness Ranger Camp, a substantial stone cabin with a covered wood porch facing the creek, which was built by Hollywood horror film actor Lon Chaney in the 1920s and is included on the National Register of Historic Places. Mt Alice rises south across the valley.

Staying near the creek, the trail continues beneath forest shade past more orange lily and deep blue larkspur displays. Continuing up, you catch sight of imposing **Temple Crag** (12,999ft) as the trail passes through an open area, 30 minutes from the cabin. The trail crosses a small, clear stream, then makes a few switchbacks to recross the stream 15 minutes above.

A 20-minute zigzagging traverse brings you up the slope to the signed junction (9971ft) with the trail from Black Lake (to the right, or north), 3.4mi from the footbridge at the top of First Falls. Continue straight (west), following the sign for 'Lakes 1–7,' crossing the small outlet from Black Lake. A couple of minutes beyond the junction, First Lake is visible

(0.3mi) of almost level trail brings you along the lake's outlet to large, blue **Fifth Lake** (10,787ft). Less cloudy than the lower lakes, this cold and nearly clear lake has trout. *Campsites* are across the outlet beneath pines on its southwest shore. With rocky Two Eagle Peak (12,966ft) above to the west reflecting in the lake's waters, and Mt Gayley and Mt Sill above Palisade Glacier to the south, the setting is inspirational.

Side Trip: Palisade Glacier

3–4 hours, 6.2mi (10km), 1752ft (525.6m) ascent, 1752ft (525.6m) descent

A steep and strenuous 3.1mi one-way hike to the snout of the Palisade Glacier has a total elevation gain and loss of 3504ft. From Fifth Lake, return 0.3mi to the four-way junction (10,760ft) near Fourth Lake and continue back downvalley 0.3mi to the signed junction (10,600ft) with the Glacier Trail. Turn southwest onto the Glacier Trail and descend slightly to cross the outlet from Fifth Lake, then climb innumerable steep switchbacks amid boulders and pines 1.5mi to **Sam Mack Meadow** (11,080ft). The trail turns southeast, crosses the outlet stream from Sam Mack Lake (11,793ft) and ascends 1mi onto the ridge south of the meadow. The faint trail continues to the terminal moraine at the snout of Palisade Glacier (12,165ft). Retrace your steps to Fifth Lake.

Day 2: Fifth Lake to Big Pine Creek Trailhead

3–3½ hours, 7.1mi (11.4km), 73ft (21.9m) ascent, 3160ft (948m) descent

Return 0.3mi from Fifth Lake to the signed four-way junction near Fourth Lake and con-

tinue straight (north), following the sign for Black Lake. Pass around the grass-fringed south shore of Fourth Lake and crossing its outlet. The trail ascends stone steps to the top of a ridge (10,860ft), 15 minutes from Fourth Lake. Clambering onto rocks on the ridge presents a fine view of North Palisade Peak (14,242ft) and the hike's best perspective of the Palisade Glacier. The trail turns northeast and descends five minutes to **Black Lake** (10,649ft), passing along its south shore. Peaceful *campsites* in the forest near the eastern shore lack the big mountain views found at other lakes.

Descending from forested Black Lake, the trail pops out of the forest to traverse an open slope with a sweeping, exquisite perspective on First and Second Lakes and Temple Crag. Long switchbacks lead you east 30 minutes down the hot sagebrush-, chinquapin- and mahogany-covered hillside to rejoin the main trail, 1.9mi from the four-way junction near Fourth Lake. Retrace your steps downvalley 1¼ hours along North Fork Big Pine Creek 3.4mi to the wooden footbridge near the top of First Falls, and another one hour (1.5mi) farther to the Big Pine Creek trailhead (7700ft).

Sixty Lake Basin

Duration	5 days
Distance	34.1mi (56.9km)
Standard	moderate-hard
Start/Finish	Onion Valley Trailhead
Nearest Town	Independence
Public Transport	no

Summary This loop hike crosses two high passes in both directions and accesses a secluded lake-filled basin in remote Kings Canyon high country, visiting a different lake each night.

Sixty Lake Basin is one of the most gorgeous and secluded places in the Sierra Nevada. The quickest and most scenic way to the basin is from Onion Valley and across Kearsarge Pass (11,823ft) into Kings Canyon National Park. Visiting the lakes east of Kearsarge Pass, such as Gilmore or

Heart Lakes, makes a fine day hike, as does hiking to the top of the pass for spectacular views of the Kearsarge Pinnacles. But the real reward comes from continuing via the John Muir Trail across Glen Pass (11,978ft) to the marvelous Rae Lakes and then taking the little-used trail into lovely Sixty Lake Basin. In addition to offering solitude and excellent scenery, the basin is home to two endangered species, Sierra Nevada bighorn sheep and mountain yellow-legged frogs, making this hike a delight for those who love high passes, subalpine lakes and watching rare wildlife. Sixty Lake Basin can

also be visited as a side trip from the Rae Lakes Loop hike (see p219).

PLANNING
When to Hike
The hiking season is from mid-June to September, because both Kearsarge and Glen Passes rarely open before late June.

Maps
The USGS 1:24,000 *Kearsarge Peak* and *Mt Clarence King* quadrangles cover the hike, as does the SNHA 1:62,500 *Rae Lakes Loop Trail Map* ($4).

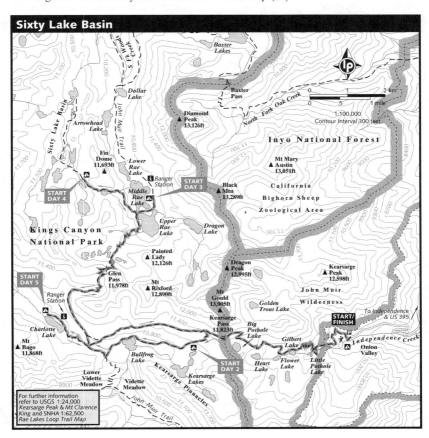

Permits & Regulations

A free wilderness permit is required for this hike (see Bishop and Lone Pine, p261, for the nearest ranger stations). Camping is prohibited at Bullfrog Lake and is limited to two nights at each of the Rae Lakes. Campfires are prohibited in the Onion Valley drainage.

The USFS requires backpackers camping east of Kearsarge Pass and along the Rae Lakes Loop to use bear-resistant food containers, which the host at Onion Valley campground rents, between 7:30am and 11:30am, for $5 per day.

NEAREST TOWN
Independence

County-run *Independence Creek Campground* ($10), on Market St half a mile west of US 395 (Edwards St), is right alongside the road. It lacks grass, but has a few shade trees and a little stream. An HI/AYH hostel is in the *Winnedumah Hotel* (☎ 760-878-2040, fax 878-2833, ⓔ winnedumah@ qnet.com, ⓦ www.winnedumah.com, 211 N Edwards St). A dormitory bed costs $18.

Two non-smoking motels with queen-sized beds are the *Independence Court House Motel* (☎ 800-801-0703), at the corner of N Edwards and Market streets across the street from Winnedumah Hotel ($38/45 singles/doubles), and the neat and tidy *Ray's Den Motel* (☎ 760-878-2122, 405 N Edwards St at Wall St) ($45 for one or two people).

Independence (3925ft) is along US 395, 16mi north of Lone Pine and 26mi south of Big Pine.

GETTING TO/FROM THE HIKE

From the junction of US 395 (Edwards St) and Market St in Independence (3925ft), drive 13mi west on Market St, which becomes Onion Valley Rd, to its end at the Onion Valley trailhead (9200ft) and USFS *Onion Valley Campground* ($11).

Two other USFS campgrounds are along Onion Valley Rd west of Independence: *Lower Grays Meadow* ($11, 6000ft), a narrow strip along Pinyon Creek 6mi west of town; and *Upper Grays Meadow* ($11, 6200ft), a well-shaded area beyond Lower Grays Meadow.

THE HIKE
Day 1: Onion Valley to Kearsarge Lakes

3½–4½ hours, 6.5mi (10.5km), 2623ft (787m) ascent, 863ft (259m) descent

Switchbacks take you from the trailhead (9200ft) up an open, manzanita-covered slope and into a stand of foxtail pines. Entering John Muir Wilderness, the trail touches flower-lined **Independence Creek** and ascends a short series of switchbacks past **Little Pothole Lake** (9900ft), whose two willow-lined inlets cascade into the small lake. Another set of switchbacks brings you up to the next lake in the chain, attractive **Gilbert Lake**. Passing along its northern shore, you ascend more gradually, through forest cover, to shallow Flower Lake.

Beyond, the trail turns north to ascend switchbacks that bring you above pretty **Heart Lake**, from where more switchbacks take you up to the top of a large granite wall. Traverse above Big Pothole Lake and make two long final switchbacks to **Kearsarge Pass** (11,823ft), 5.5mi from the trailhead. The spectacular view ahead of the Kearsarge Pinnacles and Kearsarge Lakes is one of the Sierra Nevada's grandest. Descend west and take the spur trail left (south) to *campsites* at the **Kearsarge Lakes** (10,960ft), 1mi below the pass.

Day 2: Kearsarge Lakes to Middle Rae Lake

4–5 hours, 7.9mi (12.7km), 1338ft (401.4m) ascent, 1748ft (524.4m)descent

From Kearsarge Lakes follow the trail west, along the north shore of **Bullfrog Lake**, continuing 2.4mi to a signed junction with the John Muir Trail (10,640ft) along the north side of the lake's outlet. This is the last reliable water source until just below Glen Pass.

Turn right (north) and make a short ascent via switchbacks over a slight ridge 0.7mi to a level sandy area and a signed four-way junction (10,720ft), where the trail to Charlotte Lake turns left (west) and another trail to Kearsarge Pass branches right (northeast). Kearsarge Pass itself is visible to the east.

Continue straight (north) on the John Muir Trail 0.2mi to a junction with yet another trail leading east to Kearsarge Pass.

Again staying on the John Muir Trail, traverse northwest, high above forested Charlotte Lake, then turn east into a steep-walled rocky canyon. The trail drops down to pass above a snow-fed pool, then turns north and ascend to a larger, aquamarine tarn at the base of Glen Pass. Well-graded switchbacks take you up the steep scree slope to **Glen Pass** (11,978ft), 2.1mi from the previous junction.

The view ahead is inspiring. Numerous tarns dot the basin below and the Rae Lakes beckon beyond. Descend the steep talus slope on solid switchbacks, then follow a small stream down toward Upper Rae Lake and reach the junction with the trail to Sixty Lake Basin 2mi below the pass. Continue north 0.5mi across the isthmus between Upper Rae and Middle Rae Lakes to *campsites* at **Middle Rae Lake** (10,550ft), just west (left) of the trail.

Day 3: Middle Rae Lake to Sixty Lake Basin

1½–2 hours, 2.5mi (4km), 650ft (195m) ascent, 240ft (72m) descent

Retrace your steps 0.5mi back across the isthmus to the junction with the trail to Sixty Lake Basin, marked by an information signboard. The backcountry ranger usually posts a hand-drawn map on it that shows the trail. The Sixty Lake Basin trail is no longer maintained, but it is still easy to follow and presents no navigational difficulties. Leaving the John Muir Trail, turn northwest (right) onto a faint trail that circles a pond in a counterclockwise direction to avoid a marshy area. The trail around the pond is shown incorrectly on some maps.

Once on the pond's west side, the trail zigzags up a grassy slope, steep in places, to a knoll overlooking the Rae Lakes with good views of colorfully banded Dragon Peak (12,995ft) to the east. The trail traverses north toward Fin Dome (11,693ft), then follows switchbacks up and west to a small tarn, reaching it one hour after leaving the John Muir Trail. Skirting the north shore of the tarn, you come to a slight saddle (11,200ft) and begin your 15-minute descent into Sixty Lake Basin. The first good *camp-*

site (10,960ft) is above the north end of the northernmost lake in the upper basin, 2mi from the John Muir Trail.

The trail continues another 2mi down through Sixty Lake Basin to its lower end. You can continue to any of the lakes lower in the basin and camp in perfect solitude in this incredibly scenic subalpine basin.

Alternatively, spend an extra day here to explore its many lakes. The southeast-facing sheer cirque wall of Mt Clarence King (12,905ft), at the basin's northern end, draws your attention and also offers rock climbers a serious challenge. Mt Cotter (12,721ft) and other 12,000ft peaks of the Kings Spur frame the western side of Sixty Lake Basin.

Day 4: Sixty Lake Basin to Charlotte Lake

4–5 hours, 7.6mi (12.2km), 1668ft (500.4m) ascent, 2258ft (677.4m) descent

Retrace your steps out of the basin, over the ridge, and past the small tarn. Descend easily

---

Frogs & Fish: Friends or Foes?

In late summer 2001, the mountain yellow-legged frog *(Rana muscosa)* was placed on the federal endangered species list. One of the Sierra Nevada's few high-elevation amphibians, this frog is never more than a few hops from water. Living in lakes, ponds and streams between 4500ft and 12,000ft, they also favor moist meadows in lodgepole pine and conifer forests. This curious amphibian is essentially mute, having only an underwater call.

Mountain yellow-legged frogs are prey to garter snakes and non-native trout, who eat their tadpoles. Where non-native trout have been introduced, scientists are working to trap and remove them. In Sixty Lake Basin, a gill-net program has been established to remove trout from lakes in hopes of restoring the amphibian population. Swimming is not allowed in these lakes, to prevent entanglement in the gill nets.

to rejoin the John Muir Trail in one hour (2mi). From the junction, turn right (south) and retrace your steps back over **Glen Pass** and down to the signed four-way junction (10,720ft) with the trail to Charlotte Lake, 4.3mi from the Sixty Lake Basin trail junction.

Turn right (west) and descend amid foxtail pines that quickly yield to lodgepole pines as you near the meadows along Charlotte Lake's lovely eastern shore. The trail continues along the northeast shore, passing the ranger station to *campsites* at the northwest end of **Charlotte Lake** (10,370ft), 1.3mi from the four-way junction.

Day 5: Charlotte Lake to Onion Valley

5–5½ hours, 9.6mi (15.5km), 1453ft (435.9m) ascent, 2623ft (786.0m) descent

Retrace your steps along the lakeshore, 1.3mi back to the four-way junction. Cross the John Muir Trail and continue straight (northeast) 0.4mi on a connector trail to join another connector from the John Muir Trail. Turn right, heading east, and traverse the rocky slope high above Bullfrog and Kearsarge Lakes 2.4mi to **Kearsarge Pass**. After savoring a last look at the beautiful lake-dotted high country, descend east 5.5mi to the Onion Valley trailhead (9200ft).

Mt Whitney

Duration	3 days
Distance	22mi (35.4km)
Standard	hard
Start/Finish	Whitney Portal
Nearest Facilities	Whitney Portal
Public Transport	no

Summary This hugely popular trail rises more than 6000ft in 10.7mi to the summit of Mt Whitney, the highest peak in the contiguous US.

Mt Whitney (14,496ft), named for Josiah Dwight Whitney, who headed the California State Geological Survey from 1860 to 1874, is the Sierra Nevada's highest peak. Nearby, five other southern Sierra peaks tower above 14,000ft. The well-marked and maintained trail to the summit gains a challenging 6000ft over 10.7mi. Hikers in good physical condition can reach the summit, although only superbly conditioned, previously acclimatized and psychologically prepared hikers should attempt this as a gargantuan day hike. (If you go for it, bring a flashlight in case you don't make it all the way down by sunset.) With 200 permits issued daily during summer (50 for backpackers and 150 for day hikers), no one is likely to be alone making their way to Mt Whitney's summit.

PLANNING
When to Hike

The trail is usually snowfree from July to September, although patchy ice can remain above Trail Camp year-round.

What to Bring

Early in the season, an ice axe and crampons may be necessary. A bear-resistant food container is required to protect your food from marmots as well as bears.

Maps

The USGS 1:24,000 *Mt Whitney* and *Mt Langley* quadrangles cover the hike, as does Tom Harrison Maps 1:63,360 *Mt Whitney High Country Trail Map* ($8.95).

Permits & Regulations

A free wilderness permit for the Whitney Zone, a designated region jointly managed by Inyo National Forest and Sequoia and Kings Canyon National Parks, is required for day hikers and backpackers between May 15 and November 1, when a quota system is in effect. The 3-sq-mile zone encompasses NPS and USFS land around the summit. Self-issuing permits, which are available at any ranger station, are required from November 2 to May 14. From Whitney Portal, the Whitney Zone starts above Lone Pine Lake.

Advance reservations are available (for a $15 per-person reservation fee) during the quota period for 100% of the permits. The permits, however, are assigned on a lottery basis due to high demand. You can submit a

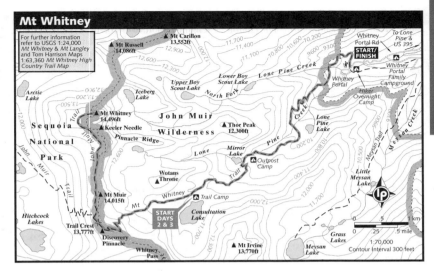

Mt Whitney

For further information refer to USGS 1:24,000 Mt Whitney & Mt Langley and Tom Harrison Maps 1:63,360 Mt Whitney High Country Trail Map

lottery application by fax (fax 760-873-2484) or mail (Wilderness Reservation Office, Inyo National Forest, 873 N Main St, Bishop, CA 93514), and only in February; applications with any other date or postmark are discarded. Lottery applications can be downloaded from the Inyo National Forest website at ⓦ www.r5.fs.fed.us/inyo/vvc/permits.htm.

The lottery process begins February 15, and notification is made by late March. Successful applicants must then pick up their permits in person from the Mt Whitney ranger station (☎ 760-876-6200) on US 395 at Inyo St at the south end of Lone Pine.

The unfortunate reality is that not everyone who wants a permit gets one. A few last-minute cancellations and no-shows can happen, so you if don't get a confirmation through the lottery, you can always go to the Mt Whitney ranger station and try your luck. Day hikers who show up midweek often do have a chance of getting a permit for the next day, either by filling a cancellation or by getting the occasional lottery allotment that was not initially filled by the lottery system.

An alternative strategy for getting a permit for Mt Whitney is to approach the mountain

from a trailhead other than Whitney Portal on a longer hike.

For example, west-to-east traverses of Sequoia National Park are possible from Crescent Meadow (see the High Sierra Trail, p228) and Mineral King. Alternatively, from the eastern Sierra, try starting from Kearsarge Pass (see the Sixty Lake Basin hike, p270) and following the John Muir Trail south to Mt Whitney, or via New Army or Cottonwood Passes (see the New Army & Cottonwood Passes hike, p277) and heading north on the PCT.

Don't despair entirely if you cannot get a permit on your own. Contact the companies listed under Organized Hikes, p38, in the Facts for the Hiker chapter to join one of their scheduled departures.

You are required to store all food and refuse in a bear-resistant food container. Campfires are prohibited. Camping is prohibited at Mirror Lake or Trailside Meadow. Outpost Camp and Trail Camp have toilets.

NEAREST FACILITIES
Whitney Portal

Within the USFS Whitney Portal Recreation Area, west of Lone Pine, are two attractive campgrounds tucked into a pine forest along Lone Pine Creek: *Whitney Portal Family Campground* ($14, 8000ft); and the first-come, first-served walk-in only *Hiker Overnight Camp* ($6, 8300ft), which is at the Whitney Portal trailhead.

The campgrounds are only open mid-May to mid-October. The nearby Whitney Portal Store sells a good selection of groceries and snacks, and there you can also rent bear-resistant food containers ($2 per day). The cafe serves hot meals. The store has public showers.

If the above campgrounds are full, try those closer to Lone Pine. Two camp-grounds are west of Lone Pine's Alabama Hills. The BLM *Tuttle Creek Campground* (by donation, 4000ft) is 1mi south of Whitney Portal Rd off Horseshoe Meadow Rd, 5mi from Lone Pine. The USFS *Lone Pine Campground* ($12, 6000ft) is along the south side of Whitney Portal Rd 7mi west of Lone Pine.

From Lone Pine's only intersection that has a traffic light, you need to drive west from US 395 on Whitney Portal Rd for about 13mi to the dramatic granite canyon at Whitney Portal, where the road comes to an end .

GETTING TO/FROM THE HIKE
The trailhead for this hike is at Whitney Portal (see above).

THE HIKE
Day 1: Whitney Portal to Trail Camp
4–5 hours, 6.2mi (10km), 3635ft (1090.5m) ascent
Start early and carry water, as the east-facing trail gets hot by midmorning. From Whitney Portal (8365ft), the Mt Whitney Trail ascends switchbacks through forest to cross North Fork Lone Pine Creek and enter John Muir Wilderness after half a mile. It continues steeply up open switch-backs, then eases off to pass through stands of forest and open fields of flowers en route to a crossing of Lone Pine Creek 2mi from the trailhead. Beyond the creek, a side trail leads east to Lone Pine Lake.

The main trail heads west and ascends to a boggy meadow. Beyond *Outpost Camp* (10,365ft), at the west end of this meadow (labeled Bighorn Park on most maps) and 3.8mi from the trailhead, the trail crosses Lone Pine Creek and ascends switchbacks for 0.5mi to ford the outlet of Mirror Lake (10,640ft), which lies in a cirque beneath **Thor Peak**. The trail climbs out of the cirque and leaves the last trees behind as it follows the creek beside huge boulders and granite outcrops. A final ascent up concrete steps leads to *Trail Camp* (12,000ft), beneath Wotan's Throne and above large **Consulta-tion Lake**, 1.9mi beyond Mirror Lake. Trail Camp has the last reliable water source along the hike.

Day 2: Trail Camp to Mt Whitney Summit to Trail Camp
6–7 hours, 9.6mi (15.5km), 2496ft (748.8m) ascent, 2496ft (748.8m) descent
No dependable water source exists beyond Trail Camp, so carry all your water from here. The trail follows switchbacks relent-lessly, 2.3mi up the talus slope to **Trail Crest** (13,777ft), the pass marking the eastern boundary of Sequoia National Park. To the west, the Kern River canyon and the distant Great Western Divide come into view, with the two large Hitchcock Lakes close below.

From the pass, the trail descends north along the ridgeline half a mile to meet the John Muir Trail. Many hikers leave their backpacks here and continue the final 2mi to the summit with day packs. The trail zigzags through granite blocks, with occa-sional exposure and sweeping eastern views, and finally reaches the several-acre summit plateau with its metal-roofed stone hut. Retrace your steps to *Trail Camp* or, if time and your legs allow, all the way to Whitney Portal.

Day 3: Trail Camp to Whitney Portal
3–4 hours, 6.2mi (10km), 3635ft (1090.5m) descent
Follow the trail back down, enjoying the views and savoring the memory of your ascent.

New Army & Cottonwood Passes

Duration	3 days
Distance	20.9mi (33.6km)
Standard	moderate
Start/Finish	Cottonwood Lakes Trailhead
Public Transport	no

Summary This loop hike through the southern High Sierra visits two wilderness areas and Sequoia National Park, crossing an alpine pass with foxtail pines presenting dramatic nature-sculpted wood forms along the way.

With a trailhead elevation higher than 10,000ft, the nearly level hike through Golden Trout Wilderness and southern John Muir Wilderness brings you to a series of lakes in a striking landscape of shimmering white granite. Beyond, you cross the alpine New Army Pass into the High Sierra realm of southern Sequoia National Park. A long, panoramic traverse to a lovely cirque lake and the rolling terrain and subalpine meadows of the Cottonwood Pass area complete this loop hike.

An alternative hike for those wanting a shorter or easier outing is to embark on a day hike to Lake 1 or Lake 2 in the Cottonwood Lakes Basin. Those not wanting to cross New Army Pass can also enjoy an overnight trip to Long Lake. But the rewards of crossing the pass and camping in upper Rock Creek inside the national park are the highlights of this circumambulation of Cirque Peak (12,900ft).

PLANNING
When to Hike
The hiking season for this trail is from late June to mid-October.

Maps
The USGS 1:24,000 *Cirque Peak* and *Johnson Peak* quadrangles cover the hike, as does Tom Harrison Maps 1:63,360 *Mt Whitney High Country Trail Map* ($8.95). The USGS maps depict the roads correctly

at the new trailheads, but not the realigned trail starting from the Cottonwood Lakes trailhead. Fortunately, the trailhead map and trail signs are very clear and easy to understand. The USGS map also incorrectly labels these Cottonwood Lakes: Lake 2, Lake 3 and Lake 4.

The published elevation of New Army Pass ranges from 11,900ft to 12,400ft. The pass is closer to 12,300ft, and the lower published elevation is likely due to a mislabeled contour line (the one labeled 11,800ft northwest of the pass) on the USGS *Cirque Peak* quadrangle.

Despite the fact that the eastern extent of the Tom Harrison map excludes both trailheads and the first four trail miles from each trailhead, the map is still very useful for the rest of the hike.

Permits & Regulations
A free wilderness permit is required for this hike (see Lone Pine, p262, for the nearest ranger station). Campfires are prohibited in the Cottonwood Lakes drainage and above 10,800ft in Sequoia National Park.

GETTING TO/FROM THE HIKE
From Lone Pine's only intersection with a traffic light, drive west from US 395 on Whitney Portal Rd 3.1mi and turn left (south) on Horseshoe Meadow Rd. Horseshoe Meadow Rd is a seriously engineered, wide two-lane paved road that snakes it way up the rocky eastern Sierra more than 6000ft to the middle of nowhere. Follow Horseshoe Meadow Rd a seemingly endless 18.9mi to a signed intersection.

Turn right at the intersection, following the signs for New Army Pass and Cottonwood Lakes. In 0.4mi pass the Hiker Overflow Parking area on the left, and 0.1mi farther is the *walk-in campground* ($6) on the right beyond which is the massive parking lot for the Cottonwood Lakes Trailhead (10,040ft).

From the intersection, the road continues straight, passing another *walk-in campground* ($6) in 0.2mi and reaching the Cottonwood/Trail Pass Trailhead 0.1mi farther.

THE HIKE
Day 1: Cottonwood Lakes Trailhead to Long Lake

3½–4 hours, 6.1mi (9.8m), 1100ft (330m) ascent

The trail heads west from Cottonwood Lakes Trailhead (10,040ft) across an open granite sand-and-boulder landscape amid scattered foxtail and more numerous large lodgepole pines, and quickly enters **Golden Trout Wilderness**. Turning north, you head through easy, open forest, and 30 minutes from the trailhead, approach South Fork Creek. Turning northeast, you cross the creek and continue another 20 nearly level minutes toward Cottonwood Creek. Nearing the creek, you follow along its true right (west) bank, passing the privately owned Golden Trout Camp after 15 minutes. The lovely meadows along Cottonwood Creek here are fenced off and closed to the public. The trail continues north, amid mostly lodgepole pines, leaving Golden Trout Wilderness and entering John Muir Wilderness.

Cross logs over a creek 10 minutes from the private fish camp, as the trail bends westward, ascending gently amid lodgepole and scattered foxtail pines. In 15 minutes, reach a signed junction with a trail that branches right (northwest), leading to Lake 3, Lake 4 and Lake 5 of the **Cottonwood Lakes**. The Cottonwood Lakes were named for the cottonwood trees at the original Owens Valley trailhead, which was long ago abandoned. Stay to the left (west), continuing on the trail to New Army Pass, which crosses to the true right bank of Cottonwood Creek via a log.

Ascend gently along its willow-lined true right bank, passing through a small creekside meadow where violet gentians, pink shooting stars and yellow potentillas are conspicuous. Foxtail pines become more prevalent as the trail ascends away from the cascading Cottonwood Creek toward the head of a large meadow.

At the upper end of the meadow is a signed junction (10,960ft). The trail to the left (south) leads to South Fork Lakes and Cirque Lake. Go right (southwest) toward New Army Pass and ascend on switchbacks. The trail tops a slight ridge and soon comes to **Lake 1** (11,040ft). *Campsites* are along the forested northern shore or on the rise above the eastern shore. Set in a dramatic granite landscape beneath shimmering white cliffs and peaks, the south and east shores are grassy and open meadows. The trail rolls along the southern lakeshore and, in 15 minutes, passes smaller Lake 2.

Beyond Lake 2, the trail works through a huge talus field that fills the horizon. At first glance, the landscape is intimidating, but a broad, sandy trail snakes its way southwest through the granite blocks. The easternmost of the **South Fork Lakes** is soon visible to the southeast. After 15 minutes you pass close to the attractive westernmost of the South Fork Lakes, which is unnamed. A use trail, marked by cairns, leads down one minute to the left (southwest), to forested *campsites* (11,080ft) in a secluded depression on the lake's northwest shore, beyond its inlet. This spot is an attractive alternative to the campsites a few minutes farther at Long Lake.

Continue north on the trail five minutes to a signed junction, where a small spur trail branches right along the outlet from Long Lake. The trail to New Army Pass turns left (southwest) and immediately crosses the lake's outlet on a log. Following Long Lake's south shore less than 10 minutes to *campsites* at the west end of **Long Lake** near its inlet (11,140ft). Tall pines shade the dramatic and often windy campsite.

Day 2: Long Lake to Chicken Spring Lake

5–6 hours, 10.4mi (16.7km), 1760ft (528m) ascent, 1660ft (498m) descent

From Long Lake, you might find yourself wondering, 'Where is New Army Pass?' It's not obvious and it's also not the lowest point visible at the head of the colorful granite cirque enclosing Long Lake. However, a well-graded trail ascends the cirque wall to the pass.

The sandy trail ascends from the campsite to a rocky terrace and up switchbacks

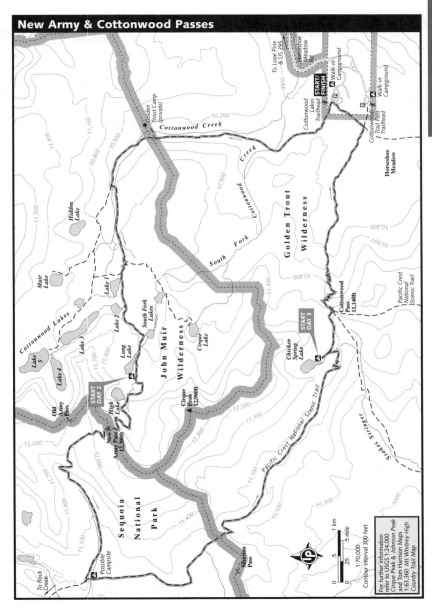

New Army & Cottonwood Passes

through stunted, wind-twisted whitebark pines, reaching High Lake in 25 minutes. Rock-enclosed, beneath towering columnar cliffs of orange and white granite, **High Lake** (11,480ft) is the highest in the chain of lakes feeding South Fork Cottonwood Creek. Now above timberline, you hop rocks across the creek's small inlet. Colorful gentians, heathers, stone crops, rock fringes and whorled penstemons catch your eye in this all-granite landscape, where a few willows line the trail.

Ascending well-graded switchbacks you pass clusters of rock fringe and primulas, which splash pink against the rock. It takes 45 minutes to steadily ascend 820ft of long switchbacks up the cirque wall to reach the barren **New Army Pass** (12,300ft), crowned by a large, almost stupa-shaped 6ft-high cairn. To the south, rising directly above the cirque, is Cirque Peak (12,900ft). To the north is massive Mt Langley (14,027ft), which is the southernmost of the Sierra Nevada's 14,000ft peaks. To the northwest, above upper Rock Creek, are **Joe Devel Peak** (13,325ft) and **Mt Pickering** (13,485ft). Far to the west, across the Kern River Canyon, are the peaks of the Kaweahs and the Great Western Divide.

Entering Sequoia National Park, the trail descends the barren granite slope, and in 15 to 20 minutes passes faint upper and lower cairn-marked trails that lead to nearby Old Army Pass. Old Army Pass was a route originally used by shepherds and was established as a trail in 1892 when the US Army patrolled Sequoia National Park. Today Old Army Pass is no longer maintained, but is still crossed as part of a cross-country route. The main trail curves west from these cairns through a marmot-infested meadow, then descends steeply to the usually dry creek bed below, 45 minutes beyond New Army Pass.

As you descend farther, water fed by springs appears in the creek, and you follow along this upper, unnamed branch of Rock Creek 15 minutes as it descends through a pleasant meadow. Cross to the creek's true right bank and descend 15 minutes into lodgepole-pine forest to a signed junction, 2.3mi from New Army Pass. The trail to the right (north) leads in 0.5mi to Rock Creek. Turn south (left) and cross the lovely creek, which flows through an attractive flower-filled meadow. This is the last water until Chicken Spring Lake, and alternative *campsites* (10,920ft) are on the forested bench just south of and above the creek. This pleasant campsite gets late afternoon sunlight as well as early morning sun. The peaks encircling Rock Creek are impressive, as are the views west to the Kaweah peaks, Great Western Divide and the Chagoopa Plateau.

The trail rises south over a slight ridge, offering fine views north of The Miter's double summits (12,770ft) and the rock walls above Rock Creek, and drops down to meet the PCT, 1.1mi from the last junction at the creek. The sign here indicates Cottonwood Pass is 3.6mi ahead, but it is actually closer to 5mi. Turning left onto the famous trail, you head east, circling around the upper end of a desolate meadow called Siberian Outpost and ascending 30 minutes southeast through mixed lodgepole and foxtail pines to the boundary (13,320ft) of Sequoia National Park and Golden Trout Wilderness. The equally expansive and desolate Big Whitney Meadow is visible to the south of Siberian Pass below.

The trail continues ascending southeast to a ridge (11,440ft) overlooking Big and Little Whitney Meadows, with views farther west of the Great Western

Divide and the Kaweahs. Gnarled, dead foxtail pines stand on the ridge crest, their bark weathered away to reveal their golden-grained wood. Descending into a basin below Cirque Peak, the trail crosses soft, sandy soil amid red-barked foxtail pines, traversing steadily southeast and rising gradually to the highest point on the ridge (11,520ft) above Chicken Spring Lake. It takes 1½ hours to reach this point from the national park boundary. Savor the panoramic views west and south from this point, then descend 10 minutes on switchbacks along a spur toward **Chicken Spring Lake** (11,240ft) and cross its outlet stream. *Campsites* are along its south side, amid pines.

Day 3: Chicken Spring Lake to Cottonwood Lakes Trailhead

2 hours, 4.4mi (6.4km), 100ft (30m) ascent, 1300ft (390m) descent

The trail from the lake descends 100ft in 15 minutes to **Cottonwood Pass** (11,140ft). No sign marks the pass, but a signed junction of the north-south PCT and the east-west trail from Horseshoe Meadow lies just west of the pass. Turning east, the trail follows switchbacks down the foxtail pine-forested slope to the head of a small willow-filled meadow. Beyond, more switchbacks lead you down into nearly level lodgepole pine forest.

Forty-five minutes below the pass, the trail crosses a small stream feeding Horseshoe Meadow to its south bank, then immediately recrosses it. The trail heads east 30 minutes through lodgepole pines along the north side of long Horseshoe Meadow. The trail on this long, level stretch is over soft, sandy soil that makes for poor footing.

Eventually you reach a signed junction where the trail to Cottonwood Lakes Trailhead turns left (northeast). The main trail, which is signed for 'Hiker Parking,' continues straight-leading in a few minutes to the Cottonwood/Trail Pass Trailhead (9940ft). Turn left at the junction and go over a small ridge, leaving Golden Trout Wilderness, past the aromatic horse corrals at the pack station and continue through the equestrian parking lot back to the Cottonwood Lakes trailhead (10,040ft).

Other Hikes

Iceberg & Cecile Lakes

Ediza Lake and Minaret Lake, two hikes described earlier in this chapter, sparkle beneath the Minarets. The Sierra Nevada's most frequently done cross-country route links these two lakes, passing even closer beneath the jagged summits of the Minarets. More adventurous hikers can combine these hikes into a three-day, near-loop trip, starting from Agnew Meadow and finishing at Devils Postpile. The more challenging cross-country segment is just 3mi long.

The first day, start from Agnew Meadows and go to Ediza Lake (see Day 1 of the Ediza Lake hike, p248). The second day, follow switchbacks from the lake's southeast shore (9265ft) along a faint trail, paralleling the willow-lined stream for a mile to Iceberg Lake (9800ft). Beyond Iceberg Lake, the rugged Class 2 route is steep and often snow-covered until mid-August. The route works around Iceberg Lake's eastern shore, then ascends along the outlet of Cecile Lake over steep talus to Cecile Lake (10,280ft), with unsurpassed views and reflections of the Minarets. Skirt its east shore and descend steeply over Class 2 to Class 3 rock and talus to campsites at Minaret Lake (9793ft). The third day, continue down to Devils Postpile (see the Minaret Lake hike, p245, for a description of the trail between Minaret Lake and Devils Postpile). Use the shuttle bus to return 4.8mi to the starting trailhead if you left your vehicle there, or to head back toward Mammoth Lakes. Campfires are prohibited between Ediza and Minaret Lakes.

The USGS 1:24,000 *Mammoth Mountain* and *Mt Ritter* quadrangles cover the hike, as does Tom Harrison Maps 1:63,360 *Mammoth High Country Trail Map* and USFS 1:63,360 *Ansel Adams Wilderness* map.

Lake Italy

Flanking the southern slopes of the Mono Divide in a remote part of John Muir Wilderness, Lake Italy (11,154ft) makes a superb base for cross-country exploration of the surrounding alpine country. The trail to Lake Italy crosses Italy Pass (12,400ft), and although beautiful, it has not been maintained in years. Crossing the pass requires some route-finding and cross-country travel on both sides, so is better suited to adventurous backpackers. The 23mi round-trip hike takes at least two days. A wilderness permit is required for this hike. Go to the ranger station in Mammoth Lakes or Bishop. The USGS 1:24,000 *Mount Tom* and *Mt Hilgard* quadrangles cover the hike.

From US 395 between Toms Place and Bishop, look for the isolated turnoff to Pine Creek Rd. Turn west and drive 10mi to the road's end at the Pine Creek trailhead (7400ft) and pack station. A dusty trail ascends steeply, merging with an unpaved road to a large, closed tungsten mine. Beyond the mine, the trail continues steeply into John Muir Wilderness and passes along the north shore of Pine Lake, 3.5mi from the trailhead. It continues 1.5mi past Upper Pine Lake to a junction (10,400ft), where the trail to Pine Creek Pass heads left and the trail to Italy Pass turns right and continues 0.5mi to Honeymoon Lake, where campsites are reached by a short spur trail.

Cross the inlet to Honeymoon Lake and continue west along the stream's north side into Granite Park, where the trail grows faint. Pass north of the highest lake (11,800ft) and follow a faintly marked route to Italy Pass. Mt Julius Caesar (13,196ft), Mt Gabb (13,711ft) and Mt Hilgard (13,361ft) are close at hand to the north and west. Mt Tom, Mt Humphreys and the Palisades are visible in the distance to the east and south. Descend toward Jumble Lake, passing well above its north shore, cross its outlet, and follow it to Lake Italy's south shore.

Long-Distance Trails

Three impressive trails traverse key segments of the Sierra Nevada in addition to the famous Pacific Crest National Scenic Trail (PCT): The Tahoe Rim Trail encircles Lake Tahoe; the Tahoe-Yosemite Trail links the western shore of Lake Tahoe with Tuolumne Meadows in Yosemite National Park; and the John Muir Trail links Yosemite Valley and Mt Whitney. These trails cover more than 550 trail miles, each ranging in length from 153mi to 218mi. These trails take weeks to complete, and relatively few hikers complete a trail in its entirety in a single trip. The majority of hikers enjoy shorter segments of a trail on day hikes or shorter backpacking trips. Though popular, the trails are rarely crowded, and apart from near trailheads and in the national parks, hikers experience much solitude.

Tahoe Rim Trail

Duration	10–17 days
Distance	153.1mi (246.3km)
Standard	moderate
Start/Finish	Tahoe City
Public Transport	no

Summary This unique ridge-top trail encircles enormous, azure Lake Tahoe, offering the ultimate in lake vistas.

Circumambulating the Lake Tahoe Basin mostly along ridge tops, the Tahoe Rim Trail bestows inspirational views of Lake Tahoe, the snowcapped peaks of the Sierra Nevada's crest to the west and Nevada's Great Basin to the east. Along the diverse glacial and volcanic terrain are subalpine meadows, aspen-lined creeks, thick conifer forests of the Crystal Range, sage and Jeffrey-pine covered slopes of the Carson Range, crystalline lakes and a delightful diversity of wildflower gardens clinging to windswept, rocky peaks.

Whether hiking one segment at a time (one to four days each), the most popular way to complete the trail, or becoming a '150-miler' at one go (10 to 17 days), the trail crosses easy passes and has the ultimate in Tahoe panoramas.

Staying between 6300ft and 10,150ft and passing through three wilderness areas, state park and national forest lands, the Tahoe

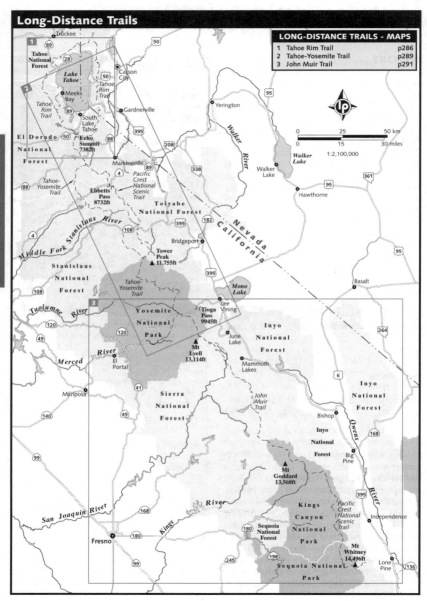

Long-Distance Trails

LONG-DISTANCE TRAILS - MAPS	
1 Tahoe Rim Trail	p286
2 Tahoe-Yosemite Trail	p289
3 John Muir Trail	p291

Rim Trail also joins segments of the Pacific Crest National Scenic Trail (PCT) and Tahoe-Yosemite Trail.

HISTORY
In 1981, USFS employee Glenn Hampton conceived the idea of a continuous trail encircling the Tahoe Basin. Construction began in 1984, and the final trail segment was completed in 2001.

PLANNING
The Tahoe Rim Trail Association (☎ 775-588-0686, fax 588-8737, e tahoerim@aol.com, w www.tahoerimtrail.org), 298 Kingsbury Grade (Hwy 207), PO Box 4647, Stateline, NV 89449, is the best information source.

When to Hike
The hiking season is from June to September. Trails in the Carson Range are snow free as early as June because they receive less snowfall than trails in the Crystal Range. Some lower-elevation trail segments along streams are beautiful in October, when fall colors come to aspen groves. Water sources can be far apart on some eastern segments, especially late in the season.

Maps
The USGS 1:24,000 *Mt Rose, Marlette Lake, Glenbrook, South Lake Tahoe, Freel Peak, Caples Lake, Echo Lake, Emerald Bay, Pyramid Peak, Rockbound Valley, Homewood, Tahoe City, Kings Beach* and *Martis Peak* quadrangles cover the hike, and are most useful when hiking individual segments. Tom Harrison Maps 1:71,280 *Recreation Map of Lake Tahoe* depicts the trail on one sheet.

Permits & Regulations
A wilderness permit is required only for the segment through Desolation Wilderness (see the Dicks & Phipps Passes hike, p111).

GETTING TO/FROM THE HIKE
Hikers can start and finish segments at any of eight trailheads. Seven trailheads, six of which are at or near passes, are along highways around the Tahoe Basin (listed clockwise, starting along the northwest shore of

Lake Tahoe): Hwy 89 at Tahoe City; Hwy 267 near Brockway Summit; Hwy 431 near Mt Rose Summit and at Ophir Creek; US 50 at Spooner Summit, called Spooner Summit North and Spooner Summit South; Hwy 207 (Kingsbury Grade) near Daggett Pass, called Kingsbury North, 2mi north of Hwy 207, and Kingsbury South, 1.3mi south of Hwy 207; Hwy 89 at Big Meadow 3.1mi west of Luther Pass (and 5.2mi southeast of the US 50/Hwy 89 intersection in Meyers); and US 50 at Echo Summit and nearby Lower Echo Lake. The eighth trailhead is toward the head of Blackwood Canyon at Barker Pass.

THE HIKE
Segment 1: Tahoe City to Brockway Summit
1–2 days, 18.5mi (29.8km)
The Tahoe City Trailhead (6300ft) is at Fairway Community Center on Fairway Drive 0.2mi off Hwy 89 just 0.1mi west of the Hwy 89/Hwy 28 intersection. The trail climbs to Painted Rock (7754ft), then traverses the southeast slopes of Mt Watson to Watson Lake in 12.5mi, and continues 6mi to Hwy 267, half a mile south of Brockway Summit (7179ft).

Segment 2: Brockway Summit to Mt Rose Summit
1–2 days, 16mi (25.7km)
The trail begins 200ft east of Hwy 267, at a sign reading 'Forest Protection Road.' It leads for 4mi east to Martis Peak (8742ft) and continues 12mi through Mt Rose Wilderness to Hwy 431. See the Mt Rose hike, p116, in the Tahoe chapter for a description of the worthwhile side trip to the top of this peak.

Segment 3: Ophir Creek to Spooner Summit North
2 days, 22mi (35.4km)
See the Tahoe Meadows to Spooner Summit hike, p114, in the Tahoe chapter for a description of this outstanding segment.

Segment 4: Spooner Summit South to Kingsbury North
1 day, 11.8mi (19km)
The trail skirts the west slopes of Duane Bliss (8658ft) and South Camp (8866ft)

LONG-DISTANCE TRAILS

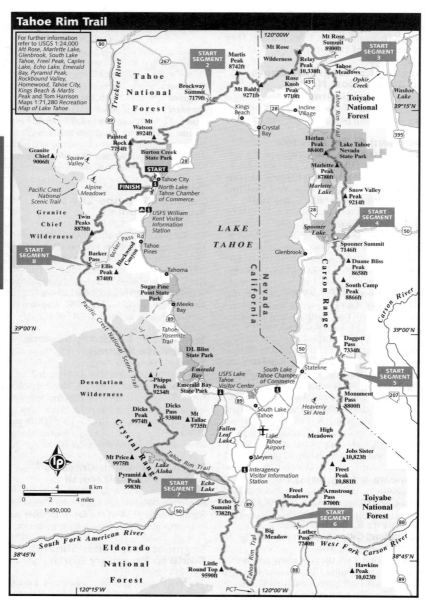

Tahoe Rim Trail

For further information refer to USGS 1:24,000 Mt Rose, Marlette Lake, Glenbrook, South Lake Tahoe, Freel Peak, Caples Lake, Echo Lake, Emerald Bay, Pyramid Peak, Rockbound Valley, Homewood, Tahoe City, Kings Beach & Martis Peak and Tom Harrison Maps 1:71,280 Recreation Map of Lake Tahoe

peaks, ending at the trailhead parking area at the end of Andria Drive, an extension of North Benjamin Drive, 1.9mi north of Hwy 207 just west of Daggett Pass.

Segment 5: Kingsbury South to Big Meadow North
2 days, 22.6mi (36.4km)

See the Freel Peak hike, p118, for this segment, which passes Tahoe's highest peak.

Segment 6: Big Meadow South to Echo Summit
2 days, 16mi (25.8km)

The trail heads south past Round Lake 5mi to a junction with the combined PCT and Tahoe-Yosemite Trail, 2.2mi north of Carson Pass. From the junction, the Tahoe Rim Trail turns north (right) to reach **Showers Lake** in 1.8mi. See the Echo Summit to Carson Pass hike, p121, in the Tahoe chapter, for a description of the trail between Showers Lake and Echo Summit.

Segment 7: Echo Summit to Barker Pass
4 days, 32.6mi (52.5km)

See Days 1 to 3 of the Dicks & Phipps Passes hike, p111 in the Tahoe chapter for a description from Echo Summit to Middle Velma Lake. From Middle Velma Lake, the Tahoe Rim Trail continues north, passing the junction where the Tahoe-Yosemite Trail turns east toward Phipps Pass after 1.5mi. The combined PCT and Tahoe Rim Trail continue north, passing the Lake Genevieve and General Creek trail junction in 4.4mi. The short side trail to Richardson Lake is 2.7mi farther, a short distance north of the Desolation Wilderness boundary. The Barker Pass Trailhead is another 7mi farther, at the head of Blackwood Canyon, 7.5mi west of Hwy 89.

Segment 8: Barker Pass to Tahoe City
1 day, 13.6mi (21.9km)

From Barker Pass, the trail continues north, entering the Granite Chief Wilderness. The Tahoe Rim Trail turns east (right), leaving the PCT, and traverses Twin Peaks (8878ft),

then descends past a 100ft waterfall at the head of Ward Creek to reach Tahoe City.

Tahoe-Yosemite Trail

Duration	19–23 days
Distance	185.7mi (297.7km)
Standard	hard
Start	Meeks Bay Trailhead
Finish	Tuolumne Meadows
Public Transport	yes

Summary Connecting Lake Tahoe with Yosemite National Park, this classic trail contours the spine of the northern Sierra, crosses seven passes, and lets hikers get deep into the wilderness, away from crowds.

Linking two Sierra gems, Lake Tahoe and Yosemite, the 185mi Tahoe-Yosemite Trail traverses four wilderness areas and crosses seven passes. It is a more varied and less frequently used trail than the John Muir Trail, or the parallel PCT. Elevations range from 5200ft, in the canyon carved by the Mokelumne River, to 10,400ft, at St Marys Pass.

Through hikers can easily cover the trail in one season, although it is more common for hikers to complete short trail segments over a few seasons. Hiking the trail by segments typically take 19 to 23 days, a slower pace than that of through hikers, who might take only 11 to 19 days. Five trans-Sierra highways provide easy access to the trail.

HISTORY
The Tahoe-Yosemite Trail, conceived by the USFS as early as 1914, was a line on a map with only partially completed segments until 1966, when John Jencks of Berkeley set out to walk it and revived interest in the route. In the 1930s, the PCT was proposed to follow the Tahoe-Yosemite Trail's route, but between northern Yosemite and Carson Pass on Hwy 88, they follow separate routes.

PLANNING
When to Hike
The hiking season for this trail is from July to mid-September.

LONG-DISTANCE TRAILS

What to Bring

All but the strongest through hikers need to resupply along the route. Lake Alpine on Hwy 4, about 70mi south of Meeks Bay, has a post office where through hikers can mail supplies to themselves. Otherwise, hikers can buy basic supplies at resorts along the highways that intersect the trail.

Maps

The USGS 1:62,500 *Tahoe, Fallen Leaf Lake, Silver Lake, Markleeville, Big Meadow, Dardanelles Cone, Sonora Pass, Tower Peak, Matterhorn Peak* and *Tuolumne Meadows* quadrangles cover the trail.

Permits & Regulations

A free wilderness permit is required for Yosemite National Park and the four wilderness areas (Desolation, Mokelumne, Carson–Iceberg and Emigrant).

Through hikers can get one permit for the entire trail. For details, hikers beginning from Yosemite should see Permits & Regulations, p167, in the Yosemite National Park chapter, and those beginning from Meeks Bay should see Permits & Regulations for the Dicks & Phipps Passes hike, p111, in the Lake Tahoe chapter.

Hikers can get permits for individual segments from the US Forest Service office that administers the corresponding wilderness area or get self-issuing permits at some trailheads.

GETTING TO/FROM THE HIKE

The hike's northern terminus is at the Meeks Bay Trailhead (see the Dicks & Phipps Passes hike, p111), along the west side of Hwy 89 on Lake Tahoe's west shore, and its southern terminus at Tuolumne Meadows on Hwy 120 (see Tuolumne Meadows, p184).

Hikers can also start and finish segments of the Tahoe-Yosemite Trail from trailheads at or near passes on any of the following four trans-Sierra highways (listed north to south): US 50 at Echo Summit or Lower Echo Lake; Hwy 88 at Carson Pass; Hwy 4 east of Ebbetts Pass; and Hwy 108 west of Sonora Pass.

THE HIKE
Segment 1: Meeks Bay to Echo Summit

4 days, 31.2mi (50.2km)
See the Dicks & Phipps Passes hike, p111, for a description of the trail through Desolation Wilderness. From Lower Echo Lake, walk a trail or a 1.5mi road to Echo Summit.

Segment 2: Echo Summit to Carson Pass

1–2 days, 13.5mi (21.7km)
See the Echo Summit to Carson Pass hike, p121, in the Tahoe chapter for a description.

Segment 3: Carson Pass to Lake Alpine

3–4 days, 26mi (41.8km)
This segment traverses the infrequently visited Mokelumne Wilderness. See the Fourth of July Lake hike, p129, for a description from Carson Pass to this lake, which is a short distance off the Tahoe–Yosemite Trail. Beyond Fourth of July Lake, hikers find splendid isolation as the trail heads 12mi south through **Summit City Canyon** to Camp Irene, which has campsites on the Mokelumne River. From this canyon, the trail ascends the northern slopes of Mt Reba (8758ft) to reach Lake Alpine, on Hwy 4.

Segment 4: Lake Alpine to Kennedy Meadow

5–6 days, 44mi (70.8km)
Traversing the Carson-Iceberg Wilderness, the trail visits the headwaters of the Stanislaus River. From the Silver Valley parking area, at the east end of Lake Alpine, the trail goes east 3mi to the North Fork Stanislaus River, then south to the upper end of long Spicer Meadow Reservoir for 7mi. The trail ascends Jenkins Canyon, going north and east of **Dardanelles Cone** (9524ft), to descend Woods Gulch and meet Clark Fork Rd at the USFS *Sand Flat Campground* in 10mi.

The trail follows Clark Fork Rd 3.7mi to its end at the Clark Fork parking area in Iceberg Meadow, then continues through beautiful upper Clark Fork Meadow and across **St Marys Pass** (10,400ft) to Hwy 108, crossing the road just west of Sonora Pass. The Tahoe-

Top Left: Wildflowers bloom on a trail near Mt Williamson, near Sequoia National Park.
Top Right: A rock climber boulders across the precipitous Thunderbolt face of Calaveras Dome, in the North Palisade area.
Bottom: Copper waters glow at sunrise at Fifth Lake, Big Pine Lakes.

Clockwise from top: An ancient White Mountain bristlecone pine frames Sierra Nevada peaks. Deep-rooted, wind-resistant Sierra Nevada native Jeffrey pines grow on top of Sentinel Dome, in Yosemite. The sun casts an orange light on this rocky crag, seen from the Whitney Portal Trail.

Yosemite Trail turns west and follows Hwy 108 about 8.5mi, a section on road that's worth hitchhiking (although not if you're alone), to Kennedy Meadow Rd, which heads southeast a mile to Kennedy Meadow.

Segment 5: Kennedy Meadow to Tuolumne Meadows
6–7 days, 71mi (114.2km)

Uncrossed by roads, this segment traverses Emigrant Wilderness and northern Yosemite NP. See Days 1 to 3 of the Brown Bear & Bond Passes hike, p145, for a description of the trail from Kennedy Meadow to **Bond Pass** via Brown Bear Pass. Also, see Days 2 to 3 of the Sawtooth Ridge hike, p148, for a description of the section between Seavey Pass and Matterhorn Canyon.

Beyond Bond Pass, the Tahoe-Yosemite Trail rejoins the PCT and descends Falls Creek through meadow-dotted Jack Main Canyon. Leaving the PCT, the trail turns east to campsites on **Tilden Lake**, then descends Tilden Canyon for 3mi to rejoin the PCT. Over a series of ridges and canyons, the trail continues past the Rock Island Pass Trail and campsites, along Benson Lake to **Matterhorn Canyon** and **Virginia Canyon**. It turns south down Cold Canyon to Glen Aulin. From this junction, it is a mere 5.5mi southeast along the cascading Tuolumne River to beautiful Tuolumne Meadows.

John Muir Trail

Duration	19–20 days
Distance	218mi (350.8km)
Standard	hard
Start	Happy Isles
Finish	Whitney Portal
Public Transport	start only

Summary Traversing the roadless crest of Muir's 'Range of Light' through three national parks and two wilderness areas across 11 passes on the John Muir Trail is an unforgettable adventure and the ultimate Sierra experience.

Offering what many consider to be very best mountain hiking in the US, the 218mi John

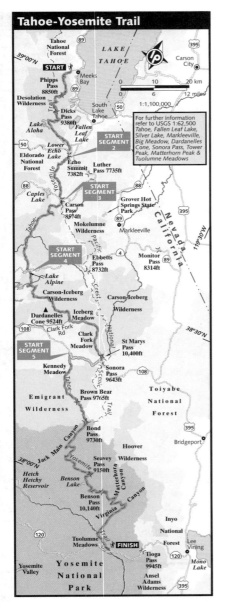

Tahoe-Yosemite Trail

LONG-DISTANCE TRAILS

Muir Trail links Yosemite Valley and Mt Whitney. Uncrossed by any roads, the trail goes through a continual wilderness comprised of Yosemite National Park, the Ansel Adams and John Muir Wilderness Areas, and Kings Canyon and Sequoia National Parks. The trail crosses 11 passes, half of which are higher than 12,000ft and all but one of which are above 10,000ft. As it traverses the timberline country of the High Sierra, the trail passes thousands of lakes and numerous granite peaks between 13,000ft and 14,000ft, and takes in the Sierra's highest peak. The trail frequently descends from the Sierra Crest into forested areas of the western Sierra, with 5000ft deep canyons.

Completing the John Muir Trail requires top physical fitness, prior backpacking experience and advance planning because of its length, substantial elevation changes and remoteness. It can be hiked in either direction. As a through hike, it is both the Sierra's most difficult and most rewarding – a once-in-a-lifetime adventure.

Many hikers choose to divide it into shorter, more manageable, but equally exhilarating segments, done at a slower pace, with layover days to enrich the experience. An average through hiker covering 12mi per day would take 19 or 20 days to complete the trail. Faster backpackers might take as few as 12 days.

HISTORY

Theodore S Solomons first imagined 'a crest-parallel trail through the High Sierra' in 1884, while herding his uncle's cattle near Fresno at the age of 14. On five journeys, undertaken between 1892 and 1897, he traversed the mountains from Yosemite to the Kings River. One of Solomons' companions, Joseph N LeConte, along with other members of the newly formed Sierra Club, continued the effort to establish a crest route. In 1915, the California legislature allocated funds to begin work on an actual trail, to be named in honor of the late president of the Sierra Club, John Muir. By the mid-1920s, Solomons' dream was realized.

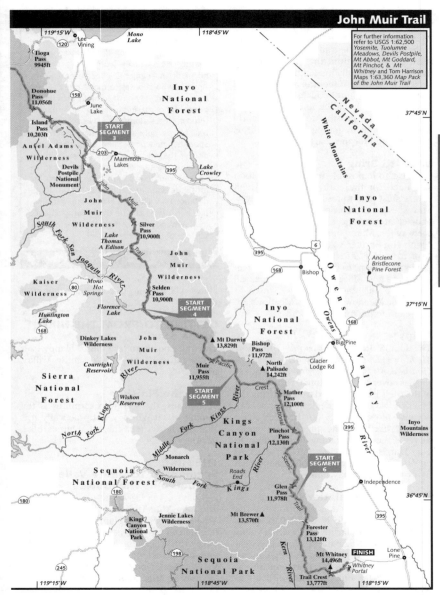

John Muir Trail

For further information refer to USGS 1:62,500 Yosemite, Tuolumne Meadows, Devils Postpile, Mt Abbot, Mt Goddard, Mt Pinchot, & Mt Whitney and Tom Harrison Maps 1:63,360 Map Pack of the John Muir Trail

Lee Vining
119°15'W
120
Mono Lake
118°45'W
Nevada
California
37°45'N

Tioga Pass 9945ft

Donohue Pass 11,056ft
158
June Lake

Island Pass 10,203ft
Ansel Adams Wilderness
START SEGMENT 3
203
Mammoth Lakes
395
Lake Crowley
White Mountains

Inyo National Forest

Devils Postpile National Monument

John Muir Wilderness

South Fork San
Silver Pass 10,900ft

Lake Thomas A Edison

John Muir Wilderness

Inyo National Forest

Joaquin River

Kaiser Wilderness
80
Mono Hot Springs

Selden Pass 10,900ft
START SEGMENT 4

Florence Lake

37°15'N

Huntington Lake
168

6
168
Bishop

Owens

Ancient Bristlecone Pine Forest

Dinkey Lakes Wilderness

John Muir Wilderness

Mt Darwin 13,829ft

Bishop Pass 11,972ft

Inyo National Forest

Big Pine
168

Courtright Reservoir

Kings River

Muir Pass 11,955ft

Pacific

North Palisade 14,242ft

Glacier Lodge Rd

Sierra National Forest

Wishon Reservoir
START SEGMENT 5

Crest

Mather Pass 12,100ft

Owens Valley

North Fork Kings

Middle Fork Kings

Kings Canyon National Park

Pinchot Pass 12,130ft

National

395

Inyo Mountains Wilderness

Monarch Wilderness

Roads End

Scenic

START SEGMENT 6

Sequoia National Forest
180
South Fork Kings

Glen Pass 11,978ft

Independence

36°45'N

180

Jennie Lakes Wilderness

Mt Brewer 13,570ft

Trail

Kern River

395

Kings Canyon National Park

Forester Pass 13,120ft

FINISH
Lone Pine

245
198
Sequoia National Park

Mt Whitney 14,496ft
Whitney Portal

Trail Crest 13,777ft

119°15'W
118°45'W
118°15'W

PLANNING
When to Hike
Most through hikers go from north to south rather than start the trail's steepest climb to its highest elevation, the summit of Mt Whitney, with a fully loaded backpack. In a typical year, most of the trail and passes are not free of snow until mid-July, and by late August hikers should be finishing the trail. Sometimes it is possible to hike into early September, but by mid-September, storms close the trail for the year.

What to Bring
It is next to impossible to carry all the food you need for the entire trail, so through hikers must plan to resupply along the way. Strategies for resupplying are mailing food to yourself at post offices near trailheads along the way (eg, Mammoth Lakes, CA 93546, or Mono Hot Springs, CA 93642), or going out to a town (eg, hitchhiking to Mammoth Lakes or Bishop) to buy supplies. Almost all towns and post offices convenient to the trail are along the eastern Sierra. Stores at Tuolumne Meadows and Reds Meadows are very close to the trail.

Maps
The USGS 1:62,500 *Yosemite, Tuolumne Meadows, Devils Postpile, Mt Abbot, Mt Goddard, Mt Pinchot* and *Mt Whitney* quadrangles cover the John Muir Trail, but not all of the trails leading to and from it. Using the USGS 1:24,000 quadrangles is impractical, because more than 26 quadrangles cover the trail, excluding the quadrangles necessary for the trails leading to and from it. Tom Harrison Maps 1:63,360 *Map Pack of the John Muir Trail* consists of 13 maps, each covering a typical day's hike.

Permits & Regulations
A wilderness permit is required for the entire trail. Yosemite National Park issues permits for those starting at Yosemite Valley (see Permits & Regulations, p167). Inyo National Forest (see Permits & Regulations, p241) issues permits for those starting at Whitney Portal, but these are difficult to obtain because of quotas. See Organized

Through Hikers

Through hikers set out to complete the entire length of a long-distance trail in one season. Many hikers complete a trail by hiking it in segments over several years. Anyone who chooses to tackle one of these trails in its entirety must carefully plan the logistics, either mailing their food and supplies to post offices along the way or leaving the trail to resupply at towns near trailheads. Specialty guidebooks and even cookbooks discuss the myriad of details. Few without previous backpacking and first-aid experience commit to a through hike, which is the most demanding approach to a long-distance trail. Through hikers form a distinctive part of the culture of the long-distance trails, embodying the mythos of the rugged, self-contained hiker.

Hikes, p38, for a list of companies that offer this hike.

GETTING TO/FROM THE HIKE
To the Start
The trail's northern terminus is Happy Isles in Yosemite Valley (see Yosemite Valley, p168).

From the Finish
Technically, the southern terminus is the summit of Mt Whitney, but practically, it is Whitney Portal (see the Mt Whitney hike, p274).

THE HIKE
Segment 1: Yosemite Valley to Tuolumne Meadows
2–3 days, 24mi (38.6km)
The John Muir Trail begins its climb out of Yosemite Valley from Happy Isles (4035ft) on the Merced River, reaching Little Yosemite Valley (6100ft) after 4.4mi. Most hikers take time for the side trip above Little Yosemite Valley to Half Dome. The trail continues past the ***Sunrise High Sierra Camp*** (9300ft) and over Cathedral Pass (9700ft) to Tuolumne

Meadows (8595ft). (See the Half Dome hike, p176, and Cathedral Lakes hike, p192, for details.)

Segment 2: Tuolumne Meadows to Reds Meadow
3 days, 33mi (53.1km)

From the backpackers' parking lot south of Hwy 120, the trail ambles south up the Lyell Fork Tuolumne River about 9mi to Lyell Base Camp (9040ft). It then climbs 5mi, out of the national park and into Ansel Adams Wilderness at **Donohue Pass** (11,056ft), and descends 3.8mi to *campsites* along Rush Creek Forks (9600ft), the only section of the John Muir Trail east of the Sierra Crest. Rising 1.5mi to Island Pass (10,203ft), the trail rolls down past Thousand Island and Garnet Lakes, beneath Banner Peak, and meets the trail linking Ediza and Shadow Lakes in 6.2mi. It continues past *campsites* along Gladys Lake to **Reds Meadow** (7600ft), half a mile north of the John Muir Trail.

Segment 3: Reds Meadow to South Fork San Joaquin River
4 days, 50mi (80.5km)

This long segment gets less use than other segments and offers tranquility, beautiful lakes and two enjoyable passes. Beyond Reds Meadow, the trail leaves Ansel Adams Wilderness and enters enormous John Muir Wilderness, ascending between the **Red Cones**, then descending to *campsites* along Deer Creek after 6.5mi. It traverses east above Cascade Valley 5.8mi to *campsites* along Duck Creek, then swings by Purple Lake and rises to beautiful Lake Virginia (10,335ft) in 4.5mi, with views across to the Silver Divide and Silver Pass. The trail drops 2mi to the meadow of Tully Hole and descends a mile to a footbridge over Fish Creek (9130ft) with nearby *campsites*. It climbs past Squaw Lake and Chief Lake 3.8mi to scenic **Silver Pass** (10,900ft), then descends by Silver Pass Lake, crossing Silver Pass Creek and North Fork Mono Creek to *campsites* in Pocket Meadow, continuing down to the bridge over Mono Creek, and *campsites* 7mi from the pass.

One can leave the John Muir Trail here to resupply by walking west a mile to Quail Meadows and 4.5mi along Lake Thomas A Edison to Vermilion Valley Resort and then following an unpaved road to Mono Hot Springs.

From the bridge over Mono Creek, the John Muir Trail continues up 4.5mi over Bear Ridge and down 1.5mi to *campsites* along Bear Creek, which it follows for 3.5mi. Crossing the creek, the trail rises through Rosemarie Meadow and past Marie Lake, 4mi to **Selden Pass** (10,900ft). Descending past Heart Lake and *campsites* at Sally Keyes Lakes (10,200ft), it crosses Senger Creek and drops to the South Fork San Joaquin River, 7mi from the pass.

Alternatively, you can leave the trail here to resupply. A westward trail leads a quarter mile to Muir Trail Ranch and Blayney Hot Springs, and then 10mi west to *campsites* at Florence Lake (7328ft), where there is a store, and a road leading to Mono Hot Springs. A boat shuttle across Florence Lake saves walking 5mi. Florence Lake is accessible by road from the western Sierra via Hwy 168 over Kaiser Pass.

Segment 4: South Fork San Joaquin River to LeConte Canyon
3 days, 26mi (41.8km)

The John Muir Trail passes the Piute Pass Trail in 1.8mi, and enters Kings Canyon National Park. See Days 2 to 6 of the Humphreys & Evolution Basins hike, p263, in the Eastern Sierra chapter for a description of the trail through Evolution Valley and Evolution Basin and over **Muir Pass** to *campsites* at Little Pete Meadow (8880ft) in LeConte Canyon.

You can resupply by heading south through Little Pete Meadow on the John Muir Trail to the Dusy Branch of the Middle Fork Kings River, and then turning east to Bishop Pass (11,972ft) via the Dusy Basin and on to South Lake (11.5mi), from where it is 22mi to Bishop.

Segment 5: LeConte Canyon to Lower Vidette Meadow
4 days, 46mi (74km)

Descending south through LeConte Canyon along the Middle Fork Kings River, the John

Muir Trail reaches the river's confluence with Palisade Creek (8020ft) and, turning east, climbs along the creek to reach *campsites* in Deer Meadow (8860ft) in 7mi. Switchbacks lead up the 'Golden Staircase' 3mi to Lower Palisade Lake (10,613ft), then past Upper Palisade Lake and up rocky trail 3.5mi to **Mather Pass** (12,100ft).

The descent south into Upper Basin goes by *campsites* and many lakes and streams at the headwaters of South Fork Kings River. The descending trail crosses the river and passes a trail heading east to Taboose Pass, 6.5mi from Mather Pass, then climbs past Lake Marjorie (11,160ft) and up steeply 3mi to **Pinchot Pass** (12,130ft), which has superb views south over Woods Creek. The trail descends to the creek and follows it down about 7mi to the junction with the Woods Creek Trail (8492ft) and *campsites* near the suspension bridge. The John Muir Trail continues south to the Rae Lakes and over **Glen Pass** (11,978ft), to Lower Vidette Meadow (9550ft) and Bubbs Creek (see Days 3 and 4 of the Rae Lakes Loop hike, p219, for a description).

You can leave the John Muir Trail to resupply at Roads End (see the Rae Lakes Loop hike for details) either by heading west on the Woods Creek Trail (15.4mi) or by heading west from Lower Vidette Meadow on the Bubbs Creek Trail (13mi). Alternatively, one can resupply at Independence by leaving the John Muir Trail 1.5mi north of Lower Vidette Meadow and heading east 7mi over Kearsarge Pass to Onion Valley.

Segment 6: Lower Vidette Meadow to Whitney Portal
3 days, 39mi (62.8km)

The John Muir Trail curves south 0.7mi to Upper Vidette Meadow (9600ft) and continues southeast along upper Bubbs Creek, rising above tree line at its headwaters, to **Forester Pass** (13,120ft) on the Kings-Kern Divide in 7.3mi. From this sweeping viewpoint, switchbacks descend into Sequoia National Park and the Kern Canyon and on 5mi to *campsites* along Tyndall Creek (10,840ft). The trail rises over panoramic Bighorn Plateau 3.7mi to *campsites* along Wright

Creek (10,790ft). It continues 0.7mi to *campsites* along Wallace Creek, where it is joined by the High Sierra Trail (see Days 6 to 8 of this hike, p228, for a description) for the final 22mi to **Mt Whitney** and Whitney Portal.

Other Hikes

The Sierra High Route and the Pacific Crest National Scenic Trail represent radically different approaches to long-distance hiking. Both require endurance and perseverance, but the PCT is a visibly marked, well-worn footpath, whereas the High Sierra Route is its polar opposite, a cross-country route with no trail and no signs, where ingenuity and experience are crucial to success.

Sierra High Route
Traversing along the north-south axis of the Sierra Nevada, the 195mi (313.8km) Sierra High Route is a rugged cross-country route that passes hundreds of lakes and skirts 14,000ft peaks from its start at Roads End in Kings Canyon National Park to its terminus at Twin Lakes near Bridgeport. The Sierra High Route stays close to timberline, never dropping below 9000ft, and avoids well-marked trails favored by traditional backpackers. Offering an extreme and low-impact alternative to the John Muir Trail, the Sierra High Route stays at higher elevations and avoids descending into forested canyons along the western Sierra, circumventing the east-west ridges protruding from the Sierra Crest.

With many Class 2 sections, the route is recommended only for experienced and adventurous backpackers who enjoy the challenges of routefinding through isolated, rigorous terrain and of serious commitment to a difficult route. Mountaineering skills, however, are not required. The route is best done from August to early September, but it may be possible to start as early as June or continue later in the season depending on snow conditions.

The Sierra High Route: Traversing Timberline Country, by Steve Roper, who conceived this route, is the definitive guidebook. Four 1:63,360 Tom Harrison Maps cover the route: *Kings Canyon High Country, Mono Divide High Country, Mammoth High Country* and *Yosemite High Country,* supplemented with the USFS 1:63,360 *Hoover Wilderness* map for the area north of Tuolumne Meadows.

The route is best done in five roughly weeklong segments, which can be done independently or consecutively: Kings Canyon to Dusy Basin; Dusy Basin to Lake Italy; Lake Italy to Devil's

Postpile (the route's easiest segment); Devil's Postpile to Tuolumne Meadows; and Tuolumne Meadows to Twin Lakes.

From Roads End, the Sierra High Route begins along the Copper Creek Trail, climbing 6000ft to the Monarch Divide, the watershed between South and Middle Forks Kings River. It parallels this long ridge until it abuts the Sierra Crest near Mather Pass. Next the route passes through three lake basins – Palisade, Dusy and Evolution – for more than 30mi. Crossing Glacier Divide, the route meanders across the Humphreys Basin, traverses the Bear Lakes area, crosses the Mono Divide at Second Recess and then crosses Silver Divide. Following the Mammoth Crest, the route crosses Mammoth Pass before dropping to Devils Postpile National Monument. It then winds through the eastern side of the Ritter Range and enters Yosemite National Park near Foerster Peak. Following seldom-used paths in the Yosemite backcountry, it crosses Vogelsang Pass before reaching Tuolumne Meadows. Heading north, it follows close to the Sierra Crest, crossing it three times before reaching the northern terminus at Twin Lakes.

Pacific Crest National Scenic Trail

The Pacific Crest National Scenic Trail (PCT) stretches 2638mi (4244.5km) from Campo, CA on the Mexican border to Manning Provincial Park in British Columbia, Canada. It hugs the crest of the glacially-carved Sierra Nevada Range in California and the volcanic Cascade Range in northern California, Oregon and Washington, crossing seven national parks, three in the Sierra Nevada and four in the Cascades, which showcase these mountains' splendor. Most of this mountainous terrain lies within 24 national forests and 33 roadless wilderness areas, with the longest unbroken stretch extending for more than 200mi. The wilderness of the High Sierra is crossed by only five roads between Walker Pass at Hwy 178 and Donner Summit at I-80, a distance of more than 275mi as the crow flies and more than 500mi on foot. As a through hike, the entire trail takes 175 days or six months to complete.

The trail skirts the Mojave Desert along the Tehachapi Range, crossing Hwy 58, where it enters the southern Sierra. The PCT joins the John Muir Trail in Sequoia National Park, just west of Mt Whitney (14,496ft), then leaves the park via Forester Pass (13,120ft), the trail's highest point. Entering Kings Canyon National Park, where imposing peaks rise above the deep canyons of the Kings River, the trail continues north, passing Devils Postpile National Monument and entering Yosemite National Park. The PCT leaves the John Muir Trail at Tuolumne Meadows on Hwy 120. Heading north out of the park and across Sonora Pass on Hwy 108, the trail then crosses Ebbetts Pass on Hwy 4, Carson Pass on Hwy 88 and Echo Summit on US 50. Entering the popular Desolation Wilderness Area west of Lake Tahoe, the trail passes Alpine Meadows and Squaw Valley ski resorts en route to Donner Summit on I-80. The trail undulates through deep river valleys in the northern Sierra, whose granite outcrops and domes come to an end a few miles north of Hwy 70. The PCT continues to Lassen Volcanic National Park, marking the southern extent of the Cascade Range.

The Sierra Nevada segment is best done in late July and August. The only accurate and comprehensive PCT guide is the highly recommended *The Pacific Crest Trail – Volume 1: California*, by Jeffrey P Schaeffer et al, which contains B&W reproductions of 1:50,000 USGS topographic trail maps. *The PCT Hiker's Handbook,* by Ray Jardine, presents Jardine's ultralight approach to long-distance hiking. Sometimes controversial and always thought-provoking, anyone considering a long hike should read this book. The USFS Pacific Southwest Region 5 (☎ 707-562-8737), 1323 Club Drive, Vallejo, CA 94592, administers the trail and provides information on the California segment. Permits are required for the national parks and wilderness areas. Through hikers can get a single permit at the start of their hike.

Glossary

AMGA – American Mountain Guides Association

Amtrak – national, government-owned railroad company

arête – a sharp-crested mountain ridge; see also *crag*

bear boxes – large metal food storage lockers that are cemented, bolted or chained into position, used to protect food and scented personal belongings from bears

bivy sack – common name for bivouac sack, an ultralightweight solo shelter system used by minimalist hikers and mountaineers instead of a tent

bench – a shelf or step-like area with steep slopes above and below it

blaze – notch in tree trunk indicating a trail, made by chipping bark away

BLM – Bureau of Land Management

bowl – a basin, sometimes glacial; see also *cirque*

cairn – a heap of stones that marks a route or pass

cirque – a bowl-shaped, steep-walled mountain basin carved by glaciation, often containing a small, round lake

col – a pass or physical depression in a mountain ridge

cornice – deposits of wind-drifted snow or ice projecting over the lee edge of mountain ridges

couloir – a steep gorge or gully on the side of a mountain

cow camp – privately leased or owned summer grazing meadows for cattle

crag – an *arête*

crevasse – a fissure or deep cleft or crack in glacial ice

divide – mountain ranges, usually running east-west, that are perpendicular or at oblique angles to the Sierra Crest and mark the drainage of different watersheds

drift fence – barbed wire fence that keeps pack stock from drifting either too far away from a campsite or entering fragile meadows or streamsides at night

erratic – a boulder carried by glacial ice and deposited some distance from its place of origin

ford – crossing a river by wading because there is no bridge or cable

fork – the place where a trail or river divides into branches

forty-niner – prospector who came to California for the gold rush in 1849

glacier – an extended mass of ice formed from snow falling and accumulating over the years that flows/moves slowly down a mountain or valley

gully – see *couloir*

IFMGA – International Federation of Mountain Guides Association

NPRS – National Park Reservation Service

NPS – National Park Service

pack string – the traveling line of animals and people that comprise guided trips into the mountains led by cowboys, where guests ride horses and mules carry gear

PCT – Pacific Crest National Scenic Trail

route – a course for traveling where no visible trail exists

RV – recreational vehicle

saddle – a low place in a ridge

scree – small rock accumulated on a slope, usually collected in a gully, that spreads into a fan-shaped cone

SNHA – Sequoia Natural History Association

switchback – a trail or route that follows a zigzagging course up a steep grade

talus – large boulders accumulated on a slope, fanning out at its base

tarn – a small mountain lake in a cirque

TART – Tahoe Area Regional Transport

technical – referring to climbing or mountaineering skills and techniques required to complete a route

terminus – the lowest part of a glacier, where melting produces an outwash stream

trail – a visible path for walking

tree line – uppermost (natural) level to which tree cover extends on a mountainside

true left – the actual left bank of a river or glacier when facing downstream or downvalley

true right – looking downstream or downvalley, the actual right bank of a river or glacier

use trail – any non-constructed path created by the passage of hikers that is not inventoried or maintained by the NPS or USFS, does not appear on published maps, and is allowed to remain where it does not cause negative impact to the environment, critical species or heritage resources; more formally termed 'user-created trail'

USFS – United States Forest Service

USFWS – United States Fish and Wildlife Service

USGS – United States Geological Survey

YARTS – Yosemite Area Regional Transportation System

Index

Bold indicates maps.

Boxed Text

Map Legend

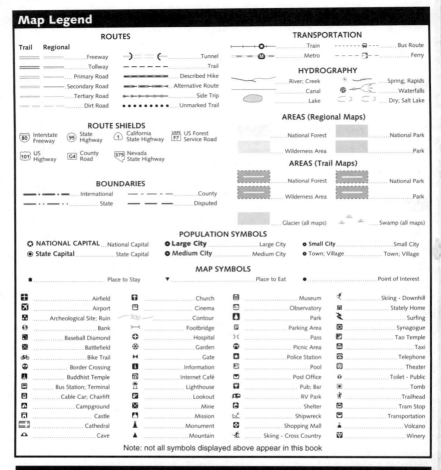

ROUTES

Trail	Regional	
		........Freeway
		........Tollway
		....Primary Road
		....Secondary Road
		....Tertiary Road
		....Dirt Road

Tunnel
Trail
Described Hike
Alternative Route
Side Trip
Unmarked Trail

ROUTE SHIELDS

80	Interstate Freeway	95	State Highway	1	California State Highway	F7	US Forest Service Road
101	US Highway	G4	County Road	375	Nevada State Highway		

BOUNDARIES

International ... County
State ... Disputed

TRANSPORTATION

Train ... Bus Route
Metro ... Ferry

HYDROGRAPHY

River; Creek ... Spring; Rapids
Canal ... Waterfalls
Lake ... Dry; Salt Lake

AREAS (Regional Maps)

National Forest ... National Park
Wilderness Area ... Park

AREAS (Trail Maps)

National Forest ... National Park
Wilderness Area ... Park
Glacier (all maps) ... Swamp (all maps)

POPULATION SYMBOLS

✪ NATIONAL CAPITAL ... National Capital	● Large City ... Large City	● Small City ... Small City
◉ State Capital ... State Capital	● Medium City ... Medium City	○ Town; Village ... Town; Village

MAP SYMBOLS

▪ ... Place to Stay   ▼ ... Place to Eat   ● ... Point of Interest

... Airfield	... Church	... Museum	... Skiing - Downhill
... Airport	... Cinema	... Observatory	... Stately Home
... Archeological Site; Ruin	... Contour	... Park	... Surfing
... Bank	... Footbridge	... Parking Area	... Synagogue
... Baseball Diamond	... Hospital	... Pass	... Tao Temple
... Battlefield	... Garden	... Picnic Area	... Taxi
... Bike Trail	... Gate	... Police Station	... Telephone
... Border Crossing	... Information	... Pool	... Theater
... Buddhist Temple	... Internet Café	... Post Office	... Toilet - Public
... Bus Station; Terminal	... Lighthouse	... Pub; Bar	... Tomb
... Cable Car; Chairlift	... Lookout	... RV Park	... Trailhead
... Campground	... Mine	... Shelter	... Tram Stop
... Castle	... Mission	... Shipwreck	... Transportation
... Cathedral	... Monument	... Shopping Mall	... Volcano
... Cave	... Mountain	... Skiing - Cross Country	... Winery

Note: not all symbols displayed above appear in this book

LONELY PLANET OFFICES

Australia
Locked Bag 1, Footscray, Victoria 3011
☎ 03 8379 8000 fax 03 8379 8111
email talk2us@lonelyplanet.com.au

USA
150 Linden Street, Oakland, California 94607
☎ 510 893 8555, TOLL FREE 800 275 8555
fax 510 893 8572
email info@lonelyplanet.com

UK
10a Spring Place, London NW5 3BH
☎ 020 7428 4800 fax 020 7428 4828
email go@lonelyplanet.co.uk

France
1 rue du Dahomey, 75011 Paris
☎ 01 55 25 33 00 fax 01 55 25 33 01
email bip@lonelyplanet.fr
www.lonelyplanet.fr

World Wide Web: www.lonelyplanet.com or AOL keyword: lp
Lonely Planet Images: lpi@lonelyplanet.com.au